Sixth Edition

CRIMINOLOGICAL THEORY

Frank P. Williams III

University of Houston–Downtown;
California State University—San Bernardino

Marilyn D. McShane

University of Houston–Downtown

Boston   Columbus   Indianapolis   New York   San Francisco   Upper Saddle River
Amsterdam   Cape Town   Dubai   London   Madrid   Milan   Munich   Paris   Montréal   Toronto
Delhi   Mexico City   São Paulo   Sydney   Hong Kong   Seoul   Singapore   Taipei   Tokyo

Vice President and Executive Publisher: Vernon Anthony
Senior Acquisitions Editor: Gary Bauer
Editorial Assistant: Tanika Henderson
Director of Marketing: David Gesell
Marketing Manager: Mary Salzman
Senior Marketing Coordinator: Alicia Wozniak
Production Manager: Romaine Denis
Creative Director: Jayne Conte
Cover Designer: Karen Noferi
Media Project Manager: Karen Bretz
Full-Service Project Management/Composition: George Jacob/Integra Software Services Pvt. Ltd.
Printer/Binder: Courier, Inc.
Cover Printer: Courier, Inc.

Credits and acknowledgments borrowed from other sources and reproduced, with permission, in this textbook appear on appropriate page within text.

Library of Congress Cataloging-in-Publication Data
Williams, Franklin P.
  Criminological theory/Frank P. Williams III, Marilyn D. McShane.—6th ed.
    p. cm.
  Includes bibliographical references and index.
  ISBN-13: 978-0-13-298702-8
  ISBN-10: 0-13-298702-3
  1. Criminology.   I. McShane, Marilyn D., 1956-   II. Title.
HV6018.W48 2014
364.2—dc23
                                          2012042343

10 9 8 7 6 5 4 3 2 1

ISBN-13: 978-0-13-298702-8
ISBN-10:   0-13-298702-3

CONTENTS

Preface   vii

Chapter 1 INTRODUCTION   1
Introduction to Theory   1
What Is Good Theory?   4
Kinds of Theory   6
Social Context and Theory   9
Theory, Research, and Policy   10
A Note on Evidence, Theory, and Reality   11
> *Summary   11   •   Questions and Weblinks   12*
> *Related Websites   13   •   Bibliography   13*

Section I   The Roots of Criminology

Chapter 2 THE CLASSICAL SCHOOL   14
Introduction   14
The Heritage of the School   15
The Perspective of the School   17
Classification of the School   19
> *Summary   20   •   Epilogue: Current Directions and Policy*
> *Implications   21   •   Questions and Weblinks   23*
> *Related Websites   23   •   Bibliography   23*
> *Research Bibliography   24*

Chapter 3 THE POSITIVE SCHOOL   27
Introduction   27
The Heritage of the School   28
The Perspective of the School   29
Classification of the School   34
> *Summary   34   •   Epilogue: Current Directions and Policy*
> *Implications   35   •   Questions and Weblinks   40   •   Related*
> *Websites   40   •   Bibliography   40   •   Research Bibliography   43*

Section II   The Foundations of American Criminology

Chapter 4 THE CHICAGO SCHOOL   46
Introduction   46
The Heritage of the School   47
The Perspective of the School   48

Classification of the School   55

    Summary   56   •   Epilogue: Current Directions and Policy
    Implications   56   •   Questions and Weblinks   59
    Related Websites   59   •   Bibliography   59
    Research Bibliography   61

Chapter 5   DIFFERENTIAL ASSOCIATION THEORY   64

Introduction   64

The Heritage of the Theory   65

The Theoretical Perspective   67

Classification of the Theory   70

    Summary   71   •   Epilogue: Current Directions and Policy
    Implications   72   •   Questions and Weblinks   73
    Related Websites   74   •   Bibliography   74
    Research Bibliography   75

Chapter 6   ANOMIE THEORY   77

Introduction   77

The Heritage of the Theory   79

The Theoretical Perspective   81

Classification of the Theory   84

    Summary   84   •   Epilogue: Current Directions and Policy
    Implications   85   •   Questions and Weblinks   88
    Related Websites   88   •   Bibliography   89
    Research Bibliography   90

Section III   Building on the Foundation

Chapter 7   SUBCULTURE THEORIES   91

Introduction   91

The Heritage of the Theories   92

Cohen's Subculture of Delinquency   93

Cloward and Ohlin's Differential Opportunity Theory   96

Other Subculture Theories   100

    Summary   103   •   Epilogue: Current Directions and Policy
    Implications   103   •   Questions and Weblinks   106
    Related Websites   106   •   Bibliography   106
    Research Bibliography   107

Chapter 8   LABELING THEORY   109

Introduction   109

The Heritage of the Theory   110

The Theoretical Perspective   111

Classification of the Theory   118

> *Summary   119   •   Epilogue: Current Directions and Policy*
> *Implications   120   •   Questions and Weblinks   123*
> *Related Websites   124   •   Bibliography   124*
> *Research Bibliography   125*

Section IV   Modern Criminology

Chapter 9   CONFLICT THEORY   127

Introduction   127

The Heritage of the Theory   128

The Theoretical Perspective   129

Classification of the Theory   137

> *Summary   137   •   Epilogue: Current Directions and Policy*
> *Implications   138   •   Questions and Weblinks   140*
> *Related Websites   141   •   Bibliography   141*
> *Research Bibliography   142*

Chapter 10   GENDER-BASED THEORIES   145

Introduction   145

The Heritage of the Theory   146

The Theoretical Perspective   146

Classification of the Perspective   154

Policy Implications   155

> *Questions and Weblinks   155*
> *Related Weblinks   156   •   Bibliography   156*
> *Research Bibliography   158*

Chapter 11   SOCIAL CONTROL THEORY   160

Introduction   160

The Heritage of the Theory   161

The Theoretical Perspective   162

Classification of the Theory   169

> *Summary   169   •   Epilogue: Current Directions and Policy*
> *Implications   170   •   Questions and Weblinks   172*
> *Related Weblinks   172   •   Bibliography   172*
> *Research Bibliography   174*

Chapter 12   SOCIAL LEARNING THEORY   177

Introduction   177

The Heritage of the Theory   178

The Theoretical Perspective   179

Classification of the Theory 184

    Summary 184 • Epilogue: Current Directions and Policy Implications 185 • Questions and Weblinks 187 Related Websites 187 • Bibliography 187 Research Bibliography 188

Chapter 13 RATIONAL THEORIES 191

Introduction 191

The Heritage of the Theory 191

The Theoretical Perspective 193

Classification of the Theory 196

    Epilogue: Current Directions and Policy Implications 197 Questions and Weblinks 198 Related Weblinks 198 • Bibliography 198 Research Bibliography 200

Section V Contemporary Perspectives

Chapter 14 CONTEMPORARY THEORIES OF PROCESS 203

Introduction 203

The Heritage of Contemporary Theory 203

Modern Strain Theory 204

Modern Social Control Theory 205

Modern Developmental Theories 209

    Summary 212 • Questions and Weblinks 212 Related Website 212 • Bibliography 213 Research Bibliography 215

Chapter 15 CONTEMPORARY INTEGRATIVE AND CRITICAL THEORIES 221

Introduction 221

The Heritage of Contemporary Theory 222

Integrative Theories 223

Postmodern Theories 228

Conclusions 230

    Questions and Weblinks 233 Related Websites 233 • Bibliography 233 Research Bibliography 235

Index 237

PREFACE

As its title implies, this book is about the major sociological theories of crime. While there are other approaches to the study of crime, since the 1920s, criminology has been oriented toward sociology. There are, however, some comments on biological and psychological theories of crime and delinquency in the text, and those comments have been expanded in response to instructors' requests. However, we still intend the book to be representative of what criminological theory has *been* because a course in criminological theory is mainly a course in history. When we first developed the concept of this text, we wanted to provide undergraduates with a brief but clear description of the most popular criminological theories. We continue to hear from students and colleagues who have used the first five editions that many graduate students find the text valuable as a primer or as a study guide in their theory classes and for studying for comprehensive exams. The research references included in this edition are a valuable resource for a graduate student writing a research paper, thesis, or dissertation, or preparing for qualifying exams. As before, we have included an update of current theory. The intent of the first edition was to focus on traditional theories, and we only briefly mentioned contemporary versions in the concluding chapter. In the second and third editions we added chapters that summarized a number of new theoretical directions. However, as time goes on and theory testing and integration continues, we have found it necessary to split some of these concluding chapters into their own distinct theoretical areas. In this edition, Chapter 14 covers contemporary social process approaches. Chapter 15 discusses the broader context of integrative theories as well as metatheory.

The format of the first five editions has been retained in most chapters. We include a discussion of the social and intellectual heritage of the theory, highlight and explain the perspective and major concepts of the theory, and summarize and list the theory's major points. The lists of major points are intended to clarify earlier commentary and to demonstrate the logical connections among the various elements of each theory. The chapter summaries may also serve as review material for examinations. Graduate students may find the major points helpful in determining the background assumptions of the theories, comparing theories, and locating hypotheses for empirical testing.

NEW TO THIS EDITION

- The bibliographies have been expanded to include a number of related sources that would be useful to those doing research in a particular theoretical area. These are called Research Bibliographies and they follow the general references section.
- In most chapters we have included brief biographies of the major theorists. We believe that it will interest the student to see the similarities and differences between the theorists' careers and how becoming a criminologist is not always a deliberate or dedicated path.
- We have added practice essay questions that will help students prepare for exams and may serve as possible essay work for online courses. These can also be used to stimulate class discussion that emphasizes creative thinking about the applications of theory in our society today.
- We have listed informative weblinks at the end of each chapter that can be used for exercises in class or for researching special assignments. Students are also encouraged to find relevant websites on their own.

- The examples of how theory can be seen and applied today have been updated to draw on current events and incidents from the news that students will be familiar with.
- Finally, we have reduced the number of chapters from sixteen to fifteen in recognition that most semesters are 15 weeks and it is difficult if not impossible to always get to that last summative chapter. The final chapter has been significantly revised and updated to serve as a summative essay and to transition students to whatever theoretical developments occur in the years to come.

As in the earlier editions, we attempt in most chapters to provide a classification of the theoretical perspective. These areas of the book continue to draw the most discussion. In one sense, we find this appropriate. There are so many methods of classifying theories that it is inevitable that instructors and others who use the text would find some conflict with their own positions. Rather than hide such conflicts, we believe it is more instructive to bring them out into the open for students. Thus, we continue to provide theory classifications and encourage instructors to tell students how and why their approaches differ from ours.

And as always, we welcome any feedback on the book. The numerous versions of each form of theory, as well as the various perspectives on them, make critical commentary inevitable. Since this book is designed primarily to be *used*, we invite readers, students, and teachers alike to provide us with their ideas on how to make it even more useful. We feel very fortunate that we were able to acquire firsthand the comments and advice of some of the original authors of the theories. Our sincere gratitude and heartfelt appreciation goes out to the many distinguished criminologists, some of whom are no longer with us, who patiently offered us their insights and commentary. We would also like to recognize the continued support and guidance of scholars and colleagues Freda Adler, Ron Akers, Al Cohen, the late Gil Geis, Hal Pepinsky, Jeff Ferrell, Mark Hamm, Frank Scarpitti, and Austin Turk and thank them for their helpful feedback and advice. Special thanks are also in order to those who used the text in their classes and provided us commentary, or otherwise helped with their ideas and thoughts, including a number of very bright students and colleagues. And as is Richard Quinney, we are once again grateful to the Lone Ranger.

INSTRUCTOR SUPPLEMENTS

A Test Generator, and PowerPoint Lecture Package can be downloaded from our Instructor's Resource Center. To access supplementary materials online, instructors need to request an instructor access code. Go to www.pearsonhighered.com/irc, where you can register for an instructor access code. Within 48 hours of registering you will receive a confirming e-mail including an instructor access code. Once you have received your code, locate your text in the online catalog and click on the **Instructor Resources** button on the left side of the catalog product page. Select a supplement and a log-in page will appear. Once you have logged in, you can access instructor material for all Pearson textbooks.

Frank P. Williams III
and Marilyn D. McShane

1

Introduction

LEARNING OBJECTIVES

Objective 1.1: Describe some of the characteristics of a good theory.

Objective 1.2: Summarize the various ways to classify criminological theories.

Objective 1.3: Explain the difference between a macro- and a microtheory.

Objective 1.4: Discuss the relationship between theory, research, and policy.

Objective 1.5: Explain what is meant by the social context of a crime theory.

INTRODUCTION TO THEORY

The study of criminological theory is an opportunity to analyze and critique the way others have looked at crime through history. Today, the quest to understand crime is as close to us as the latest newspaper headlines and television reports. As we will see, however, theory is not just a popular belief, opinion, or value-driven explanation. Instead, theory as we will discuss it here is a product of the scientific approach.

The effective use of theory is found in the everyday activities of the criminal justice system. Police departments have designed their patrol patterns around various theories that predict criminal events. Each day judges hand down sentences based on their understanding of the character of a defendant and the environment in which that defendant lives. Jurors decide whether to give the death penalty based on their assumptions about the future dangerousness of the defendant. Probation officers send their clients to treatment programs to improve work skills or to resolve their use of drugs or alcohol. Prison authorities attempt to instill discipline, teach proper work habits, and deter inmates from future criminality. Finally, as reflected in the media, the public seems to attribute criminal behavior to such things as drug use, a depressed economy, poor family life, and the influence of bad friends. All of these activities and explanations are found in the implications of various criminological theories over the past century.

As you can see, theory does not have to be abstract. Furthermore, and despite public opinion to the contrary, theory is applicable to the "real world." We all use theory; theory is part of everyday life. When you see a dark cloud in the sky and say that it is going to rain, you have just expressed a theory. To be sure, it is a relatively simple theory, but it does express the relationships among clouds in general, clouds that are dark, and the falling of drops of water from the sky. This simple explanation meets two criteria for the simplest version of theory: (1) the use of objective evidence and systematic observation and (2) a rational explanation of that evidence. In other words, we know from many observations that dark clouds are systematically associated with rain, and a rational person could assume that if dark clouds occur first, then rain will follow. Similarly, if you have been about to go in a door when someone on the other side of door bursts through (and you were then hit in the face by the door), you associate the sound of someone on the other side of a door as a reason to be cautious. Here, you are theorizing on the basis of evidence (your past experience) that sounds indicating the presence of someone could be followed by their opening the door.

Theories can be very simple or very complex, depending upon the number and types of relationships expressed by them. A more complex theory of rain would be that, under certain circumstances, surface water evaporates and rises into the atmosphere. Certain atmospheric conditions cause the water to condense, first into "clouds" and ultimately into drops of rain. The complexity in this version of a theory of rain is in specifying the conditions and processes involved in evaporation and condensation.

Theories can also be concrete or abstract. Theories about rain tend to be concrete, even if complex. Theories about simple behaviors such as throwing a ball through a window also tend to be concrete. Abstract theories, however, are more difficult to tie directly to reality. For instance, Einstein's theory of relativity is an abstract concept. We have difficulty in directly testing the concept that time gets slower the faster one travels, and certainly we cannot test velocities beyond the speed of light. Similarly, theories about the effect of social structure on crime rates are abstract. Social structure is an invented concept (we doubt that you have ever seen a social structure), and crime rates are a mathematical concept derived from dividing the number of crimes by some standard population size.

The most important thing about theories is that we need them to live or to live better. Theories allow us to develop and test potential solutions to problems we encounter in life. True, some of the problems are more critical than others; for example, addressing global warming versus predicting who will win an Oscar. But we do need the many theories we have learned about our environment to accumulate knowledge and effectively allocate resources. Imagine what life would be like if you could never generalize about things, if every time you saw a cloud you had to get wet to conclude that it was going to rain. And suppose you could not assume that a door represents a way to enter a building. Theories, then, are really generalizations of a sort; they explain how two or more events are related to each other and the conditions under which the relationship takes place. For example, the statement that seat belts reduce deaths in automobile accidents expresses a relationship between two events. The seat belts alone will not reduce deaths, however. There must be a condition that they be worn (we could also add that the seat belts have to be installed properly, worn correctly, etc.).

The way we express these generalizations, or think about things, depends on the form of knowledge we are using at the time. We know things through experience (often referred to as "empirical knowledge"), intuition, common sense, or science, or because someone important to us (or even an important book) has told us so. The causes of crime, for instance, are assumed to be "known" by everyone. They include broken homes, lack of religion, hanging around with the wrong crowd, poor upbringing, and so forth. While you probably don't think of these explanations as theories, they all are. At the same time, they are not good theories because they are too simplistic. If they were correct, then everyone whose life has these causes would be criminal (or delinquent), and, of course, we know that is not true. Even more important is the fact that such theories also imply the reverse; that is, people who are raised in a good family environment, who are religious, and who associate with the right people will *not do* anything criminal (or delinquent). This is not true either, since self-report studies (Akers, 1964; Gold, 1970; Reiss & Rhodes, 1961; Short & Nye, 1958) tell us that most young people at one time or another do things that are against the law.

The problem with most of our day-to-day theories is they are often illogical or they are the product of selective observations. They may work some of the time and even often enough to be used as a general rule of thumb for making decisions. But when we need to be accurate or more careful about making policies, these theories will fail us. Human behavior is complex, and any simplistic theory will be incorrect. Therefore, theories about crime and criminals tend to be complex and are based on what we know (or in the case of older theories, what was known at the time) from research on crime and criminals. This, then, is a characteristic of scientific theories that is not normally shared by everyday theories. In fact, everyday theories are rather speculative and are rarely based on careful observation and evidence. In this regard, many people mistake the lay use of the word "theory"—as a speculative wondering about something—for scientific theory and think that scientists also use the word "theory" in the same way. Actually, the two uses of the word are quite different.

As a rule, scientific theories reflect systematic observation (observation made through the use of certain rules), repeated evidence, and careful logic. Indeed, scientific theories are frequently "factual" but share a dislike for saying that they are "proven." Even though the evidence may have been in favor of a scientific theory for each of 1,000 tests, there is still the possibility that the next test will not be supportive and that the theory needs to be modified. Theories as we will discuss them here, then, are never proven—primarily because scientists are too conservative to use that word. But, they are always supported by observable evidence. This notion that a theory must be "proven" to be valid is one of the main reasons that nonscientists misunderstand theory. Scientists talk in terms of probability and, for them, a likelihood of something being true 95% of the time is a (usually standard) minimum criterion for accepting it. That's the same thing as saying scientists prefer to have a maximum of 5% error in their statements.

Another issue in criminological theory lies in the sheer variety of behavior defined as criminal. When we use the term "crime," the reference is often to a wide range of illegal behavior. The individual criminal acts, though, may have very little in common except that someone, at some time, disliked each of them enough to have a law passed against them (of course, sometimes the reverse occurs and criminal behaviors are made legal again). Murder and petty theft, for example, have about as much in common as a rock and an orange. Just because one can find a common thread— they are both matter, for instance—doesn't mean that they are alike in any meaningful sense.

Another problem is that criminal behavior may be merely one of a variety of similar behaviors. For instance, if we argue that some criminal behavior is thrill-seeking behavior, then a theory that predicts behavior on that basis must also include legal behavior. Assuming that any thrill-seeking behavior is equally likely committing a crime would be no more likely than someone going bungee jumping, skydiving, or hang gliding. From this perspective, even though a thrill-seeking behavior might be relatively predictable, any one of those behaviors—such as crime—remains relatively unpredictable. Thus, theories of crime and criminal behavior must encompass a wide range of human activity. For this reason, some criminologists advocate limiting theories to specific criminal acts or harmful behaviors.

WHAT IS GOOD THEORY?

Because more than one theory usually purports to explain criminality at any given time, how do we know which one is best? In fact, how can we tell what is good theory in general? The most common answer is that a good theory is one that *can be tested* and that best *fits the evidence of research* (Akers & Sellers, 2008; Blalock, 1969; Gibbs, 1972). This makes sense, because our theories are scientific and should already be based on research evidence. In fact, these criteria are derived from the natural sciences, where they are used as the standard for good theory. There is really no difference between the natural and social sciences in determining good theory. There are, however, measurement problems in the social sciences because some variables, such as social class, cannot be as accurately measured as can distance, time, or hardness and the like. Under these generally accepted criteria, if a theory is not testable or if evidence does not support it, then the theory is not a good one. While this sounds clear enough, the issue is, unfortunately, not that simple.

Suppose, for a moment, that Einstein had lived and had proposed his theory of relativity two centuries before he did. It would not have been testable at that time, nor would the theory have fit the research evidence. Obviously, his theory would not have been considered a good theory at that time. Therefore, as changes in research evidence and the ability to measure and test occur, so do the common criteria for a good theory. In other words, it sometimes takes a while before our ability to measure and produce evidence catches up with a theory. Until that time, the theory may appear to be a "bad" one because evidence will not be available to support it. This means we might discard theories that are really good ones because our measuring capabilities cannot yet adequately test them and provide the necessary support. Therefore, as our measuring capabilities and techniques change, we may need to reexamine and retest theories to see if new research evidence provides a better fit. Of one thing we can be sure, however: If there is no current way to measure something, it is unlikely to appear in a theory—regardless of how important that something might be.

Another concern with testing is the use of a single approach to measure theoretical concepts. If one uses only one measure, and that measure is not a good one or does not adequately represent the theoretical concept, the theory may be rejected (even though the theory may be valid). A similar problem arises when a theory is affirmed by a single-test approach or measure. What is being measured may generate an erroneous result, but if the measurement is done the same way time after time, the result will always be the same, thereby creating the false impression of consistently valid results. Multiple methods and measures are always better ways of testing than any single approach.

If our approach to assessing a theory is based on measuring and testing, we refer to it as quantitative validation. A different approach, one that focuses on the substance of a theory, is called qualitative validation. It is these qualitative criteria that help us resolve the problem of time-specific and measurement-specific evidence. They include such factors as *logical soundness, the ability to make sense out of several conflicting positions,* and even *the degree to which the theory may sensitize people to things they otherwise would not see.* While these criteria are not often mentioned, they are no less important for the utility of a theory than quantitative tests are. Most theories of criminology do not do well on the criterion of empirical testing.[1] On the other hand,

---

[1] Of course, as the previous discussion suggests, the problem with "fitting" the research evidence may be as much with the way we test and measure as it is with the theory itself. However, we are certainly not taking the position that all criminological theories are simply ahead of their time and merely waiting for research capabilities to "catch up" to them. There are similar problems with using existing research evidence to create theory. If the existing research has systematic errors, thus producing what appears to be valid evidence, then any theory created to explain that evidence is actually explaining a phenomenon that doesn't exist. In one sense, then, all theory is a product of what we believe to be true, using our most valid information at the time.

almost all these theories made sense out of things that had been puzzling people before, and they sensitized criminologists to new and important ways of looking at the phenomenon of crime. Let's explore these qualitative criteria more closely.

Logical soundness means that the theory does not propose illogical relationships, and that it is internally consistent. One of the most common logic problems is that of time order, in which an event that occurs after another event is assumed to have caused the first event. For instance, if we ask marijuana users about the chance of being arrested for drug use, they will probably tell us that the probability of arrest is low. We might then think that people use marijuana because they think they have very little chance of being arrested (i.e., they are not deterred). In reality, however, a low estimate of the chance of arrest is really a reflection of the fact that they have used marijuana many times and have not been arrested. The low estimate of being arrested, then, came after the drug use and could not have caused it. In a more general example of logical soundness, if someone examined evidence that criminals in an institution for the criminally insane have irrational thinking patterns and then proposed that irrational thinking causes criminal behavior, the theory would be illogical. Very few criminals are insane, and those who are placed in insane institutions are different by their very nature. Actually, if the theory were correct, the author of the theory would then be engaged in irrational thinking, and we would expect him or her to become a criminal! In another example, criminologists DeFleur and Quinney (1966) even used a special form of logic called "set theory" to analyze the logical soundness of one of the more popular theories of criminal behavior (they found that it was, indeed, internally consistent).

The ability to make sense out of several conflicting positions means that when evidence seems to indicate that there are two or more opposing facts, a theory that can reconcile those facts is a good one and is better than having different theories to account for each fact. Differential association theory (Chapter 5), for instance, brings together the concepts of disorganized social areas and organized interaction in small, intimate groups and makes sense out of differing crime rates among various groups of people. As another example, official crime statistics and self-report studies (asking people what they have done) suggest two different pictures of "the criminal." Labeling theory (Chapter 8) makes sense of both forms of evidence by pointing out that official statistics give a picture only of those who have been reacted to and that self-report information gives a picture of those who are officially criminal as well as those who have not yet been caught. A noted philosopher and historian of science, Thomas Kuhn (1970), said that accepted new theories almost always make sense out of conflicting evidence that older theories cannot explain.

Sensitizing ability refers to focusing people's attention on a new, or even forgotten, direction of inquiry, or perhaps suggesting a different way of looking at and interpreting a fact they already know. Sometimes we concentrate so hard on a particular direction for explaining crime that we need to be reminded that there are other directions as well. One value of a sensitizing theory is that it serves to reacquaint criminologists with other facets of the problem. Using labeling theory again to illustrate, theorists in the 1950s were so focused on lower-class, urban, male, gang delinquents that all delinquency seemed to be a product of those kids. Labeling sensitized criminology to the importance of asking who gets reacted to and how we react to them. This served to remind criminologists that certain types of people are more likely to be closely observed and arrested for their behavior. In other words, labeling theory sensitized criminologists to the fact that criminality is due as much to how we react to people as it is to their personal characteristics. Thus, there was another explanation for urban, minority, male delinquency than the strain and stress of social structure.

Finally, one other qualitative criterion for a "good" theory is worthy of discussion. This criterion is very different from the others, and it should be used with a great deal of caution.

This one is *popularity*. Simply put, if a theory becomes popular with criminologists, then by definition it seems to be a "good" theory. The problem here is that popularity comes from a variety of factors, some of which have little to do with any of the other criteria mentioned. For instance, a theory can simply echo our gut-level feelings about the causes of crime, and we would tend to give it credence regardless of its logical soundness and empirical support. In fact, it is just this problem that we must watch for. The notion that something must be correct because it seems correct is one of the biggest mistakes that laypeople make about theories. Nevertheless, popularity must be included as one of the criteria for determining a "good" theory because many criminological theories do not meet the testability requirement very well yet were, and still are, very popular.

Good theory, then, is logically constructed, is based on the evidence at hand, and is supported by subsequent research. Empirical evidence should not be confused with personal ideology, such as religious sentiments or political leanings, or even with what some authority figure tells us. Theory development allows us to make sense out of various facts and serves to make us aware of the surrounding circumstances of the phenomenon it is attempting to explain. In making your assessment of how valid a theory seems to be, keep in mind the problems associated with each of these criteria and be flexible in making your final judgment.

KINDS OF THEORY

One distinction needs to be made before engaging in a discussion about kinds of theories. There are two general forms of theory: unit theory and metatheory (see Wagner, 1984). By and large, this is a book about unit theories. "Unit theories" emphasize a particular problem (such as crime and delinquency) and make testable assertions about that problem. Metatheories, on the other hand, are rarely testable and are best viewed as ways of looking at and interpreting reality. In another sense, they can be seen as "theories about theories." They discuss the kinds of concepts that should be used in unit theories, the general approach to using those concepts, and the way unit theories should be constructed. As an example, a criminological metatheory might specify that explanations of criminal behavior should emphasize social concepts rather than psychological and biological ones, and that social class should be used as the dominant variable. Furthermore, our metatheoretical example might specify that official statistics should be used as appropriate evidence for unit theories and that "good" unit theories should be developed in a propositional format. While there is an occasional discussion about metatheory in contemporary criminology, when the word "theory" is used, in most cases a unit theory is meant. Therefore, we drop the term "unit" and simply use "theory." Any reference to a metatheory will use the full term.

There are different varieties of theory, but there is no single, accepted scheme that describes the kinds of theory. As if the problem of understanding the various theories were not difficult enough, attempts by various writers to group them by some simple differences have, ironically, made matters worse by making those differences appear to be the most important characteristics of the theories. Nevertheless, categorizing and classifying theories is a necessary endeavor.

Because theories are complex and because the threads from which they are woven are not always self-evident, theories can be classified in many ways. Students of criminology will read one textbook and think that they know the theories pretty well; then they look at another textbook, find theories classified differently, and end up confused. In fact, almost every criminology textbook offers a somewhat different twist to classifying theories. Most use a system of three basic types of theories: biological, psychological, and social (although they devote most of their coverage to social perspectives). Within the discussion of sociological theories, there is a tendency to divide perspectives into social process and social structural approaches (Adler, Mueller, & Laufer, 2009; Reid, 2011; Tibbets, 2011; Vito & Maahs, 2011). Other common schemes include the use of various forms of sociological and social-psychological categories or a variety of broad approaches with numerous subcategories (Beirne & Messerschmidt, 2010). With all these different approaches, students may begin to feel that their instructor does not know the subject unless he or she uses a classification scheme that matches their textbook. Clearly, the classification of theories has done as much as anything to muddy the theoretical waters for beginning students. It has also been a problem for some of the more experienced criminologists.

Since these classifications exist, however, they must be dealt with. It should be noted that no classification is *real,* because the world does not exist in black and white. There are many factors to consider, and the result is a forcing of theories into one category or the other when they might not fit any category very well. The end result is almost always an artificial scheme of classification (Williams, 1984). In addition, by "changing" the classification of theories, a theory may be viewed in a way its author never intended. Regardless, and even though it may sound strange to say so, such diversity is probably good. The reason for categorizing theories is to establish similarities and differences among them. If many different categorizations are being used, it means that the theories are rich enough to defy simple classification and therefore they contain many valuable nuances, concepts, and ideas.

We discuss three different methods for categorizing theories. Hopefully, they will assist those new to criminology in understanding the relationships and connections among the various theories. At the same time, a warning is in order: treat each classification scheme as nothing more than an attempt to highlight similarities and differences. These schemes are not to be used as the last word in grouping, or establishing types of, theories.

Levels of Abstraction

As we have already noted, some theories are more abstract than others. The most abstract can be called macrotheories. Macrotheories are broad in their scope and perhaps are best characterized as those that *explain social structure and its effects.* They paint a picture of the way the world works, fit the structure of society into that picture, and suggest how crime is related to that structure. Macrotheories focus on rates of crime (called "epidemiology") rather than on criminals and their behavior. Macrotheories are simply not interested in individual behavior. Examples of macrotheory are anomie and conflict theories.

Other, more concrete theories can be referred to as microtheories. These theories are based on the assumption that a particular way of characterizing society is best; that characterization is then used directly to *explain how people become criminals* (called "etiology"). The focus may be on specific groups of people (but usually *small* groups) or on the individual. Likewise, microtheories may range from purely social to purely psychological to purely biological. In any case, they tell us how people become criminal. Microtheories are not interested in social structure and crime rates. Examples of microtheory are social control and social learning theories.

Finally, as is the case with any classification scheme, there are theories that do not fit neatly into either of the two categories and are "in-between." We will call these bridging theories. These theories attempt to tell us both *how social structure comes about and how people become criminal.* In fact, bridging theories are often both epidemiological (explaining differing rates of crime) and etiological (explaining criminal behavior itself). Examples of bridging theory are subculture theory and differential opportunity theory. Depending on the way in which they are viewed, or the direction of emphasis a writer finds in the theory, bridging theories can be classified as either macrotheories or microtheories. Doing so establishes one focus of the theory as more dominant than the other but, because it is not the author of the theory who is specifying the dominant focus, be aware that the emphasis on a focus may be because of a vested interest of the person doing the classification.

Levels of Explanation

These three general forms of theories can be further examined on the basis of their explanatory focus. What, for instance, is a theory attempting to explain: social structure in general, classes of people in society, small groups, or individual criminality? This problem is referred to as the level of explanation of a theory, or what the theory attempts to explain. Most theories cannot be directly compared with each other because they do not focus directly on the same subject.

Theories are often said to compete with each other in best accounting for crime and criminals. It should make sense that, in most instances, this is really not the case. Some theories explain how social events give rise to crime in society but do not attempt to explain how particular individuals become criminals; others do the opposite. Some explain the social factors important in creating criminality, others explain the psychological factors, and still others the internal biological factors. Further, some theories attempt to account for *crime* as a social phenomenon or a legal phenomenon, while many focus directly on *criminals* and their behavior. Obviously, these various theories are not in competition because they apply to different levels of the crime-and-criminals problem.

Unfortunately, criminology has done little thus far to integrate these various explanatory levels (but Elliott, Huizinga, & Ageton, 1985 and Pearson & Weiner, 1985, have tried). And, except for Williams's (1999) critical incident metatheory, there is no metatheory that puts them all together in a coherent fashion. The problem of which level a theory explains has not yet been generally recognized in criminology, although James Short (1985) commented on the issue over 25 years ago. For those beginning the study of criminological theory, however, the idea of levels of explanation is crucial because it helps to make sense out of the differences among theories. A good understanding of the area each theory deals with will help you grasp what the theorists were writing about.

Other Common Classification Schemes

The more popular classification schemes usually have two mutually exclusive categories, or dichotomies. One of the oldest of the classification schemes is to separate theories into "classical" and "positive." The names come from two schools of thought in the eighteenth and nineteenth centuries (and the subject of Chapters 2 and 3). Classical theories focus on legal statutes, governmental structures, and the rights of humans. A classical orientation to a theory suggests that the theory is less concerned about traditional scientific notions of testability and more concerned about the essence of the human condition. Positivist theories focus on pathology in criminal behavior, on treatment, and on the correction of criminality within individuals. Positivism also derives from the use of the scientific method to study phenomena. In that sense, most of today's theories are positivist ones.

Another common scheme is to separate theories into those of structure and those of process. Structural theories are those that focus on the way society is organized and its effect on behavior. Some of these are also referred to as *strain theories* (a term popularized by Travis Hirschi, 1969, and Ruth Kornhauser, 1978) because of their assumption that a disorganized society creates strain that leads to deviant behavior. Not all strain theories are structural theories though; for example,

Robert Agnew (1985, 2005) has created a strain theory that is clearly focused on the process of developing delinquency. Process theories attempt to explain how people become criminal or delinquent. While it is sometimes difficult to classify theories in this scheme, the major orientation is on the starting point of the theory. As a rule, a structural theory does not emphasize the individual criminal and a processual theory does not emphasize social structure. These two forms correspond closely to the macrotheories and microtheories we have already discussed.

The final major classification approach is that of consensus and conflict, once even referred to as the "old" and the "new" criminology (Gibbs, 1966). Consensus theories are those based on the assumption that there is agreement among people in a society. At the least, they assume that members of a society hold common values. You could point to the fact that most people believe we need traffic laws as evidence of consensus in our society. Also, surveys asking respondents to rank the seriousness of various crimes often find tremendous consensus about what people believe the most serious crimes are. Conflict theories, on the other hand, are based on the assumption that disagreement is common and people hold conflicting values. Laws that seem to benefit only small groups of elites or powerful business owners are often pointed to as evidence of a conflict orientation. As we will see, most conflict theories emphasize the differences that are found among social classes in our country. Since any society may have agreement and conflict at the same time, the crux is not whether agreement exists but whether it *originally* existed. A conflict theorist may discuss a society in agreement (Marx's false consciousness), or a consensus theorist may explain how conflict exists (Cohen's delinquent subculture). Thus, this scheme is somewhat like the chicken-and-egg controversy: one simply believes that either conflict or consensus is more natural to society and asserts that humans are naturally oriented toward one or the other.

SOCIAL CONTEXT AND THEORY

The final approach to understanding theory lies in an examination of social history. Writers commonly discuss theories in the abstract, especially in introductory textbooks. Because they do, it may seem that the theorist sits in isolation, inventing and creating his or her new theory. Nothing could be further from the truth. Just as there are people who have helped mold your thoughts and views of the world, so there are for the theorist. Indeed, it should be clear that any important influence in your life will leave its mark on the way you perceive the world. Your college courses, for instance, are designed to do exactly that. Your parents also provided important attitudes and viewpoints for you. Moreover, just as you respond to the latest fads and social events, so does the theorist. In short, those who create theories are probably as susceptible as you are to influences in their lives. Criminological theorists are practicing social scientists and may be even more sensitive to social movements and trends than most of us. As a result, no theory can really be understood and appreciated without an awareness of the context within which it was created.

Further, each theorist makes certain assumptions about the way the world really is, the nature of humans, and the value of particular concepts (an unspoken metatheory). Gouldner (1970) argues that these assumptions so severely affect the direction of theorizing that entire areas of evidence and thought can be ignored. For this reason, the effect of assumptions can be seen as similar to blinders on a horse: You can see only what is right in front of you, everything else might as well not exist. If a theorist's assumptions were spelled out, this might not represent a major problem because you could see what was included and what was omitted. Unfortunately, assumptions are not always obvious, and even the theorist may not be aware of them. Therefore, to better understand any theory, we must find ways to determine what the assumptions of that theory are. One of the best ways of doing this is to examine the context within which the theory was created.

Context has two major forms, social and intellectual. Both are handy terms for identifying areas of influence on an individual. Social context refers to the world about us: the ways people in a society are thinking, the things they are doing, the events taking place, the fads and fashions that are popular, and even the way society is structured. For example, right after World War II, it would have been difficult for people in the United States to criticize either the nation or the government; there was a general feeling of satisfaction with ourselves and a relative agreement about how good our values were. During the early 1970s, the opposite was common; people were uncertain about government, their lives, and their values. In both times, a theorist would have been affected by the events of the time and written into the theory some of the contemporary ideas (Williams, 1981). Since 1980, social conservatism has become more popular and you might expect recent theories to be influenced by that perspective.

The second form of context, the intellectual, refers to the personal influence of teachers, friends, family, and colleagues. Sometimes that influence extends to people whom the theorist has never even met; but the theorist has read their work and has been impressed with what they had to say. For this reason, many people have been said to follow in the footsteps of their teachers. The major criminological theorists have undeniably done some "footstep following," but at the same time, their theories are popular at least in part because these theorists were also creative.

Now it is time for a statement that may surprise you. The above-mentioned comments about social and intellectual context are actually part of a metatheory we developed when outlining the first edition of this book. That metatheory says the way people (theorists) respond to information has to be viewed through the lens of what they believe. Their beliefs are colored by their intellectual and social context. Even how they view evidence and, in particular, how they characterize evidence as good evidence is a product of this context. Thus, you may find theorists looking at the same evidence and perceiving its meaning in multiple ways. Acceptance of theory is governed in a similar fashion. As a result, this book discusses theories in a chronological order primarily because of a need to set each theory into its social context as a mechanism for understanding it. You will find it difficult to understand a theory, and its policy implications, unless you also have an appreciation of the times and major social movements. With this in hand, you can imagine the forces producing the theory and the reception it received from those at the time. If you try to understand a theory using today's perspectives, you will misunderstand it.

THEORY, RESEARCH, AND POLICY

Theory is the logical starting point for any examination of potential strategies for improving the criminal justice system. With our theory, we can develop experiments or research protocols that allow us to test the ideas to see if any are promising or worthwhile. Carefully constructed research studies that are based on rigorous scientific principles will give us insight into the areas of a theory that may need to be clarified and revised. Once we have identified some of the significant theoretical concepts that have been supported by research evidence, and these studies have been replicated and perhaps generalized across different population groups, we may begin to design programs and policies to address the needs of the criminal justice system. The process can be seen as a linear model with feedback between the research and the theory, thus allowing the theory to be refined and redirected with additional research. Policy should not be formulated or implemented without proper research to evaluate the costs and the benefits of certain endeavors.

$$\text{THEORY} \rightarrow \text{RESEARCH} \rightarrow \text{POLICY}$$

Realistically, however, we know that policymakers and politicians often implement laws, programs, and policies without the benefit of theory or research. Many of these efforts are later found to be inadequate and are eventually abandoned because they were instituted before sufficient research had been done to validate them, as was perhaps the case with boot camps, scared straight programs, and even three-strikes laws.

A NOTE ON EVIDENCE, THEORY, AND REALITY

Is theory a product of evidence? Yes, but, as you will see in future chapters, the issue of evidence is not so clear-cut as it would seem. Every major theoretical school has defined some forms of evidence as "proper" and eschewed others. In fact, Thomas A. Kuhn's concept of paradigms is based on a combination of methodology and accepted procedure in determining proper evidence. Those working in areas within disciplines essentially prescribe what evidence is proper and how to think about that evidence. Information that is contradictory or inconvenient tends to be either ignored or proclaimed as false by those within the paradigm. While it would seem that there is not much to quibble about in an objective reality, the fact is that reality is a product of belief and perception. We do not mean to imply there is no reality; reality requires interpretation, and humans bring their strongly held beliefs to that interpretation. Frequently, these beliefs are buried so deeply in our minds that we do not even know they are there. For example, some of us declare that human nature is inherently good and others declare that it is inherently evil. This is not something that can be established one way or the other, it is merely the product of a belief system (or a paradigm); it does serve, however, to establish a type of reality. From this starting point, then, theories are proposed to explain criminal or delinquent behavior based on we think is true about human nature. Evidence is then selectively accepted or ignored based on one's view of a "proper" reality. Where do these strongly held beliefs come from? We would say that they are a product of the cultural milieu in which people are raised, their experiences, their parents, their mentors, and even perhaps their neurochemistry. This is why, in the chapters to follow, you will read about the social and intellectual context surrounding each of the theories or schools. But more to the point, what evidence you lean toward is a product of your predispositions as much as it is good old hard facts.

Summary

One commentator on social thought (Nisbet, 1966) has noted that it is possible to discuss theory in terms of specific schools (classifying periods of time), ideas or concepts themselves (such as anomie), or *dramatis personae* (the major theorists). We contend that to appreciate and understand theory, it is necessary to look at all of these. Because any review of theories is in reality a history of social thought, a combination of factors needs to be taken into account. The ideas should be followed from theory to theory, the various classifications examined to see how they overlap and how they differ, and the contexts analyzed to gain a feel for the assumptions made by the theorists. Therefore, each of the following chapters examines the social and intellectual context before discussing the theory. After the theoretical presentation, the classification schemes explored in this chapter are applied to the theory.

We contend that theory is to be used—not read, memorized, and filed away for future recital. Ideas and concepts are not anyone's exclusive property; they should be rethought, reworked, and applied where needed. No one theory takes in a complete view of crime and criminals, much less a complete view of the world. For this reason, theories should be merged and integrated to form new approaches to the problems before us. And theories should be flexible enough that citizens, police officers, and judges, as well as criminologists, can use them to understand crime and criminals in our society. This doesn't mean, however, that theories of crime and criminal behavior should be simple ones. Indeed, reality is complex so we should assume that the reasons for criminal behavior are, too. Moreover, one should make a point of understanding what a theory is actually explaining. Robert Agnew (1991), for instance, was trying to make sense of the research on social control theory and realized that different researchers were variously testing the start-up of offending, the rate of offending (prevalence), the stopping of offending (desistance), and different types of crimes. No wonder he found that the evidence on the theory was complicated.

Finally, we want to caution readers that the simple presentation of each of the theories in this book cannot capture the richness of those theories. In the interest of those being exposed to theory for the first time, we have emphasized simplicity and straightforward presentation. Each of the theories is much more complex, vastly more interesting, and has many more nuances than our presentation suggests. Students should read the original works to gain a real appreciation for the theories. Anthologies are also available with the original works or excerpts from them (see, for example, Williams & McShane (1998). *Criminology Theory: Selected Classic Readings,* 2nd ed.; Suzette Cote (2002). *Criminological Theories: Bridging the Past to the Future*; Claire Renzetti, Daniel Curran, & Patrick Carr (2008). *Theories of Crime: A Reader*; Nicole Rafter (2009). *The Origins of Criminology: A Reader*; Cullen & Agnew (2010). *Criminological Theory: Past to Present,* 4th ed).

Questions and Weblinks

Critical Thinking Questions

1. Identify current policies in effect in the criminal justice system today that would be important to conduct research on. What theories or assumptions seem to underlie these policies and why they were put in place?
2. How much weight should scientists give to a theory's popularity? How is it even possible that theories without any concrete evidence can be popular?
3. If you were to construct a theory of crime, what elements or factors do you think would be important to your theory and why?
4. Should a theory of crime be able to explain all types of crime or criminals? Why or why not?

Practice Essay Questions

1. What is the relationship between theory, research and policy and how has that relationship been misused in the past?
2. What are the qualities of a good theory?
3. Explain why a popular theory may not always be best. Use examples to illustrate your points.
4. What are the various ways that we can classify theories and why is it important to do so?

Related Websites

www.crimtheory.com

http://integral-review.org/documents/Wallis,%20
Toward%20a%20Science%20of%20Metatheory,%20
Vol.%206,%20No.%203.pdf

Bibliography

Adler, F., Mueller, G., & Laufer, W. (2009). *Criminology* (7th ed.). Boston: McGraw Hill.

Agnew, R. (1985). A revised strain theory of delinquency. *Social Forces, 64*, 151–167.

Agnew, R. (1991). A longitudinal test of social control theory and delinquency. *Journal of Research in Crime and Delinquency, 28*, 126–156.

Agnew, R. (2005). *Pressured into crime: An overview of general strain theory.* New York: Oxford University Press.

Akers, R. L. (1964). Socio-economic status and delinquent behavior: A retest. *Journal of Research in Crime and Delinquency, 1*, 38–46.

Akers, R. L., & Sellers, C. (2008). *Criminological theories: Introduction and evaluation* (5th ed.). New York: Oxford University Press.

Beirne, P., & Messerschmidt, J. (2010). *Criminology: A sociological approach* (5th ed.). New York: Oxford.

Blalock, H. M. (1969). *Theory construction.* Englewood Cliffs, NJ: Prentice Hall.

Cote, S. (Ed.). (2002). *Criminological theories: Bridging the past to the future.* Thousand Oaks, CA: Sage.

Cullen, F. T., & Agnew, R. (Eds.). (2010). *Criminological theory: Past to present* (4th ed.). Los Angeles, CA: Roxbury.

DeFleur, M. L., & Quinney, R. (1966). A reformulation of Sutherland's differential association theory and a strategy for empirical verification. *Journal of Research in Crime and Delinquency, 3*, 1–22.

Elliott, D. S., Huizinga, D., & Ageton, S. (1985). *Explaining delinquency and drug use.* Beverly Hills, CA: Sage.

Gibbs, J. P. (1966). Conceptions of deviant behavior: The old and the new. *Pacific Sociological Review, 9*, 9–14.

Gibbs, J. P. (1972). *Sociological theory construction.* Hinsdale, IL: Dryden.

Gold, M. (1970). *Delinquent behavior in an American city.* Belmont, CA: Brooks/Cole.

Gouldner, A. W. (1970). *The coming crisis of western sociology.* New York: Basic Books.

Hirschi, T. (1969). *Causes of delinquency.* Berkeley: University of California Press.

Kornhauser, R. R. (1978). *Social sources of delinquency.* Chicago: University of Chicago Press.

Kuhn, T. (1970). *The structure of scientific revolutions* (2nd ed.). Chicago: University of Chicago Press.

Nisbet, R. A. (1966). *The sociological tradition.* New York: Basic Books.

Pearson, F. S., & Weiner, N. A. (1985). Toward an integration of criminological theories. *Journal of Criminal Law and Criminology, 76*, 116–150.

Rafter, N. (Ed.). (2009). *The origins of criminology: A reader.* London: Routledge.

Reid, S. T. (2011). *Crime and criminology* (13th ed.). New York: Oxford.

Reiss, A. J., Jr., & Rhodes, A. L. (1961). The distribution of juvenile delinquency in the social class structure. *American Sociological Review, 26*, 720–732.

Renzetti, C., Curran, D., & Carr, P. (2008). *Theories of crime: A reader.* Englewood Heights, NJ: Prentice Hall.

Short, J. F., Jr. (1985). The level of explanation problem in criminology. In R. F. Meier (Ed.), *Theoretical methods in criminology* (pp. 51–72). Beverly Hills, CA: Sage.

Short, J. F., Jr., & Nye, F. I. (1958). Extent of unrecorded juvenile delinquency: Tentative conclusions. *Journal of Criminal Law, Criminology, and Police Science, 49*, 296–302.

Tibbets, S. (2011). *Criminological theory: The essentials.* Thousand Oaks, CA: Sage.

Vito, G., & Maahs, J. (2011). *Criminology: Theory, research and policy* (3rd ed.). Sudbury, MA: Jones and Bartlett Publishers.

Wagner, D. G. (1984). *The growth of sociological theories.* Beverly Hills, CA: Sage.

Williams, F. P., III. (1981). The sociology of criminological theory: Paradigm or fad. In G. F. Jensen (Ed.), *Sociology of delinquency: Current issues* (pp. 20–28). Beverly Hills, CA: Sage.

Williams, F. P., III. (1984). The demise of the criminological imagination: A critique of recent criminology. *Justice Quarterly, 1*, 91–106.

Williams, F. P., III. (1999). *Imagining criminology: An alternative paradigm.* New York: Garland.

Williams, F. P., III, & McShane, M. D. (Eds.). (1998). *Criminology theory: Selected classic readings* (2nd ed.). Cincinnati, OH: Anderson.

The Classical School

LEARNING OBJECTIVES

Objective 2.1: Outline the factors that contributed to the rise of classical thought.

Objective 2.2: Explain the contributions to criminology made by Jeremy Bentham.

Objective 2.3: Discuss the writing of Cesare Beccaria and its impact.

Objective 2.4: Summarize what is meant by the social contract.

Objective 2.5: Describe the concept of deterrence and how it might be measured today.

INTRODUCTION

The particular conceptions of crime and criminal justice that emerged in the eighteenth century are collectively known as the Classical School of criminology. The name derives from common references to that entire period of time as the "classical period." The term "criminology" is a misnomer since there was no criminology as we now know it until the late nineteenth century. Nonetheless, the term is commonly used because the period gave rise to some of the basic ideas for the operation of a criminal justice system and the processing of criminals. It also provided the first broadly understood theory of criminal behavior. Criminology is the study of crime and criminals, with some study of lawmaking included. The Classical School was not interested in studying criminals *per se*, so it gained its association with criminology through its focus on lawmaking and legal processing.

Two writers of this period, Cesare Beccaria (1738–1794) and Jeremy Bentham (1748–1832), wrote the best-known works and they are considered to have had the most influence. In their writings, they opposed the arbitrary and capricious nature of the criminal justice systems of the time. They proposed that both the law and the administration of justice should be based on rationality and human rights, neither of which was then commonly applied.

Among the major ideas that descend from this school are the concepts of humans as free-willed, rational beings; utilitarianism (the greatest good for the greatest number); civil rights and due process of law; rules of evidence and testimony; determinate sentencing; and deterrence. C. Ray Jeffery (1956,

Cesare Beccaria (1738–1794)

Cesare Bonesana, Marchese di Beccaria (known simply as Cesare Beccaria), was born in Milan, Italy, in 1738 to an aristocratic family with little remaining political power. He was schooled by Jesuits, receiving a degree in law from the University of Pavia in 1758. Shortly thereafter, he joined a society of intellectuals formed by his friends Alessandro and Pietro Verri, who were advocates of social reform. After studying with and listening to the discussions of the group, Beccaria began to read the works of French Enlightment scholars. It was this literature that ultimately served as the foundation for his *On Crimes and Punishments* in 1764. After publication of his famous treatise, the Austrian government gave him a faculty position at the Palatine School in Milan. He spent two years in that role and subsequently occupied a series of patronage-based public offices, never writing another work for public consumption. He died in 1794.

1972), speaking of classical criminology, emphasizes the school's focus on a legal definition of crime rather than on a concern with criminal behavior. In addition, both the Declaration of Independence and the U.S. Constitution reflect the concerns of the classical movement. Because of this, most of our law is classical in nature.

THE HERITAGE OF THE SCHOOL

The Social Heritage

The eighteenth century was a period of major change in Europe. The reign of the Catholic Church and aristocratic feudal structure, dating from the Middle Ages and before, was about over. The new social order was criticizing the old aristocracy, both for its claim to natural superiority and for its corrupt political practices. A new and soon-to-be powerful middle class was rising from the profits of mercantilism and the beginnings of the Industrial Revolution. Societies were becoming urbanized. Traditional conceptions of property and ownership were also being disrupted. For example, enclosure movements, the practice of claiming sole use of and fencing off previously open lands, deprived the common people of what had been their traditional rights to use the land and its resources (such as game and firewood). These changes placed stress on the poor and created a resentment that affected the agricultural and rural power base of the aristocracy.

At the same time, an emphasis on commonalities among people served to minimize national differences. With this, the rule of the Church and the aristocracy was seriously threatened. The rise of the Protestant ethic allowed people to expect success for hard work in this world and not in some Church-promised afterlife. Before this time, the common person simply had to accept his or her lot in life. The Protestant ethic promised that hard work would result in an improvement in one's life and led people to expect a direct connection between hard work and success.

Certain powerful families attempted to gain the support of the middle class in a relatively successful battle with the feudal aristocracy to establish dominance over the thrones of Europe. These ruling families were known as monarchies. For instance, German nobility ruled in England, Poland, Russia, and Sweden. All of this led to the emergence of a new and highly volatile political system. The aristocracy found itself besieged by both the monarchies and the emerging middle class, and its hold on the reins of power began to loosen.

The classical period was, in many areas of life, an era of great thought and expression. In close proximity to the time when people were reading Beccaria's great treatise, *On Crimes and Punishments* (1764), J. S. Bach had composed and performed; the young colonies were about to erupt into the American Revolution; and the Declaration of Independence, the U.S. Constitution, and the Bill of Rights were written.

Writers of the classical period examined not only human nature but social conditions as well. In the late 1700s, John Howard wrote *The State of the Prisons of England and Wales*, Immanuel Kant produced his great essay *Foundations of the Metaphysics of Morals*, and Bentham introduced his *An Introduction to the Principles of Morals and Legislation*. Revolutions took place in both the American colonies and France.

The judicial system was also marked by changes. Founded on the religious structures of the Middle Ages, pre-classical law was mainly the product of judicial interpretation and caprice (Maestro, 1942). The accused often faced secret accusations, torture, and private trials; arbitrary and overly harsh sanctions were often applied to the convicted (Barnes, 1930). Generally, there were few written laws, and existing law was applied primarily to those who were not of the aristocracy. In fact, law was often used as a political tool to suppress those who spoke out against the aristocracy or the Church. Indeed, the Spanish Inquisition of the late fifteenth century and the Italian Roman Inquisition of the early sixteenth century testified to the vigorous use of law in the defense of Church and state.

The Intellectual Heritage

The prevailing ideas of the eighteenth century were those of reform. A group of philosophers called the Naturalists believed experience and observation could determine much about the world, especially when fortified by the human ability to reason. They rebelled against the authority of the Church and emphasized an order to things that was separate from religious revelation. Morals, ethics, and responsibilities became major topics of discussion. The application of science to the physical world had begun to reveal "truths," and people were certain that the same effort brought to bear on moral and political questions would yield similar fruit.

The major explanation for human behavior was hedonism. Under this theory, people are assumed to automatically attempt to maximize pleasure and minimize pain. According to Bentham (1789, p. 29), the value of any pleasure or pain would be determined by its intensity, duration, and certainty. This theory of behavior became the basis for the concept of deterrence. Bentham's elaboration on deterrence is the essence of today's rational perspectives.

One of the major new philosophical viewpoints rested on so-called natural human rights and justified the existence of government as a social contract between the state and its citizens (see, for example, the work of John Locke). This justification came close to reversing the previous

Jeremy Bentham (1748–1832)

Jeremy Bentham was born in London, England, in 1748. He attended Westminster School until enrolling at Queen's College, Oxford, at the age of 12 and received his degree at the age of 15. Thereafter Bentham studied law at Lincoln's Inn, but ultimately decided not to pursue law as a career. As a well-to-do and self-made scholar, Bentham spent most of his time in Westminster, where he wrote prolifically in philosophy, economics, and law. He was said to have produced 10–20 pages of manuscript each day.

He was the earliest proponent of utilitarianism and was considered somewhat of a political radical for his critiques of legal and common law traditions. He suggested a broad range of reforms such as animal welfare, prison management through architecture (the panopticon), and the decriminalization of homosexuality. Upon his death, per his instructions, his body was embalmed and fitted with a wax head likeness and then placed in a glass-fronted case on display at University College, London.

political belief that people existed to serve the government and, instead, made service to the people the rationale for government. Under this social contract, a person surrendered to the authority of the state only the amount of freedom necessary to ensure protection of the rights of other citizens. Although it was not really new, the idea of a social contract between people and their government served the needs of the new middle class.

Growing specialization in trade and industry required more services such as roads, ports, municipal services, and policing, and the government made an ideal provider of those services. The increasing secularization of society, in turn, fit in well with both the social contract conception of a rational human and the rising middle class. Secularism immediately suggested reforms in institutions, which was all to the benefit of the new classes.

Finally, an emphasis on human dignity, stemming from the Enlightenment, was characteristic of the period. A humanistic current of thought, chiefly from England and France, aroused the young intellectuals of the day. Those works that expressly influenced Beccaria were Montesquieu's *The Spirit of the Laws* (1748) and the various pamphlets and letters of Voltaire (Maestro, 1942, pp. 17–18). In addition to Beccaria and Montesquieu, such writers and thinkers as Hume, Montaigne, Rousseau, Helvetius, Diderot, and Condorcet were the new champions of the common people and produced eloquent writings glorifying *people* rather than the Church or state. A concern with improving social conditions accompanied this growth of interest in humanity, making possible the rise of the social sciences.

THE PERSPECTIVE OF THE SCHOOL

The Classical School, then, generally gave us a humanistic conception of how law and criminal justice systems should be constructed. It did not give rise to theories of criminal behavior; instead, the prevailing assumption of hedonism was used as a theory of human nature and was incorporated into the rationale for building legal structures. Crime and law were its essence, not criminal behavior (although they assumed rationality, hedonism, and deterrence). Law was to protect the rights of both society and individual, and its chief purpose was to deter criminal behavior. Therefore, classical law emphasized moral responsibility and the duty of citizens to consider fully the consequences of behavior before they acted. This thinking, of course, required a conception of humans as possessing free will and a rational nature. Indeed, rationality was critical to the classical position. Any individual should be able to weigh the pleasure to be gained from an illegal behavior against the punishment (pain) decreed by law and subsequently to decide against the act.

The role of punishment, according to Bentham, in itself was evil and should be used only to exclude some greater evil (1789, p. 170). Thus, the only justification for punishment was deterrence. The Classical School saw two forms of deterrence: a specific or individual form and a general or societal form. *Specific* deterrence applied to the individual who committed an offense. The idea was to apply just enough pain to offset the amount of pleasure gained from the offense. In fact, many suggested that punishments should be restricted to the same degree of pain as the degree of pleasure gained from the offense. They saw punishment in excess of this calculated amount as unnecessary, for it put the state in the position of despot. *General* deterrence, on the other hand, was to apply to other potential offenders by showing them that a punished individual would not gain from his or her offense. Through watching, or otherwise knowing about an individual receiving punishment for committing an offense, others would learn that such behavior is not profitable and thus would not commit similar acts.

These theorists saw three components to deterrence: celerity, certainty, and severity. *Celerity* is the speed with which a punishment is applied. Theoretically, at least, the closer in time a punishment is to the act, the better the result. Therefore, if an undesirable act is punished immediately, the individual would most likely be deterred. *Certainty* is the concept of making a punishment sure to happen whenever an undesirable act is committed. Classical theorists believed if every undesirable act were sure to be punished, then any rational person would immediately see the lack of profit in such actions. *Severity* is the amount of pain to be inflicted on those who do harmful acts. The greater the potential severity, the more a rational person should avoid doing harm. Thus, our system of criminal punishments is set up to match severity with the harm of an offense. Finally, Beccaria and Bentham clearly saw deterrence as most likely to occur when celerity and certainty were maximized (swift and certain punishment). They viewed severity, on the other hand, as less important and only something to be used when celerity and certainty were diminished. There was also danger in relying on severity—punishments that are too severe are likely to make the citizenry view government as despotic and become unruly. The current U.S. system of government has, primarily because of a concern for the citizenry's civil rights, made severity important because of the justice system's lengthy process and a seeming uncertainty of being arrested. Politicians also have bought into severity as a way of appearing to be tough on crime and have managed to upset original formulas relating severity of crime and incremental punishment.

According to the thought of the Classical School, the criminal justice system should respect the rights of all people. Since government drew its authority from the social contract, all individuals were equal before the law. This meant the operation of criminal justice had to be aboveboard, due process of law had to be followed, evidence had to be obtained from facts, and equality had to be maintained. They proposed that all punishments be specified by law, thus limiting judicial discretion. Scholars such as Beccaria suspected judges of following personal whim and not the law when determining guilt. He wanted the discretion of judges limited and the process of conviction and sentencing fully spelled out by law. In response to those who argued that exactly the same treatment of all offenders would result in inequities, Becarria said some inequities would certainly result, but not the overwhelming inequity of the old system (Beccaria, 1764, p. 16).

Like Beccaria, Bentham argued against great judicial discretion but saw the need to allow for some forms of decreased rationality among offenders. Punishments, he added, should not be inflicted if they are groundless, ineffective (i.e., administered to a person who was drunk or insane at the time of the offense), unprofitable, or needless. Bentham, a writer trained in the law, sought the systematic organization of legal procedures. He divided offenses into classes and types, distinguishing between private and public wrongs, crimes against person and against property, and violations of trust. In addition, he created what he called the felicific calculus, an elaborate schedule of punishments designed to take into account a combination of pleasure, pain, and mitigating circumstances. This latter endeavor reflected one of the major problems of the Classical School: how to calculate the exact degree of punishment needed to offset the gain from criminal behavior. Bentham also recognized the problems that occur when lesser offenses are punished more severely than serious offenses. Indeed, these problems continue to plague us today, as judges and legislatures seek to find appropriate sentences for various crimes. The major difference seems to be that today's legislators have little of Bentham's understanding of how deterrence works and escalate sentences for lesser offenses at whim (or in response to special interest groups of voters).

Although Beccaria was not opposed to the use of corporal punishment, particularly for those convicted of violent personal crimes, he specifically decried the use of torture in interrogation to elicit confessions (Beirne, 2006). He supported time limits on case preparation for both the defense and the prosecution. This is another example of these theorists' conviction that swiftness of punishment, not its severity, is the strength of its deterrent value. Beccaria was also opposed to the imprisonment of those not yet convicted of crimes. Languishing in the filthy, disease-ridden prisons, many of the accused died even before being tried, a situation repugnant to the humanitarian as well as to the rational thinker of the time. The writings of Beccaria and John Howard, who toured prisons and jails and described their conditions, inspired sweeping reforms of prison conditions and incarceration practices.[1]

Finally, members of the Classical School were generally opposed to capital punishment. Beccaria argued that no citizen has the right to take his or her own life and, therefore, citizens could not give this right to the state under the social contract. Moreover, if the state can take a life, where is the profit in allowing the state to govern for us? Capital punishment was, as a result, not part of the state's base of authority. Using a more pragmatic approach to capital punishment, Bentham pointed out that the death penalty might tend to make members of a jury exercise leniency out of humane motives, therefore subverting the law. Using this same line of reasoning, he also thought witnesses might perjure themselves out of the same humane motives. In short, by being humane, jurors in capital cases could spread a message that it is acceptable to ignore the law. Thus, he thought capital punishment was simply not worth the potential havoc it could create for the justice system and law.

The impact of the Classical School may be seen in the results of the French and American revolutions (Newman & Morongiu, 2009). Both embraced the equality of people, the right to life and liberty, fairness in the administration of justice, and restrictions on the actions of the state. Criminal law in the United States is largely classical, with its strong emphasis on individual responsibility for actions and on due process of law. In our contemporary criminal justice system, not until the sentencing stage is there a move away from the classical emphasis, with some sentences designed to treat the offender. Even here the current trend is toward a more punitive form of sentencing.

CLASSIFICATION OF THE SCHOOL

Since the Classical School was, in reality, a movement designed to reform society, it was both conflict-oriented and structural. The *conflict* classification derives from the fact that philosophers and scholars of this era saw human nature as needing to be restricted and controlled. They believed that people were basically self-interested and, without restraint, would act in ways that conflict with the interests of others. Proponents of these versions of human nature simply could not accept the idea of individuals naturally being in a state of consensus or agreement with each other. The promotion of social contract forms of government is an example of the way in which classical theorists felt societies could most humanely control their citizens and their governments. In addition, the majority of their ideas were at odds with existing political and legal structures, and their reforms were aimed at existing social arrangements. The new philosophy of the common people was in conflict with religious and economic systems, the old governmental structure, and forms of knowledge based on religious revelation.

We classify the Classical School as predominantly *structural* because it emphasizes the effect of societal institutions on people in general. The theorists' main concern focused on the way governments make law and how law affects the rights of citizens. The fact that the Classical

---

[1] There is some contention about the importance of Beccaria's work. Philip Jenkins (1984) argues that it was Beccaria's "conservative" bent that provided the support for the essay. Similarly, Graeme Newman and Pietro Marongiu (1990, 2009) hold that Beccaria's work is vastly overrated today. They suggest that all the ideas in his essay were present in others' works, from which Beccaria liberally borrowed. Piers Beirne (1991, 1993, 1994, 2006) also argues there was no real Classical School and that Beccaria has been continuously misinterpreted by scholars. Other critics have noted that the very processes and behaviors Beccaria objected to were being reformed both before and as he wrote.

An Example of Classical Thought

(Excerpts from the Virginia Bill of Rights, adopted June 12, 1776)

SECTION 1.   That all men are by nature equally free and independent, and have certain inherent rights, of which, when they enter into a state of society, they cannot, by any compact, deprive or divest their posterity; namely, the enjoyment of life and liberty, with the means of acquiring and possessing property, and pursuing and obtaining happiness and safety.

SECTION 2.   That all power is vested in, and consequently derived from, the people; that magistrates are their trustees and servants....

SECTION 3.   That government is, or ought to be, instituted for the common benefit, protection, and security of the people, nation or community; of all the various modes and forms of government, that is best which is capable of producing the greatest degree of happiness and safety....

SECTION 4.   That no man, or set of men, are entitled to exclusive or separate emoluments or privileges from the community....

SECTION 8.   That in all capital or criminal prosecutions a man hath a right to demand the cause and nature of his accusation, to be confronted with the accusers and witnesses, to call for evidence in his favor, and to a speedy trial by an impartial jury of twelve men of his vicinage, without whose unanimous consent he cannot be found guilty; nor can he be compelled to give evidence against himself; that no man be deprived of his liberty, except by the law of the land or the judgment of his peers.

School was interested in the legislation of criminal law and in the criminal justice system, rather than in criminal behavior, is characteristic of a fully structural approach. Indeed, since most of the criminological theories of the period were political theories, the Classical School was predominantly *macrotheoretical* in its orientation.

There is also a processual and microtheoretical side to the Classical School. Some argue that the Classical School should be categorized as processual because of its emphasis on the rational, and hedonistic, behavior of individuals. Indeed, the justification for punishment and the construction of criminal law were based on showing a rational person that there would be no profit in transgressing on the rights of others. The entire classical legal structure is founded on the concept of a rational person and responsibility for one's own actions. Clearly, the Classical School had something to say about the process of committing crime and why crime takes place. It is also true, however, that every theoretical position begins with (often unstated) assumptions about human nature. Those assumptions form a foundation for theories but do not constitute the essence of a theory. Therefore, we believe that the rational pursuit of pleasure is best seen as an assumption rather than the real focus of classical theory. Those who focus on the writings of Jeremy Bentham are more likely to see a microtheoretical, and processual, focus to the school.

Summary

The Classical School is characterized by (1) an emphasis on free will choices and human rationality, (2) a view of behavior as hedonistic, (3) a focus on morality and responsibility, (4) a concern with political structure and the way in which government deals with its citizens, and (5) a concern for the basic rights of all people. These generic ideas and concerns were applied to criminal justice to produce concepts such as deterrence, civil rights, and due process of law; but it is the general characteristics, not the specific ones of criminal justice, that contain the essence of classical thought.

MAJOR POINTS OF THE SCHOOL

1. People exist in a world with free will and make their own rational choices, although they have a natural tendency toward self-interest and pleasure.
2. People have certain natural rights, among them life, liberty, and ownership of property.
3. Governments are created by the citizens of a state to protect these rights, and they exist as a social contract between those who govern and those who are governed.
4. Citizens give up only the portion of their natural rights that is necessary for the state to regulate society for the benefit of all and to protect society against the natural self-interest of individuals.
5. To ensure civil rights, legislators enact law that both defines the procedures by which transgressions will be handled and specifies the exact behaviors that make up those transgressions. This law specifies the process for determining guilt and the punishment to be meted out to those found guilty.
6. Crime consists of a transgression against the social contract; therefore, crime is a moral offense against society.
7. Punishment is justified only to preserve the social contract. Therefore, the purpose of punishment is to prevent future transgressions by deterring socially harmful behavior. Only that amount of punishment necessary to offset the gains of harmful behavior is justified.
8. All people are equal in their rights and should be treated equally before the law.

Epilogue: Current Directions and Policy Implications

The Classical School still has a dominant effect on today's criminal justice system policies. Most Western nations still adhere to most of the classical inventions under due process of law and the rights of individuals, largely because these concepts are imbedded in various constitutions. Two of the major concepts of the Classical School, deterrence and rationality, are still alive and well.

Deterrence has had two separate rebirths over the last four decades. In the first, the public, in moving toward a more conservative and punitive mode, has embraced the concept of deterrence and clamored for harsher sentences. The assumption, of course, is that tougher sentences will deter would-be criminals from committing crimes and make those caught and convicted reconsider their behavior. Deterrence has been the favored approach to the crimes of drunken driving and drug dealing. One of the problems with deterring criminals is that our criminal justice system does not proceed quickly. The federal system and many states have attempted to solve this problem by enacting speedy trial laws.

In the second renewal of interest in deterrence, many scholars have been engaged in research to see if deterrence works. Three of the favorite research topics have been the death penalty, drunken driving, and drug use. At this time, the collective evidence points to a short-term effect for drunken driving, probably no effect for the death penalty, and little, if any, effect for drug use. There is still controversy over the proper way to test for the effects of deterrence, and the jury is still out on most of the issues. However, it should be noted the vast majority of deterrence research has failed to find any substantial deterrent effect for legal sanctions. In fact, Ray Paternoster, a criminologist who has been engaged in deterrence research for more than 30 years, characterizes the body of evidence for deterrence as more than a little flimsy (2010, p. 766). Similarly, a new review of the deterrent effect of the death penalty by the National Research Council (Nagin and Pepper, 2012) concludes that existing research can be used to make *any* conclusions. In the face of this evidence, contemporary legislatures and the public continue to act as if deterrence were alive and well, and the primary factor in keeping crime in check.

Researchers have also recognized that legal punishments do not stand alone, and some have argued for a version of deterrence combining both legal and informal punishment systems. In fact, the usual direction is to combine deterrence with concepts from social control theories (Chapter 11).

Social learning theory (Chapter 12) can also be interpreted as a close cousin of deterrence because it includes punishment as one of the stimuli involved in the learning process. When legal deterrence is combined with informal social controls, the research results usually show only a slight effect attributable to legal deterrence. Informal controls seem to have a stronger effect on individuals, particularly when the informal controls include shaming.

The public and the government have embraced the notion of a rational criminal. This makes it easier to blame the offender for all aspects of a crime, rather than share some of that blame with society for creating conditions that force some people into crime. If it is an individual's decision to commit crime, then he or she is morally responsible and deserves to be punished. The great advantage of this reasoning is that we do not have to do anything other than punish while the individual is in our control. Thus, from the mid-1970s to about 2000, rehabilitation and skill training were no longer part of what a prison should do. In addition, with deterrence as our goal, we do not have to engage in expensive social programs to improve conditions that create crime, nor do we have to engage in even more expensive social reform. An assumption that individuals make fully rational decisions to engage in criminal behavior can save a lot of money. If this assumption is incorrect, and research on the effects of prison warehousing of offenders seems to have invalidated it, these savings may be short-term ones. A failure to rectify social conditions, if they are also important, will simply make matters worse and over the long term will cost much more in increased crime, suffering, and deterioration of neighborhoods. In the past few years, administrators of most state correctional systems have recognized the problem. Ironically, many of the politicians who still support the concepts of deterrence and rational criminals are now supporters of skills training and rehabilitation because they think it saves money by reducing the number of offenders who return to prison.

Criminologists have also granted a good deal of popularity to the concept of rational offenders. We now have rational choice theories (Chapter 13) and theories of punishment called "just deserts." The rational choice theories generally suggest a connection between opportunities for offending, the environmental conditions at the time, and the readiness of the offender to engage in the offense. That is, they assert that, given the situation and the circumstances, offenders make informed decisions to commit crimes. Just deserts punishment theory returns to the classical concept of retribution and argues that, because offenders make the choice to offend, punishment is deserved. The just portion of the theory restates the classical notion of equitable punishment—no more or less punishment than what is required to correct the harm from the crime.

One might argue that our criminal justice system has become so punitive and unwieldy that we need a similar period of reform and revision in order to insure fairness and proportionality in our law. Most jurisdictions have gradually increased the possible aggravating circumstances that make capital punishment an option in murder cases. There is even talk of capital punishment for certain homeland security crimes. Also, zero-tolerance policies and mandatory punishments have made a wide range of behaviors criminal, and those behaviors vary significantly from state to state, making it difficult to know what specific conduct is allowed or proscribed. In one school, a six-year-old girl with mental health problems was arrested for kicking her teacher. In New Haven, Connecticut, an eighth grader was removed from his position of class vice-president, banned from participating in an honors dinner, and suspended for a day because he violated the school district's wellness policy by purchasing a serving of candy. The youth, who simply bought a small bag of Skittles from a classmate, admitted he did not even know that he broke a rule. In another instance, a child who gave an aspirin to a classmate who complained of a headache was suspended from school for distributing drugs. Too many rules and laws, the classical scholars would argue—and the ability for everyone to know and understand them and the way they are interpreted and enforced—leads to abuses of punishment and ineffective governance. The bottom line for the Classical School though is that these 200-year-old ideas are applicable to our latest policy and theoretical notions. Obviously, we are still engaged in debates about these ideas.

Questions and Weblinks

Critical Thinking Questions

1. How relevant do you think the ideas of the Classical School are to the criminal justice system today? What classical ideas could be developed and implemented today that we are not currently using?
2. What do you think deters someone from committing a crime? What evidence can you think of that indicates people are or are not deterred? Are there people who are "most deterred"?
3. Do we have a viable and meaningful sense of "social contract" in our society today? Why or why not? How important is it for society to have a strong social contract and what barriers do we face in developing such sentiments?
4. Examine some of the more notable criminal cases in the news today and the punishments that were handed down. How do the sentences today compare to those of the classical period or even to sentences of 100 or 50 years ago? What factors seem to shape the way we view punishments?

Practice Essay Questions

1. What were punishments like before the influence of the classical philosophers?
2. Discuss some of the classical concepts and ideas that we still see in our criminal justice system today.
3. Who were some of the major contributors to classical thought and what were their specific contributions?
4. How were ideas about the basic nature of all men related to the way we determine criminal punishment.

Related Websites

http://www.utilitarianism.com/bentham.htm
http://www.ucl.ac.uk/Bentham-Project/who
http://www.constitution.org/cb/beccaria_bio.htm

http://academicearth.org/lectures/
classical-utilitarianism-and-distributive-justice

Bibliography

Barnes, H. E. (1930). *The story of punishment: A record of man's inhumanity to man.* Boston: Stratford.

Beccaria, C. (1963). *Of crimes and punishments* (H. Paolucci, Trans.). Indianapolis, IN: Bobbs-Merrill. (Original work published 1764.)

Beirne, P. (1991). Inventing criminology: The "science of man" in Cesare Beccaria's *Dei delitti e delle pene* (1764). *Criminology, 29,* 777–820.

Beirne, P. (1993). *Inventing criminology: Essays on the rise of "homo criminalis."* Albany, NY: State University of New York Press.

Beirne, P. (1994). *The origins and growth of criminology: Essays in intellectual history, 1760–1945.* Aldershot, UK: Dartmouth.

Beirne, P. (2006). Free will and determinism? Reading Beccaria's *Of Crimes and Punishments* (1764) as a text of Enlightenment. In S. Henry & M. Lanier (Eds.), *The essential criminology reader* (pp. 3–17). Boulder, CO: Westview Press.

Bentham, J. (1830). *The rationale of punishment.* London: Robert Heward.

Bentham, J. (1905). *Theory of legislation.* London: Kegan Paul.

Bentham, J. (1948). *An introduction to the principles of morals and legislation.* New York: Kegan Paul. (Original work published 1789.)

Bentham, J. (Ed.). (1995). *The panopticon writings,* edited and introduced by M. Bozovic. London, UK: Verso.

Howard, J. (1929). *The state of the prisons of England and Wales.* London: J. M. Dent. (Original work published 1777.)

Jeffery, C. R. (1956). The structure of American criminological thinking. *Journal of Criminal Law, Criminology, and Police Science, 46,* 658–672.

Jeffery, C. R. (1972). The historical development of criminology. In H. Mannheim (Ed.), *Pioneers in criminology* (2nd ed., pp. 458–498). Montclair, NJ: Patterson Smith.

Jenkins, P. (1984). Varieties of enlightenment criminology. *British Journal of Criminology, 24,* 112–130.

Kant, I. (1959). *Foundations of the metaphysics of morals.* New York: Bobbs-Merrill. (Original work published 1785.)

Locke, J. (1937). *Treatise of civil government and a letter concerning toleration.* New York: D. Appleton-Century. (Original work published 1690.)

Maestro, M. T. (1942). *Voltaire and Beccaria as reformers of criminal law.* New York: Columbia University Press.

Maestro, M. T. (1973). *Cesare Beccaria and the origins of penal reform.* Philadelphia: Temple University Press.

Montesquieu, C. L. De Secondat. (1878). *The spirit of the laws* (Vols. 1–2). London: G. Bell. (Original work published 1748.)

Montesquieu, C. L. De Secondat. (1964). *The Persian letters.* New York: Bobbs-Merrill. (Original work published 1721.)

Newman, G., & Marongiu, P. (1990). Penological reform and the myth of Beccaria. *Criminology, 28,* 325–346.

Newman, G., & Marongiu, P. (Trans.). (2009). *Cesare Beccaria, on crimes and punishments.* Translation, annotations, and introduction. New Brunswick, NJ: Transaction.

Paternoster, R. (2010). How much do we really know about criminal deterrence? *Journal of Criminal Law & Criminology, 100,* 765–823.

Research Bibliography (from 1990)

Aldarondo, E. (1996). Cessation and persistence of wife assault: A longitudinal analysis. *American Journal of Orthopsychiatry, 66,* 141–151.

Anwar, S., & Loughran, T. A. (2011). Testing a Bayesian learning theory of deterrence among serious juvenile offenders. *Criminology, 49,* 667–698.

Bailey, W. C. (1990). Murder, capital punishment, and television: Execution publicity and homicide rates. *American Sociological Review, 55,* 628–633.

Benson, B., Kim, I., & Rasmussen, D. W. (1994). Estimating deterrence effects: A public choice perspective on the economics of crime literature. *Southern Economic Journal, 61,* 161–168.

Berk, R. A., Campbell, A., Klap, R., & Western, B. (1992). The deterrent effect of arrest in incidents of domestic violence: A Bayesian analysis of four field experiments. *American Sociological Review, 57,* 698–708.

Birks, D., Townsley, M., & Stewart, A. (2012). Generative explanations of crime: Using simulation to test criminological theory. *Criminology, 50,* 221–254.

Burkett, S. R., & Ward, D. A. (1993). A note on perceptual deterrence, religiously based moral condemnation, and social control. *Criminology, 31,* 119–134.

Buzawa, E. S., & Buzawa, C. G. (Eds.). (1996). *Do arrests and restraining orders work?* Thousand Oaks, CA: Sage.

Canela-Cacho, J. A., Blumstein, A., & Cohen, J. (1997). Relationship between the offending frequency of imprisoned and free offenders. *Criminology, 35,* 133–175.

Caplan, J., Kennedy, L., & Petrossian, G. (2011). Police-monitored CCTV cameras in Newark, NJ: A quasi-experimental test of crime deterrence. *Journal of Experimental Criminology, 7,* 255–274.

Crank, J., Koski, C., Johnson, M., Ramirez, E., Shelden, A., & Peterson, S. (2010). Hot corridors, deterrence, and guardianship: An assessment of the Omaha metro safety initiative. *Journal of Criminal Justice, 38,* 430–438.

Decker, S. H., & Kohfeld, C. W. (1990). The deterrent effect of capital punishment in the five most active execution states: A time series analysis. *Criminal Justice Review, 15,* 173–191.

Decker, S. H., Wright, R., & Logie, R. (1993). Perceptual deterrence among active residential burglars: A research note. *Criminology, 31,* 135–147.

Dölling, D., Entorf, H., Hermann, D., & Rupp, T. (2009). Is deterrence effective? Results of a meta-analysis of punishment. *European Journal on Criminal Policy & Research, 15*(1/2), 201–224.

Dundes, L. (1994). Punishing parents to deter delinquency: A realistic remedy? *American Journal of Police, 13,* 113–133.

Dunford, F., Huizinga, D., & Elliott, D. S. (1990). The role of arrest in domestic assault: The Omaha experiment. *Criminology, 28,* 183–206.

Elis, L. A., & Simpson, S. S. (1995). Informal sanction threats and corporate crime: Additive versus multiplicative models. *Journal of Research in Crime and Delinquency, 32,* 399–424.

Gartin, P. R. (1995). Examining differential officer effects in the Minneapolis domestic violence experiment. *American Journal of Police, 14*, 93–110.

Gertz, M. G., & Gould, L. C. (1995). Fear of punishment and the willingness to engage in criminal behavior: A research note. *Journal of Criminal Justice, 23*, 377–384.

Grasmick, H. G., & Bursik, R. J., Jr. (1990). Conscience, significant others, and rational choice: Extending the deterrence model. *Law and Society Review, 24*, 837–861.

Grasmick, H. G., Bursik, R. J., Jr., & Arneklev, B. J. (1993). Reduction in drunk driving as a response to increased threats of shame, embarrassment, and legal sanctions. *Criminology, 31*, 41–67.

Grasmick, H. G., Davenport, E., Chamlin, M., & Bursik, R. J., Jr. (1992). Protestant fundamentalism and the retributive doctrine of punishment. *Criminology, 30*, 21–45.

Gray, T. (1994). Using cost-benefit analysis to measure rehabilitation and special deterrence. *Journal of Criminal Justice, 22*, 569–575.

Guerette, R. T., & Santana, S. A. (2010). Explaining victim self-protective behavior effects on crime incident outcomes: A test of opportunity theory. *Crime & Delinquency, 56*, 198–226.

Hamdani, A., & Klement, A. (2008). Corporate crime and deterrence. *Stanford Law Review, 61*, 271–310.

Jacobs, B. A. (1996a). Crack dealers' apprehension avoidance techniques: A case of restrictive deterrence. *Justice Quarterly, 13*, 359–381.

Jacobs, B. A. (1996b). Crack dealers and restrictive deterrence: Identifying narcs. *Criminology, 34*, 409–431.

Joo-Hee, J., Ekland-Olson, S., & Kelly, W. R. (1995). Recidivism among paroled property offenders released during a period of prison reform. *Criminology, 33*, 389–410.

Kirchgässner, G. (2011). Econometric estimates of deterrence of the death penalty: Facts or ideology? *Kyklos, 64*, 448–478.

Koper, C. S. (1995). Just enough police presence: Reducing crime and disorderly behavior by optimizing patrol time in crime hot spots. *Justice Quarterly, 12*, 649–672.

Lott, J. R., Jr., & Mustard, D. B. (1997). Crime, deterrence, and right-to-carry concealed handguns. *Journal of Legal Studies, 26*, 1–68.

Maltz, M. D. (1996). From Poisson to the present: Applying operations research to problems of crime and justice. *Journal of Quantitative Criminology, 12*, 3–61.

Marvel, T. B., & Moody, C. E. (1995). The impact of enhanced prison terms for felonies committed with guns. *Criminology, 33*, 247–281.

Marvel, T. B., & Moody, C. E. (1996). Determinate sentencing and abolishing parole: The long-term impacts on prisons and crime. *Criminology, 34*, 107–128.

Maxson, C. L., Matsuda, K. N., & Hennigan, K. (2011). "Deterrability" among gang and nongang juvenile offenders: Are gang members more (or less) deterrable than other juvenile offenders? *Crime & Delinquency, 57*, 516–543.

McDowall, D., Lizotte, A., & Wiersema, B. (1991). General deterrence through civilian gun ownership. *Criminology, 29*, 541–559.

Nagin, D. S., & Paternoster, R. (1991). The preventive effects of the perceived risk of arrest: Testing an expanded conception of deterrence. *Criminology, 29*, 561–585.

Nagin, D. S., & Pepper, J. V. (Eds.) (2012). *Deterrence and the death penalty*. Washington, DC: National Academies Press.

O'Connell, D., Visher, C. A., Martin, S., Parker, L., & Brent, J. (2011). Decide your time: Testing deterrence theory's certainty and celerity effects on substance-using probationers. *Journal of Criminal Justice, 39*, 261–267.

Pate, A. M., & Hamilton, E. E. (1992). Formal and informal deterrents to domestic violence: The Dade County spouse assault experiment. *American Sociological Review, 57*, 691–697.

Paternoster, R., & Nagin, D. S. (1994). Personal capital and social control: The deterrence implications of a theory of individual differences in criminal offending. *Criminology, 32*, 581–606.

Paternoster, R., & Piquero, A. (1995). Reconceptualizing deterrence: An empirical test of personal and vicarious experiences. *Journal of Research in Crime and Delinquency, 32*, 251–286.

Paternoster, R., & Simpson, S. (1996). Sanction threats and appeals to morality: Testing a rational choice model of corporate crime. *Law and Society Review, 30*, 549–583.

Peterson, R. D., & Bailey, W. C. (1991). Felony murder and capital punishment: An examination of the deterrence question. *Criminology, 29*, 367–395.

Piquero, A., & Pogarsky, G. (2002). Beyond Stafford and Warr's reconceptualization of deterrence: Personal & vicarious experiences, impulsivity, & offending behavior. *Journal of Research in Crime and Delinquency, 39*, 153–186.

Pogarsky, G. (2007). Deterrence and individual differences among convicted offenders. *Journal of Quantitative Criminology, 23*, 59–74.

Pogarsky, G., & Piquero, A. R. (2003). Can punishment encourage offending? Investigating the "Resetting" effect. *Journal of Research in Crime and Delinquency, 40*, 92–117.

Ross, H. L., & Klette, H. (1995). Abandonment of mandatory jail for impaired drivers in Norway and Sweden. *Accident Analysis and Prevention, 27*, 151–157.

Saridakis, G., & Spengler, H. (2012). Crime, deterrence and unemployment in Greece: A panel data approach. *Social Science Journal, 49*, 167–174.

Sherman, L. W., & Berk, R. A. (1984). The specific deterrent effects of arrest for domestic assault. *American Sociological Review, 49*, 261–272.

Sherman, L. W., & Rogan, D. P. (1995a). Deterrent effects of police raids on crack houses: A randomized controlled experiment. *Justice Quarterly, 12*, 755–781.

Sherman, L. W., & Rogan, D. P. (1995b). Effects of gun seizures on gun violence: "Hot spots" patrol in Kansas City. *Justice Quarterly, 12*, 673–693.

Sherman, L. W., Schmidt, J., Rogan, D., Gartin, P., Cohn, E., Collins, D., et al. (1991). From initial deterrence to long-term escalation: Short custody arrest for poverty ghetto domestic violence. *Criminology, 29*, 821–850.

Sherman, L. W., & Weisburd, D. (1995). General deterrent effects of police patrol in crime "hot spots": A randomized, controlled trial. *Justice Quarterly, 12*, 625–648.

Sitren, A. H., & Applegate, B. K. (2012). Testing deterrence theory with offenders: The empirical validity of Stafford and Warr's model. *Deviant Behavior, 33*, 492–506.

Socia, K. M. (2012). The efficacy of county-level sex offender residence restrictions in New York. *Crime & Delinquency, 58*, 612–642.

Stack, S. (1994). Execution publicity and homicide in Georgia. *American Journal of Criminal Justice, 18*, 25–39.

Tauchen, H., Witte, A. D., & Griesinger, H. (1994). Criminal deterrence: Revisiting the issue with a birth cohort. *Review of Economics and Statistics, 76*, 399–412.

Tavares, A., Mendes, S., & Costa, C. (2008). The impact of deterrence policies on reckless driving: The case of Portugal. *European Journal on Criminal Policy & Research, 14*, 417–429.

Thomson, E. (1997). Deterrence versus brutalization: The case of Arizona. *Homicide Studies, 1*, 110–128.

Tittle, C., Botchkovar, E., & Antonaccio, O. (2011). Criminal contemplation, national context, and deterrence. *Journal of Quantitative Criminology, 27*, 225–249.

Tolnay, S. E., & Deane, G. (1996). Vicarious violence: Spatial effects on southern lynchings, 1890–1919. *American Journal of Sociology, 102*, 788–815.

Traub, S. H. (1996). Battling employee crime: A review of corporate strategies and programs. *Crime and Delinquency, 42*, 244–256.

Trivizas, E., & Smith, P. T. (1997). The deterrent effect of terrorist incidents on the rates of luggage theft in railway and underground stations. *British Journal of Criminology, 37*, 63–74.

Tunnell, K. D. (1990). Choosing crime: Close your eyes and take your chances. *Justice Quarterly, 7*, 673–690.

Veneziano, C., & Veneziano, L. (1995). Reasons for refraining from criminal activity. *American Journal of Criminal Justice, 19*, 185–196.

Veneziano, C., & Veneziano, L. (1996). Factors accounting for not engaging in illegal acts in relationship to type of crime. *Journal of Crime and Justice, 19*, 167–178.

Waldorf, D., & Murphy, S. (1995). Perceived risks and criminal justice pressures on middle class cocaine sellers. *Journal of Drug Issues, 25*, 11–32.

Watling, C. N., Palk, G. R., Freeman, J. E., & Davey, J. D. (2010). Applying Stafford and Warr's reconceptualization of deterrence theory to drug driving: Can it predict those likely to offend? *Accident Analysis & Prevention, 42*, 452–458.

Weisburd, D., & Green, L. (1995). Policing drug hot spots: The Jersey City drug market analysis experiment. *Justice Quarterly, 12*, 711–735.

Weisburd, D., Waring, E., & Chayet, E. (1995). Specific deterrence in a sample of offenders convicted of white-collar crimes. *Criminology, 33*, 587–607.

Wiersma, E. (1996). Commercial burglars in the Netherlands: Reasoning decision-makers? *International Journal of Risk Security and Crime Prevention, 1*, 217–225.

Wikström, P. H., Tseloni, A., & Karlis, D. (2011). Do people comply with the law because they fear getting caught? *European Journal of Criminology, 8*, 401–420.

Wittebrood, K., & Nieuwbeerta, P. (2000). Criminal victimization during one's life course: The effects of previous victimization and patterns of routine activities. *Journal of Research in Crime and Delinquency, 37*, 91–123.

3

The Positive School

LEARNING OBJECTIVES

Objective 3.1: Describe the development of biological theories of crime.

Objective 3.2: Discuss the work of Cesare Lombroso and what he contributed to criminology.

Objective 3.3: Explain what is meant by atavism and whether it is a still a relevant concept to the study of crime.

Objective 3.4: Compare and contrast the major principles of the classical and positivist school.

Objective 3.5: Summarize some of the topics in criminology studied by psychologists.

INTRODUCTION

While the champions of the classical period were writers and philosophers, the Positivists were more likely to be scientists, mathematicians, doctors, and astronomers. While the classical reformers sought to modernize and civilize the system within which they lived, the Positivists reached out to order and explain the world around them. The earlier concentration on building a moral and fair system of justice and government was thus displaced by the scientific exploration and discovery of other aspects of life.

Although the Classicalists believed that humans possess a rational mind and thus have free will to choose good over evil, the Positivists saw behavior as determined by its biological, psychological, and social traits. The primary characteristics of positivist criminological thought are a deterministic view of the world, a focus on criminal behavior instead of on legal issues such as rights, and the prevention of crime through the treatment and rehabilitation of offenders.

The use of scientific research techniques was common to those who studied criminals from a positivist perspective. In scientific analyses, data were collected to describe and explain different types of individuals as well as different social conditions. The theory of evolution, proposed by naturalists and anthropologists, formed a basis for the study of human behavior and, more specifically, of criminal behavior.

Most criminological texts limit their consideration of the Positive School to the work of three Italian writers and thus create confusion among students when the term "positivism" is applied to later and broader theories. This chapter focuses on positivism as a more general approach and delves into the essence of what positivism *is*. In this way, one gains a more general understanding of positivism than the theories of a few people, and this view helps students transcend the biological emphasis usually associated with the Positive School. In reality, positivism is a philosophical system that emphasizes the "positive" application of science to knowledge production. Therefore, the Positive School is an all-encompassing scientific perspective. The school is also known today as the "modernist" perspective (a term used by those scholars who consider themselves to be "postmodern").

THE HERITAGE OF THE SCHOOL

The Social Heritage

The years at the beginning of the twentieth century were alive with invention and discovery. Science became a major tool of scholars, and the world experienced a revolution in knowledge that brought countless changes to everyday life. Advanced communications put once-separate cultures in close contact. The Statue of Liberty was unveiled, the Eiffel Tower was completed, Henrik Ibsen wrote, Giuseppe Verdi composed, and Vincent van Gogh painted. The automobile, the airplane, the phonograph, and electric lighting were introduced. Medicine embraced science, and researchers discovered germs and how to combat them. Sigmund Freud developed psychoanalysis, and Albert Einstein pronounced his theory of relativity.

The application of science to problems of everyday life was central to the creations of the late nineteenth and early twentieth centuries. Perhaps as never before, a method of gaining knowledge was almost deified. With the great strides made by the application of science to industry, it was to be expected that those concerned with human affairs would have a vision of perfecting humanity through scientific study.

Of great importance was the transformation of the agriculturally based aristocracies of the eighteenth century into complex, industrialized, urban societies. The French and American revolutions helped foster a new climate in which the concerns of the Classical School could be addressed. People became less concerned with their governments than previously was the case and focused more attention on social rather than on political problems. Social historian David Rothman (1971, pp. 59–62), for example, points out that Americans saw crime as the product of inequities in British colonial rule and expected crime to be reduced with the institution of the new democracy. When crime rates failed to drop, Americans were forced to acknowledge that crime might have other bases in human behavior. Positivism provided the answers to that new concern.

The Intellectual Heritage

Although some see little connection between the Classical and Positive Schools, it was the classical reaffirmation that people could develop and verify their own knowledge that led to the widespread use of science in the positivist era. Among the various intellectual influences in this direction was the rise of a (positive) philosophy that underscored the importance of tested and systematized experience rather than pure speculation, or metaphysics. Humans were seen as responsible for their own destinies, and they were fully capable of adapting their own behaviors and social institutions to create a society that would fulfill those destinies.

A second important ingredient in the rise of positivist criminology was the concept of evolution that emerged even before the writing of Charles Darwin. Evolution became a standard form of thinking about subjects, popularized to the extent that human societies were seen as evolving. Western societies were seen as the pinnacle of human accomplishment, and all else was less evolved. Criminals were viewed as individuals who were not as fully evolved as more civilized people ("normal" members of Western societies). Leonard Savitz (1972, p. viii) even suggests that this evolutionary perspective contributed to the development of a racist view of criminality and fueled the popularity of the field of eugenics.

A final influence on positivist criminology was the emergence of anthropology. Still in its infancy as an academic discipline, anthropology presented evidence that other societies were more "primitive." The chief purveyors of this evidence were missionaries and colonial administrators, who were not well trained in the art of observation. Failing to look deeply into the societies they reported on, they assumed that complex organization would resemble their own European societies. Failing to find European-style social organization, they concluded that other societies were less evolved, more primitive, and closer to original human nature. Their observations were then used by other disciplines and incorporated into social science theories of how societies develop and why humans behave as they do.

THE PERSPECTIVE OF THE SCHOOL

Positivism itself is more accurately called a philosophy than a theory. Even as a philosophy, there are several varieties of positivism. Abraham Kaplan (1968, p. 389) identifies two major forms. The first is a product of eighteenth-century Enlightenment philosophy (the Classical School), with its emphasis on the importance of reason and experience. The second is a twentieth-century version known as "Logical Positivism," with a close association with mathematical reasoning and formal models of thought. This is the version that is referred to as "modernism." Many today also associate positivism with various forms of statistical analysis. Within sociology alone, there have been several different understandings about the meaning of positivism (Halfpenny, 1982). One important underpinning of almost any form of positivism is an interest in classifying (or establishing categories for) any subject of interest.

Many criminologists use the term "positivism" to mean an approach that studies human behavior through the use of the traditional scientific method. The focus is on systematic observation and the accumulation of evidence and objective fact within a deductive framework (moving from the general to the specific). Positivists, then, may study behavior from a biological, a psychological, or a sociological perspective. The point is not the perspective from which the study is done but the assumptions that underlie the methodology for doing the study.

Auguste Comte and the Methodology of Positivism

Much of the system of analysis that constitutes sociological positivism today was developed by Auguste Comte, a nineteenth-century French philosopher and social scientist who is credited with being the father of sociology. His approach to the study of social phenomena included an insistence on testable hypotheses, the use of comparative methods, the careful classification of societies, a systematic approach to the study of social history, and the study of abnormality as a means to understanding normality (Fletcher, 1975, pp. ix–xi). Comte's work, among that of others, prompted scientific studies of human social behavior.

Early Nineteenth-Century Positivist Work

Perhaps the earliest of positivistically oriented work on the subject of crime was that of two statisticians, Adolphe Quetelet of Belgium and Andre Guerry of France, in the 1820s and 1830s. Each examined the social statistics that were available in some European countries as if they were data from the physical sciences. Quetelet, a mathematician, applied probability theory to these data to produce a concept of the "average person," something we might take for granted today in our use of actuarial data and in our projections of crime risk over time. His adherence to the idea of a normal distribution (bell curve) of events seemed to stand in contrast to the idea of free will. Applying predictive models to the study of crime rates, he found variations in crime rates by climate and season and observed the same age and sex differences we find today among criminals (Quetelet, 1831/1984).

Other early work was largely that of biologists and anatomists who studied the human body in hopes of establishing some relationship between it and human behavior. Some of this work distinctly predates any of the usual claims to the founding of criminology. A physiognomist of the sixteenth century, G. Baptista della Porta, related characteristics of the body to criminality (Schafer, 1976, p. 38). In the early nineteenth century, phrenologists measured and studied the shape of the head in an attempt to determine the relationship between brain and behavior. The chief practitioners of phrenology, Franz Joseph Gall and Johann Gaspar Spurzheim, believed that the characteristics of the brain are mirrored in bumps on the skull. They and their followers set about documenting the relationship between these bumps and behavior, especially abnormal behavior. For a short period in the 1830s, the United States even had a journal devoted to the science of phrenology, the *American Journal of Phrenology*. In its day, phrenology was a reasonable scientific approach.

The Italian Positivists

The beginnings of criminological positivism are usually traced (although with questionable accuracy, as we have mentioned) to the work of three Italian thinkers, Cesare Lombroso, Enrico Ferri, and Raffaele Garofalo.

Lombroso, often called the father of modern criminology, was a surgeon who conducted systematic observations and measurements of soldiers, criminals, the insane, and the general population. His initial data collection on over 54,000 subjects included not only the living, but measures from cadavers as well (Parmelee, 1908). The descriptive data he painstakingly collected represented the use of an experimental method in "legal" medicine that was similar to criminal anthropology. Trying to account for mental and physical differences, he pointed out that criminals have multiple physical abnormalities of an atavistic (subhuman or primitive) or degenerate nature. These physical inferiorities characterized a biological throwback that Lombroso called the born criminal. He also reported that criminals manifest traits of sensory impairment; a lack of moral sense, particularly the absence of remorse; and the use of slang and tattoos.

In accord with the positivist tendency to categorize traits, Lombroso distinguished other types of criminals: the insane criminal, the epileptic criminal, and the occasional criminal, who for no biological reason but by the influence of circumstances or surroundings was drawn to crime. This classification scheme was later modified by Ferri, one of Lombroso's students, to include the born criminal, those who committed crimes of passion, and the habitual criminal. Lombroso quickly embraced the "born criminal" term because it fit his previous description of the major cause of criminality. Later in life, he acknowledged his numerous critics and included

Excerpt from Lombroso's *Crime: Its Causes and Remedies*

Atavism

The born criminal shows in a proportion reaching 33% numerous specific characteristics that are almost always atavistic.... [C]haracteristics presented by savage races are very often found among born criminals. Such, for example, are:... low cranial capacity; retreating forehead; highly developed frontal sinuses;... the thickness of the bones of the skull;... prognathism; obliquity of the orbits; greater pigmentation of the skin; tufted and crispy hair; and large ears. To these we may add... anomalies of the ear;... great agility; relative insensibility to pain; dullness of the sense of touch; great visual acuteness; ability to recover quickly from wounds; blunted affections; precocity as to sensual pleasures; greater resemblance between the sexes; greater incorrigibility of the woman; laziness; absence of remorse; impulsiveness; physiopsychic excitability; and especially improvidence, which sometimes appears as courage and again as recklessness changing to cowardice. Besides these there is great vanity; a passion for gambling and alcoholic drinks; violent but fleeting passions; superstition; extraordinary sensitiveness with regard to one's own personality; and a special conception of God and morality. Unexpected analogies are met even in small details, as, for example the improvised rules of criminal gangs;... the custom of tattooing, the not uncommon cruelty of their games; the excessive use of gestures...

social and economic factors in his list of causes of crime. He continued to insist, however, that these causes were secondary in nature to biological factors. *[handwritten margin note: Lombroso biological]*

Enrico Ferri's conception of criminal causality went beyond that of his teacher. While responsible for the term "born criminal" that Lombroso used, he introduced other important causal factors into Italian Positivism. According to Ferri, crime was caused by a number of factors including physical (race, geographics, temperature, and climate), anthropological (age, sex, organic, and psychological), and social factors such as customs, religion, economics, and population density. To study them, he argued, one would need to use positive observation that would include criminal statistics and penal law in a "synthetic science" that he called "criminal sociology" (Ferri, 1917).

Ferri supported the notion that in any given social environment, with generally fixed conditions, only a certain amount of crime could be realized. This was called the Law of Criminal Saturation. He also developed a fourfold classification of murders that appears in his book *Homicide*, based on the insane, the occasional, and the born criminal, as well as the crime of passion.

Raffaele Garofalo (1914) also built on the work of Lombroso and, of the three, was perhaps the most skeptical about biological explanations of criminal behavior. Garofalo believed that civilized people have certain basic sentiments about the values of human life and property; absence of these sentiments indicates a lack of concern for fellow humans. Finding a combination of environmental, circumstantial, and organic reasons for criminal behavior, he termed such behavior psychic or moral "anomaly," a deficiency of altruistic sensibility. He assumed that this psychic variation, which he carefully distinguished from insanity or mental illness, is more frequent among members of "certain inferior races" (Allen, 1972). In essence, he believed that certain people are morally less developed than others. Garofalo also commented on the legalistic nature of definitions of crime, believing that these definitions limit them in application and situation. Instead, he formulated the more universal notion of natural crime, by which he referred to acts that all civilized societies would readily recognize as offensive. He believed that the dangerousness of the criminal was the criterion on which social crime-fighting priorities should be based.

Twentieth-Century Positivism

Following the work of the Italian positivists, a good deal of effort was expended in the biological area. The family histories of criminals were examined and criminal heredity traced to certain ancestors (Dugdale, 1877; Estabrook, 1916; Goddard, 1913; Goring, 1913). Richard Dugdale's study of six generations of the Juke family was used to infer that criminal (and antisocial) behavior is inherited. He was able to trace a number of criminals, prostitutes, and paupers in the family line, all derived from the original criminal father. Intelligence tests were developed by Alfred Binet and subsequently used to explain criminality through the concept of inherited feeblemind-edness, or lack of intelligence (Burt, 1925; Goddard, 1914). Henry Goddard's well-known study of the Kallikak family was similar to that of Dugdale's. He matched the histories of two family lines produced by a soldier (from a well-to-do family) in the Revolutionary War. One lineage derived from a liaison with a "feebleminded" barmaid, the other from marriage to an honorable Quaker woman. Goddard traced numerous antisocial, deviant, and criminal offspring from the liaison with the barmaid and "none" from the marriage.

The obvious implication was that feeblemindedness was inherited and a cause of criminality. As a result, sterilization programs were advocated and implemented across the country during the 1930s and 1940s. In fact, a recent task force in North Carolina pressed the state to compensate surviving victims of state-imposed sterilizations. North Carolina not only moved to apologize for the ill-advised eugenics program but has organized reparations for the 72 remaining subjects of the 7,600 cases documented in that state alone. Although eugenics proponents claimed to have targeted those deemed "mentally diseased, feebleminded or epileptic," Elaine Riddick acknowledges that she was sterilized following the birth of her son, who resulted from being raped at the age of 14 (Waggoner, 2012).

Other more contemporary studies of genetics and heredity have involved the examination of twins (Lange, 1919/1930), general body types (Glueck & Glueck, 1950, 1956, 1974; Hooten, 1939; Kretschmer, 1926; Sheldon, 1949), and even endocrinology (Schlapp & Smith, 1928). The body type theories suggest that certain physical features result in a propensity to crime often studied as constitutional psychology. The most quoted of this work is that of William Sheldon, who proposed three categories of a combination of body types and personality temperaments that he called somatotypes. An *ectomorph* is a person who is small-boned, lean, and frail, with a sensitive and introverted (shy) personality. A *mesomorph* is a person of muscular, larger-boned body build with an aggressive, action-oriented, outgoing (extroverted) personality. The third type, an *endomorph,* has a rather soft and fat build with a relaxed, jovial, and extroverted personality. Sheldon found that delinquents were most often of the mesomorph body type. The platform of Sheldon's work has been criticized for its eugenic nature (supportive of racial "cleansing"), and his conclusions of biological devolution in studies sponsored by the National Council on Religion in Higher Education were also criticized. Scientific reviews condemned his small and suspect samples, the lack of rigor in his work, and the subjective assessments in his conclusions (Rafter, 2007).

Still, strains of the body type/temperament approach are found in more recent times in the work of Juan Cortes and Florence Gatti (1972) and psychologists who have tied body type and self-perceptions of physical attractiveness with self-esteem and self-concept (see, for example, Catell & Metzner, 1993). These may be personality traits that are indirectly linked to behavior including deviance and delinquency.

The twin research is perhaps the most interesting of the genetic studies. In this form of research, the behavior of identical twins (who have identical genetic heritage) is compared.

Fraternal twins (who have a different genetic heritage just like any two siblings) have also been used. The reasoning is that if one twin is criminal, then the other also should be criminal. Johannes Lange's study of prisoner twins and their noninstitutionalized counterparts found a high degree of concordance (both twins had engaged in criminal behavior). Identical twins produce concordant results in a higher proportion than do fraternal twins. Several other studies have produced similar results (for reviews of this research see Christiansen, 1968, 1970, 1977b; Cortes & Gatti, 1972; Dalgaard & Kringlen, 1976; Ellis, 1982, 1985). The question that remains unanswered, however, is the effect of environment in creating likeness among twins. Comparable studies of adopted siblings have also been undertaken (Crowe, 1972, 1974; Hutchings & Mednick, 1977; Schulsinger, 1972). The logic is that if genetic theories hold true, the children should behave more like their biological parents than their adoptive parents. To some extent these results were found.

Much of the literature on psychological influences on behavior has been the result of the ground-breaking work of Sigmund Freud. While Freud himself said little about crime, other psychiatrists have examined the effect of unconscious conflict on criminal behavior (Abrahamsen, 1944; Aichhorn, 1925/1935; Friedlander, 1947). Perhaps, the most notable work has been that of William Healy (1915; Alexander & Healy, 1935; Healy & Bronner, 1936). Healy and other psychiatric workers examined juveniles in a psychiatric institution (which he directed) and after numerous sessions determined that each juvenile had experienced emotional trauma at some point in life. For comparison, the brothers and sisters of the delinquents were then briefly interviewed, and very little evidence of emotional trauma was found in their histories. Healy concluded that emotional trauma is responsible for creating psychological conflicts that lead to delinquent behavior.

Other approaches have included the examination of personality differences, as with the Minnesota Multiphasic Personality Inventory (MMPI) (a complex personality test), and of psychopathic personalities (Hathaway & Monachesi, 1953, 1963). The MMPI contains a psychopathic personality subscale that was created by finding questions to which institutionalized delinquents gave uniformly different answers (i.e., scored higher) than "normal" juveniles. Subsequent researchers have found that institutionalized juveniles almost always score higher on the psychopathic personality subscale of the MMPI than normal juveniles do, thereby justifying psychopathy as a cause of delinquency. There is, of course, a certain irony in this research because the scale was created from questions on which the delinquents originally scored higher.

On the sociological side, some early positivistic approaches encompassed both explanations of individual behavior and rates of behavior in society. The notion that behavior, including criminal acts, involves a process of imitating others was proposed by Gabriel Tarde (1890). He theorized that there is short-term behavior (fashion) and long-term behavior (custom). People who are inferior, that is, less successful, imitate those who are superior and copy their behavior. Thus, he argues that the use of new techniques for committing offenses, such as today's carjackings and home invasion robberies, spreads by others hearing about and copying the crimes. Tarde also suggested that as the population becomes more dense, behavior will be oriented more toward fashion than toward custom. On the statistical side, the ecological studies begun by Guerry and Quetelet blossomed into a sociological criminology that set out to investigate the effect of social structure on crime. Since the 1920s, the American tradition of criminology has used the positivist technique of analyzing population data and crime rates as well as the systematic study of criminal behavior.

CLASSIFICATION OF THE SCHOOL

The Positive School is characterized by a *consensus* perspective. All the theories developed under its mantle assume the existence of a core set of values in society that can be used to determine and treat deviance. Positivists did not question the validity of their categories of harmful acts or the desirability of treating people. In fact, their assumption of consensus was so strong that they rarely ever questioned their own actions, even when "exterminating" groups of people designated as socially harmful. Other than the consensus perspective, the wide range of positivist theories makes any attempt at categorizing them very difficult. Positivist theories can be either structural or processual, so no definitive classification is possible. However, we can state that sociological theories have, as a rule, been *structurally oriented* and *macrotheoretical*, while biological and psychological theories have been *processual* and *microtheoretical*.

Summary

The work of the Positive School, diverse as it was, represented the first real concern with studying the behavior of the criminal. As Rafter (2006) explains, before Lombroso, crime was studied only by metaphysicians, moralists, and penologists. His work turned the field into a truly biosocial science. Embracing the scientific method, positivists took a deterministic stance toward behavior and left behind the Classical School's insistence that humans are rational beings with free will. In the process, the notion of punishment for deterrence began to make less sense. If an individual's behavior was not predicated on rational decisions, then how could that individual be deterred? The thing to do, obviously, was to find those factors that cause the criminal behavior and remove (or treat) them. Further, the ability to predict which individuals would be likely to become criminal and to treat them before they could harm themselves and society would be valuable in creating a better society.

Comparison of Classical and Positive Schools

Point	Classical School	Positive School
View of human nature	Hedonistic; free-willed rationality, morally responsible for own behavior	Malleable; determined by biological, psychological, and social environment; no moral responsibility; consensus oriented
View of justice system	Social contract; exists to protect society; due process and concern with civil rights; restrictions on system	Scientific treatment system to cure pathologies and rehabilitate offenders; no concern with civil rights
Form of law	Statutory law; exact specification of illegal acts and sanctions	Social law; illegal acts defined by analogy; scientific experts determine social harm and proper form of treatment
Purpose of sentencing	Punishment for deterrence; sentences are determinate (fixed length)	Treatment and reform; sentences are indeterminate (variable length until cured)
Criminological experts	Philosophers; social reformers	Scientists; treatment experts

Positivists left behind the legal focus and concerns of the Classical School. In fact, for them the only reasonable definition of criminality was a social one. Legality simply got in the way of treatment because behavioral categories did not necessarily fit legal categories. If behaviors were socially undesirable, then individuals exhibiting them should be treated and returned to normalcy. Civil rights were of no concern if the real purpose of treatment was that of help. After all, how can one object to being helped; when a physician treats us, do we feel our civil rights have been violated? Thus, early positivists reasoned that criminals have no need to object when they are being treated by correctional experts.

Finally, positivism, as we have seen, is represented not only by biological theories of causality but by psychological and sociological theories as well. In fact, most of the theories of criminology throughout the 1950s were positivistic in nature. As a general perspective, then, positivism has had an enormous effect on the way criminological theories have been constructed and the way that research has been conducted. While this chapter has focused on the Positive School (or the Italian School), positivism itself is much larger than that school. Indeed, the Positive School is called that because it was the first criminological use of the "positive application of science." In that regard, it is the application of scientific tenets to establish and solve problems that is the essential ingredient of positivism. This approach is now frequently referred to as "modernism" by today's *postmodernist* theorists.

MAJOR POINTS OF THE SCHOOL

1. Humans live in a world in which cause and effect operate. Attributes of that world exhibit order and can be uncovered through systematic observation.
2. Social problems, such as crime, can be remedied by means of a systematic study of human behavior. Through the application of science, human existence is perfectible, or at the least the human condition can be made better.
3. Criminal behavior is a product of abnormalities. These abnormalities may be within the person, or they may exist as external social forces.
4. Abnormal features can be found through comparison with those that are normal.
5. Once abnormalities are found, it is the duty of criminology to assist in their correction. Abnormalities should be treated and the criminal reformed.
6. Treatment is desirable both for the individual, so that he or she may become normal, and for society, so that members of society are protected from harm.
7. The purpose of sanctions against criminals, then, is not to punish but to provide for treatment.

Epilogue: Current Directions and Policy Implications

CURRENT DIRECTIONS

The more conservative attitudes of the mid-1970s through the present gave rise to an assumption of consensus in values, favoring the reemergence of nonsocial theories. A major impetus was that American society was doubtful of the value of reform and rehabilitation and had no desire to pay for the massive social programs suggested by existing social theories. Thus, theories that cast the blame for crime on something more intrinsic were received favorably. A renewed interest in biological/biochemical and psychological theories of crime ensued.

BIOLOGY

Work in the biology of crime was especially focused during the 1970s and 1980s with research by Christiansen (1977a), Mednick and Christiansen (1977), Mednick and various associates (Hutchings & Mednick, 1977; Kirkegaard-Sorensen & Mednick, 1977; Mednick, Gabrielli, & Hutchings, 1984, 1987; Mednick, Moffitt, & Stack, 1987), the biosocial theorizing of C. Ray Jeffery (1977, 1979, 1989a, 1998), and defense provided by James Q. Wilson and Richard Herrnstein (1985). Mednick's (1977) work, referred to as a biosocial theory, is an excellent example of the orientation of modern biological theorists. He views the biological characteristics of an individual as only one part in the equation of behavior—other parts are the physical and social environment. Mednick assumes that all individuals must learn to control natural urges toward antisocial and criminal behavior. This learning takes place in the family and with peer groups and is based on the punishment of undesirable behaviors. The punishment response is mediated by the autonomic (involuntary) nervous system. If the reaction is short lived, the individual is said to have rewarded himself or herself, and criminal behavior is inhibited. However, a slow physiological recovery from punishment (and fear of it) does little to teach the individual to refrain from undesirable behavior. Mednick views criminals as having slow autonomic nervous system responses to stimuli.

As part of a series of writings, C. Ray Jeffery also offered an interdisciplinary biosocial theory of criminal behavior in *Advances in Criminological Theory* (1989a) and a criminology text (1989b). His perspective is that sociological, psychological, and biological characteristics should be seen as interacting together in a systems model to produce criminal behavior. Three basic systems produce the total organism: genetics, brain structure and function, and learning (1989a, pp. 72–73). He posits that individuals are born with particular biological (genetic) and psychological characteristics that not only may predispose but may actually cause certain forms of behavior. This "nature" is independent of the socialization process present in the social environment. There is, however, a good deal of interplay between nature and nurture through the physical environment and the feedback mechanisms that exist in human biochemical systems. For example, Jeffery notes that poverty translates to a certain type of diet and exposure to pollutants. The resulting nutrients and chemicals are transformed by the biochemical system into neurochemical compounds within the brain. Thus, poverty indirectly leads to behavioral differences (and, potentially, criminal behavior) through the interaction of individual and environment. Jeffery's general scheme can be summed up in an equation he provides (1989a, p. 73):

$$Genetics \leftrightarrow Brain \leftrightarrow Behavior\ (Learning/Personality)$$
$$\updownarrow \qquad\quad \updownarrow$$
$$Environment$$

In a controversial book, *Crime and Human Nature* (1985), Wilson and Herrnstein offer a similar biosocial version of the causes of street crime. They combine genetic factors with psychological dispositions and personality traits, drug usage, and socialization factors. Their final explanation of crime not only leans heavily toward individual human nature but also has a deterrence-like component: An offender makes a decision that the potential gain from crime will outweigh any possible punishment. Thus, Wilson and Herrnstein's criminals are born with and, throughout their life continue to gain, predispositions toward crime, but it is ultimately the criminal's own decision to commit an act that is important. Other similar work has focused on neuropsychological functioning and its connection to behavior (Fishbein, 1990, 2000).

Another approach to biological effects is work on intelligence and crime. Also referred to as mental deficiency, intelligence has been implicated in criminality for a long time. The "feeblemindedness" work of Dugdale, Goddard, and Goring is discredited today, however. Most criminologists see intelligence not as a cause of crime but as a predisposing factor in decisions to commit crime, but they do not discuss it very often. For a long time, interest in intelligence was based on a controversial position, taken in the late 1960s, that intelligence is genetically based and that differences in IQ can be used to explain different criminal propensities between races (see Jensen, 1969; Shockley, 1967). One criminologist, Robert Gordon (1986), used the position to argue that IQ is the best predictor of delinquency rates among various groups. In 1977, criminologists Travis Hirschi and Michael Hindelang published an article that reviewed studies on IQ and delinquency. They found that, as a predictor of delinquency, IQ is at least as good as any of the other major social variables. Further, they noted that IQ is also strongly related to social class and race. Because delinquency is viewed as the province of lower-class, minority youths, this relationship implies that lower-class, minority delinquents have lower

IQs. Responding to the IQ and delinquency position, Scott Menard and Barbara Morse (1984) argued that IQ is merely one of the ways in which juveniles are disadvantaged in American society. They see the societal and institutional response to these disadvantages as the real causal agent in delinquent behavior. Critics of IQ tests have noted that the way in which the tests are constructed provides advantages to those who are middle class and white. Moreover, they argue that these tests do not measure innate intelligence but rather some other ability, such as facility in language or cultural concepts.

The most recent work on IQ and delinquency relies on an indirect relationship model that argues that IQ may influence school performance, which will then impact overall school adjustment and the positive social control mechanisms related to education. Vulnerability to the pressures of delinquent peers and one's own self-control mechanisms are also indirectly related to IQ (McGloin, Pratt, & Maahs, 2004; Ward & Tittle, 1994). This research implies that if IQ can be addressed and improved, children may be able to develop more resistance to delinquency through stronger ties to school and stronger valuation of academic achievement.

Newer gene-based evolutionary theories are no longer postulating that genetic structures directly affect behavior. Because behavior is complex, these theories assume that genetic effects are indirect. They view the role of genes as affecting brain functioning, which governs behavior. Learning theories may be used in specifying how brain functioning is translated into behavior or there may be a propensity toward certain forms of learning. Even socialization may be affected by propensities toward such things as psychological or physiological traits, antisocial behaviors, and so on. These factors, then, influence how an individual will react in certain settings and make criminal behavior more or less probable. In sum, modern biosocial criminology is a complex perspective but is characterized by the way it emphasizes social context rather than straightforward biogenetic factors (Beaver, 2009; Walsh & Beaver, 2009a; Walsh & Beaver, 2009b). There are even those who advocate crime prevention on the basis of this approach (Rocque, Welsh, & Raine, 2012).

There is also a form of biological research that may not be properly called "biology" anymore because it is quite different from the earlier positions. This research is virtually all brain based and is a form of neurochemistry. The essence of the position is that much of delinquency may be a product of immature brain function, particularly in the ability to judge consequences of actions. This immature brain function is related to the fact that the sheathing (myelin) that covers nerve fibers does not fully form until approximately age 24. The myelin acts as an insulator and contains the electric impulses flowing along the nerves. In the brain, with so many nerves in such close proximity, the myelin is critical to preventing what we might think of as "short-circuits." Apparently, accurate and thoughtful assessments of the consequences of behavior fall victim to poor myelination, and impulsive behavior is the result. While there is much good research developing in this area, it remains to be seen whether general delinquency can be construed as primarily a neurological issue and to what extent that is modified by environment.

The issue of a connection between the brain and violence appears to be on much firmer ground than the connection with delinquency in general. The most recent work on the brain and violence/psychopathology uses brain imaging (CAT and MRI scans) techniques to locate both differences in brain structure and electroneural activation among violent and nonviolent individuals. A review of much of that research by Wahlund and Kristiansson (2009) shows that neurological researchers have produced fairly strong documentation of a link between dysfunctional portions of the brain's frontal and temporal lobes and past violence behavior.

PSYCHOLOGY

Some recent psychological work argues that there may be a "criminal personality," or a different thinking pattern among criminals. Samuel Yochelson, a psychiatrist, and Stanton Samenow, a clinical psychologist, in a widely publicized study (1976, 1977), reintroduced the case for a criminal personality. After thorough case studies of between 230 and

270 inmates at St. Elizabeth's Hospital for the criminally insane in Washington, DC, Yochelson and Samenow pronounced that the causes of crime are not social, economic, or psychological inner conflicts. Instead, they claimed that all criminals are born with abnormal thinking patterns that affect their ability to make decisions.[1] This "criminal personality" seeks excitement, has an inordinately high opinion of self, is exploitative and selfish, manipulates others, is amoral, and so forth. An attack on the criminal's self-image tends to produce a violent reaction. All in all, Yochelson and Samenow claimed to have found 52 different criminal thinking patterns. The theoretical position that all criminals have different thinking patterns was very popular in federal government circles for a while, and some of the crime policies of the 1980s were based on it.

COGNITIVE THEORY

The best example of psychologically based cognitive theory is one proposed by Glenn Walters and Thomas White (1989; and Walters, 1990). In a 1989 critique, Walters said that criminology had not adequately recognized the role of cognition in the individual. His point is that social and environmental conditions serve to limit individual options rather than determine behavior. If social and environmental factors are a backdrop for choice, then behavior can be seen as patterned by these factors while individual rationality determines the *form* of patterned activity. In short, "life conditions place effected [*sic*] individuals at increased (or decreased) risk for later criminality" (Walters, 1989, p. v).

Walters and White jointly argue that criminal behavior is the product of faulty, irrational thinking and deny that environmental factors determine criminal behavior, except for limiting options. Focusing on career criminals, Walters and White point out that these individuals are characterized in most, if not all, of their interactions by irresponsibility, self-indulgence, interpersonal intrusiveness, and social rule breaking. Lifestyle criminals appear to have similar thought patterns to those of early adolescents and, thus, have little conception of responsibility and self-discipline. The arrested development of the cognition process, regardless of whether the source is constitutional or environmental, tends to set these individuals up for failure. This failure applies not only to criminal situations but also to a wide range of common situations, such as school, work, and home.

Locating eight "primitive cognitive characteristics," Walters and White examined the thinking patterns of lifestyle criminals and found that from an early age these individuals present chronic management problems. Because of their adolescent-like motives, lifestyle criminals rationalize their behavior and are preoccupied with short-term hedonism, which is destructive in the long run. Finally, Walters and White argue that lifestyle criminals direct their behavior toward "losing in dramatic and destructive ways" (1989, p. 8). In consistently choosing self-interested and hedonistic alternatives, criminals perpetuate their behavior.

PERSONALITY DIMENSIONS

Another approach to the personality issue has been generated by Hans Eysenck (1977, 1989, 1996, Eysenck & Gudjonnson, 1990). His theory is that there are three major personality dimensions: *psychoticism, extraversion,* and *neuroticism* (now popularly known as the P-E-N system). Criminality in general is correlated with high degrees of all three, although certain types of crime may be correlated differently. Where age is concerned, the younger offender is more likely to have high levels of extroversion than neuroticism. Older offenders, on the other hand, exhibit higher levels of neuroticism. In all age groups, psychoticism is always important. Eysenck documents these relationships across various studies and countries and notes that "antisocial" traits (smoking, legal or illegal drug use) as well as criminality are correlated with these personalities. Finally, he connects these personality traits with the development of a conscience through a learning

---

[1] One of the major problems of this study is that Yochelson and Samenow overgeneralized the evidence. While there is little disagreement with the position that the criminally *insane* have different thinking patterns, Yochelson and Samenow did not perform similar studies on criminals who were *not* insane. Therefore, they can say nothing about "normal" criminals and certainly nothing about *all* criminals.

process called conditioning and a high need for external stimulation. Criminals' condition poorly and as a result are slow to develop an effective conscience. The most recent research on his personality system (Bulten, Nijman, & van der Staak, 2009; Ireland & Ireland, 2011) continues to lend support.

LEARNING THEORY

A final popular psychological approach to criminal behavior is through learning theory, particularly social learning theory. Developed by Albert Bandura (1973), the perspective adds to B. F. Skinner's earlier version of operant learning theory by including imitation and modeling of behavior. That is, social learning asserts that we learn by watching others receive rewards and punishments for certain forms of behavior. We then imitate or model those behaviors that are rewarded. This theory has been heavily used in studies of aggression, family violence, and the effect of television in encouraging aggression. There is some evidence that such behavior is indeed learned from others. Criminology picked up social learning theory in the 1960s, and we examine that approach in Chapter 11.

POLICY IMPLICATIONS

Positivist theories, old and new, are full of policy implications. Because of the theoretical emphases on treatment and pathology, they are often the backbone of social reform programs. They have even been used to argue that people are innately different and uncorrectable, thus lending themselves to extreme strategies of social reform, such as Hitler's genocide programs.

Because the biological versions have not been very popular over much of the past half-century, until recently there have been few biologically oriented crime policies. Perhaps the closest the United States has gotten to these policies in the past several decades is the war on drugs. Not only has drug use been viewed as a major cause of crime by at least two presidential administrations, but the implicit suggestion is that neurochemical compounds (drugs) cause people to behave in ways that they would not normally behave. That is, crime is a product of the effect of drugs on human physiology and neurological

systems. Thus, in the fight against crime, there is no need to implement expensive social reform policies; we merely need to eliminate drugs and crime rates will drastically decrease.

On the other hand, modern biosocial criminology has recently been applied to crime prevention policy with several suggestions by Michael Rocque, Brandon Welsh and Adrian Raine (2012). Using what they refer to as "developmental crime prevention," they argue that, by targeting risk factors during child and adolescent developmental periods, propensities toward delinquency might be overcome. Illustrative policies compatible with this approach include identifying risk factors early and treating them in pre-school and school programs, school nutrition programs, health and nutrition care for pregnant women, parenting classes, antismoking and antidrug (during pregnancy) programs, and cognitive therapy programs.

Psychological perspectives have found much more favor with policymakers as a standard approach to criminal behavior. Indeed, they have become a routine part of our criminal justice system. As a matter of course, sentenced individuals are required to attend treatment sessions of various sorts. Offenders on probation receive diagnostic tests to determine what forms of counseling and treatment they need. Such services are now being offered to victims of crimes as well. The newer forms of psychological theories, especially cognitive approaches, have been well received by policymakers. Cognitive theory dwells on the differences in thinking patterns between "normal" and criminal individuals, thus contributing to the assumption that criminal behavior is a result of some thinking failure of the individual. This has been translated into "bad people bring on their own bad behavior and deserve to be punished for their own decisions." In short, policymakers see punishment as the way to impress on bad individuals that their thinking needs correcting; no treatment programs are needed. Psychologists, however, have generally not subscribed to the no-treatment philosophy and have created techniques designed to teach offenders how to think rationally and realistically (see, for example, MacPhail, 1989). Interestingly, the DARE drug prevention program originally subscribed to the "just say no" perspective and after finally admitting that it had no effect, subsequently took up a cognitive thinking skills approach.

Sociological versions of positivist theory have been the cornerstone of many of our crime policies for the past 30 years. We examine most of these under the various sociologically based theories in the coming chapters. An example or two, however, may assist in understanding their utility. Exemplified by the Great Society programs of the 1960s, reforms were instituted to provide greater opportunities to those who were socially disadvantaged. The assumption was that increased opportunities would reduce social strains producing crime. These programs resulted in educational programs such as Project Head Start and in job training programs such as the Job Corps and Comprehensive Employee Training Act (CETA). More recently, social control theories have led to renewed emphasis on the importance of school and family (especially proper parenting skills) in the fight against crime. The "family values" issue of the 1992 presidential campaign can be seen, in part, as an extension of this perspective.

Questions and Weblinks

Critical Thinking Questions

1. How have the developments of science and the influence of scientific thinking changed the way we view crime and criminals?
2. Which disciplines or academic fields do you feel offer the strongest explanations of criminal behavior?
3. What should we continue to appreciate about the work of Cesare Lombroso?
4. The work of the early positivists has been criticized as racist, sexist, and elitist. Would you agree with that? Why or why not?

Practice Essay Questions

1. What would be some of the policy implications of an approach toward criminal behavior and punishment that is "deterministic" in nature?
2. Which aspects of the early positivists work discussed in this chapter would you argue are outdated and why?
3. What does the term "positivism" mean to you and why is it important in our study of crime today?
4. Compare and contrast the Classical school with the work of the early positivists in terms of what their motivations and priorities were.

Related Websites

http://www.socialresearchmethods.net/kb/positvsm.php
http://plato.stanford.edu/entries/legal-positivism/
http://www.kheper.net/topics/typology/somatotypes.html
http://criminology.fsu.edu/crimtheory/samenow.htm

Bibliography

Abrahamsen, D. (1944). *Crime and the human mind*. New York: Columbia University Press.

Aichhorn, A. (1935). *Wayward youth*. New York: Viking. (Original work published 1925.)

Alexander, F., & Healy, W. (1935). *Roots of crime*. New York: Knopf.

Allen, F. A. (1972). Raffaele Garofalo. In H. Mannheim (Ed.), *Pioneers in criminology* (2nd ed., pp. 318–340). Montclair, NJ: Patterson Smith.

Bandura, A. (1973). *Aggression: A social learning approach*. Englewood Cliffs, NJ: Prentice Hall.

Beaver, K. M. (2009). *Biosocial criminology: A primer.* Dubuque, IA: Kendall/Hunt.

Bulten, E., Nijman, H., & van der Staak, C. (2009) Psychiatric disorders and personality characteristics of prisoners at regular prison wards. *International Journal of Law and Psychiatry, 32,* 115–119.

Burt, C. (1925). *The young delinquent.* New York: Appleton.

Catell, P., & Metzner, R. (1993). Associations among somatotype, temperament and self-actualization. *Psychological Reports, 72*(2), 1165–1166.

Christiansen, K. O. (1968). Threshold of tolerance in various population groups illustrated by results from a Danish criminological twin study. In A. V. S. de Reuck & R. Porter (Eds.), *CIBA Foundation Symposium on the Mentally Abnormal Offender* (pp. 107–116). London: I. and J. Churchill.

Christiansen, K. O. (1970). Crime in a Danish twin population. *Acta Genetical Medical Gemellologial, 19,* 323–326.

Christiansen, K. O. (1977a). A preliminary study of criminality among twins. In S. A. Mednick & K. O. Christiansen (Eds.), *Biosocial bases of criminal behavior* (pp. 89–108). New York: Gardner.

Christiansen, K. O. (1977b). A review of studies of criminality among twins. In S. A. Mednick & K. O. Christiansen (Eds.), *Biosocial bases of criminal behavior* (pp. 45–88). New York: Gardner.

Cortes, J., & Gatti, F. M. (1972). *Delinquency and crime, a biopsychosocial approach: Empirical, theoretical and practical aspects of criminal behavior.* New York: Seminar Press.

Crowe, R. R. (1972). The adopted offspring of women criminal offenders: A study of their arrest records. *Archives of General Psychiatry, 27,* 600–603.

Crowe, R. R. (1974). An adoption study of anti-social personality. *Archives of General Psychiatry, 31,* 785–791.

Dalgaard, O. S., & Kringlen, E. (1976). A Norwegian twin study of criminality. *British Journal of Criminology, 16,* 213–232.

Dugdale, R. L. (1877). *The Jukes: A study in crime, pauperism, disease, and heredity.* New York: Putnam's.

Ellis, L. (1982). Genetics and criminal behavior: Evidence through the end of the 1970s. *Criminology, 20,* 43–66.

Ellis, L. (1985). Genetic influences and crime. In F. H. Marsh & J. Katz (Eds.), *Biology, crime and ethics: A study of biological explanations for criminal behavior* (pp. 65–92). Cincinnati, OH: Anderson.

Estabrook, A. (1916). *The Jukes in 1915.* Washington, DC: Carnegie Institute.

Eysenck, H. J. (1977). *Crime and personality.* London: Routledge and Kegan Paul.

Eysenck, H. J. (1989). Personality and criminality: A dispositional analysis. *Advances in Criminological Theory, 1,* 89–110.

Eysenck, H. J. (1996). Personality and crime: Where do we stand? *Psychology Crime and Law, 2*(3), 143–152.

Eysenck, H. J., & Gudjonnson, G. H. (1990). *The causes and cures of crime.* New York: Plenum.

Ferri, E. (1917). *Criminal sociology* (J. Killey & J. Lisle, Trans.). Boston: Little, Brown. (Original work published 1881.)

Fishbein, D. H. (1990). Biological perspectives in criminology. *Criminology, 28,* 27–72.

Fishbein, D. H. (2000). Neuropsychological function, drug abuse, and violence: A conceptual framework. *Criminal Justice and Behavior, 27,* 139–159.

Fletcher, R. (1975). Introduction. In K. Thompson (Ed.), *Auguste Comte: The foundation of sociology* (pp. ix–xi). New York: Halsted.

Friedlander, K. (1947). *The psychoanalytic approach to juvenile delinquency.* London: Kegan Paul, Trench and Trubner.

Garofalo, R. (1914). *Criminology* (R. W. Millar, Trans.). Boston: Little, Brown. (Original work published 1885.)

Glueck, S., & Glueck, E. T. (1950). *Unraveling juvenile delinquency.* New York: Commonwealth Fund.

Glueck, S., & Glueck, E. T. (1956). *Physique and delinquency.* New York: Harper and Row.

Glueck, S., & Glueck, E. T. (1974). *Of delinquency and crime.* Springfield, IL: Charles C. Thomas.

Goddard, H. H. (1913). *The Kallikak family: A study in the heredity of feeblemindedness.* New York: Macmillan.

Goddard, H. H. (1914). *Feeblemindedness: Its causes and consequences.* New York: Macmillan.

Gordon, R. A. (1986). Scientific justification and the race-IQ-delinquency model. In T. Hartnagel & R. Silverman (Eds.), *Critique and explanation: Essays in honor of Gwynne Nettler* (pp. 91–131). New Brunswick, NJ: Transaction.

Goring, C. B. (1913). *The English convict.* London: H.M. Stationery Office.

Guerry, A. M. (1833). *Essai sur la statistique sorale.* Paris: Crochard.

Halfpenny, P. (1982). *Positivism and sociology: Explaining social life.* Boston: Allen and Unwin.

Hathaway, S. R., & Monachesi, E. D. (1953). *Analyzing and predicting juvenile delinquency with the MMPI.* Minneapolis, MN: University of Minnesota Press.

Hathaway, S. R., & Monachesi, E. D. (1963). *Adolescent personality and behavior: MMPI patterns of normal, delinquent, dropout and other outcomes.* Minneapolis, MN: University of Minneapolis Press.

Healy, W. (1915). *The individual delinquent.* Boston: Little, Brown.

Healy, W., & Bronner, A. (1936). *New light on delinquency and its treatment.* New Haven, CT: Yale University Press.

Hirschi, T., & Hindelang, M. J. (1977). Intelligence and delinquency: A revisionist view. *American Journal of Sociology, 42,* 571–587.

Hooten, E. A. (1939). *The American criminal: An anthropological study* (Vol. 1). Cambridge, MA: Harvard University Press.

Hutchings, B., & Mednick, S. A. (1977). Criminality in adoptees and their adoptive and biological parents: A pilot study. In S. A. Mednick & K. O. Christiansen (Eds.), *Biosocial bases of criminal behavior* (pp. 127–141). New York: Gardner.

Ireland, J. L., & Ireland, C. A. (2011). Personality structure among prisoners: How valid is the five-factor model and can it offer support for Eysenck's theory of criminality? *Criminal Behavior and Mental Health, 21,* 35–50.

Jeffery, C. R. (1977). *Crime prevention through environmental design* (Rev. ed.). Beverly Hills, CA: Sage.

Jeffery, C. R. (1979). *Biology and crime.* Beverly Hills: Sage.

Jeffery, C. R. (1989a). An interdisciplinary theory of criminal behavior, *Advances in Criminological Theory, 1,* 69–87.

Jeffery, C. R. (1989b). *Criminology: An interdisciplinary approach.* Englewood Cliffs, NJ: Prentice Hall.

Jeffery, C. R. (1993). Biological perspectives. *Journal of Criminal Justice Education, 4,* 291–306.

Jeffery, C. R. (1998). Prevention of juvenile violence: A critical review of current scientific strategies. *Journal of Offender Rehabilitation, 28,* 1–28.

Jensen, A. R. (1969). How much can we boost IQ and scholastic achievement? *Harvard Educational Review, 39,* 1–123.

Kaplan, A. (1968). Positivism. In D. L. Sills (Ed.), *International encyclopedia of the social sciences* (Vol. 12, pp. 389–395). New York: Macmillan.

Kirkegaard-Sorensen, L., & Mednick, S. A. (1977). A prospective study of predictors of criminality: A description of registered criminality in high-risk and low-risk families. In S. A. Mednick & K. O. Christiansen (Eds.), *Biosocial bases of criminal behaviors* (pp. 229–243). New York: Gardner.

Kretschmer, E. (1926). *Physique and character* (W. J. H. Sprott, Trans.). New York: Harcourt and Brace.

Lange, J. (1930). *Crime and destiny* (C. Haldane, Trans.). New York: Charles Boni. (Original work published 1919.)

Lombroso, C. (1876). *L'uomo delinquente.* Milan: Hoepli.

Lombroso, C. (1918). *Crime: Its causes and remedies* (H. P. Horton, Trans.). Boston: Little, Brown.

MacPhail, D. D. (1989). The moral education approach in treating adult inmates. *Criminal Justice and Behavior, 16,* 81–97.

McGloin, J. M., Pratt, T., & Maahs, J. (2004). Rethinking the IQ-delinquency relationship: A longitudinal analysis of multiple theoretical models. *Justice Quarterly, 21*(3), 603–635.

Mednick, S. A. (1977). A biosocial theory of the learning of law-abiding behavior. In S. A. Mednick & K. O. Christiansen (Eds.), *Biosocial bases of criminal behavior* (pp. 1–8). New York: Gardner.

Mednick, S. A., & Christiansen, K. O. (Eds.). (1977). *Biosocial bases of criminal behavior.* New York: Gardner.

Mednick, S. A., Gabrielli, Jr., W. F., & Hutchings, B. (1984). Genetic influences in criminal convictions: Evidence from an adoption cohort. *Science, 224,* 891–893.

Mednick, S. A., Gabrielli, Jr., W. F., & Hutchings, B. (1987). Genetic factors in the etiology of criminal behavior. In S. A. Mednick, T. E. Moffitt, & S. Stack (Eds.), *The causes of crime: New biological approaches* (pp. 74–91). Cambridge: Cambridge University Press.

Mednick, S. A., Moffitt, T. E., & Stack, S. (Eds.). (1987). *The causes of crime: New biological approaches.* Cambridge: Cambridge University Press.

Menard, S., & Morse, B. J. (1984). A structuralist critique of the IQ-delinquency hypothesis: Theory and evidence. *American Journal of Sociology, 89,* 1347–1378.

Parmelee, M. (1908). *The principles of anthropology and sociology in their relations to criminal procedure.* New York: MacMillan.

Quetelet, A. (1984). *Research on the propensity for crime at different ages* (S. F. Sylvester, Trans.). Cincinnati, OH: Anderson. (Original work published 1831.)

Rafter, N. (2006). Cesare Lombroso and the origins of criminology: Rethinking criminological tradition. In S. Henry & M. Lanier (Eds.), *The essential criminology reader* (pp. 33–42). Boulder, CO: Westview Press.

Rafter, N. (2007). Somatotyping, antimodernism and the production of criminological knowledge. *Criminology, 45*(4), 805–833.

Rocque, M., Welsh, B. C., & Raine, A. (2012). Biosocial criminology and modern crime prevention. *Journal of Criminal Justice, 40,* 306–312.

Rothman, D. (1971). *The discovery of the asylum: Social order and disorder in the New Republic.* Boston: Little, Brown.

Savitz, L. D. (1972). Introduction to the reprint edition. In G. Lombroso-Ferrero (Ed.), *Criminal man: According to the classification of Cesare Lombroso* (Reprint ed., pp. v–xx). Montclair, NJ: Patterson Smith.

Schafer, S. (1976). *Introduction to criminology.* Reston, VA: Reston.

Schlapp, M. G., & Smith, E. H. (1928). *The new criminology.* New York: Boni and Liveright.

Schulsinger, F. (1972). Psychopathy, heredity and environment. *International Journal of Mental Health, 1,* 190–206.

Sheldon, W. H. (1949). *Varieties of delinquent youth: An introduction to constitutional psychiatry.* New York: Harper and Row.

Shockley, W. (1967). A "try simplest cases" approach to the heredity-poverty-crime problem. *Proceedings of the National Academy of Sciences of the United States of America, 57,* 1767–1774.

Tarde, G. (1890). *Penal philosophy* (R. Howell, Trans.). Boston: Little, Brown. (Reprinted 1912)

Waggoner, M. (2012, January 11). Eugenics panel backs compensation. *Houston Chronicle,* p. A3.

Wahlund, K., & Kristiansson, M. (2009). Aggression, psychopathy and brain imaging—Review and future recommendations. *International Journal of Law & Psychiatry, 32*(4), 266–271.

Walsh, A., & Beaver, K. M. (2009a). Biosocial criminology. In M. D. Krohn, A. J. Lizotte, & G. P. Hall (Eds.), Handbook on crime and deviance (pp. 79–101). New York: Springer.

Walsh, A., & Beaver, K. M. (2009b). *Biosocial criminology: New directions in theory and research.* New York: Taylor & Francis.

Walters, G. D. (1989). Putting more thought into criminology. *International Journal of Offender Therapy and Comparative Criminology, 30,* v–vii.

Walters, G. D. (1990). *The criminal lifestyle.* Beverly Hills, CA: Sage.

Walters, G. D., & White. T. W. (1989). The thinking criminal: A cognitive model of lifestyle criminality. *Criminal Justice Research Bulletin, 4,* 1–10.

Ward, D. A., & Tittle, C. (1994). IQ and delinquency: A test of two competing explanations. *Journal of Quantitative Criminology, 10,* 189–212.

Wilson, J. Q., & Herrnstein, R. J. (1985). *Crime and human nature.* New York: Simon and Schuster.

Yochelson, S., & Samenow, S. E. (1976). *The criminal personality: A profile for change* (Vol. 1). New York: Jason Aronson.

Yochelson, S., & Samenow, S. E. (1977). *The criminal personality: The change process* (Vol. 2). New York: Jason Aronson.

Research Bibliography

Biological Research (from 2000)

Aigner, M., Eher, R., Fruehwald, S. S., Frottier, P., Gutierrez-Lobos, K. K., & Dwyer, S. (2000). Brain abnormalities and violent behavior. *Journal of Psychology & Human Sexuality, 11*(3), 57–64.

Åslund, C. C., Nordquist, N. N., Comasco, E. E., Leppert, J. J., Oreland, L. L., & Nilsson, K. K. (2011). Maltreatment, MAOA, and delinquency: Sex differences in gene-environment interaction in a large population-based cohort of adolescents. *Behavior Genetics, 41,* 262–272.

Beaver, K. M. (2011). Environmental moderators of genetic influences on adolescent delinquent involvement and victimization. *Journal of Adolescent Research, 26,* 84–114.

Beaver, K. M., DeLisi, M., Vaughn, M. G., & Wright, J. (2010). The intersection of genes and neuropsychological deficits in the prediction of adolescent delinquency and low self-control. *International Journal of Offender Therapy & Comparative Criminology, 54,* 22–42.

Beaver, K. M., DeLisi, M., Wright, J., & Vaughn, M. G. (2009). Gene-environment interplay and delinquent involvement: Evidence of direct, indirect, and interactive effects. *Journal of Adolescent Research, 24,* 147–168.

Beaver, K. M., Gibson, C. L., DeLisi, M., Vaughn, M. G., & Wright, J. (2012). The interaction between neighborhood disadvantage and genetic factors in the prediction of antisocial outcomes. *Youth Violence & Juvenile Justice, 10,* 25–40.

Boutwell, B. B., & Beaver, K. M. (2008). A biosocial explanation of delinquency abstention. *Criminal Behaviour & Mental Health, 18,* 59–74.

Button, T. M., Stallings, M. C., Rhee, S., Corley, R. P., Boardman, J. D., & Hewitt, J. K. (2009). Perceived peer delinquency and the genetic predisposition for substance dependence vulnerability. *Drug & Alcohol Dependence, 100*(1/2), 1–8.

El-Sheikh, M., Hinnant, J., & Erath, S. (2011). Developmental trajectories of delinquency symptoms in childhood: The role of marital conflict and autonomic nervous system activity. *Journal of Abnormal Psychology, 120,* 16–32.

Fazel, S., Philipson, J., Gardiner, L., Merritt, R., & Grann, M. (2009). Neurological disorders and violence: A systematic review and meta-analysis with a focus on epilepsy and traumatic brain injury. *Journal of Neurology, 256,* 1591–1602.

Guang, G., Xiao-Ming, O., Roettger, M., & Shih, J. C. (2008). The VNTR 2 repeat in MAOA and delinquent behavior in adolescence and young adulthood: Associations and MAOA promoter activity. *European Journal of Human Genetics, 16,* 626–634.

Guo, G., Roettger, M. E., & Cai, T. (2008). The integration of genetic propensities into social-control models of delinquency and violence among male youths. *American Sociological Review, 73,* 543–568.

Harden, K., & Mendle, J. (2012). Gene-environment interplay in the association between pubertal timing and delinquency in adolescent girls. *Journal of Abnormal Psychology, 121,* 73–87.

Ilhong, Y., Jinseong, C., & Walsh, A. (2011). Genetic and environmental influences in delinquent peer affiliation: From the peer network approach. *Youth Violence & Juvenile Justice, 9,* 241–258.

Kumar, R. (2003). Violence begets violence; or does it? A brain enzyme protects victims of childhood abuse from becoming antisocial and criminal. *Clinical Genetics, 63*(3), 180–183.

Kumari, V., Barkataki, I., Goswami, S., Flora, S., Das, M., & Taylor, P. (2009). Dysfunctional, but not functional, impulsivity is associated with a history of seriously violent behaviour and reduced orbitofrontal and hippocampal volumes in schizophrenia. *Psychiatry Research: Neuroimaging Section, 173,* 39–44.

Mead, H. K., Beauchaine, T. P., & Shannon, K. E. (2010). Neurobiological adaptations to violence across development. *Development & Psychopathology, 22,* 1–22.

Narayan, V. M., Narr, K. L., Kumari, V., Woods, R. P., Thompson, P. M., Toga, A. W., et al. (2007). Regional cortical thinning in subjects with violent antisocial personality disorder or schizophrenia. *American Journal of Psychiatry, 164,* 1418–1427.

Raine, A., Park, S., Lencz, T., Bihrle, S., LaCasse, L., Widom, C., et al. (2001). Reduced right hemisphere activation in severely abused violent offenders during a working memory task: An fMRI study. *Aggressive Behavior, 27,* 111–129.

Rossby, P. (2002). The biology of violence: Serotonin, alcoholism, hypoglycemia. *Criminal Justice, 17,* 20–24.

Simpson, J. A., Griskevicius, V., I-Chun Kuo, S., Sung, S., & Collins, W. (2012). Evolution, stress, and sensitive periods: The influence of unpredictability in early versus late childhood on sex and risky behavior. *Developmental Psychology, 48*(3), 674–686.

Psychological Research (from 2000)

Buist, K. L. (2010). Sibling relationship quality and adolescent delinquency: A latent growth curve approach. *Journal of Family Psychology, 24,* 400–410.

Chin-Chih, C., Symons, F. J., & Reynolds, A. J. (2011). Prospective analyses of childhood factors and antisocial behavior for students with high-incidence disabilities. *Behavioral Disorders, 37,* 5–18.

Dean, K. K., Mortensen, P. B., Stevens, H. H., Murray, R. M., Walsh, E. E., & Agerbo, E. E. (2012). Criminal conviction among offspring with parental history of mental disorder. *Psychological Medicine, 42,* 571–581.

Eklund, J. M., Liljeberg, J., & af Klinteberg, B. (2011). Delinquent behaviour patterns in adolescence: Development and associated personality traits. *Personality & Mental Health, 5*(3), 169–185.

Elonheimo, H., Sourander, A., Niemelä, S., & Helenius, H. (2011). Generic and crime type specific correlates of youth crime: A Finnish population-based study. *Social Psychiatry & Psychiatric Epidemiology, 46,* 903–914.

Ezinga, M. J., Weerman, F. M., Westenberg, P. M., & Bijleveld, C. H. (2008). Early adolescence and delinquency: Levels of psychosocial development and self-control as an explanation of misbehaviour and delinquency. *Psychology, Crime & Law, 14,* 339–356.

Goldweber, A., Dmitrieva, J., Cauffman, E., Piquero, A., & Steinberg, L. (2011). The development of criminal style in adolescence and young adulthood: Separating the lemmings from the loners. *Journal of Youth & Adolescence, 40,* 332–346.

Jackson, D. B. (2012). The role of early pubertal development in the relationship between general strain and juvenile crime. *Youth Violence & Juvenile Justice, 10,* 292–310.

Kennedy, T. D., Burnett, K. F., & Edmonds, W. A. (2011). Intellectual, behavioral, and personality correlates of violent vs. non-violent juvenile offenders. *Aggressive Behavior, 37,* 315–325.

Laak, J., de Goede, M., Aleva, L., Brugman, G., van Leuven, M., & Hussmann, J. (2003). Incarcerated adolescent girls: Personality, social competence, and delinquency. *Adolescence, 38,* 251–265.

LaGasse, L. L., Hammond, J., Jing, L., Lester, B. M., Shankaran, S., Bada, H., et al. (2006). Violence and delinquency, early onset drug use, and psychopathology in drug-exposed youth at 11 years. *Annals of the New York Academy Of Sciences, 1094,* 313–318.

Maughan, D., & Moore, S. C. (2010). Dimensions of child neglect: An exploration of parental neglect and its relationship with delinquency. *Child Welfare, 89,* 47–65.

Mellin, E. A., & Hong-Ning, F. (2010). Exploration of the pathways to delinquency for female adolescents with depression: Implications for cross-systems collaboration and counseling. *Journal of Addictions & Offender Counseling, 30*(2), 58–72.

Mordre, M., Groholt, B., Kjelsberg, E., Sandstad, B., & Myhre, A. (2011). The impact of ADHD and conduct disorder in childhood on adult delinquency: A 30 years follow-up study using official crime records. *BMC Psychiatry, 11,* 57–66.

Nederlof, E., van der Ham, A., Dingemans, P., & Oei, K. (2010). The relation between dimensions of personality and personality pathology and offence type and severity in juvenile delinquents. *Journal of Forensic Psychiatry & Psychology, 21,* 711–720.

Pullmann, M. M. (2010). Predictors of criminal charges for youth in public mental health during the transition to adulthood. *Journal of Child & Family Studies, 19,* 483–491.

Sibley, M. H., Pelham, W. E., Molina, B. G., Gnagy, E. M., Waschbusch, D. A., Biswas, A., et al. (2011). The delinquency outcomes of boys with ADHD with and without comorbidity. *Journal of Abnormal Child Psychology, 39,* 21–32.

Van Dam, C., De Bruyn, E. J., & Janssens, J. M. (2007). Personality, delinquency, and criminal recidivism. *Adolescence, 42,* 763–777.

Wilkinson, D., Jones, T., & Caulfiend, L. (2011). Time to reason about crime: Assessing the impact of schizotypal tendencies on a crime-based reasoning task. *Howard Journal of Criminal Justice, 50,* 393–405.

The Chicago School

LEARNING OBJECTIVES

Objective 4.1: Outline the contributions of the Chicago School to the study of crime.

Objective 4.2: Explain the term "social disorganization" and how it is measured.

Objective 4.3: Describe how symbolic interactions take place and why they are important.

Objective 4.4: Discuss how culture conflict is related to crime and delinquency.

Objective 4.5: Summarize the use of concentric zones for studying urban areas.

INTRODUCTION

The University of Chicago established the first department of sociology in 1892, and through the mid-twentieth century it was one of the dominant forces in American sociological thought. The diverse group of scholars associated with the department were collectively referred to as the "Chicago School" of sociology and criminology. Although we focus on their work in criminology, many of the major themes running through their studies are also found in the related fields of social psychology and urban sociology.

One recurrent theme of the school is that human behavior is developed and changed by the social and physical environment of the person rather than by genetic structure. As David Matza (1969) wrote, it was assumed people are complex creatures who are capable of great diversity in their lifestyles. In support of this view, the Chicago School scholars considered the community to be a major influence on human behavior. They believed a city is a natural human environment, "a microcosm of the human universe."

The methods by which the Chicago School studied the individual and the city were in themselves contributions to sociology and criminology. Developing an *empirical sociology*, researchers moved beyond social philosophy and armchair theory and began to study individuals in their social environment. At the same time, they examined people in the aggregate and as individuals. The *life history* provided a method of reaching deeply into the cumulative factors and events shaping the lives of individuals. The *ecological study* technique allowed them to transcend individuality and, through the collection of social data, gain a sense of the characteristics of large groups of people. Combining the information gathered from individual cases with population statistics, the Chicago School thereby constructed a framework that has been the basis for most of our criminological theories ever since.

THE HERITAGE OF THE SCHOOL

The Social Heritage

Those who worked in the social sciences during the early twentieth century dealt with the development of the big cities, rapid industrialization, mass immigration, the effects of World War I, Prohibition, the Great Depression, and more. Through it all, the members of the Chicago School looked to the city of Chicago as a source of questions and answers. Indeed, the urbanization of the nation led many scholars to believe the city was responsible for most of the problems of society.

From a small settlement of the early 1800s, Chicago grew rapidly as "cheap labor" rushed to take advantage of canal work and inexpensive land. Opportunity attracted the abundant unskilled workers necessary to encourage industrial growth. Chicago doubled its population in the three decades between 1898 and 1930 as waves of immigrants transformed the simpler fabric of small-town uniformity into complex and conflicting patterns of urban life (Cressey, 1938, p. 59). When the limits of industrialization were reached and the displacement of workers by technology began, the demand for a large, mobile, unskilled population disappeared, leaving a tangle of social problems ranging from inadequate housing and sanitation to homelessness, juvenile gangs, and vice.

Away from their closely knit families and familiar communities, many people found that there was no one to whom they could turn in troubled times. Thousands of unemployed people—male and female, young and old—became transients to avoid burdening relatives or friends. To counter these problems, many social work organizations and relief programs emerged between 1920 and 1930. Based on an implicit faith in the value of case work and rehabilitation, they sought to employ and thus reform the troubled masses. Though much attention was focused on the needs of the poor, it was also recognized that crime seemed to be fostered in the slums. The study of the slums, the immigrants living there, and crime became politically and socially relevant (Kobrin 1959, and in Laub, 1983a, p. 89). In addition, the mobster in organized crime syndicates was a stereotype image of Chicago and to many it seemed the crime capital of the world (Valier, 2003).

Representing the last major wave of immigrants to the United States, southern and eastern Europeans received much of the blame for the nation's conditions. Among an existing population derived largely from western and northern Europe, the new immigrants were discriminated against and looked on as inferior stock. Aside from the prejudices inspired by peculiar customs and mannerisms, immigrants' loyalties were always suspect, particularly in times of war and political conflict. Children of immigrants, adapting more rapidly to the change in culture than their parents and grandparents, were often embarrassed by their families and drew away from them, forming their own support groups and gangs (Whyte, 1943).

The melting pot of the American dream was also a law-enforcement nightmare as it became apparent that city neighborhoods had few purposes or customs in common at any one time.

People often felt the law was not theirs and refused to support or contribute to its enforcement. The search for a solution to these problems turned the city into a human laboratory for the new sociologists at the University of Chicago.

The Intellectual Heritage

Until the early twentieth century, American criminology had drawn from its European (Italian and English) heritage and supported popular positivist explanations of crime, usually of the biological variety. Much of the previous research had linked feeblemindedness and hereditary factors with delinquency (Shaw & McKay, 1931, p. 4). A change in this perspective came with the rise of cultural (rather than biological) theories of the behavior of individuals and groups.

As sociology moved into the study of crime, German influence began to take hold. As Martin Bulmer (1984, p. 38) notes in his history of the Chicago School, the leading figures in sociology had studied in Germany and were profoundly influenced by that experience. The German approach (as well as that of the French sociologist Emile Durkheim), in contrast to the approach of the Italian positivists, was preeminently social and cultural. At the same time, anthropology, under the leadership of Franz Boas and his students, had dedicated itself to demonstrating that human nature is almost solely a product of culture, not of biology (Edgerton, 1976). Under this general social science umbrella, the foundation was being laid for a new sociological criminology.

In addition to the substance of their work, American sociologists were trying to establish a reputation for scientific analysis in their field, to counteract the image of sociology as philosophical and speculative (Short, 1971, p. xii). The scientific study of social problems, especially of crime, became one way for sociologists to enhance their academic and scientific credibility. Painstakingly, they gathered facts about urban life, watching and recording the growth and structure of the developing city.

THE PERSPECTIVE OF THE SCHOOL

Methodological Contributions

Two major methods of study were employed by the Chicago School. The first was the use of official data (crime figures, census reports, housing and welfare records). This information was applied to geographical layouts of the city, indicating areas of high crime, truancy, and poverty. Charts and graphic portraits of social phenomena were maintained over periods of time, and the figures displayed a stability that led to a revolutionary thought in crime causation: Certain areas of the city remained crime prone even though various ethnic populations came and went.

The second method of study was the life history. W. I. Thomas first studied this form of folk psychology in Germany (Bulmer, 1984, p. 36) and developed it into "ethnography" at the University of Chicago (Thomas & Znaniecki, 1918). This type of study shifted away from theoretical abstracts to the more intimate aspects of the real world. The life history or case study approach presented the social-psychological process of becoming a criminal or delinquent. Sociologists became research explorers; they met, talked with, ate with, and virtually lived with their subjects. As the everyday lives of addicts, hobos, and delinquents unfolded, the observers were invited to analyze the characters as they appeared in their natural environment, be it a slum, a street corner, or a railroad car. Borrowing the idea of studying plants and animals in their natural habitat, Robert Park and Ernest Burgess (1924) saw the ecological symbiosis present in interdependent plant and animal life and attempted to present a human ecology, to interpret people in time and space as they naturally appear. For this reason, the Chicago School

Clifford Robe Shaw (1896–1957)

Shaw was born in the farming town of Luray, Indiana. He received an A.B. from Albion College in 1919, although his studies were interrupted by his service in the Navy during World War I. He went on to earn an M.A. in sociology in 1921 at the University of Chicago and completed most of the work for his Ph.D., although he never finished the degree. He immersed himself in life within the immigrant neighborhoods of Chicago and worked as a parole officer and a probation officer with juvenile populations. In 1926, Shaw was appointed director of the new sociology department at the Institute for Juvenile Research and held the position until his death in 1957. He taught as an adjunct professor at George Williams College in Chicago and the Central YMCA College from 1926 to 1941 and at the University of Chicago from 1941 to 1957.

In keeping with the traditions of the Chicago School, Shaw experimented with sociological theories of communities and self-governance. In the early 1930s, he founded the Chicago Area Project (CAP) as a way to study delinquency intervention strategies and oversaw its successful growth over the following two decades.

was often referred to as the "Ecological School." In fact, Chicago School researchers maintained that observation of the neighborhood and community was as important as observing the people who lived there.

Ecological and Social Disorganization Theory

Perhaps as important as any other contribution of the Chicago School was the organic approach to the study of the community taken by Robert Park. Working under the assumption that the city is similar to a body with its different organs, Park sent his students out to examine the various organs, or "social worlds," of the metropolis (Farris, 1967, p. 52). From these investigations and others, Park and Ernest Burgess (1924) produced a conception of the city as a series of distinctive concentric circles radiating from the central business district. The farther one moved away from the center of these concentric zones, the fewer social problems were found. The basic idea was that the growth of cities, and the location of various areas and social problems, is not random but instead is part of a pattern. Burgess's (1925) conception of the concentric zone pattern of city growth provided the foundation for later Chicago School explanations of crime and delinquency.

Using the ecological concepts of dominance, invasion, and succession from plant and animal ecology, the general theory maintained there are dominant uses of land within the zones. When those uses characteristic of an inner zone encroach on the adjacent outer zone, invasion occurs and that territory becomes less desirable. In time, the invading land uses replace the existing land uses, resulting in a new social and physical environment. In this way, the inner zone grows to include the adjacent outer zone, thus causing a ripple effect among all the zones.

The first zone was the *central business district*, with its businesses and factories but few residences. The zone next to it was referred to as the *zone of transition* because businesses and factories were encroaching on this area. This zone was not desirable as a location for residences and homes but owing to its deterioration was the cheapest place to live. Immigrants, then, usually settled into this second zone because it was inexpensive and near the factories where they could find work. As they could afford to move, they moved into the third zone, the *zone of workingmen's homes*, and were themselves replaced in the zone of transition by another wave of immigrants. Other zones radiating out from there were increasingly more expensive to live in.

Subsequent research noted that social ills seemed to follow a pattern in which the most problems were found in the first zone and progressively fewer problems were found in each succeeding zone. Clifford Shaw and Henry McKay (1931), for instance, documented that rates of delinquency, tuberculosis, and infant mortality followed the same decreasing pattern as one moved away from the central business district. The ethnographic and life history work of the Chicago School was then, in part, devoted to explaining the effect of these ecological areas on social life.

The observations made by researchers provided a picture of the city as a place where life is superficial, people are anonymous, relationships are transitory, and kinship and friendship bonds are weak. The Chicago School saw the weakening of primary social relationships as a process of social disorganization. In turn, social disorganization became the primary explanation for the emergence of crime. Shaw and McKay's (1942) version of social disorganization is based on a conception of primary relationships similar to those found in a village. If relationships in the family and friendship groupings are good, neighborhoods are stable and cohesive, and people have a sense of loyalty to the area, then social organization is sound. In other words, intact homes and proper family values are part of a socially organized community. Without these characteristics, a community or neighborhood is socially disorganized. Normal social control, which prevents crime and delinquency, cannot do its job. Robert Sampson and Byron Groves (1989) list four elements that constitute social disorganization: (1) low economic status, (2) a mixture of different ethnic groups, (3) highly mobile residents moving in and out of the area, and (4) disrupted families and broken homes. Thus, social disorganization is an explanation of the distribution of rates (or epidemiology) of crime and delinquency.

Shaw and McKay also noted that the zone of transition was more socially disorganized than other areas, primarily because of the high degree of mobility, the decaying neighborhoods, and the encroachment of the business and factory district. This was a particularly serious matter in the zone of transition because of the number of immigrants. Faced with the difficulty of maintaining primary relationships (and the difficulty of financially succeeding in a relatively class-bound society), immigrants retreated to the safety of their own native cultures. The relationship between immigrants and crime was finally seen not as a product of heredity but as a dual problem of social disorganization and of *conflict* with existing American culture.

Another contribution made by Shaw and McKay[1] was their explanation of the process by which social disorganization affects juveniles and leads to delinquency, commonly referred to as "cultural transmission theory." According to this theory, juveniles who live in socially disorganized areas have greater opportunities for exposure to those who espouse delinquent and criminal values. Indeed, one of the primary characteristics of those areas is that a delinquent tradition has developed. This delinquent tradition provides a way of transmitting delinquent values, as Shaw and McKay (1942, p. 168) explain:

> The importance of the concentration of delinquents is seen most clearly when the effect is viewed in a temporal perspective. The maps representing distribution of delinquents at successive periods indicate that, year after year, decade after decade, the same areas have been characterized by these concentrations. This means that delinquent boys in these areas have contact not only with other delinquents who are their contemporaries but also with

---

[1] See Reiss (1976) for an overview of Henry McKay's life and work. Also see Short's (1972) introduction to Shaw & McKay's classic book as an excellent source of the context of the theory and work.

older offenders, who in turn had contact with delinquents preceding them, and so on back to the earliest history of the neighborhood. This contact means that the traditions of delinquency can be and are transmitted down through successive generations of boys, in much the same way that language and other social forms are transmitted.

In later chapters of this book, the similarity of social disorganization theory and cultural transmission theory to differential association theories and social control becomes evident. Thus, it can easily be argued that Shaw and McKay exerted a great deal of influence on the criminological theories following them.

The social disorganization perspective was especially attractive to African American sociologists studying crime. Monroe Work (1866–1945), one of the first African American graduates of the University of Chicago's Sociology master's program, explained that during the period following slavery, African Americans experienced a disorientation with societal norms. He focused on changing social conditions during emancipation and reconstruction which resulted in disorganization. This was particularly true in southern states where lawlessness was reflected in higher crime rates, as well as lynchings (Work, 1939). However, as more people migrated to northern cities, arrests there increased. Work also noted that during prohibition, crime rates in the South declined.

One of the most noted of African American sociologists, E. Franklin Frazier (1894–1962) suggested that black adolescent boys learn criminality from older peers or family members and begin patterns of delinquent behavior around 11 or 12 years of age. While he argued that a lack of collective environmental controls in urban lower-class neighborhoods was at the root of this delinquency, he also blamed absentee fathers, separated parents, and a lack of parental control for creating high-risk environments. Like others of this time, Frazier saw the city divided into zones with varied levels of disorganization which corresponded with rates of delinquency (Frazier, 1939). The interesting note here is that he was echoing the same kind of thoughts that were to come from Edwin Sutherland in the theory of differential association. In 1948, Frazier was elected President of the American Sociological Society (later American Sociological Association).

The third African American theorist, Earl R. Moses (1901–1968), obtained his master's in sociology at the University of Chicago in 1932. Moses researched family and community factors that influenced what he called "indigenous" and "transplanted" criminal behaviors. Using case studies of young males, as well as statistical data, he noted that while the population of African Americans in Chicago grew, the rates of delinquency grew disproportionately faster. Delinquency appeared to be related not to race but to mobility, which he characterized as the frequent movement of delinquency-prone families within dilapidated housing areas that were more deteriorated and disorganized than those of surrounding zones (Moses, 1936). Moses later completed his Ph.D. in Sociology at the University of Pennsylvania. (For other theoretical commentary during this period see Gabbidon & Greene, 2001; Gabbidon, Greene, & Young, 2002.)

Symbolic Interactionism

The social-psychological theory of symbolic interactionism has been one of the more lasting of the Chicago School's theoretical perspectives. Although the Chicago School theorists who developed it never referred to it by this name (Blumer, 1969, p. 1), symbolic interactionism developed from a belief that human behavior is the product of purely social symbols communicated between individuals. A basic idea of symbolic interactionism is that the mind and the self are not innate but are products of the social environment. It is in the process of communicating, or symbolizing, that humans come to define both themselves and others. These symbols have meanings affecting the way we see the world. If, for example, we are introduced to a juvenile delinquent, we may not see the person but may view him or her as "the standard juvenile delinquent"; that is, we see someone who is all the things we expect a juvenile delinquent to be.

Further, we pick up our own self-concept from our perception of what others think about us. These others are not necessarily specific individuals but, often, generalized types of people (George Mead [1934] called this abstract person the "generalized other"). Thus, we create our own identities by reflection from others. W. I. Thomas's addition of situations led to the understanding that we can have many identities, or self-concepts, depending on the setting in which we find ourselves. In the school setting, one may be a student; at home, a parent; at work, an insurance salesperson; at play, the team captain; in our parents' house, a child; and so forth. Each situation demands its own role, its own identity, and its own behaviors. Moreover, in social life, one may incorrectly define the situation and behave inappropriately. To paraphrase Thomas's famous saying, a proper definition of the situation is necessary for one to respond with acceptable behavior.

This recognition of the complexity and relativity of social life, with its multiplicity of required roles, gave the Chicago School an understanding of deviance. Such an understanding required the ability to view human behavior, and guidelines for that behavior, as *relative*. For the Chicago School, there were no absolutes, no set of universal rules governing human behavior. First, there are places where normal behaviors would be defined by those outside of the place as deviant, in the "hobo jungles," for example. There people engage in "deviant" behavior by correctly defining the situation and following the roles expected of them. The behavior is not, of course, deviant from the perspective of that specific setting but only from the perspective of outside society. Second, people can misdefine situations, act inappropriately, and become deviant. Thus, a misreading of situational guidelines can lead to rule-violating behavior. For instance, at the street corner near your home you may legally make a right turn at a red light. Elsewhere, you may erroneously assume, much to your dismay when you get a ticket, that right turns are also allowed.

Symbolic interactionism, then, provided a true social origin for both self-concepts and behaviors. It also gave us a relativistic (i.e., situational) understanding of the rules and guidelines that govern behavior. The Chicago School gave criminology an appreciation of the effect of social settings and situational values on crime and deviant behavior, which served to offset the universal rule approach of the Positive School. The appearance of the labeling perspective in the criminological writing of the 1960s was directly related to this theoretical approach.

Culture Conflict

Having taken a relativistic position on human values and behavior, it was only natural for the Chicago School to recognize that conflict is common in society. After all, contact between people of different values and lifestyles will almost always lead to some type of conflict. Robert Park, impressed by the thoughts of a dominant German conflict sociologist, Georg Simmel, incorporated the notion of conflict as a central component of an influential sociology textbook that he wrote with Ernest Burgess (1924) and specifically used the term "culture conflict" in a 1930 article. Here conflict is viewed as a major social process, set in motion by the differences in values and cultures among groups of people. Louis Wirth, one of Park's students, wrote his

Thorsten Sellin (1896–1994)

Thorsten Sellin was born in Ornskoldsvik, Sweden. His family moved to Ontario, Canada, when he was 17. He received his B.A. in 1915 from Augustana College, Illinois, and his M.A. in sociology from the University of Pennsylvania in 1916 and his Ph.D. in 1922. Sellin began his career teaching at the University of Pennsylvania and remained there until his retirement in 1967. He had an excellent command of languages, with expertise in Swedish, English, German, and French. He served as long-time editor of the *Annals of the American Academy of Political and Social Science*. His interest in crime statistics and a crime index was tied to his service as a consultant and special agent with the U.S. Census Bureau, where he advocated for states to adopt the uniform collection and maintenance of crime statistics in the 1930s. His career was highlighted by his work on international crime and punishment issues. Distinguished accomplishments include leadership in the International Society of Criminology (President 1956–1965), the International Penal and Penitentiary Commission (Secretary General), and the United National Social Defense Section. His policy critiques of capital punishment include some of his best-known writings.

thesis on cultural conflicts in immigrant families (1925), and a few years later (1931) wrote about the relationship of the conflict of cultures to crime and delinquency (see Reiss, 1964, for an overview of Wirth's work). Another graduate (and subsequently a faculty member) of the Chicago School, Edwin Sutherland, also wrote (1929) on conflicting values and how criminal behavior arises from them.

The best statement of culture conflict theory, however, came from a scholar who was not a member of the Chicago School. In his book *Culture Conflict and Crime* (1938), Thorsten Sellin produced what is seen today as the seminal work on culture conflict. Although the book was to have been written with Sutherland as a project of the Social Science Research Council, Sellin alone completed the work. The central thesis of culture conflict, though, was borrowed from the writings and teachings of Park, Wirth, and others at the University of Chicago (Sellin, in Laub, 1983b).

Sellin's culture conflict theory revolves around the idea of conduct norms, or rules that govern behavior. In this sense, conduct norms are similar to W. I. Thomas's concept of definitions for behavior. According to Sellin, one is reared with cultural values about proper conduct. The content of those norms varies from culture to culture. Groups with social and political power can even use their conduct norms to control the definition of crime. Thus, the legal definition of crime is but the conduct norm for one particular social group. People come in conflict with these legal definitions of behavior accidentally or intentionally. If one's own culture approves an act but the dominant culture does not, the stage is set for criminal behavior.

An Example of Primary Culture Conflict

In Sunrise, Florida, a community official claiming to be protecting innocent animals moved to ban Muslims from sacrificing lambs and goats in a celebratory rite. However, the ceremony commemorating Abraham's willingness to offer his son's life and the pilgrimage to Mecca appeared to be consistent with laws protecting religious freedoms. Still, the public controversy resulted in the event being moved from that private property site to another undisclosed venue.

Source: Bryan, S. (2011, November 6). City official stops Muslims' animal sacrifice. *Houston Chronicle*, p. A30.

Sellin suggested that there are two main forms of culture conflict. The first, called primary conflict, occurs when two different cultures govern behavior, for example, when someone from one culture emigrates to another cultural area. The "old" culture cannot simply be cast off, and for a while it continues to influence the person's behavior. Sellin's classic example of this involves an "Old World" family who moved to New Jersey: The daughter was seduced by a young man, and her father, following an Old World tradition, killed him to protect the family honor. The father was arrested, yet he could not understand why, because from his cultural perspective he had committed no crime. Another example of primary conflict is when one country conquers another and imposes its laws on the conquered people. Citizens of the conquered nation run afoul of some of the new laws simply because they are not yet accustomed to the new laws or they find them too restrictive. For example, Mexico's Metlatonoc Indians have fought the government to retain their practice of offering a bride's family money up to $500 upon her marriage. The custom, frowned upon by contemporary Mexican society, has been one of the many issues leading to rebel uprisings and the attempt to enact an Indian Rights Law that would allow native villages to retain their ancient traditions. However, human rights groups throughout the area argue that the presence of wealthy drug traffickers in these opium-growing regions has increased the value of selling women often into lives of abuse and degradation (Lloyd, 2001).

Sellin's other form of culture conflict is called secondary conflict. Here, he was referring to smaller cultures existing within a larger culture; the term we might use today is "subculture." People who live in a geographic area begin, over a period of time, to create their own set of values (conduct norms). While these values are not wholly different from those of the larger culture, there are enough differences to give rise to conflict. The people within an urban, center-city neighborhood, for example, may develop values leading to lawbreaking. The agents of the law, of course, respond from the framework of laws based on middle-class values, laws that do not allow for subcultural differences. Thus, some subcultures see gambling

Two Examples of Secondary Culture Conflict

An Ethiopian father charged in Duluth, Georgia, with cruelty to a child and aggravated battery for cutting the genitals of his 2-year-old daughter was sentenced to 10 years in prison. The father was convicted of using a pair of scissors to perform the operation in his apartment without the consent of the mother. The practice is traditionally used to curtail the sex drive and to preserve the virginity of a young woman, proof of which is often a prerequisite for marriage. Although Congress outlawed the practice in 1996, Georgia did not have a law in place at the time of Khalid Adem's offense, thus the alternate charges. Had the mutilation taken place after Georgia passed its female circumcision ban, the sentence would have likely been more severe.

Source: Mungin, L. (2006, November 2). Dad guilty of genital mutilation: Ten years in prison for circumcising daughter. *Atlanta Journal Constitution*, p. B1.

In the heart of Amish country a series of violent attacks has highlighted the growing schism between two religious groups. The majority Amish culture adheres to their interpretations of Biblical instructions for both men and women to refrain from cutting their hair. A breakaway faction of members have been accused of breaking into the homes of traditional Amish families and cutting the hair and beards of the men as well as the hair of the women. The spiritual conflict has led to charges of kidnapping and burglary. The attacks have terrorized an otherwise peaceful and cohesive community.

Source: Spector, A. (2012, March 19). Amish case has odd focal point: Sissors reportedly used to cut beards. *Dayton Daily News*, p. B4.

and prostitution as legitimate behaviors, but the larger society has usually declared them illegal. Because of their values, then, the members of such subcultures are more likely to be arrested for gambling and prostitution than are other members of society whose values are more closely represented in law.

The notion of conflict, and culture conflict, as it grew from the Chicago School, has strongly influenced American sociological criminology. In his book *Explaining Crime* (1974, p. 141), Gwynn Nettler states that all subsequent social explanations have been based on the assumption that culture conflict is the fundamental source of crime. While his point may be arguable, the relativistic conflict approach of the Chicago School has been critical to the further development of criminology.

CLASSIFICATION OF THE SCHOOL

As diverse in its viewpoints as it was, the Chicago School still shared a few commonalities. The main thrust of its work, for instance, was *positivist* in character, albeit of a "newer" social variety. The assumption of determinism strongly characterized all the work of the school, from the initial symbolic interactionism of Mead and Thomas to the statistical work of Shaw and McKay. Further, the positivist emphasis on systematic observation and testing is clearly reflected in the work of the Chicago School. It is clear that Chicago criminologists saw pathology in the city, and they conducted their studies in an effort to learn what was wrong. Ultimately, they wanted to correct the social ills of the city, and crime and delinquency were high on their list. The Chicago School also helped create what may be the best criminological examples of using theory to develop reform and treatment programs.

Classifying the Chicago School as either structural or processual is difficult, largely because different members of the school stressed different factors in their explanations of society. Regardless of any assumptions they might have made about the structure of society (seen most clearly in the later work of Shaw and McKay [1942]), the dominant orientation was that of *process*. All those associated with the Chicago School stressed the processes involved in behavior, the ways that people come to act in response to other people, real or imagined. Even the reliance on social disorganization (in reality a structural element) was derived from a different source from that of the anomie-strain theories that followed later (see Chapter 6). For the Chicago School, the product of social disorganization was a variety of conduct norms and behavior rules, not societal strain. These various norms result in deviance as members of different groups or subcultures apply different definitions to the situations they commonly shared. Thus, the school's focus was on the process of gaining definitions, and its underlying question was, How do individuals use their definitions of self and situation to produce behavior?

Chicago School theorists were, at heart, *consensus* theorists. This does not mean that they did not emphasize conflict—they did. The assumption, however, was that consensus, or a natural conformity to cultural lifeways, is the initial pattern of human behavior. This was demonstrated by their appreciation of diversity in human behavior, yet it was a patterned diversity, one shared by the members of the culture to which one belongs. It was only where one group came into contact with another that conflict developed. And, of course, these theorists recognized that society is made up of a variety of cultural groups; therefore, conflict is simply a fact of life.

Finally, the Chicago School produced chiefly *microtheories* (with the exception of culture conflict, which is a macrotheory). The social-psychological approach to the study of human behavior dominated almost all the work of these theorists and became the common thread that wound through the diverse positions they espoused. They focused more on the process of becoming deviant than on explaining how the structure of society affects deviant behavior. This is somewhat ironic, given that members of the Chicago School developed the study of ecological rates and prepared the evidence for most of the macrotheoretical work that followed.

Summary

Although the sociological approach to studying modern social problems began as an interest of a small group of professors and students, the second generation of scholars expanded their interest into the realm of city programs and local research offices. Sampson (2002a) summarizes the characteristics of the work of the Chicago School as (1) an emphasis on the area or place of social activity; (2) a view of the community as well as the city as a complex social organism; (3) a preference for studying the dynamic and variable social organizations of the people rather than just their traits or characteristics; (4) data collection that focuses on a variety of methods and techniques with a focus on direct observation; and (5) a concern for public affairs and community improvement through empowerment.

The theoretical positions advanced by the Chicago School became the basis for much of the criminological work of the next three decades (1940s through the 1960s). The theoretical explanations that the Chicago School theorists (and their followers) gave to their research data can still be found behind many contemporary criminological theories. In short, because of its widespread influence, the Chicago School was the discipline of criminology prior to the late 1950s.

MAJOR POINTS OF THE SCHOOL

1. Humans are social creatures, and their behavior is a product of their social environment.

2. Social environments provide cultural values and definitions that govern the behavior of those who live within them.

3. Urbanization and industrialization have created communities that have a variety of competing cultures, thus breaking down older and more cohesive patterns of values.

4. This breakdown, or disorganization, of urban life has resulted in the basic institutions of family, friendship groups, and social groups becoming more impersonal.

5. As the values provided by these institutions become fragmented, several opposing definitions about proper behavior arise and come into conflict. Continued disorganization makes the potential for conflict even more likely.

6. Deviant or criminal behavior generally occurs when one behaves according to definitions that conflict with those of the dominant culture.

7. Social disorganization and social pathology are most prevalent in the center-city area, decreasing with distance from that area.

8. Crime and delinquency are transmitted by frequent contact with criminal traditions that have developed over time in disorganized areas of the city.

Epilogue: Current Directions and Policy Implications

CURRENT DIRECTIONS

The work of the Chicago School, with its focus on cities, communities, and social organization, continued through the 1940s. After that time, two different approaches became dominant. Stressing individual deviance on the one hand, and the effect of cultural and societal structures on the other, the majority of criminologists spent their time on the theories of labeling, control, and anomie.[2] The community-based theories of the Chicago School did not disappear, however. Disciples of the Chicago School continued their work. In the late 1970s, the tradition gained renewed attention. The interest can probably be attributed to the emergence of victimization data. Whatever the reason, the Chicago School is still with us, with ecological/social disorganization theory currently enjoying a resurgence of popularity.

Some of the concerns of ecological criminology reappeared in the 1970s under the headings of environmental design and geographical criminology. Drawing from Jane Jacobs's ideas on urban renewal, C. Ray Jeffery suggested in 1969 that crime prevention should focus on changing the physical environment rather than on changing the offender (something he saw as much more difficult). Oscar Newman (1972), an architect, further elaborated on environmental design with his notion of defensible space. Newman's idea was that any physical area would be better insulated against crime if those who live there recognize it as their territory and keep careful watch over the area. Because of the simplicity of the defensible space concept, the federal government adopted many of the architectural components into their regulations for constructing public housing. Moreover, the entire concept of environmental design generated many of today's crime prevention programs and served as the impetus for the neighborhood watch program. While Jeffery (1971, 1976, 1977) decries the emphasis on hardware, he and Newman are responsible for what may have been the main approach to crime control and prevention throughout the 1970s and beyond.

The late 1970s saw a renewed interest in the ecological and social disorganization perspective. Studies using data from the National Crime Victim Survey, coupled with an article by Lawrence Cohen and Marcus Felson on "routine activities" (see Chapter 13), were instrumental in reviving research on the location of crime. Cohen (with others) followed this two

decades later with a complex theory called "evolutionary ecology theory." Not only were ecological studies popular again, but criminologists also set out to extend the ideas of Shaw and McKay (see Bursik, 1988). One of the major new directions has focused on the stability of ecological areas over time. Applying the concept of criminal careers to ecological areas, Albert Reiss, Jr., (1981) and others began researching and writing about community crime careers. Spurred by examinations of urban renewal and crime rates, this new direction asks how changes inside and outside of urban areas affect their crime rate patterns. The task now is to determine which natural social changes result in which kind of crime patterns (Bottoms & Wiles, 1986; Kobrin & Schuerman, 1982; Reiss, 1986; Schuerman & Kobrin, 1986). Others have combined environmental design, community ecological features, and criminal opportunities to explain rates of offending in areas that are identified as "hot spots" for crime.

In a perspective related to both environmental design and social disorganization, several criminologists (Hunter, 1978; Taylor & Gottfredson, 1986; Wilson & Kelling, 1982) have posited that physically deteriorated neighborhoods are related to social disinterest in the neighborhood (incivility). This, in turn, creates a greater climate of fear and crime, which then results in fewer social controls and a more deteriorated neighborhood. In a similar vein, Rodney Stark (1987) presents an ecological theory that he calls *deviant places*. Stark's theory is contained in a detailed list of 30 propositions that capture much of the concept of incivility. Generally, he elaborates on the ecological theory claims of Shaw and McKay that varying neighborhood controls and structure result in varying crime rates. Moreover, Stark reiterates the Chicago School's position that "kinds-of-places" explanations are more important in understanding crime rates than "kinds-of-people" explanations. Other criminologists (Esbensen & Huizinga, 1990; Laub, 1983b; Sampson, 1985, 1986a, 1986b) have reported research results that led them to

---

[2] It is not quite true to say that the Chicago School ideas fell into decline during the 1950s and 1960s. Two dominant theories, Albert Cohen's subculture theory and Richard Cloward and Lloyd Ohlin's differential opportunity theory, attempted to integrate the concepts of social disorganization and cultural transmission with anomie theory. A review of these theories can be found in Chapter 7. In addition, labeling theory is an offshoot of the Chicago School's symbolic interactionism and was the dominant theory of the 1960s. See Chapter 8 for an explanation of the relationship between symbolic interactionism and labeling theories.

believe that rather than an either-or choice between people and places, a better explanation of crime rates combines both approaches. Robert Sampson (2002a) reinforces the notion that neighborhoods and communities are themselves deserving of theoretical attention. Without a social theory of community, crime theories risk reducing their focus to individuals without recognizing larger forces at work. New research in Chicago by Sampson suggests that old forms of social disorganization may no longer be applicable in some communities (1992, 2000, 2002b). For instance, Sampson's (2008) research on immigrant communities in Chicago fails to find the traditional immigrant–crime link and instead provides evidence that the presence of immigrants reduces crime, and especially violent crime, in areas where they live.

Today, sophisticated statistical analyses with advanced computer capabilities, geospatial software, and access to large government datasets have enhanced the work begun by the Chicago School. Research that once began with push pins pressed into crude paper maps of the city now utilizes complex ecological models that allow not only the correlation of many neighborhood and resident traits but the development of models that might predict future trends in social disorganization.

POLICY IMPLICATIONS

The work of the Chicago School has been directly relevant to policies at the neighborhood and city level as well as statewide and nationally. Shaw and McKay, working for the state of Illinois's Institute of Juvenile Research, implemented their theories almost from the very beginning. As Ruth Kornhauser (1978), Charles Tittle (1983), and Robert Bursik (1984, 1986) have pointed out, Shaw and McKay felt that the critical problem in social disorganization is the community's inability to regulate itself. Their long-lasting Chicago Area Project attempted to reorganize neighborhoods and provide the social organization they felt was lacking. Because Shaw and McKay felt that renewal and reorganization had to come from within, they worked to get people in the neighborhoods to institute and oversee the changes. They did this by helping create community organizations and committees, offering workers who could teach political skills, and helping the community reach out to city

hall. They assisted communities in gaining political power and establishing control of their neighborhoods. Neighborhoods were encouraged to clean up the environment, and workers helped juveniles in trouble with the authorities. The projects that came out of this approach often involved the construction of recreation facilities and areas for juveniles in a community. This general approach to delinquency prevention spread widely throughout the United States and still constitutes one of the most popular solutions to delinquency (and other social problems).

In a 1986 article, Albert Reiss discusses several forms that policies derived from ecological theories may take. Generally, he notes that interventions focus on either the social structures or the social controls in the community (1986, p. 23). Examples of such policies are those that intercede in juvenile peer groups to diminish their power and the establishment of housing regulations that distribute certain types of individuals throughout a complex, rather than grouping them. Reiss even suggests that public policies be questioned when they prevent or restrict a community from exercising control over itself. Of interest is his suggestion that impact reviews be required when proposed policies result in changes in social life, just as environmental impact reviews are now required before physical changes can take place.

In short, the ideas of the Chicago School are alive and well and probably living in your neighborhood. The "new" environmental design concepts, based on ecological evidence, are used by developers in the design and construction of subdivisions. The neighborhood convenience store has also used environmental design concepts to reduce victimization opportunities. Further, police departments have for years used a Chicago School invention called "spot maps" to help them pinpoint criminal activity. Now, the newer ecological approaches have contributed a variation on the old spot maps called "hot spot" analysis (discussed in Chapter 13). Crime analysts, using geospatial computer programs, are now common in major police departments and provided community-level data as the basis for New York City's CompStat program. It should be evident from these remarks that the scholars of the Chicago School have provided us with a rich mixture of ideas, and we are just now beginning to tap some of them.

Questions and Weblinks

Critical Thinking Questions

1. Discuss examples of social disorganization that you see in your community or in the news. What types of interventions, policies, or programs are needed to address them?
2. Think of some incidents or cases that have occurred recently that seem to be attributed to culture conflict and what might have been done to prevent it.

3. What factors may influence whether a city today will reflect the same concentric zone traits as researchers demonstrated in early 1900s' Chicago? Use a large city near you as an example.
4. Are there areas near you that you would identify as "crime prone"? What are the characteristics or traits of those areas that create the impression of "crime proneness"?

Practice Essay Questions

1. What were the various social challenges facing the growing American urban environment in the early 1900s?
2. What methods did the Chicago School researchers use to study the urban environment and what were the advantages of these approaches?

3. What is symbolic interaction and what role does it play in the creation or interpretation of deviance?
4. Why is the Chicago School model of sociological research also referred to as the Ecological School?

Related Websites

http://prohibition.osu.edu

http://www.pbs.org/wgbh/amex/rails/timeline/index_3.html

http://www.chicagoareaproject.org/about.html

http://www.memory.loc.gov/learn/features/timeline/progress/prohib/prohib.html

Bibliography

Blumer, H. (1969). *Symbolic interactionism: Perspectives and method.* Englewood Cliffs, NJ: Prentice Hall.

Bottoms, A. E., & Wiles, P. (1986). Housing tenure and residential community crime careers in Britain. In A. Reiss & M. Tonry (Eds.), *Crime and justice: A review of research, Vol. 8, Communities and crime* (pp. 101–162). Chicago: University of Chicago Press.

Bulmer, M. (1984). *The Chicago School of sociology.* Chicago: University of Chicago Press.

Bulmer, M. (1986). The ecological fallacy: Its implications for social policy analysis. In M. Bulmer (Ed.), *Social science and social policy* (pp. 223–256). London: Allen and Unwin.

Burgess, E. W. (1925). The growth of the city. In R. E. Park, E. W. Burgess, & R. D. McKenzie (Eds.), *The city* (pp. 47–62). Chicago: University of Chicago Press.

Bursik, R. J., Jr. (1984). Urban dynamics and ecological studies of delinquency. *Social Forces, 63,* 393–413.

Bursik, R. J., Jr. (1986). Ecological stability and the dynamics of delinquency. In A. Reiss & M. Tonry (Eds.), *Crime and justice: A review of research, Vol. 8, Communities and crime* (pp. 35–66). Chicago: University of Chicago Press.

Bursik, R. J., Jr. (1988). Social disorganization and theories of crime and delinquency: Problems and prospects. *Criminology, 26,* 519–551.

Cressey, P. F. (1938). Population succession in Chicago: 1898–1930. *American Journal of Sociology, 44,* 59–69.

Edgerton, R. (1976). *Deviance: A cross-cultural perspective.* Menlo Park, CA: Cummings.

Esbensen, F., & Huizinga, D. (1990). Community structure and drug use: From a social disorganization perspective. *Justice Quarterly, 7,* 691–709.

Farris, R. E. L. (1967). *Chicago sociology: 1920–1932.* Chicago: University of Chicago Press.

Frazier, E. F. (1939). *The Negro family in the United States.* Chicago: University of Chicago Press.

Gabbidon, S., & Greene, H. T. (2001). The presence of African American scholarship in early American criminological texts (1918–1960). *Journal of Criminal Justice Education, 12,* 301–308.

Gabbidon, S., Greene, H. T., & Young, V. (2002). *African American classics in criminal justice.* Thousand Oaks, CA: Sage.

Hunter, A. (1978). *Symbols of incivility.* Paper presented at the annual meeting of the American Society of Criminology, Dallas, TX.

Jeffery, C. R. (1969). Crime prevention and control through environmental engineering. *Criminologica, 7,* 35–58.

Jeffery, C. R. (1971). *Crime prevention through environmental design.* Beverly Hills, CA: Sage.

Jeffery, C. R. (1976). Criminal behavior and the physical environment. *American Behavioral Scientist, 20,* 149–174.

Jeffery, C. R. (1977). *Crime prevention through environmental design* (Rev. ed.). Beverly Hills, CA: Sage.

Kobrin, S. (1959). The Chicago Area Project—A 25-year assessment. *Annals of the American Academy of Political and Social Science, 322,* 19–29.

Kobrin, S., & Schuerman, L. (1982). *Interaction between neighborhood change and criminal activity* (Draft final report). Los Angeles: University of Southern California, Social Science Research Institute.

Kornhauser, R. R. (1978). *Social sources of delinquency.* Chicago: University of Chicago Press.

Laub, J. (1983a). Interview with Solomon Kobrin. In J. Laub (Ed.), *Criminology in the making: An oral history* (pp. 87–105). Boston: Northeastern University Press.

Laub, J. (1983b). Urbanism, race, and crime. *Journal of Research in Crime and Delinquency, 20,* 283–298.

Lloyd, M. (2001, March 4). Some Mexican Indian traditions seen as shocking. *Houston Chronicle,* p. 28A.

Matza, D. (1969). *Becoming deviant.* Englewood Cliffs, NJ: Prentice Hall.

Mead, G. H. (1934). *Mind, self, and society.* In C. W. Morris (Ed.). Chicago: University of Chicago Press.

Moses, E. R. (1936). Community factors in Negro delinquency. *Journal of Negro Education, 5,* 220–227.

Nettler, G. (1974). *Explaining crime.* New York: McGraw-Hill.

Newman, O. (1972). *Defensible space: Crime prevention through urban design.* New York: Macmillan.

Park, R. E. (1930). Personality and culture conflict. In *Race and culture.* Glencoe, IL: Free Press.

Park, R. E., & Burgess, E. W. (1924). *Introduction to the science of sociology* (2nd ed.). Chicago: University of Chicago Press.

Reiss, A. J., Jr. (Ed.). (1964). *Louis Wirth on cities and social life.* Chicago: University of Chicago Press.

Reiss, A. J., Jr. (1976). Settling the frontiers of a pioneer in American criminology: Henry McKay. In J. F. Short, Jr. (Ed.), *Delinquency, crime and society* (pp. 64–88). Chicago: University of Chicago Press.

Reiss, A. J., Jr. (1981). Towards a revitalization of theory and research on victimization by crime. *Journal of Criminal Law and Criminology, 72,* 704–713.

Reiss, A. J., Jr. (1986). Why are communities important to understanding crime? In A. Reiss & M. Tonry (Eds.), *Crime and justice: A review of research, Vol. 8, Communities and crime* (pp. 1–33). Chicago: University of Chicago Press.

Sampson, R. J. (1985). Structural sources of variation in race-age-specific rates of offending across major U.S. cities. *Criminology, 23,* 647–673.

Sampson, R. J. (1986a). Crime in cities: The effects of formal and informal social control. In A. Reiss & M. Tonry (Eds.), *Crime and justice: A review of research, Vol. 8, Communities and crime* (pp. 271–311). Chicago: University of Chicago Press.

Sampson, R. J. (1986b). Neighborhood family structure and the risk of criminal victimization. In J. Byrne & R. J. Sampson (Eds.), *The social ecology of crime* (pp. 25–46). New York: Springer-Verlag.

Sampson, R. J. (1992). Family management and child development: Insights from social disorganization theory. *Advances in Criminological Theory, 3,* 63–94.

Sampson, R. J. (2000). What "community" supplies. In R. F. Ferguson & W. T. Dickens, (Eds.), *Urban problems and community development* (pp. 241–292). Washington, DC: Brookings Institution Press.

Sampson, R. J. (2002a). Transcending tradition: New directions in community research, Chicago style. *Criminology, 40,* 213–230.

Sampson, R. J. (2002b). Studying modern Chicago. *City and community, 1,* 45–48.

Sampson, R. J. (2008). Rethinking crime and immigration. *Contexts, 7*(1), 28–33.

Sampson, R. J., & Groves, B. W. (1989). Community structure and crime: Testing social disorganization theory. *American Journal of Sociology, 94,* 774–802.

Schuerman, L., & Kobrin, S. (1986). Community careers in crime. In A. Reiss & M. Tonry (Eds.), *Crime and justice: A review of research, Vol. 8, Communities and crime* (pp. 67–100). Chicago: University of Chicago Press.

Sellin, T. (1938). *Culture conflict and crime.* New York: Social Science Research Council.

Shaw, C. R., & McKay, H. D. (1931). *Report on the causes of crime: Social factors in juvenile delinquency, National Commission on Law Observance and Enforcement*

(Vol. 2, Tech. Rep. No. 13). Washington, DC: U.S. Government Printing Office.

Shaw, C. R., & McKay, H. D. (1942). *Juvenile delinquency in urban areas.* Chicago: University of Chicago Press.

Short, J. F., Jr. (Ed.). (1971). *The social fabric of the metropolis: Contributions of the Chicago School of urban sociology.* Chicago: University of Chicago Press.

Short, J. F., Jr. (1972). Introduction to the revised edition. In C. R. Shaw & H. D. McKay (Eds.), *Juvenile delinquency and urban areas* (Rev. ed., pp. xxv–liv). Chicago: University of Chicago Press.

Stark, R. (1987). Deviant places: A theory of the ecology of crime. *Criminology, 25,* 893–909.

Sutherland, E. H. (1929). Crime and the conflict process. *Journal of Juvenile Research, 13,* 38–48.

Taylor, R. B., & Gottfredson, S. D. (1986). Environmental design, crime and prevention: Examination of community dynamics. In A. Reiss & M. Tonry (Eds.), *Crime and justice: A review of research, Vol. 8, Communities and crime* (pp. 387–416). Chicago: University of Chicago Press.

Thomas, W. I., & Znaniecki, F. (1918). *The Polish peasant in Europe and America.* Chicago: University of Chicago Press.

Tittle, C. (1983). Social class and criminal behavior: A critique of the theoretical foundation. *Social Forces, 62,* 334–358.

Valier, C. (2003). Foreigners, crime and changing mobilities. *British Journal of Criminology, 43,* 1–21.

Whyte, W. F. (1943). *Street corner society: The social structure of an Italian slum.* Chicago: University of Chicago Press.

Wilson, J. Q., & Kelling, G. L. (1982). Broken windows: The police and neighborhood safety. *Atlantic Monthly, 249,* 29–38.

Wirth, L. (1925). *Culture conflicts in the immigrant family.* Unpublished master's thesis, Sociology Department, University of Chicago, Chicago.

Wirth, L. (1931). Culture conflict and misconduct. *Social Forces, 9,* 484–492.

Work, M. (1939). Negro criminality in the south. *Annals of the American Academy of Political and Social Sciences, 49,* 74–80.

Research Bibliography (from 1990)

Bachman, R. (1991). An analysis of American Indian homicide: A test of social disorganization and economic deprivation at the reservation county level. *Journal of Research in Crime and Delinquency, 28,* 456–471.

Bowen, N. K., & Brown, G. L. (1999). Effects of crime and violence in neighborhoods and schools on the school behavior and performance of adolescents. *Journal of Adolescent Research, 14,* 319–343.

Bui, H. N. (2009). Parent–child conflicts, school troubles, and differences in delinquency across immigration generations. *Crime & Delinquency, 55,* 412–441.

Bursik, R. J., Jr., & Grasmick, H. G. (1993). *Neighborhoods and crime: The dimensions of effective community control.* New York: Lexington Books.

Cantillon, D., Davidson, W. S., II, & Schweitzer, J. H. (2003). Measuring community social organization: Sense of community as a mediator in social disorganization theory. *Journal of Criminal Justice, 31,* 321–340.

Cohen, L. E., Vila, B. J., & Machalak, R. (1995). Expropriative crime and crime policy: An evolutionary ecological analysis. *Studies on Crime and Crime Prevention, 4,* 197–219.

D'Allesio, S., & Stolzenberg, L. (1990). A crime of convenience: The environment and convenience store robbery. *Environment and Behavior, 22,* 255–271.

DeFronzo, J. (1996). Welfare and burglary. *Crime and Delinquency, 42,* 223–230.

Einat, T., & Herzog, S. (2011). A new perspective for delinquency: Culture conflict measured by seriousness perceptions. *International Journal of Offender Therapy & Comparative Criminology, 55,* 1072–1095.

Elliott, D. S., Wilson, W. J., Huizinga, D., Samson, R. J., Elliott, A., & Rankin, B. (1996). The effects of neighborhood disadvantage on adolescent development. *Journal of Research in Crime and Delinquency, 33,* 389–426.

Fraser, M. W. (1996). Aggressive behavior in childhood and early adolescence: An ecological-developmental perspective on youth violence. *Social Work, 41,* 347–361.

Gottfredson, D. C., McNeil, R. J., III, & Gottfredson, G. D. (1991). Social area influences on delinquency: A multilevel analysis. *Journal of Research in Crime and Delinquency, 28,* 197–226.

Grauerholz, L. (2000). An ecological approach to understanding sexual revictimization: Linking personal, interpersonal, and sociocultural factors and processes. *Child Maltreatment, 5,* 5–18.

Harries, K. D. (1995). The ecology of homicide and assault: Baltimore city and county, 1989–91. *Studies on Crime and Crime Prevention, 4,* 44–60.

Heimer, K., & Matsueda, R. I. (1994). Role-taking, role commitment, and delinquency: A theory of differential social control. *American Sociological Review, 59*, 365–390.

Hesseling, R. B. P. (1992). Using data on offender mobility in ecological research. *Journal of Quantitative Criminology, 8*, 95–106.

Ingram, A. L. (1993). Type of place, urbanism, and delinquency: Further testing the determinist theory. *Journal of Research in Crime and Delinquency, 30*, 192–212.

Kennedy, L. W., Silverman, R. A., & Forde, D. R. (1991). Homicide in urban Canada: Testing the impact of economic inequality and social disorganization. *Canadian Journal of Sociology, 16*, 397–410.

Kposowa, A. J., & Breault, K. D. (1993). Reassessing the structural covariates of U.S. homicide rates: A county level study. *Sociological Focus, 26*, 27–46.

Lee, N. (1995). Culture conflict and crime in Alaskan native villages. *Journal of Criminal Justice, 23*, 177–189.

Lopes, G., Krohn, M. D., Lizotte, A. J., Schmidt, N. M., Vasquez, B. E., & Bernburg, J. G. (2012). Labeling and cumulative disadvantage: The impact of formal police intervention on life chances and crime during emerging adulthood. *Crime Delinquency, 58*, 456–488.

Lowenkamp, C. T., Cullen, F. T., & Pratt, T. C. (2003). Replicating Sampson and Grove's test of social disorganization theory: Revisiting a criminological classic. *Journal of Research in Crime and Delinquency, 40*, 351–373.

Lynch, J. P., & Cantor, D. (1992). Ecological and behavioral influences on property victimization at home: Implications for opportunity theory. *Journal of Research in Crime and Delinquency, 29*, 335–362.

Markowitz, F. E., Bellair, P., Liska, A., & Liu, J. (2001). Extending social disorganization theory: Modeling the relationships between cohesion, disorder, and fear. *Criminology, 39*, 293–319.

Meares, T., & Kahan, D. (1998). Law and (norms of) order in the inner city. *Law and Society Review, 32*, 805–838.

Miethe, T. D., Hughes, M., & McDowall, D. (1991). Social change and crime rates: An evaluation of alternative theoretical approaches. *Social Forces, 70*, 165–185.

Miles-Doan, R., & Kelly, S. (1997). Geographic concentration of violence between intimate partners. *Public Health Reports, 112*, 135–141.

Morenoff, J. D., & Sampson, R. J. (1997). Violent crime and the spatial dynamics of neighborhood transition: Chicago, 1970–1990. *Social Forces, 76*, 31–65.

Morenoff, J. D., Sampson, R. J., & Raudenbush, S. W. (2001). Neighborhood inequality, collective efficacy, and the spatial dynamics of urban violence. *Criminology, 39*, 517–560.

Moriarty, L. J. (1994). Social disorganization theory, community empowerment, and coalition building: Exploring the linkages. *Criminal Justice Policy Review, 6*, 229–240.

Nelson, A. L., Rosemary, D. F., Bromley, R. D. F., & Thomas, C. J. (1996). The geography of shoplifting in a British city: Evidence from Cardiff. *Geoforum, 27*, 409–423.

Osgood, D., & Chambers, J. M. (2000). Social disorganization outside the metropolis: An analysis of rural youth violence. *Criminology, 38*, 81–115.

Perkins, D. D., Meeks, J. W., & Taylor, R. B. (1992). The physical environment of street blocks and resident perceptions of crime and disorder: Implications for theory and measurement. *Journal of Environmental Psychology, 12*, 21–34.

Perkins, D. D., Wandersman, A., & Rich, R. C. (1993). The physical environment of street crime: Defensible space, territoriality and incivilities. *Journal of Environmental Psychology, 13*, 29–49.

Petee, T. A., Kowlaski, G. S., & Duffield, D. W. (1994). Crime, social disorganization, and social structure: A research note on the use of interurban ecological models. *American Journal of Criminal Justice, 19*, 117–132.

Pogrebin, M. R., & Poole, E. D. (1990). Culture conflict and crime in the Korean-American community. *Criminal Justice Policy Review, 4*, 69–78.

Raudenbush, S. W., & Sampson, R. J. (1999). "Ecometrics": Toward a science of assessing ecological settings, with application to the systematic social observation of neighborhoods. *Sociological Methodology, 29*, 1–41.

Reisig, M., & Cancino, J. (2004). Incivilities in nonmetropolitan communities: The effects of structural constraints, social conditions and crime. *Journal of Criminal Justice, 32*(1), 15–30.

Rose, D., & Clear, T. (1998). Incarceration, social capital, and crime: Implications for social disorganization theory. *Criminology, 36*(3), 441–479.

Sampson, R. J., & Jeglum-Bartusch, D. (1998). Legal cynicism and (subcultural?) tolerance of deviance: The neighborhood context of racial differences. *Law and Society Review, 32*, 777–804.

Sampson, R. J., Morenoff, J. D., & Earls, F. (2000). Beyond social capital: Spatial dynamics of collective efficacy for children. *American Sociological Review, 64*, 633–660.

Sampson, R. J., Morenoff, J. D., & Gannon-Rowley, T. (2001). Assessing "neighborhood effects": Social processes and new directions in research. *Annual Review of Sociology, 28*, 443–478.

Sampson, R. J., & Raudenbush, S. W. (1999). Systematic social observation of public spaces: A new look at disorder in urban neighborhoods. *American Journal of Sociology, 105*, 603–651.

Sampson, R. J., Raudenbush, S. W., & Earls, F. (1997). Neighborhoods and violent crime: A multilevel study of collective efficacy. *Science, 277*, 918–924.

Shihadeh, E. S., & Steffensmeier, D. J. (1994). Economic inequality, family disruption, and urban black violence: Cities as units of stratification and social control. *Social Forces, 73*, 729–751.

Silver, E. (2000). Extending social disorganization theory: A multilevel approach to the study of violence among persons with mental illnesses. *Criminology, 38*, 1043–1073.

Stack, S. (1995). The effect of temporary residences on burglary: A test of criminal opportunity theory. *American Journal of Criminal Justice, 19*, 197–214.

Stern, S. B., & Smith, C. A. (1995). Family processes and delinquency in an ecological context. *Social Service Review, 69*, 703–731.

Sun, I. Y., Triplett, R., & Rainey, R. (2004). Neighborhood characteristics and crime: A test of Sampson and Groves' model of social disorganization. *Western Criminology Review, 5*(1), 1–16.

Taylor, R. B. (1997). Social order and disorder of street blocks and neighborhoods: Ecology, microecology, and the systemic model of social disorganization. *Journal of Research in Crime and Delinquency, 34*(1), 113–155.

Taylor, R. B., & Covington, J. (1993). Community structural change and fear of crime. *Social Problems, 40*, 374–397.

Tienda, M. (1991). Poor people and poor places: Deciphering neighborhood effects on poverty outcomes. In J. Huber (Ed.), *Macro-micro linkages in sociology* (pp. 244–262). Newbury Park, CA: Sage.

Toy, C. (1992). Coming out to play: Reasons to join and participate in Asian gangs. *Gang Journal, 1*, 13–29.

Triplett, R. A. (1993). The conflict perspective, symbolic interactionism, and the status characteristics hypothesis. *Justice Quarterly, 10*, 541–558.

Triplett, R. A., Sun, I., & Gainey, R. R. (2005). Social disorganization and the ability and willingness to enact control: A preliminary test. *Western Criminology Review, 6*(1), 89–103.

Velez, M. (2001). The role of public social control in urban neighborhoods. *Criminology, 39*, 837–863.

Veysey, B. M., & Messner, S. F. (1999). Future testing of social disorganization theory: An elaboration of Sampson and Grove's "Community structure and crime." *Journal of Research in Crime and Delinquency, 36*, 156–174.

Vila, B. J., & Cohen, L. E. (1993). Crime as strategy: Testing an evolutionary ecological theory of expropriative crime. *American Journal of Sociology, 98*, 873–912.

Walker, J. T. (1992). *Ecology and delinquency in 1990: A partial replication and update of Shaw and McKay's study in Little Rock, Arkansas.* Unpublished dissertation. Huntsville, TX: Sam Houston State University.

Walker, J. T. (1994). Human ecology and social disorganization revisit delinquency in Little Rock. In G. Barak (Ed.), *Varieties of criminology: Readings from a dynamic discipline* (pp. 47–78). Westport, CT: Praeger.

Warner, B. D. (2003). The role of attenuated culture in social disorganization theory. *Criminology, 41*, 73–98.

Weisheit, R. A., & Wells, E. L. (1996). Rural crime and justice: Implications for theory and research. *Crime and Delinquency, 42*, 379–397.

Differential Association Theory

LEARNING OBJECTIVES

Objective 5.1: Discuss some of the influences on Sutherland's work in criminology.

Objective 5.2: Explain what is meant by the term "differential association."

Objective 5.3: Describe the role that learning plays in the potential for delinquency.

Objective 5.4: Identify aspects of Sutherland's theory that are related to conflict in society.

Objective 5.5: Compare and contrast differential identification with differential association.

INTRODUCTION

Edwin H. Sutherland presented his theory of differential association in two versions, the first in 1939 and the final version in 1947. The latter is still found in its original form in Sutherland and Donald Cressey's *Criminology* (1978, in its tenth edition and with David Luckenbill added as third author in the eleventh edition, 1992). Sutherland created a general theory of criminal behavior by insisting behavior is *learned* in a social environment. In fact, for Sutherland, all behavior is learned in much the same way. Therefore, the major difference between conforming and criminal behavior is in *what* is learned rather than in *how* it is learned.

In the 1920s and 1930s, it was still common to assert that crime is the result of individual biological or mental defects. In the first two editions of his *Principles of Criminology*, Sutherland criticized and rejected both of these positions and, in so doing, advanced the cause of sociological criminology. Criminologist C. Ray Jeffery (1977, p. 97) has even said criminology is allied with the discipline of sociology today because of Sutherland.

Within the sociological criminology of the period, however, multiple-factor theories were popular. Sutherland provided a much less complex and more coherent approach to the cause of crime and delinquency, yet his ideas were well grounded in existing evidence. In a sense, his work set the tone for what we study and how we study it. Thus, we gain many fundamental theoretical concepts from Sutherland, and his theory may be the most popular of the twentieth century.

THE HERITAGE OF THE THEORY

The Social Heritage

Many of the insights that shaped Sutherland's theory came from events of the 1920s and 1930s. The Federal Bureau of Investigation had begun to produce yearly reports of crimes known to the police, the *Uniform Crime Reports*, and evidence was growing that certain categories of people are more likely to be criminals than others are. Because these people matched the Chicago School ecological data, official statistics seemed to support the view that crime is a part of the sociological domain rather than of the biological or psychological disciplines.

The Great Depression also served as fertile ground for sociological observations. As the Depression began, Sutherland served for a year with the Bureau of Social Hygiene in New York. He saw that people who previously had not been criminal, or even who had not been in contact with criminals, committed criminal acts as a direct result of their impoverished situation during the Depression. Others, comparatively well off, took advantage of the economic situation and manipulated banks and stocks. All these are forms of "crime" in which Sutherland had an interest since the 1920s. Crime and other criminal behaviors were obviously not inborn or the results of feeblemindedness (a popular "intelligence" explanation of crime during the 1910s and 1920s). Criminality was the product of situation, opportunity, and, of course, values.

In addition, two other events occurred that may have affected Sutherland's views on criminal behavior: prohibition and the criminalization of drug use. A colleague at the University of Indiana, Alfred Lindesmith, was working in both of these areas and had a great deal of interaction with Sutherland. These "new" forms of crime taught the astute observer that criminality is, in part, governed by the legal environment. Individuals who engaged in behavior that was not criminal at one point could become criminals by engaging in the same behavior subsequent to the mere passage of law. The focus on crime as defined by the legal codes was important to Sutherland largely because he saw society continually evaluated conduct in terms of adherence to the law. Though many positivists of this time preferred expanded sociological (or nonlegal) interpretations of crime, Sutherland saw the practical importance of working within legal parameters.

Edwin Hardin Sutherland (1883–1950)

Edwin Sutherland was born in Nebraska, and was the son of a rural minister. He graduated with (a) Ph.D. in Sociology and Political Economy from the University of Chicago and taught at a number of small colleges before taking positions at the University of Illinois, the University of Minnesota and, finally, Indiana University (1935–1950). He was head of the sociology department at Indiana in all but his final year there. Sutherland was the 29th President of the American Sociological Association (ASA) to which he presented an address on white-collar crime in 1939. The next year he served as President of the Sociological Research Association. He also was a member of an ASA subcommittee in the early days of World War II to determine how sociologists could assist in the emergency needs of the country during the war (his *Principles of Criminology* was republished as a manual for military police). He published the classic book *White Collar Crime* in 1949, although, under threat of lawsuit, the publisher removed the actual business names. Yale University Press later published the uncut version in 1983.

The Intellectual Heritage

The major intellectual influences on Sutherland's thinking came from the members of the Chicago School, particularly W. I. Thomas. The editor of a collection of Sutherland's papers even comments in his introduction that "Sutherland's theory of criminal behavior...may be regarded as an adaptation of the interactional sociology expounded by W. I. Thomas" (Schuessler, 1973, p. xi). In addition, specific influences on Sutherland included symbolic interactionist materials developed by George Mead (Gongaware & Dotter, 2005), Robert Park and Ernest Burgess's conception of the city as a multifaceted organism, the ecological work of Clifford Shaw and Henry McKay, and Sutherland's association with Thorsten Sellin. Indeed, it was while Sutherland and Sellin worked together on a project for the Social Science Research Council to make criminology more scientific that they settled on culture conflict as the orienting strategy. Sutherland's critique of the final product led him to more thoroughly focus his own ideas. Sutherland himself taught at the University of Chicago from 1930 to 1935 and, throughout his life, never went far from the Chicago area (Vold, 1951). The fact that Sutherland was born, raised, and educated in a religious, rural Midwestern setting is also said to have influenced his perspective (Schuessler, 1973, p. x). His father was a religious fundamentalist and stern disciplinarian who was at various times a minister, a college professor, and a college president. Mark Gaylord and John Galliher (1988) have made a case that his father was very influential in helping develop Sutherland's critical stance toward theory and evidence.

The two chief methodologies developed by the Chicago School, the examination of statistical information and the life history, were also important to Sutherland. Using the former approach, members of the Chicago School had already shown that, as the central area of a city was subjected to succeeding waves of immigrants, the high crime rates remained in the same *location*. Since the same high rates did not follow the residents who moved out into other areas of the city, it was obvious something (values) was being transmitted that kept the crime rates high (Shaw & McKay, 1931).

In the search for the causes behind high crime rates in certain areas, several theorists proposed that the answer lay in the conflict between different cultural groups (Sellin, 1938; Sutherland, 1929; Wirth, 1931). Because the central-city area was inhabited largely by immigrants (it was the cheapest place to live and closest to the factories and businesses where they worked), culture conflict theorists suggested their values and norms were simply different from those of the general population of Chicago. The source of the high crime rates, then, was not the area itself but the way in which the immigrants had been socialized to their native or "private" cultures in contrast to American or "public" culture (Schuessler, 1973, p. 98).

The life history approach was also practiced by Sutherland in a collection of case histories from incarcerated immigrants and in a series of interviews and contacts with a professional thief beginning in about 1930. In a book based on this work, the thief Chic Conwell talked about learning the trade and the apprenticeship and recognition within the almost-institutionalized profession of thieves. This was, perhaps, for Sutherland the first analysis of how a group associating itself differently, isolating and reinforcing its values, could grow out of the general culture. This was also the first appearance of the term "differential association." There is, however, some controversy over the way the term is used in *The Professional Thief* (1937) and the theoretical usage appearing later. Our own readings and the commentaries of others (Gibbons, 1979, p. 50; Snodgrass, 1973, pp. 4–5) suggest the earlier use of the term was much narrower than the concept Sutherland conveyed in his theory. Indeed, in a discussion of the common, but mistaken, belief that Sutherland was referring to the members of groups who kept themselves apart from others, Cressey (in Sutherland & Cressey, 1978, p. 86) said: "This kind of error may stem from Sutherland himself, for in his work on the professional thief he used the term 'differential association' to characterize the members of the behavior system, rather than to describe the process presented in the first statement of his theory, two years later."

In formulating his theory, then, Sutherland drew on three major theories from the Chicago School: ecological and cultural transmission theory, symbolic interactionism, and culture conflict theory. In doing so, he was able to make sense of both the varying crime rates in society (the culture conflict approach) and the process by which individuals became criminal (the symbolic interactionist approach). Within this context, Sutherland formulated a theory that was an attempt to explain both individual criminal behavior and the variation in group (societal) rates of crime. He had to take into account that (1) criminal behavior is not necessarily different from conventional behavior, (2) values are important in determining behavior, and (3) certain locations and people are more crime prone than others.

A final major influence on Sutherland's thinking was an important critique of criminology written in 1933 by Jerome Michael and Mortimer J. Adler (Cressey, 1979; Sutherland, 1973c). They reviewed criminology and argued it had failed to produce sufficient scientific evidence, had developed no coherent theories, and had no rigorous standards. After first defending criminology against their critique, Sutherland set out to create a theory based on rigorous scientific standards. Differential association theory was the result. In keeping with his critical stance, Sutherland revised his theory in at least three drafts between 1939 and the publication of the last version in 1947. Even that last version was not meant to be final (Sutherland, 1973a).

THE THEORETICAL PERSPECTIVE

Even the first edition of Sutherland's textbook, *Criminology* (1924), contains discussions of the importance of interaction among people and the conveyance of values from one person to another. Given his deep immersion in the Chicago School, such commentary is not surprising. Nonetheless, there was no organized discussion of the effects of these factors on crime and delinquency (actually, a major thrust of this edition was to critique psychological and biological explanations of crime). The first suggestion of differential association theory came in the second edition of *Principles of Criminology* (1934, with a change of name, hereafter *Principles*). There, Sutherland (1934, pp. 51–52) stated:

> First, any person can be trained to adopt and follow any pattern of behavior which he is able to execute. Second, failure to follow a prescribed pattern of behavior is due to the inconsistencies and lack of harmony in the influences which direct the individual. Third, the conflict of cultures is therefore the fundamental principle in the explanation of crime.

This statement became the basis for differential association theory, which Sutherland developed more fully. Some versions attribute the "discovery" of differential association in this preliminary statement to Henry McKay (Sutherland, 1973b, p. 16). Gaylord and Galliher (1988) suggest Sutherland clearly knew what he was doing and his inherent modesty led him to credit his friends. If the statement is read closely, it is also evident that Sutherland viewed cultural conflict as producing social disorganization (the "inconsistencies and lack of harmony") and, thus, crime.

The first full version of the theory was proposed in 1939, with the publication of the third edition of *Principles*. This version referred to systematic criminal behavior and focused equally on cultural conflict and social disorganization and on differential association. Sutherland would later eliminate the reference to systematic criminal behavior and limit the discussion of cultural conflict. When Sutherland used the term "systematic," he meant either "criminal careers or organized criminal practices" (1939, p. 4). It is the latter that causes the most problems of understanding. Based on his commentary in the 1939 edition of *Principles*, as well as on later sources (Cressey, 1960b, p. 3; Sutherland, 1973b, pp. 21–22), the reference to organized criminal practices seems to have meant those behaviors with supporting definitions readily available in the community and not just organized crime as we think of it today. This interpretation is supported by his choice of the term "adventitious" for nonsystematic criminal behavior. The difference from the final version of the theory, where he dropped the term "systematic," is not so marked as it would seem. Sutherland evidently felt systematic criminal behavior includes almost all forms of criminal behavior (Cressey, 1960b, p. 3).

Differential Association

By the term "differential association," Sutherland meant that "the contents of the patterns presented in association" with others would differ from individual to individual (1939, p. 5). Thus, he never meant mere *association* with criminals would cause criminal behavior. Instead, the content of communications from others (the "contents of the patterns presented") was given primary focus. Sutherland viewed crime as a consequence of conflicting values; that is, the individual followed culturally approved behavior that was *disapproved* (and set in law) by the larger American society. Sutherland's own summary (1939, p. 9) of the first version of differential association says, "Systematic criminal behavior is due immediately to differential association in a situation in which cultural conflicts exist, and ultimately to the social disorganization in that situation." As an individual-level explanation, differential association theory is entirely a product of the social environment surrounding individuals and the values gained from important others in that social environment.

Differential Social Organization

The first version of differential association theory clearly explained more than the process of how individuals become delinquent. It was also an epidemiological theory of the distribution of crime rates and delinquency rates in society. Sutherland used the concepts of differential social organization and culture conflict to offer an explanation of why rates vary from group to group (Reinarman & Fagan, 1988). He believed, with his mentors in the Chicago School, that culture conflict is rampant in society. This conflict, in part a product of a disorganized society separated into many groups, creates many values and interests among the different societal groups. Inevitably, many of these values come into conflict, and some of them deal with values about the law. Groups with different values about the law (and lawful behavior) come into conflict with the authorities more often, resulting in higher rates of crime and delinquency. Indeed, high rates of crime can be used as an indicator of socially disorganized areas. Moreover, as Craig Reinarman and Jeffrey Fagan point out, the probability of differential association itself (and thus the learning of conflicting definitions) is a "function of differential social organization" (1988, p. 311).

The Final Version of the Theory

The second, and final, version of the theory was proposed in the fourth edition of *Principles* in 1947. There Sutherland expressly incorporated the notion that all behavior is learned and, unlike other theorists of the time, moved away from referring to the varied cultural perspectives as "social disorganization." He used the term "differential social organization" or "differential group organization" instead. This allowed him to more clearly apply the learning process to a broader range of American society. The final version of differential association was proposed in nine points.

Sutherland's first point was that "criminal behavior is learned." And, more importantly, he maintained in his second point that learning took place "in interaction with other persons in a process of communication." This process, would involve all types of contacts and exchanges, some overt and direct while others could be subtle and indirect. The key was that the content was meaningful for the participants who held shared values. For Sutherland, it was critical that the teaching and learning of criminal behaviors took place in "intimate personal groups," the focus of his third point.

In Sutherland's fourth point, he draws our attention to the learning process, explaining that in some cases, it is complex and in others it can be quite simple. Overall, two basic things are learned: the techniques for committing criminal behavior and the definitions (values, motives, drives, rationalizations, attitudes) supporting such behavior. Sutherland stressed a *relationship* must exist; that is, the transfer of skills or values cannot be accomplished merely by reading books or watching movies. The techniques may be thought of as the "how's," or the content of an act, and the definitions as the "why's," or the reasons for doing it.

The learning of techniques is important, but Sutherland focused less on that than on the learning of definitions. Bill McCarthy (1996) argued that tutelage by those already skilled in criminal methods is crucial to understanding the theory. As an example, it makes no difference what definitions a would-be criminal has about the desirability of safe-cracking if he or she is unable to break into the safe. It is also obvious that criminal tutors provide definitions as well as the "motives and drives" that may be favorable to breaking the law, which is the essence of the fifth point. However, as Sutherland emphasized, most criminal behaviors require nothing more than what is normally learned during the course of daily activity. In other words, he saw most criminal behaviors as having essentially the same techniques that one learns from conventional behavior.

The sixth point, according to Sutherland, was that criminal behavior often results when there is an excess of definitions favoring criminal behavior, as opposed to those definitions favoring conventional behavior. The phrase "excess of definitions," however, does not mean a simple quantity as we might think of in numbers, but instead, the *weight* of definitions as determined by the quality and intimacy of interaction with others (frequency, priority, duration, and intensity). Sutherland saw individuals as operating on a balance or ratio of potential good and bad behavioral definitions. One could become a shoplifter in the same manner as one becomes a bricklayer. The resulting behavior often may be determined not only by the persons to whom one is exposed but also by the *absence* of alternative (criminal or noncriminal) patterns to fall back on.

The seventh point simply clarifies that the associations that provide the opportunity to learn criminal behavior may "vary in frequency, duration, priority, and intensity." Obviously, interactions that are more intense or those that occur more regularly and for longer periods of time are thought to have more impact on participants. Sutherland assures us in his next proposition that this process "involves all of the mechanisms that are involved in any other learning." And finally, Sutherland addresses concerns about economic disadvantage and theoretical focus on social-class by explaining that for him, while "criminal behavior is an expression of general needs and values, it is not explained by those general needs and values, since noncriminal behavior is an expression of the same needs and values" (Sutherland and Cressey, 1978, p. 82).

In short, the theory of differential association does not necessarily emphasize *who* one's associates are; rather, it focuses on the *definitions* provided by those associations. Indeed, it suggests that once the techniques of criminal behavior are learned, the values (definitions) supporting that behavior may be learned from *anyone*. However, definitions provided by close, intimate others remain important to determining the weight of that learning.

The different social organizations to which individuals belong provide the associations from which a variety of forms of behaviors, both favoring and opposing legal norms, can be learned. Thus, the term "differential association" implies that individuals as well as groups are exposed to differing associations with people who vary in the importance they attach to respect for the law or law-abiding behavior. Individuals, then, will lean toward or away from crime according to the cultural standards of their associates, especially those with whom they spend frequent and long periods of time (Schuessler, 1973). In this vein, it is important to remember that Sutherland was an advocate of culture conflict. To the extent that the social organizations (anything from one's neighborhood to a sorority) are culturally different from each other or the majority norms, they increase the likelihood of criminal definitions.

Once certain definitions exist, an individual tends to be more susceptible to similar behavioral definitions (Sutherland, 1973d). This means an individual with an excess of criminal definitions will be open to new criminal definitions. Moreover, that individual will be less receptive to anticriminal definitions. Over time, as individuals interact within different groups, their patterns of definitions toward any behavior will change. Highly organized areas will have stable patterns of associations and offer consistent definitions to their residents. Unorganized areas will have high mobility and a mixture of cultural groups, resulting in inconsistent definitions and a greater likelihood that the ratio of criminal to anticriminal definitions will change frequently.

CLASSIFICATION OF THE THEORY

Differential association is a *positivist* theory in that it focuses on criminals and their behavior. For Sutherland, the real questions concern criminal behavior, not how criminal law came to be or even how the criminal justice system should be changed. Because of this approach, differential association is a *microtheory* when applied to etiological issues of criminal behavior. There is clearly a macrotheoretical component to Sutherland's theory, however. The theory is based on the concepts of differential social organization and culture conflict. As we have noted earlier, differential association also has a societal and group explanation of crime and delinquency that predicts differing rates of crime. That component has, until recently, been largely ignored in favor of the processual, microtheoretical aspects of the theory.

In addition, the theory is oriented toward *conflict*. Sutherland's main objective was to explain how normative and cultural conflicts influence the learning of criminal behavior (Cressey, 1979). His work thus focused on conflicting values, not on groups or classes with conflicting interests. In this sense, then, the theory is not a contemporary conflict theory. The key to classifying Sutherland's differential association as a conflict theory lies in his recognition that a large number of values or definitions exist in society, some of which are favorable to law-abiding behavior and some of which are not. This version of society does not suggest a consensus of values, and Sutherland, in fact, referred to some laws as a product of the values of certain segments of society.

Finally, differential association is a theory of *process,* rather than of structure. Granted, it takes into account facts about the structure of society and even argues for a structural explanation of crime rates, but the focus of the final version of the theory is on the process of becoming criminal. That is, Sutherland emphasizes the behavior itself and the processes operating to create criminal behavior as opposed to conventional behavior. It is this area of the theory that has contributed to its classification by many criminologists as a symbolic interactionist theory.

Summary

Sutherland's differential association theory was one of the most popular theories of criminal behavior for more than a half-century. The late Donald Cressey carried on as a champion of the theory (1952, 1953, 1960a, 1964, 1965, 1966, 1968, 1972) and as coauthor of Sutherland's textbook. The theory itself is two-fold. First, it states that differential group organization explains varying crime rates and, second, that differential association explains individual criminal behavior. The former has been largely ignored because criminal behavior was the express focus of Sutherland's nine propositions.

According to this theory, criminal behavior is based on interactions we have with others and the values we receive from others during those interactions. We learn values from important people (parents, spouses, close friends, important business associates, etc.) around us. Those values either support or oppose criminal behavior. To the extent that the weight of values is against criminal behavior, we will be law abiding. On the other hand, if the weight of values supports criminal behavior, we will commit crime. Finally, an excess of values supporting criminal behavior does not mean we will commit *any* criminal behavior, just the one(s) specifically supported by the definitions.

MAJOR POINTS OF THE THEORY

1. Criminal behavior is learned in the same way as any other behavior.

2. Learning takes place in social settings and through what the people in those settings communicate.

3. The largest part of learning takes place in communication with those who are most important to us.

4. The intimate social environment provides a setting for learning two things: the actual way to accomplish a behavior (if necessary) and the values or definitions concerning that behavior.

5. These values about certain behavior may be in opposition to the established legal codes. To the extent we receive many statements about values, the *weight* of those statements (the importance and closeness of those who convey them) is more important than the actual number of statements.

6. Criminal behavior takes place when the weight of the values concerning a particular behavior is in opposition to the legal codes.

7. The great number of groups and cultures in society makes possible the learning of different types of values or definitions. The greater the number of groups and cultures in a specific area, the greater is the likelihood of learning definitions conducive to criminal behavior.

8. Some groups in society have more values in opposition to the legal codes than others (some are more in conflict); thus, some groups have higher crime rates than others.

Epilogue: Current Directions and Policy Implications

CURRENT DIRECTIONS

There have been three general trends in the way differential association theory has been treated over the years.[1] In the 1950s, the trend was to focus on delinquent subcultures as a means of transmitting definitions conducive to delinquency. This meant explaining how delinquent subcultures form, why they continue, and how they transmit delinquent definitions and values. The work of Albert Cohen, and of Richard Cloward and Lloyd Ohlin, exemplify this approach. We treat both of these perspectives in greater detail in Chapter 7.

A second trend, in the 1950s and 1960s, was to return to the Chicago School roots of the theory and explain the symbolic interactionist relationships within differential association. An allied perspective, role theory, was an obvious candidate for merger into differential association. Cressey (1954), in replying to criticisms that differential association did not apply to crimes of passion and "compulsive crimes," used symbolic interactionism and role theory as a means of extending the direct propositions of the theory. Cressey's argument was rationalizations and verbalizations exist that motivate behavior. This "vocabulary of motives" combines with the role an individual identifies himself or herself as playing at the moment. Because learning a vocabulary of motives is achieved in the same way as learning any other set of values, Cressey felt compulsive crimes are well within the province of differential association theory. Another criminologist, Daniel Glaser (1956), combined the theory with the symbolic interactionist concept of identification to create differential identification. In this approach and later adaptations, Glaser (1960, 1978) used the differential association proposition relating to intensity of associations and specified the degree and strength of identification with another person as a key ingredient in the learning of values.

The stronger the identification with another person, the more likely an individual is to accept the other's values. This extended to the learning of values from those who are not direct associates of an individual, such as public figures, actors, and athletes. Because the media in Sutherland's day were not as pervasive as they are today, he rejected the idea that the media could be a source of definitions. However, if Sutherland had lived longer, it is very likely that he would have accepted Glaser's addition to his theory.

The third trend, from the mid- until the late 1960s, attempted to explain the processes involved in the learning component of differential association through the use of psychologically based social learning theories. C. Ray Jeffery (1965), Robert Burgess and Ronald Akers (1966), and later Akers (1973, 1977, 1985, 1998) were the foremost examples. The major reason for these reinterpretations of the theory lay in the popular criticism that the major concepts in differential association are untestable because of their abstract nature. Social learning theories are described in detail in Chapter 12.

More recently, interest in differential association theory has focused on testing the theory's various theoretical concepts, particularly the notion of associations. Almost invariably, this research has demonstrated that an association with delinquent or criminal peers has a major effect on illegal behavior. A major criticism of this research is that we do not know which came first—the association with delinquent others or the illegal behavior itself. Research has now begun to incorporate measures of time order (when the associations and behaviors occurred) and even has attempted to distinguish between romantic and traditional friendship relationships in influencing delinquent conduct (Haynie, Giordano, Manning, & Longmore, 2005). A wider variety of crimes, beyond traditional delinquency, has also been examined

---

[1] A trend we are not referencing here involves a reconstruction of differential association theory by Travis Hirschi and Ruth Kornhauser as "cultural deviance" theory. This approach actually makes testing differential association theory more difficult because it confuses the issues (Akers, 1996).

using differential association. Computer hacking (Dalal & Sharma, 2007), corporate crime (Piquero, Tibbetts, & Blankenship, 2005), and cheating among college students (Vowell & Chen, 2004) have all been examined. Differential association theory appears to be supported in most of these studies.

Another direction corresponds to the renewed interest in social disorganization, as we noted in the previous chapter. Sutherland's theory, with its use of differential social organization to explain crime rates, corresponds nicely with social disorganization concerns. Now past its seventieth birthday, differential association theory still retains its popularity.

POLICY IMPLICATIONS

In the area of policy, Sutherland's theory has implications for treatment and even the study of alternative "types" of crime. Cressey has pointed to prison programs that could use the concept of associating with role models who provide conventional definitions for behavior. Standard conditions of both probation and parole include warnings to keep away from criminal associations. Juvenile delinquency projects invariably stress the importance of avoiding "undesirables," and school programs uniformly make use of role models for youngsters. The Big Brother/Big Sister mentoring program is another good example of providing role models, and thus proper definitions, for children. Finally, virtually all contemporary models of parenting suggest that parents watch and supervise their children's choice of friends.

In another area, Sutherland generated interest and research in white-collar crime, a term he is credited with inventing. He used his theory to explain how those of higher social standing learn crime in the same manner as those in the lower classes, who largely commit street crimes. The difference in type of crimes between the two groups can be explained by a combination of definitions from differential organizations and the learning of different techniques of behavior. In the past two decades, research in white-collar crime and theory has become a staple in criminology. Governmental concern with white-collar and corporate criminality has grown to the point where corporations often receive criminal punishments for their illegal actions. Those accused of white-collar crime, such as ENRON executives Kenneth Lay, Jeffrey Skilling, and Andrew Fastow, as well as Bernie Madoff, Jack Abramoff, and Allen Stanford have become synonymous with financial fraud, greed, and pyramid schemes. Training programs in corporate ethics are direct offshoots of differential association theory.

Questions and Weblinks

Critical Thinking Questions

1. Are friends more important than family in determining whether a youth will become delinquent? Why or why not?
2. Does differential association seem to be a theory that only explains delinquency and not adult crime? Why or why not?

3. Sutherland was convinced that direct face-to-face communication in intimate groups was essential for transmitting the values conducive to committing crime. Do you think so? Is society that much different today than when he developed this theory?

Practice Essay Questions

1. According to differential association, what types of policies and programs would best be able to reduce delinquency?
2. What is the relationship between the concepts of symbolic interaction and differential association?

3. Argue for or against the idea that crime is learned the way you would learn anything else.

Related Websites

http://www.familyfirstaid.org/peer-pressure.html
http://www.idtheft.gov/reports/IDTReport2008.pdf

http://www.fbi.gov/about-us/investigate/white_collar
https://www.ncjrs.gov/pdffiles1/ojjdp/232272.pdf

Bibliography

Akers, R. L. (1973). *Deviant behavior: A social learning approach*. Belmont, CA: Wadsworth.

Akers, R. L. (1977). *Deviant behavior: A social learning approach* (2nd ed.). Belmont, CA: Wadsworth.

Akers, R. L. (1985). *Deviant behavior: A social learning approach* (3rd ed.). Belmont, CA: Wadsworth.

Akers, R. L. (1996). Is differential association/social learning cultural deviance theory? *Criminology, 34*, 229–247.

Akers, R. L. (1998). *Social learning and social structure: A general theory of crime and deviance*. Boston: Northeastern University Press.

Burgess, R. L., & Akers, R. L. (1966). A differential association–reinforcement theory of criminal behavior. *Social Problems, 14*, 128–147.

Cressey, D. R. (1952). Application and verification of the differential association theory. *Journal of Criminal Law, Criminology, and Police Science, 43*, 43–52.

Cressey, D. R. (1953). *Other people's money*. New York: Free Press.

Cressey, D. R. (1954). The differential association theory and compulsive crimes. *Journal of Criminal Law and Criminology, 45*, 49–64.

Cressey, D. R. (1960a). Epidemiology and individual conduct: A case from criminology. *Pacific Sociological Review, 3*, 47–58.

Cressey, D. R. (1960b). The theory of differential association: An introduction. *Social Problems, 8*, 2–6.

Cressey, D. R. (1964). *Delinquency, crime and differential association*. The Hague, Netherlands: Martinus Nijhoff.

Cressey, D. R. (1965). Social psychological foundations for using criminals in the rehabilitation of criminals. *Journal of Research in Crime and Delinquency, 2*, 49–59.

Cressey, D. R. (1966). The language of set theory and differential association. *Journal of Research in Crime and Delinquency, 3*, 22–26.

Cressey, D. R. (1968). Culture conflict, differential association, and normative conflict. In M. E. Wolfgang (Ed.), *Crime and culture* (pp. 43–54). New York: Wiley.

Cressey, D. R. (1972). Role theory, differential association and compulsive crimes. In A. M. Rose (Ed.), *Human behavior and social processes: An interactionist approach* (pp. 443–467). London: Routledge and Kegan Paul.

Cressey, D. R. (1979). Fifty years of criminology. *Pacific Sociological Review, 22*, 457–480.

Dalal, A. S., & Sharma, R. (2007). Peeping into a hacker's mind: Can criminological theories explain hacking? *ICFAI Journal of Cyber Law, 6*(4), 34–47.

Gaylord, M. S., & Galliher, J. (1988). *The criminology of Edwin Sutherland*. New Brunswick, NJ: Transaction.

Gibbons, D. C. (1979). *The criminological enterprise: Theories and perspectives*. Englewood Cliffs, NJ: Prentice Hall.

Glaser, D. (1956). Criminality theories and behavioral images. *American Journal of Sociology, 61*, 433–444.

Glaser, D. (1960). Differential association and criminological prediction. *Social Problems, 8*, 6–14.

Glaser, D. (1978). *Crime in our changing society*. New York: Holt, Rinehart and Winston.

Gongaware, T. B., & Dotter, D. (2005). Developing the criminal self: Mead's social psychology and Sutherland's differential association. *Sociological Spectrum, 25*, 379–402.

Haynie, D., Giordano, P., Manning, W., & Longmore, M. (2005). Adolescent romantic relationships and delinquency involvement. *Criminology, 43*(1), 177–210.

Jeffery, C. R. (1965). Criminal behavior and learning theory. *Journal of Criminal Law, Criminology and Police Science, 54*, 294–300.

Jeffery, C. R. (1977). *Crime prevention through environmental design* (2nd ed.). Beverly Hills, CA: Sage.

McCarthy, B. (1996). The attitudes and actions of others: Tutelage and Sutherland's theory of differential association. *British Journal of Criminology, 36*, 135–147.

Piquero, N., Tibbetts, S., & Blankenship, M. (2005). Explaining the role of differential association and techniques of neutralization in explaining corporate crime. *Deviant Behavior, 26*(2), 159–188.

Reinarman, C., & Fagan, J. (1988). Social organization and differential association: A research note from a longitudinal study of violent juvenile offenders. *Crime and Delinquency, 34*, 307–327.

Schuessler, K. (Ed.). (1973). *Edwin H. Sutherland: On analyzing crime.* Chicago: University of Chicago Press.

Sellin, T. (1938). *Culture conflict and crime* (Bulletin 41). New York: Social Science Research Council.

Shaw, C. R., & McKay, H. D. (1931). *Report on the causes of crime: Social factors in juvenile delinquency. National Commission on Law Observance and Enforcement* (Vol. 2, Tech. Rep. No. 13). Washington, DC: U.S. Government Printing Office.

Snodgrass, J. (1973). The criminologist and his criminal: The case of Edwin H. Sutherland and Broadway Jones. *Issues in Criminology, 8,* 2–17.

Sutherland, E. H. (1924). *Criminology.* Philadelphia: Lippincott.

Sutherland, E. H. (1926). The biological and sociological processes. *Papers and Proceedings of the Twentieth Annual Meeting of the American Sociological Society, 20,* 58–65.

Sutherland, E. H. (1929). Crime and the conflict process. *Journal of Juvenile Research, 13,* 38–48.

Sutherland, E. H. (1934). *Principles of criminology* (2nd ed.). Philadelphia: Lippincott.

Sutherland, E. H. (1937). *The professional thief: By a professional thief.* Chicago: University of Chicago Press.

Sutherland, E. H. (1939). *Principles of criminology* (3rd ed.). Philadelphia: Lippincott.

Sutherland, E. H. (1947). *Principles of criminology* (4th ed.). Philadelphia: Lippincott.

Sutherland, E. H. (1949). *White collar crime.* New York: Dryden.

Sutherland, E. H. (1973a). Critique of the theory. In K. Schuessler (Ed.), *Edwin H. Sutherland on analyzing crime* (pp. 30–41). Chicago: University of Chicago Press.

Sutherland, E. H. (1973b). Development of the theory. In K. Schuessler (Ed.), *Edwin H. Sutherland on analyzing crime* (pp. 13–29). Chicago: University of Chicago Press.

Sutherland, E. H. (1973c). The Michael-Adler report. In K. Schuessler (Ed.), *Edwin H. Sutherland on analyzing crime* (pp. 229–246). Chicago: University of Chicago Press.

Sutherland, E. H. (1973d). Susceptibility and differential association. In K. Schuessler (Ed.), *Edwin H. Sutherland on analyzing crime* (pp. 42–43). Chicago: University of Chicago Press.

Sutherland, E. H., & Cressey, D. R. (1978). *Criminology* (10th ed.). Philadelphia: Lippincott.

Sutherland, E. H., Cressey, D. R., & Luckenbill, D. F. (1992). *Principles of criminology* (11th ed.). Dix Hills, New York: General Hall.

Vold, G. B. (1951). Edwin Hardin Sutherland: Sociological criminologist. *American Sociological Review, 16,* 3–9.

Vowell, P., & Chen, J. (2004). Predicting academic misconduct: A comparative test of four sociological explanations. *Sociological Inquiry, 74*(2), 226–249.

Wirth, L. (1931). Culture conflict and misconduct. *Social Forces, 9,* 484–492.

Research Bibliography (from 2000)

Alarid, L. F., Burton, V. S., Jr., & Cullen, F. T. (2000). Gender and crime among felony offenders: Assessing the generality of social control and differential association theories. *Journal of Research in Crime and Delinquency, 37,* 171–201.

Baron, S. W. (2009). Differential coercion, street youth, and violent crime. *Criminology, 47,* 239–268.

Church, I. T., Wharton, T., & Taylor, J. K. (2009). An Examination of Differential Association and Social Control Theory: Family Systems and Delinquency. *Youth Violence & Juvenile Justice, 7*(1), 3–15.

Church, W. T., Jaggers, J. W., & Taylor, J. K. (2012). Neighborhood, poverty, and negative behavior: An examination of differential association and social control theory. *Children & Youth Services Review, 34,* 1035–1041.

Erickson, K. G., Crosnoe, R., & Dornbusch, S. M. (2000). A social process model of adolescent deviance: Combining social control and differential association perspectives. *Journal of Youth and Adolescence, 29,* 395–425.

Gunter, W. D. (2009). Internet scallywags: A comparative analysis of multiple forms and measurements of digital piracy. *Western Criminology Review, 10*(1), 15–28.

Haynie, D. (2002). Friendship networks and delinquency: The relative nature of peer delinquency. *Journal of Quantitative Criminology, 18,* 99–134.

Heidensohn, F. (2010). The deviance of women: A critique and an enquiry. *British Journal of Sociology, 61,* 111–126.

Higgins, G. E., Tewksbury, R., & Mustaine, E. (2007). Sports fan binge drinking: An examination using low self-control and peer association. *Sociological Spectrum, 27,* 389–404.

Hochstetler, A., Copes, H., & DeLisi, M. (2002). Differential association in group and solo offending. *Journal of Criminal Justice, 30,* 559–566.

Kissner, J., & Pyrooz, D. C. (2009). Self-control, differential association, and gang membership: A theoretical and empirical extension of the literature. *Journal of Criminal Justice, 37*, 478–487.

Kobayashi, E., & Kerbo, H. R. (2012). Differences in perceived levels of informal punishments for noncompliance and rewards for compliance: A comparison of Japanese and American workers. *Deviant Behavior, 33*, 40–57.

Miller, H. (2010). If your friends jumped off of a bridge, would you do it too? Delinquent peers and susceptibility to peer influence. *Justice Quarterly, 27*, 473–491.

Miller, W. J., & Matthews, R. A. (2001). Youth employment, differential association, and juvenile delinquency. *Sociological Focus, 34*, 251–268.

Minke, L. (2011). The effects of mixing offenders with non-offenders: Findings from a Danish quasi-experiment. *Journal of Scandinavian Studies in Criminology & Crime Prevention, 12*, 80–99.

Moon, B., Hwang, H., & McCluskey, J. D. (2011). Causes of school bullying: Empirical test of a general theory of crime, differential association theory, and general strain theory. *Crime & Delinquency, 57*, 849–877.

Piquero, N., Tibbetts, S., & Blankenship, M. (2005). Examining the role of differential association and techniques of neutralization in explaining corporate crime. *Deviant Behavior, 26*, 159–188.

Rebellon, C. J. (2012). Differential association and substance use: Assessing the roles of discriminant validity, socialization, and selection in traditional empirical tests. *European Journal of Criminology, 9*, 73–96.

Ulmer, J. T. (2000). Commitment, deviance, and social control. *Sociological Quarterly, 41*, 315–337.

Vermeersch, H., T'Sjoen, G., Kaufman, J. M., & Vincke, J. J. (2008). Gender, parental control, and adolescent risk-taking. *Deviant Behavior, 29*, 690–725.

6

········· ─────────────────────────────

Anomie Theory

LEARNING OBJECTIVES

Objective 6.1: Summarize Durkheim's view of the causes of crime.

Objective 6.2: Explain what the term "anomie" means and where it comes from.

Objective 6.3: Outline Merton's view of how people adapt to anomie in different ways.

Objective 6.4: Discuss the role of social structure in the creation of deviance.

Objective 6.5: Describe some of the policy implications that can be drawn from anomie theory.

INTRODUCTION

Anomie is a concept closely associated with two theorists, Emile Durkheim and Robert K. Merton. When Durkheim introduced the term in his 1893 book *The Division of Labor in Society,* he used it to describe a condition of "deregulation" occurring in society. By this he meant that the general procedural rules of a society (the rules that say how people ought to behave toward each other) have broken down and that people do not know what to expect from each other. This deregulation, or normlessness, easily leads to deviant behavior. Durkheim later used the term *anomie,* in *Suicide: A Study in Sociology* (1897/1951), to refer to a morally deregulated condition in which people have inadequate moral controls over their behavior (see Olsen, 1965). Thus, a society may be anomic if people do not know when to quit striving for success, or how to treat other people along the way. Whichever of these two descriptions of anomie is used—a breakdown in either the rules of society or the moral norms—it is clear that Durkheim was talking about a disruption of normal societal conditions.

Durkheim's central thesis in *The Division of Labor in Society* was that societies evolved from a simple, nonspecialized form (mechanical) toward a complex, highly specialized form (organic). In both cases, he referred to the way in which people interact with each other and the way in which labor is carried out. In the mechanical society, people behave and think similarly and, except for a division of labor along gender lines, perform most of the same work tasks and have group-oriented goals. As a society becomes more complex, work also becomes more complex and specialized. Modern, organic societies are characterized by highly interactive sets of relationships, specialized labor, and individual goals. For example, one person's work skills are rarely sufficient to provide all that is necessary to live. People depend on each other to produce various items. The distribution of these items, once produced, is a problem. Highly complex relationships are required to distribute the products of each person's skills. This, for Durkheim, suggested that an organic society is a contractual society, and he saw almost all relationships as contractual ones. By this he meant that people are no longer tied together by bonds of kinship and friendship but, because of the impersonality of modern society, by various types of contractual bonds. The problem with such societies is that these bonds are constantly being broken (the concept of bonds reappears in our discussion of social control theories in Chapter 11). In sum, the rules governing how people in organic societies interact with each other (the contracts) are continually in flux, and social conditions are constantly in danger of disruption. When disruption occurs, we have anomie.

Anomie, then, refers to the breakdown of social norms and a condition in which those norms no longer control the activity of societal members. Without clear rules to guide them, individuals cannot find their place in society and have difficulty adjusting to the changing conditions of life. This in turn leads to dissatisfaction, frustration, conflict, and deviance. Studying France and Europe after the Industrial Revolution, Durkheim saw economic crises, forced industrialization, and commercialization as factors producing anomie. Durkheim was fairly sure that contemporary Western societies had reached such a point of complexity that they were in a constant state of anomie. Even so, he saw that a period of social disruption, such as an economic depression, would make matters worse and result in greater anomie and, of course, higher rates of crime, suicide, and deviance.

Robert K. Merton (1910–2003)

Robert K. Merton was born in Philadelphia on July 4, 1910, to Jewish immigrant parents from Russia. He lived in an apartment over the dairy shop that his father owned until it was destroyed by fire and his father had to work as a carpenter's assistant. Although he immersed himself in the area's art, music, and library resources, Merton also dabbled in magic tricks. When he was 14 years old, Merton decided to change his name, which was originally Meyer R. Schkolnick, to Robert Merlin, after Merlin, the wizard of King Arthur's legendary court. However, friends prevailed upon him to choose something more practical and, therefore, he became Robert King Merton.

Merton received an A.B. from Temple College (1931) and his masters and doctorate from Harvard University (1936). Merton taught at Harvard until 1939, when he left to become Chair of the Department of Sociology at Tulane University. A few years later, he was invited to join the faculty at Columbia University, where he was named Associate Director of the Bureau of Applied Social Research (1942–1971). He was an adjunct professor at Rockefeller University and was also the first Foundation Scholar at the Russell Sage Foundation. He was elected President of the American Sociological Association in 1957. In 1963, Merton was named a Giddings Professor of Sociology at Columbia. He was awarded the university's highest academic rank, University Professor, in 1974, and he became a Special Service Professor upon his "retirement" in 1979, although he continued to teach for five more years. Merton was also named one of the prestigious MacArthur Foundation Fellows in August, 1983. In 1990, Columbia University established the Robert K. Merton Professorship in the Social Sciences.

In a ceremony hosted by President Bill Clinton, Merton received the National Medal of Science for Behavioral and Social Science in 1994. Three years later, one of his sons, Robert C. Merton, won the Nobel Prize in economics. Merton died in 2003 at the age of 92.

In 1938, Merton borrowed the concept of anomie to explain deviance in the United States. His concept, however, differed from that of Durkheim. Merton disagreed that changes and deregulation within society created anomie; instead, he felt that the critical ingredient was the ability of the social system to exercise control in the form of social norms. Dividing social norms (or values) into two types, Merton talked of societal *goals* and the acceptable *means* for achieving those goals. In addition, he redefined anomie as a disjuncture (or split) between those goals and means as a result of the way society is structured; for example, with class distinctions. Deviance, then, could be explained as a symptom of a social structure within which "culturally defined aspirations and socially structured means" are separated from each other. Or, in other words, deviance is a product of anomie. It is Merton's treatment of anomie that we consider in this chapter.

Before we leave this brief introduction to both Durkheim and Merton, it is perhaps best to precisely distinguish between the two approaches to anomie, as Merton saw it. According to Merton (quoted in Cullen & Messner, 2007, p. 21), Durkheim focused on *social conditions* in society (such as economic depressions) where rules lost their value. Merton, on the other hand, saw his approach as focusing on embedded social structure and cultural disparities in society, which generate anomie. In other words, Durkheim was more interested in changing social conditions and Merton more so in permanent features of the social structure of a society.

THE HERITAGE OF THE THEORY

The Social Heritage

Like the Industrial Revolution, the Great Depression of the 1930s produced insights for social scientists. An entire generation of sociologists could observe the collapse and deregulation of social traditions and the effect this had on both individuals and the institutions of society. As did Edwin Sutherland, Merton noted that crime was not necessarily an intrinsic part of the person, and he rejected individualistic views of pathology (Merton & Ashley-Montagu, 1940). The increasing popularity of Durkheim's discussion of anomie, when combined with the Depression, provided sociological insights into the connection between social structure and deviant behavior. Similarly, the notion of the division of labor opened up possibilities for an examination of the role of aspirations and opportunities in American society.

The importance of analyzing social structure itself became firmly grounded when the government's New Deal reform efforts focused on rearranging society. Sociologists and others found themselves moving away from the narrower applications of sociology and toward an examination of social structure as a whole (Merton, 1964, p. 215). Given the popular belief of the time—that government was largely responsible for society's problems—Durkheim had provided social scientists with a readymade explanation: society was simply in a state of deregulation.

Another factor affecting criminology during the 1930s was the emergence of, and emphasis on, the collection of demographic data (information about people). Moreover, in examining both the ecological data collected by Clifford Shaw and Henry McKay and the newly created Uniform Crime Reports, it was evident that certain segments of society were burdened with high crime rates. These were the very same segments of society in which a relatively permanent state of deregulation could be observed. An obvious explanation was that, somehow, deregulation led to deviance. Finally, the idea that social class might be a crucial sociological factor in explaining societal events was gaining popularity. Just as sociologists were viewing other behavior as being influenced by social class position (Dollard, 1937; Lynd & Lynd, 1929), it occurred to theorists that an explanation of deviance based on social class differences might be productive.[1]

The Intellectual Heritage

Merton was influenced by two sociologists during the 1930s. He was first introduced, as a student and research assistant at Harvard, to Durkheim's concept of anomie by Pitirim Sorokin, whose 1928 book *Contemporary Sociological Theories* called attention to Durkheim's use of the term "anomic suicide" (Merton, 1964, p. 215). Merton also worked with a young Talcott Parsons at Harvard and assisted in the production of his seminal work, *The Structure of Social Action,* (1937), which explained social events by emphasizing the way society is structured. This approach became known as "structural-functionalism." As an undergraduate at Temple University, Merton had also studied under George Simpson, who was to write the popular English-language translation of Durkheim's *Division of Labor in Society* in the 1930s (Martin, Mutchnick, & Austin, 2009). Merton, then, was well prepared to adopt Durkheim's interest in anomie.

Parsons saw society as the product of an equilibrium of forces (like a pendulum) that served to produce order. When the various components of the social structure became "unbalanced"—that is, when the pendulum swung too far to either side—society became disorganized. Durkheim's concept of anomie fit nicely into the Parsonian framework and was a major focus of Parsons's book, *The Structure of Social Action* (1937). With Simpson's translation of Durkheim's *Division of Labor* in 1930, the use of social structure in explaining social behavior became accepted.

Two strains of psychological/biological positivism during the 1930s also exerted an influence on Merton. Freudian psychotherapy, with its emphasis on internal conflicts, was exceedingly popular. Moreover, Earnest Hooton had created a stir with his controversial books on the biological inferiority of criminals. Merton reacted strongly to these approaches and, with anthropologist Ashley-Montagu, published a rebuttal to them in 1940. In sharpening criticism against the nonsociological positions, Merton more clearly focused his thoughts on the effects of social structure. In addition, Merton was very familiar with the works of Karl Marx during the 1930s. The Marxist influence can be seen most clearly in Merton's focus on the American capitalist system's excessive attention to financial success goals.

Finally, there is the question of whether a linkage exists between Sutherland's differential association theory and Merton's anomie theory. Merton (1997, p. 519; as quoted in Cullen & Messner, 2007, p. 17) himself said that he views the two theories as complementary. In one sense, then, the individual-level process (the sociopsychological, in Merton's words) had already been developed by the Chicago School and its followers. Merton wanted to explain what he felt was the missing part—"how those patterns of criminal preferences and behaviors emerged in the first place." Thus, the theory of anomie was partly an avoidance of processual elements and partly a push to explain the structural components of deviance.

---

[1] It is worth noting that Robert Merton grew up in the Philadelphia slums and certainly was aware of the issues of class yet did not characterize his experiences as culture conflict, instead preferring to refer to it as a sort of benign slum (Merton quoted in Cullen & Messner, 2007, p. 15).

THE THEORETICAL PERSPECTIVE

Merton's anomie theory is, above all, a theory of deviance; that is, it does not focus on criminality. Further, Merton's approach to deviance itself is relatively general. When one conceives of a society that emphasizes well-structured goals for its members and equally structured avenues to reach those goals, deviance becomes any behavior that does not follow commonly accepted values. For example, Merton uses the term "deviance" to refer to bureaucratic behavior as well as to criminal behavior.

Merton notes that certain goals are strongly emphasized throughout society (he uses the example of financial success). Society also emphasizes (legitimizes) certain means to reach those goals (such as hard work, education, starting at the bottom and working one's way up). When these goals are too strongly stressed, as Merton said financial success was in the United States, the stage is set for anomie. Not everyone has equal access to the achievement of legitimate financial success and, as a result, these people may search for other, perhaps illegitimate, ways of succeeding. Because of social inequality, the approved means to reach the success goals are not readily available to certain groups in society, even though the goals are said to apply equally to all. Certain groups of people, the lower social class and minorities, for instance, may be at a disadvantage in gaining business positions that would allow them to pursue the goal of financial success.

According to Merton, when this inequality exists because of the way society is structured, the social structure is anomic. Given the evidence that there are several segments of society in which legitimate avenues to success are severely restricted without a corresponding reduction in the emphasis on achievement, U.S. society seems to be in a permanent state of anomie. The individuals caught in these anomic conditions (largely the lower classes) are then faced with the strain of being unable to reconcile their aspirations with their limited opportunities. As with Durkheim's formulation of anomie, this does not mean that anomic conditions are constant. As social conditions change, thereby resulting in greater or lesser inequality, so does the degree of anomie.

We should note, however, that legitimate means are not necessarily the most efficient methods of reaching the goals. Other means, although perhaps illegitimate or de-emphasized by society, may be both available and more efficient. These other means are, however, not compatible with Merton's true success goals in that the emphasis is on *legitimately* reaching them. It is also important to keep in mind that Merton focuses on financial success only as an *example* throughout his work; he did not mean to imply that it was the only major goal that exists in American society. In fact, Merton later stated:

> The theory holds that *any* extreme emphasis upon achievement—whether this be scientific productivity, accumulation of personal wealth or, by a small stretch of the imagination, the conquests of a Don Juan—will attenuate conformity to the institutional norms governing behavior designed to achieve the particular form of "success," especially among those who are socially disadvantaged in the competitive race. It is the conflict between cultural goals and the availability of using institutional means—whatever the character of the goals—which produces a strain toward anomie. (1968, p. 220)

The success goals themselves are not necessarily applicable to all social classes at the same time. Indeed, each class may have its own brand of success goals, and a number of different goals are possible. Rather than a reference to specific goals, Merton talks about the presence of a cultural message that legitimates upward striving and the alleged mobility that is available to all those who desire to achieve. It is then the *emphasis* on reaching the goals that becomes important. Because of this, any test of the theory that concentrates on one goal or concept of success will invariably be deficient.

It is at this point that Merton's scheme can be related to Sutherland's differential association. According to Merton (1997), Sutherland's definitions can be interpreted as values related to legal or illegal means. Thus, at the neighborhood level, the presence of values conducive to delinquency or crime essentially tells those who live there that legitimate opportunities are scarce and encourages illegal means to reach goals. Conversely, conventional values in the neighborhood support legitimate means.

The Modes of Adaptation

Merton presents five ways (modes) of adapting to strain caused by restricted access to the socially approved goals and means. If the emphasis on goals and means is maintained even in the face of a realization that the means are restricted, an individual will remain conforming. Most people follow this adaptation, Merton maintains; if they did not, the very existence of society would be threatened. The remaining four modes, however, represent a departure from this all-endorsing adaptation and thus are the "real" deviant modes of adaptation.

First is the case in which the emphasis on the approved goals of society is maintained while legitimate means are replaced by other, nonapproved means. This mode of adaptation, called innovation, is the most common of the four deviant types. Interestingly, for some segments of society, innovative means may be *more efficient* in reaching a goal than the approved means for doing so. For example, instead of saving money and letting it slowly earn interest in a bank, a faster way of accumulating a lot of money is to rob the bank. The primary characteristic of innovation can also be seen in the familiar statement, "The end justifies the means."

Merton's Typology of Adaptations to Anomie

	Culture Goals	Institutionalized Means
I. Conformity	+	+
II. Innovation	+	−
III. Ritualism	−	+
IV. Retreatism	−	−
V. Rebellion	±	±

(+) signifies "acceptance," (−) signifies "elimination," and (±) signifies "rejection and substitution of new goals and standards."

However, when the goals themselves are rejected and the focus is shifted to the means, the mode of adaptation is that of ritualism. In this mode, the means can become the aspirations of an individual, as when one attempts to treat a job (means) as a form of security instead of using the job as a means of achieving success. In this example, keeping the job has become the goal, resolving the frustration of unsuccessfully chasing the original goal. Ritualism can also be seen in bureaucratic behavior, in which an employee has no power to actually do anything for anyone and instead focuses on the fact that the paperwork must be correctly filled out.

The fourth mode, retreatism, involves a rejection of *both* the goals and means. Retreatists are those individuals who opt not to be innovative and, at the same time, need to resolve their inability to reach the important goals in life. Their solution is that they simply quit trying to get ahead and retreat from standard modes of behavior. This pattern is best seen as dropping out of society and is exemplified by vagrants, alcoholics, and drug addicts. In 1938, Merton saw retreatism as the least common mode of adaptation. Today, perhaps, it is more common.

The final mode of adaptation, rebellion, is of a different type from the other four. While those modes emphasize rejection of means or goals, or both, rebellion focuses on the *substitution* of new goals and means for the original ones. Merton's conception suggests that rebellion "leads men outside the environing social structure to envisage and seek to bring into being a new, that is to say a greatly modified, social structure. It presupposes alienation from reigning goals and standards" (1968, p. 209). These individuals, then, are precisely what the term indicates: rebels and revolutionaries.

In short, Merton's anomie theory explains how social structure contributes to the creation of deviance on all levels, although the primary focus of the theory is on the lower class. Because of the societally induced disjunction (separation) between cultural aspirations and the approved methods of attaining those aspirations, the lower class is most likely to exhibit deviant, nonapproved, adaptive behavior. Merton (1997, p. 519) summarizes anomie theory in the following way:

It holds that rates of various types of deviant behavior (not only crime) are high in a society where, as with the American Dream, the culture places a high premium on economic success and upward mobility for *all* its members, although in brute social fact large numbers of people located in the lower reaches of the social structure have severely limited access to legitimate resources for achieving those culturally induced or reinforced goals. Since the key question in this theory focuses on the socially structured sources and consequences of deviant behavior, it says next to nothing about the social mechanisms for transmitting such patterns of behavior or about the ways in which individuals' initial departures from the norms crystallize into deviant careers.

Finally, the difference between two types of conformity—the conformity mode of adaptation and "real" conformity—is worth exploring. Real conformity would be found in those individuals for whom there is no problem in accessing the means for achieving goals: primarily the rich and elite. Merton included conformity as a deviant mode of adaptation because inequality causes an anomic split between goals and access to means. The victims of this inequality who nonetheless remain committed to society and its rules/laws therefore are actually deviant. A dominant number of these conformists are required to keep society from falling apart. Therefore, it is in the interests of those for whom the social structure works best (the real conformists) to keep a large share of the population believing in the system and with some small degree of access to legitimate means.

Merton continued, throughout his life, rethinking and adding commentary to his original 1938 essay (Merton, 1995). In particular, he rethought the theory in his book *Social Theory and Social Structure* (1957a, 1968). In 1964, he added the notion that the increasing degree of deviance precipitated by a class-structured anomic society would, ultimately, result in a feedback effect. This effect would essentially subvert the original norms justifying the institutionally-approved means, resulting in more anomie and more deviance. Different types of deviance were also explored, on purpose, to demonstrate the utility of his theory in explaining more than class-based deviance (for instance, he discussed scientific fraud in 1957b). He also, in 1997, reconciled differential association and anomie by noting that each explained a different but complementary piece of the deviance-generating process.

CLASSIFICATION OF THE THEORY

Anomie theory is a *positivist* theory. In contrast to positivist theories locating pathology within the individual, anomie theory locates pathology within the social structure. Merton explains how a pathological social structure (one in which there is an undue emphasis on goals, especially economic ones, without corresponding avenues of access available to all members of the society) serves to create a strain in certain segments of society and, ultimately, a push toward deviance. Because of this concern with structural strain, anomie theory is often referred to as a "strain theory" (see the discussion of strain theory later in this chapter).

The assumption of a *consensus* of values also characterizes anomie theory. American society imposes on us the "right" things to do and the "right" ways to do them. Unless there is considerable unanimity about societal goals and means, there can be no anomic condition that results in adaptations to those goals and means. In other words, adaptations or deviations would merely be alternate modes of success or achievement.

Anomie theory is a *structural* theory. It focuses on the way society is structured and how that structure serves to create deviance within American society. It does not, nor did Merton intend it to, specify the process by which *individuals* become deviant. Instead, anomie theory deals with the pathology of existing social structure and the subsequent forms of deviance arising in the various segments of society as a whole. In short, Merton intends to explain variations in rates of deviance (1968, p. 186) among societal groups and not how the process of choosing among adaptations takes place. This broad scope and emphasis on explaining social structure also makes anomie theory a *macrotheory*.

Finally, and outside of our usual classification scheme, anomie theory is often called a *functionalist* theory. Functionalism presumes that it is desirable to explain a social phenomenon in terms of its effect on, and its consequences for, the social structure in which it exists. In other words, Merton uses the concepts of cultural goals and norms to explain how they serve to produce both conformity *and* deviance within the social structure.

Summary

Merton's theory of anomie is still among the most influential of all criminological theories, although presented as long ago as 1938. It continues to draw commentary and research, and several modifications have been offered (Richard Cloward's [1959] addition of an illegitimate opportunity structure is probably the most important; see the discussion of differential opportunity theory in Chapter 7). Further, elements of anomie theory are, at least in part, found in more contemporary criminological theories (e.g., Hirschi, 1969, p. 198).

Anomie theory comments on extreme emphases on cultural goals and accompanying cultural messages that assert the importance of striving for those goals. Unless the means to reach the goals are equitably distributed in society, the overemphasis on goals and inequality of means will result in socially structured and patterned rates of deviance. Groups who have the greatest access to the approved means are mostly conforming. Conversely, those groups with the least access to the means have higher rates of deviance. In U.S. society this suggests that structured inequality leads to deviance and crime, with the highest rates among the lower classes. Indeed, the theory's premise is that the lower class suffers the most anomic conditions and therefore has the highest level of involvement in deviant behavior.

MAJOR POINTS OF THE THEORY

1. Most members of society share (or are socialized into) a common system of values.

2. This common value system teaches us both the things we should strive for (cultural goals) and the most appropriate ways (societal means) to achieve those goals.

3. If the goals and the means to achieve them are not equally stressed, an anomic condition is created.

4. In a disorganized society, different degrees of access to these goals and means exist. Thus, the means are not equally distributed within a disorganized society.

5. Some societies, such as that of the United States, may place too much stress on success goals. In a disorganized society, this results in a striving toward those goals, but not enough access to the means to achieve them.

6. Without reasonable access to the socially approved means, members of society will attempt to find some way to resolve the pressure to achieve. These alternative solutions are called "modes of adaptation."

7. The various modes of adaptation are formed by combinations of accepting, rejecting, or substituting for the goals and the means.

   a. If, in the face of moral pressure, the individual continues to "accept" the value of both the goals and the means, the form of behavior exhibited will be *conforming*. This is the most common form of adaptation.

   b. If the individual accepts the goals but rejects the means to achieve them, the form of behavior will be deviant and *innovative*. Here, more available and faster ways of achieving the goals are created.

   c. If the individual sees the goals as unattainable (rejects them) but accepts the means anyway, the form of behavior will be deviant and *ritualistic*. In this case, the focus of the individual becomes the means rather than the ends.

   d. If the individual rejects both the goals and the means, the form of behavior will be deviant and *retreatist*. A person engaged in this behavior will no longer strive toward the goals and not even continue in the normal stream of life.

   e. If both the goals and the means are rejected and then substituted for, the form of behavior will be deviant and *rebelling*. This form of deviance actually rejects the way society is currently set up and attempts to create a new form of society.

Epilogue: Current Directions and Policy Implications

CURRENT DIRECTIONS

Alarm over the recent suicides of seven young people in a depressed Welsh town (Katz, 2008, p. A26) forced officials to confront many of the ideas argued by anomie theory. Comments included the area's "deepening sense of foreboding and hopelessness," the loss of jobs, high unemployment, a high level of illness, and the lack of meaningful activity for the youth that leads them to drink and take drugs. Ironically, even the recreation center cost too much to use. One resident explained the feelings of the teens "when something goes wrong in their inner circle, they feel helpless and don't know where to turn . . . nobody really knows what to do . . . society is disconnected."

These circumstances correspond well with the current theoretical emphasis of anomie theory as a form called strain theory. Although Merton uses the word "strain" in his presentation, he rejected the idea that his theory was a strain theory. To his way of thinking, strain tends toward psychosocial and microlevel analysis and anomie theory was never meant to be an explanation of that (as quoted in Cullen & Messner, 2007, p. 21). In a similar vein, Albert K. Cohen (himself referred to as a strain theorist) argues that Travis Hirschi, in his 1969 book *Causes of Delinquency* "invented" the category of modern strain theory (Cohen, personal communication, January 29, 1993) and vehemently denies that he wrote about "strain." The term was also used by Ruth Kornhauser (1978) in her critique of criminological theories. Featherstone and Deflem (2003) even present a case for Merton's theory having two parts:

anomie, which is the structural component of the disjunction between goals and means which causes normlessness, and strain, which is the adaptation to blocked opportunities.

This category of theories is defined by its focus on *motivation*. That is, strain theories require that people be motivated to commit criminal and delinquent acts. Without such motivation, there would be conformity. In other words, strain theories are focused on some special state of mind (or collective state of mind) such as a pathology, tension, frustration, or mental conflict. As a result, people in this state of mind "see crime as expressions, symptoms, or ways of dealing with, solving, or getting relief from whatever is troubling them" (Cohen, personal communication, January 29, 1993). Such theories include psychological and psychoanalytic versions, which explain the source of these symptoms by looking at individuals and locating answers in their own situation and history.

The sociological versions of strain theory ask the question, "Where do these strains come from?" In other words, what is it about the way in which society is organized and arranged that tends to produce the conditions and circumstances that give rise to deviant behavior? Sociological strain theories also attempt to explain the origins of motivational states (and usually are concerned with the distribution of those states). They search for the origins of strain in the way society is put together or arranged; that is, in the social structure. Theories such as Merton's place the source of strain in cultural messages and social inequalities. We refer to all these approaches as *structural* strain theories.

Other than Merton's further writing and elaboration on his theory, several theorists have added to the general strain theory perspective. Most notable are Cohen (1955, 1965), Cloward (1959), and Cloward with Ohlin (1960). These extensions are examined in detail in the chapter on subculture theories (Chapter 7). Other theorists, however, have directly added to anomie theory by suggesting new categories for the modes of adaptation (Dubin, 1959; Harary, 1966; Murphy & Robinson, 2008; and with Merton's, 1959 commentary on Dubin and Cloward's contributions). Most of these writers were concerned with Merton's use of the substitution concept and argued that it opened the door to many more than the five modes of adaptation predicted by the scheme of accepting and rejecting the goals and means. Other criminologists have critiqued the theory and conducted studies to see if the relationships implied in the theory exist. Many have noted that the theory is wanting in support, but some have argued that much of the research on anomie theory has been done with microlevel variables dealing with individuals, rather than the more appropriate use of macrolevel variables measuring characteristics of groups. As a result, the downturn of popularity for anomie theory during the 1970s is more likely the result of criminological attention turning to "newer" theories rather than any lack of supportive evidence (Lilly, Cullen, & Ball, 2010).

ASPIRATIONS AND EXPECTATIONS

One variety of newer work carries on the Mertonian tradition of examining disparities between aspirations and expectations. In this vein, aspirations are viewed as the ideal goals that one should strive for, whereas expectations are what the individual thinks he or she can actually achieve. The argument is that a disparity between aspirations and expectations leads to a sense of frustration and higher probabilities of deviant behavior. Typically, this approach is used for adolescents, because they have not had time to be rejected by the social system and thereby meet Merton's criteria for a shortage of means. Robert Agnew, in particular, has argued in his general strain theory that blockage of adolescent's goals leads to deviance.

RELATIVE DEPRIVATION

Another direction suggests that the relative discrepancy between poverty and wealth is important in determining crime rates. For instance, in areas of extreme poverty or extreme wealth, we might expect to find that such conspicuous differences create more frustration and despair and, subsequently, higher crime rates. Several studies have suggested that this variation of strain theory makes sense and, indeed, does have the anticipated effect.

IMMEDIACY OF GOALS

Yet another variety of strain theory seeks to resolve one of the major criticisms of strain theory: that the goals/means formula does not explain middle-class deviance very well.[2] While this might not be a valid criticism, Delbert Elliott and Harwin Voss (1974) added middle-class delinquency to the strain picture. They did so by focusing more on immediate goals than the long-range aspirations usually connected with strain theory. Juveniles are more likely to be concerned about their immediate goals (popularity, athletic achievement, good grades) than whether they will eventually succeed in life. Moreover, these immediate goals are not necessarily tied to social class, although middle-class juveniles are perhaps more likely to chase immediate goals that are more difficult to achieve (class president, captain of cheerleaders). When coupled with other impediments to success (physical unattractiveness, poor personality, lack of coordination, or inferior intellectual ability), the inability to achieve goals may be seen as a combination of several factors.

NEW STRAIN THEORIES

Two forms of strain theory emerged during the 1980s and 1990s. The first, Robert Agnew's *general strain theory* (1985, 2001, 2005) focuses on juveniles and adds the concept of blocked avoidance of painful situations. Just as blocked legitimate opportunities create strain, so too does the inability to avoid stressful circumstances. Thus, Agnew adds a personal level to Merton's structural explanation. The second new version, *institutional strain theory*, is from Steven Messner and Richard Rosenfeld (2007). They posit that anomie also reduces the control of most social institutions (family, school, law) over individuals and exacerbates cultural economic sources of strain. This, too, moves strain theory to a more personal level. Each of these additions to the Mertonian strain approach provides another level of explanation to the structural variables of the original perspective and demonstrates the value of relationships between cultural strain and personal factors. This acknowledgment of the complexity of strain is an important advance in combining structural factors with individual-level variables (see Chapters 14 and 15 for more detail on these theories).

POLICY IMPLICATIONS

Policy implications are easy to draw from anomie and strain theories; putting them into practice is another matter entirely. Because anomie is a macrolevel theory, the proper form of policy would be aimed at modifying the social structure. Examples would include the elimination of class structures, racism, and prejudice, all of which are factors working to limit the opportunities for reaching goals. Other approaches, as we discuss in Chapter 7, involve programs to provide increased job opportunities. Although most clearly seen in the Depression-era work programs, many programs that aimed to increase opportunities for meaningful work were also created during the 1960s. Similarly, providing greater educational opportunities would be a desirable approach under strain theory. California's education master plan of the 1960s, for example, gave all citizens free access to at least two years of college. Programs aimed at decreasing school dropout rates and increasing educational levels are also in keeping with the anomie tradition. From the perspective of Agnew's strain theory, a reasonable approach would be to find ways to decrease negative relationships in families, schools, and neighborhoods and to increase methods of avoiding other negative strains. Messner and Rosenfeld (2007) argue that more flexible work plans for parents, including family leave and working from home offices, may help restore the balance between the pressure for success and the need to devote time and energy to supportive social structures such as the family. Schools that strive to incorporate parents in special activities and companies that allow employees to devote work time to community projects also help strengthen these institutional controls.

---

[2] This critique ignores the fact that Merton was writing about a more general notion of deviance, not specifically crime or psychopathology. As a result, his use of conformity as the dominant mode of adaptation nicely captures middle-class efforts to remain true to the status quo system even in the face of self-evident lack of opportunities to gain "real" success.

A final policy implication deserves attention. Ruth Kornhauser (1978) as well as Steve Brown, Finn Esbensen, and Gil Geis (2010) have suggested that one possible policy implementation of anomie theory would be to reduce aspirations. While they do not actually suggest that we do so, some of the possibilities are intriguing. We could, for instance, introduce a caste system in which individuals remain in the caste to which they are born, never being allowed to dream of goals beyond their reach. Or, perhaps we could mount a campaign to tell everyone that the American dream is over. None of these things would, of course, be desirable—crime is not necessarily the worst ill in society. On the positive side though, we could attempt to restrict advertising that announces the availability of all sorts of luxury goods and our need to secure those goods to keep up with the proverbial "Jones family next door." In this sense, the advertising media might be blamed (under anomie theory) for magnifying the tensions between the haves and the have-nots.

Questions and Weblinks

Critical Thinking Questions

1. Do you think our current society reflects a certain level of anomie? Why or why not?
2. How does advertising and media contribute to our drive for material forms of success and is there any benefit for attempting to control that?
3. Do you think the American Dream is the same today as when Merton first wrote his theory?
4. In the late 1950s, Leo Srole developed a scale that attempted to measure individual levels of anomie. The survey asked if you agreed or disagreed with the following statements:

a) Despite what some say, the conditions of the average person are getting worse.
b) The way the future looks, it is hardly fair to bring children into this world.
c) A person has to mainly live for today and let tomorrow take care of itself.
d) Today it is hard to tell who you can really count on.
e) It is no use writing public officials, they don't care about you.

Answer the questions a–e above with agree or disagree and compare your results with those in your class.

Practice Essay Questions

1. Discuss how progress in society contributes to the development of anomie according to Emile Durkheim.
2. As described in this chapter, what are some of the different ways that people adapt to the strain of not having access to the goals or means that society offers?
3. How does social structure interfere with someone's ability to access the means to obtain the "American Dream?"

Related Websites

http://www.aacap.org/cs/root/facts_for_families/teen_suicide
http://www.samhsa.gov/prevention/

AfterSchool.Gov
http://www.afterschool.gov/

National Mentoring Center
http://www.nwrel.org/mentoring/index.php

National Mentoring Partnership
http://www.mentoring.org/

Bibliography

Agnew, R. (1985). A revised strain theory of delinquency. *Social Forces, 64,* 151–167.

Agnew, R. (2001). Building on the foundation of general strain theory: Specifying the types of strain most likely to lead to crime and delinquency. *Journal of Research in Crime and Delinquency, 38,* 319–361.

Agnew, R. (2005). *Pressured into crime: An overview of general strain theory.* New York: Oxford University Press.

Brown, S. E., Esbensen, F.-A., & Geis, G. (2010). *Criminology: Explaining crime and its context.* Cincinnati, OH: Anderson.

Cloward, R. A. (1959). Illegitimate means, anomie, and deviant behavior. *American Sociological Review, 24,* 164–176.

Cloward, R. A., & Ohlin, L. E. (1960). *Delinquency and opportunity: A theory of delinquent gangs.* New York: Free Press.

Cohen, A. K. (1955). *Delinquent boys: The culture of the gang.* New York: Free Press.

Cohen, A. K. (1965). The sociology of the deviant act: Anomie theory and beyond. *American Sociological Review, 30,* 5–14.

Cullen, F. T., & Messner, S. F. (2007). The making of criminology revisited an oral history of Merton's anomie paradigm. *Theoretical Criminology, 11,* 5–37.

Dollard, J. (1937). *Caste and class in a Southern town.* New Haven, CT: Yale University Press.

Dubin, R. (1959). Deviant behavior and social structure: Continuities in social theory. *American Sociological Review, 24,* 147–164.

Durkheim, E. (1930). *The division of labor in society* (G. Simpson, Trans.). New York: Free Press. (Original work published 1893.)

Durkheim, E. (1951). *Suicide: A study in sociology* (J. A. Spaulding & G. Simpson, Trans.). New York: Free Press. (Original work published 1897.)

Elliott, D. S., & Voss, H. (1974). *Delinquency and dropout.* Lexington, MA: Lexington Books.

Featherstone, R., & Deflem, M. (2003). Anomie and strain: Context and consequences of Merton's two theories. *Sociological Inquiry, 73,* 471–489.

Harary, F. (1966). Merton revisited: A new classification for deviant behavior. *American Sociological Review, 31,* 693–697.

Hirschi, T. (1969). *Causes of delinquency.* Berkeley: University of California Press.

Katz, G. (2008, January 27). Loss of seven young people leave Welsh town reeling. *Houston Chronicle,* p. A26.

Kornhauser, R. R. (1978). *Social sources of delinquency.* Chicago: University of Chicago Press.

Lilly, J. R., Cullen, F. T., & Ball, R. A. (2010). *Criminological theory: Context and consequences* (5th ed.). Thousand Oaks, CA: Sage.

Lynd, R. S., & Lynd, H. M. (1929). *Middletown: A study in American culture.* New York: Harcourt, Brace and World.

Martin, R., Mutchnick, R., & Austin, T. (2009). Robert Merton. In R. Martin, R. Mutchnick, & T. Austin (Eds.), *Criminological thought: Pioneers past and present* (pp. 207–238). New York: Macmillan.

Merton, R. K. (1938). Social structure and anomie. *American Sociological Review, 3,* 672–682.

Merton, R. K. (1957a). *Social theory and social structure* (Rev. ed.). New York: Free Press.

Merton, R. K. (1957b). Priorities in scientific discovery: A chapter in the sociology of science. *American Sociological Review, 22,* 635–639.

Merton, R. K. (1959). Social conformity, deviation, and opportunity structures: A comment on the contributions of Dubin and Cloward. *American Sociological Review, 24,* 177–188.

Merton, R. K. (1964). Anomie, anomia, and social interactions: Contexts of deviant behavior. In M. B. Clinard (Ed.), *Anomie and deviant behavior* (pp. 213–242). New York: Free Press.

Merton, R. K. (1968). *Social theory and social structure* (Rev. and enlarged ed.). New York: Free Press.

Merton, R. K. (1997). On the evolving synthesis of differential association and anomie theory: A perspective from the sociology of science. *Criminology, 35,* 517–525.

Merton, R. K., & Ashley-Montagu, M. F. (1940). Crime and the anthropologist. *American Anthropologist, 42,* 384–408.

Messner, S. F., & Rosenfeld, R. (2007). *Crime and the American dream* (4th ed.). Belmont, CA: Wadsworth.

Murphy, D., & Robinson, M. (2008). The Maximizer: Clarifying Merton's theories of anomie and strain. *Theoretical Criminology, 12,* 501–521.

Olsen, M. (1965). Durkheim's two concepts of anomie. *Sociological Quarterly, 6,* 37–44.

Parsons, T. (1937). *The structure of social action.* New York: McGraw-Hill.

Sorokin, P. A. (1928). *Contemporary sociological theories.* New York: Harper and Brothers.

Research Bibliography (from 2000)

Baron, S. W. (2011). Street youths and the proximate and contingent causes of instrumental crime: Untangling anomie theory. *Justice Quarterly, 28,* 413–436.

Bernburg, J. (2002). Anomie, social change and crime. *British Journal of Criminology, 42,* 729–742.

Bjerregaard, B., & Cochran, J. (2008). Want amid plenty: Developing and testing a cross-national measure of anomie. *International Journal of Conflict & Violence, 2,* 182–193.

Braithwaite, J. (2011). Anomie and violence in Indonesia and Timor-Leste, 1997–2009. *Asian Journal of Criminology, 6,* 51–68.

Cao, L. (2007). Returning to normality: Anomie and crime in China. *International Journal of Offender Therapy and Comparative Criminology, 51,* 40–51.

Cao, L., Zhao, R., Ren, L., & Zhao, J. (2010). Social support and anomie. *International Journal of Offender Therapy and Comparative Criminology, 54,* 625–639.

Cochran, J. K., & Bjerregaard, B. (2012). Structural anomie and crime: A cross-national test. *International Journal of Offender Therapy & Comparative Criminology, 56,* 203–217.

Konty, M. (2005). Microanomie: The cognitive foundations of the relationship between anomne and deviance. *Criminology, 43,* 107–131.

Martin, R. (2000). Anomie, spirituality, and crime. *Journal of Contemporary Criminal Justice, 16,* 75–99.

Stults, B. J., & Baumer, E. P. (2008). Assessing the relevance of anomie theory for explaining spatial variation in lethal criminal violence: An aggregate-level analysis of homicide within the United States. *International Journal of Conflict & Violence, 2,* 215–247.

Young, T. (1990). Native American crime and criminal justice require criminologists' attention. *Journal of Criminal Justice Education, 1,* 111–126.

Zhao, L. (2008). Anomie theory and crime in a transitional China (1978—). *International Criminal Justice Review, 18,* 137–157.

Zhao, R., & Cao, L. (2010). Social change and anomie: A cross-national study. *Social Forces, 88,* 1209–1229.

Subculture Theories

LEARNING OBJECTIVES

Objective 7.1: Discuss what is meant by a subculture.

Objective 7.2: Describe Cohen's view of gang behavior and how it forms.

Objective 7.3: Explain what Miller meant by lower-class focal concerns.

Objective 7.4: Compare and contrast community opportunities as seen by Cloward and Ohlin and how they contribute to gang activity.

Objective 7.5: Discuss some of the programs designed to offset the negative influences of gangs in inner cities.

INTRODUCTION

With few exceptions, criminological theories of the 1950s and early 1960s focused on juvenile delinquency. Many of the theorists set out to explain what they believed to be the most common form of delinquency: gangs. They were interested in explaining the origins of delinquent gangs and the context in which different types of gangs developed. At the same time, the cultures studied by the Chicago School began to be referred to by the new sociological term "subcultures."

Combining these two topics, criminologists began studying gang delinquency and theorizing about delinquent subcultures. In separate works, Albert K. Cohen in 1955 and Richard A. Cloward and Lloyd E. Ohlin in 1960 combined the work of the Chicago School (and Sutherland) with Merton's anomie theory. Both focused on urban, lower-class, male, gang delinquency. Other theories included Walter Miller's (1958) theory of lower-class "focal concerns" and Marvin Wolfgang and Franco Ferracuti's (1967) theory of the subculture of violence.

Because of the differences among these theories, it is difficult to characterize them as a generic subculture theory. Even characterizing them as strain theories, as some writers have done, is not accurate. Cohen has long refuted a simple strain theory characterization of his work, and Frank Cullen

(1988) has made a cogent argument that Cloward and Ohlin were not primarily strain theorists. Therefore, this chapter is divided into three sections. After a discussion of the heritage of the theories, we examine, in turn, Cohen's theory of the delinquent subculture, Cloward and Ohlin's differential opportunity theory, and two other subculture theories, those of Miller, and Wolfgang and Ferracuti.

THE HERITAGE OF THE THEORIES

The Social Heritage

The 1950s were a time of prosperity and a tremendous rise in consumerism. The values of the middle class had proven their superiority in a massive war effort, and, consequently, for many it was difficult to conceive of anything other than the middle-class way as being "normal." It may even have been this same pride in "the American way" that helped create the climate for communist-chasing during the McCarthy years.

Along with this spirit, the right to education was seen for the first time as something all Americans shared. As a result of educational benefits provided to military veterans, college enrollment climbed, and the middle class began to expect a college education for its children. Public schooling captured the attention of America and, by the end of the 1950s, the Soviet success in putting into orbit the first satellite resulted in a call in the United States for better education in the sciences. These events ultimately led to changes in the U.S. educational system.

At the same time, the peaking urbanization of the United States was producing increasingly deteriorated central-city areas. Middle-class suburbs were developing, and the first housing sub-division was built outside Philadelphia. The Supreme Court outlawed segregation, but economic and territorial boundaries were already distinct. The problems of the cities were the problems of the people who lived there, principally the lower class. Delinquency was viewed as a lower-class problem, and gangs were the most visible form of delinquency. With a clear "we–they" separation, middle-class America saw itself as superior to the lower class.

As Charles Murray (1984) notes, the dominant concepts of poverty, as translated into policy during the 1950s, tended to rely on explanations of individual behavior. The popular view was that individuals were responsible for their own situations and that the poor probably had not worked hard enough. The civil rights movement and other factors already mentioned helped recast the responsibility for poverty into a social framework. With the arrival of the 1960s, the time was ripe for a reinterpretation of the effects of poverty. Bob Lilly, Frank Cullen, and Richard Ball (1989, p. 90) point out that the new social responsibility served to highlight Merton's theory and to emphasize the emerging opportunity-oriented theories of Cohen, and Cloward and Ohlin.

The Intellectual Heritage

The intellectual traditions behind the theories of the 1950s included the Chicago School theories and the Mertonian conception of anomie. Scholars who were associated with the Chicago School continued their study of crime and delinquency rates and researched the relationship between community and delinquency. Edwin Sutherland, previously the dominant figure in criminology, spread the work of the Chicago School through several graduate students who had studied with him at the University of Indiana in the 1940s. These students would become prominent criminologists.

Robert Merton's theories had also become influential. His writings in sociology, and those of Talcott Parsons, had established a concern with social structure and the examination of social class differences. Within criminology, this "structural-functionalist" approach captured the imagination of theorists who sought ways to reconcile Merton's structure with the Chicago School's process.

A final major influence on the subculture theorists of the 1950s was the writing of a researcher at the Chicago Area Project, Solomon Kobrin. He and others, in examining street gangs and studying the relationships between male generations in a lower-class community, found strong ties between the political hierarchy and organized crime. These ties were so strong that Kobrin referred to them jointly as a "single controlling group" (Kobrin, in Laub, 1983b). It was from these observations that Kobrin (1951) introduced the concept of an integrated community. According to this concept, the degree of social control present within a community is dependent on how well the criminal element is organized as well as on the character of its relationship with the community's official leadership. A community that is organized and integrated has greater social control over the behavior of juveniles than a community where integration is lacking. This control exists because organized crime members reside in the community with their families. Thus, they have an interest in controlling and preventing violence in the community. Because they have power and participate in the political arena, organized crime is able to use that political power to have the police keep the streets in their neighborhood safe. In short, they want the same things for their community that you and I do. Kobrin's insights led the way to a future combination of the Mertonian and Chicago School paradigms.

[Handwritten margin note: gangs are organized to protect resources/access for themselves]

COHEN'S SUBCULTURE OF DELINQUENCY

Albert K. Cohen's book *Delinquent Boys: The Culture of the Gang* (1955) was the first attempt at solving the problem of how a delinquent subculture could begin.[1] Cohen also attempted to integrate several theoretical perspectives, including the work of Clifford Shaw and Henry

Albert Kircidel Cohen (1918–)

Albert Cohen was born in Boston, Massachusetts, in 1918. He attended his local university, and received his BA in sociology from Harvard in 1939. While there, he became acquainted with Robert Merton and Talcott Parsons. Upon graduation, Cohen wanted to pursue a graduate degree and applied for assistantship funding at various institutions. Edwin Sutherland, at Indiana University, replied with financial assistance and Cohen went there to obtain his master's degree. After that, he went to work at a correctional facility for youth and later served in the Army in a chemical warfare unit.

Returning to graduate school, he completed his Ph.D. at Harvard and began teaching at Indiana University. In 1965, he began his distinguished tenure at the University of Connecticut (1964–1988). His accomplishments there included serving as editor of the *American Sociological Review*, a term as President of the Society for the Study of Social Problems, and a Senior Fulbright in the Philippines. Cohen won the prestigious Edwin Sutherland Award from the American Society of Criminology (ASC) in 1993 and was also named an ASC Fellow. He retired as professor emeritus in 1988.

[1] We would like to express our appreciation to Albert Cohen for his review and comments on this summary.

McKay, Edwin Sutherland, and Robert Merton.[2] Although criticized severely (see, especially, Bordua, 1960, 1961, 1962; Kitsuse & Dietrick, 1959), his work has been influential among criminologists.

After an examination of the research on juvenile delinquency, Cohen noted that delinquent behavior is most often found among lower-class males and that gang delinquency is the most common form. He also determined that gang subcultures are characterized by behavior that is nonutilitarian, malicious, and negativistic. In other words, Cohen saw in subcultural delinquency no rationale for stealing (other than seeking peer status), a delight in the discomfort of others, and an obvious attempt to flout middle-class values. The research also characterized gangs as engaged in various forms of delinquent acts (versatility), interested mainly in the present (short-run hedonism) as opposed to the future, and hostile to outsiders (group autonomy). These constitute the factors that had to be explained by a theory of the delinquent subculture.

Cohen declared that all children (indeed, all individuals) seek social status. However, not all children can compete equally for status. By virtue of their position in the social structure, lower-class children tend to lack both material and symbolic advantages. As long as they compete among themselves, the footing is relatively equal; it is in competition with middle-class children that those of the lower class fall short.

The first major status problems facing lower-class children are found in the school system. Not only do these children have to compete with middle-class children, but they are also evaluated by adults who use a "middle-class measuring rod," a set of standards that are difficult for the lower-class child to attain. These standards include sharing, delaying gratification, setting long-range goals, and respecting others' property. All of these things intrinsically relate to being brought up with property of one's own and to having parents who know firsthand the future can be better and hard work pays off. None of these standards are necessarily self-evident to the parents of lower-class children, and they cannot be expected to lie to their children. In this competitive framework, then, lower-class children lose ground in the search for status, among both fellow students and teachers. Those who most strongly feel the loss most suffer status-frustration. Employing the Freudian mechanism of reaction-formation (a defensive mechanism to overcome anxiety) as an explanation, Cohen speculated a hostile overreaction to middle-class values may occur.

Because many lower-class children are trapped in this status-frustration, various adaptations to the middle class take place. For some, adjustment to the middle-class measuring rod results in a collective solution to the problem of status. This solution, Cohen suggested, also requires a change in the way status is attained. This is accomplished by jointly establishing "new norms, new criteria of status which define as meritorious the characteristics they *do* possess, the kinds of conduct of which they *are* capable" (1955, p. 66, emphasis in original). Thus, a new cultural form, a delinquent subculture, is created to resolve problems of lower-class status.

It is this delinquent subculture that provides the nonutilitarian, malicious, and negativistic character of gang delinquency. Abandoning and inverting the middle-class value system, gang members can achieve status simply by doing those things they do well, such as showing toughness or standing up for themselves. As long as the need for status exists, the delinquent subculture will exist as an available solution for lower-class, male youths.

---

[2] Most criminologists have viewed Cohen's work as a combination of the East Coast anomie tradition and the Chicago School tradition. Although this view is correct, it is curious that Cohen's book contains only one citation to Merton's work, and this is in a footnote on social disorganization, whose primary source is Shaw and McKay.

The more a frustrated lower-class youth interacts with those in the delinquent subculture, the greater is the likelihood the youth will take up the definitions and behaviors of the subculture. Cohen is really saying, then, that the strains resulting from social disorganization (or differential social organization) create a commonly shared situation for many lower-class children. Whether such children become delinquent depends on the degree and strength of their interaction with members of the delinquent subculture. Those who have frequent interaction and begin to view gang delinquents as their significant others are most likely to view the delinquent subculture as the solution to their problems.

We should also note that Cohen proposed, albeit in few words, theories of female delinquency and middle-class male delinquency. In both instances, he used the concepts of status-frustration and reaction-formation to explain the form of delinquent subculture available to each group. He characterized females as frustrated by the sexual "double standard" and, through the reaction-formation process, as resolving their status-frustration by engaging in sexually oriented delinquent behavior. Cohen viewed middle-class males, in contrast, as anxious about their "maleness" because of the child-rearing responsibilities of the mother. The reaction-formation process in this case results in a "masculine protest" against female authority, creating a middle-class male delinquent subculture. The subculture emphasizes behavior involving masculine activities, especially those revolving around the automobile, and thus leads to joyriding, "drag racing," and being "bad."

Classification of the Theory

Cohen's subculture theory is usually referred to as a *strain*, or *structural*, theory. While the strain classification is to Cohen's mind questionable (Laub, 1983a), it is potentially usable because while the source of the delinquent subculture is strain, the theory focuses on the process by which the subculture is created. The latter part represents the influence of the Chicago School's process orientation. This duality also makes it difficult to classify the theory as either a macrotheory or a microtheory; instead, classification as a *bridging* theory is appropriate. In this respect, Cohen borrows from strain theory an explanation of social structure and proceeds to describe how delinquent subcultures come about. He does this from a *consensus* approach, meaning that society emphasizes reaching goals in the accepted middle-class way. It is only after frustration develops from an inability to reach status goals that lower-class children find a need for alternative means. Similarly, the theory is a clear example of sociological *positivism* (as are most criminological theories). In fact, Cohen (1955, pp. 21–48) tells us there are certain forms of behavior to be explained, and he then develops the concept of subculture as a means of understanding those behaviors. Cohen himself says (personal communication, January 29, 1993):

> *Delinquent Boys* is not just a strain theory and structural theory. It is also a theory that emphasizes the role of *process* and of interaction; specifically, the way in which the availability of others who are similarly circumstanced (who experience the same strain) and interaction with those others determines how the actor will deal with strain.

Major Points of the Theory

1. Members of society share a common value system that emphasizes certain values over others. In the United States, these values are closely associated with the middle class.
2. Most of these common values stress goals that result in the gaining of status; therefore, status itself becomes a generally approved goal.

3. Opportunities to reach these goals are more often available to the middle class than to the lower class.

4. Societal institutions, especially schools, reflect middle-class value goals and use them to evaluate those who come in contact with the institution.

5. Because of their limited opportunities, lower-class youths are often evaluated unfavorably by the school system, leading to frustration in their pursuit of status.

6. Unable to gain status through the use of conventional school opportunities (grades, social standing), lower-class youths rebel (reaction-formation) against middle-class values while still keeping status as a goal.

7. Over a period of time, lower-class youths collectively create a new value system in opposition to middle-class values. The standards of this new value system are mostly anticonventional and afford the youths opportunities for gaining status.

8. This "delinquent solution" is passed on through the transmission of values from youth to youth and generation to generation, fostering an ongoing delinquent subculture that provides status for behavior that is negativistic, malicious, and nonutilitarian.

→CLOWARD AND OHLIN'S DIFFERENTIAL OPPORTUNITY THEORY

The theory that became known as "differential opportunity theory" had its origins in a 1959 article by Richard Cloward. Noting Merton's anomie theory had specified only one opportunity structure, Cloward argued there is a second opportunity structure. Not only does a set of legitimate means exist to reach cultural goals, but standard illegitimate avenues exist as well (the illegitimate opportunity structure). This second source of opportunities became the background of the theory proposed in a book Cloward wrote with Lloyd Ohlin, *Delinquency and Opportunity: A Theory of Delinquent Gangs* (1960).[3]

Richard Andrew Cloward (1926–2001)

Richard Cloward was born in Rochester, New York, on Christmas of 1926. After earning his bachelor's degree from the University of Rochester in 1949, Cloward obtained his master's in social work from Columbia University in 1950. He served in both the Navy and the Army from 1951 to 1954 and after leaving the service joined Columbia University's School of Social Work as an assistant professor. While teaching at Columbia, he pursued and completed a doctorate in sociology in 1958, working with Robert Merton as his mentor. As a professor at the Columbia School of Social Work for 47 years, he helped to establish a number of community action and legal programs aimed at reducing poverty. One in particular, Mobilization for Youth (MFY), in the early 1960s became a program model for the 1960s federal War on Poverty. Other affiliations include the National Welfare Rights Organization and Service Employees Registration and Voter Education (SERVE), which he founded with his wife and coauthor, Frances Fox Piven. In 1993, he spearheaded efforts to formalize motor voter programs, which resulted in passage of the Motor Voter Act. He died of lung cancer at the age of 74.

---

[3] Lloyd Ohlin reviewed and approved this summary for substantive accuracy.

Lloyd Edgar Ohlin (1918–2008)

Lloyd Ohlin was born in Belmont, Massachusetts, in 1918, where his family owned a small chain of bakeries. He received a bachelor's degree from Brown University in 1940 and a master's in sociology from Indiana University in 1942, working with Edwin Sutherland. In World War II, Ohlin served with the Army in counterintelligence in Europe. Leaving the service, Ohlin worked as a sociologist and actuary for the Illinois Parole and Pardon Board from 1947 to 1953, earning his Ph.D. from the University of Chicago in 1954, working with Ernest Burgess. In the mid-1950s, Ohlin directed the Center for Education and Research in Corrections at the University of Chicago, after which he joined the social work faculty at Columbia University. He was later named director of the school's research center. His work with Mobilization for Youth, a $12.9 million antipoverty program designed to prevent delinquency, was rooted in the ideas set forth in "Delinquency and Opportunity" and encompassed job training, psychological counseling, a narcotics program, legal assistance, and other services. It became a model for federal antipoverty programs of the 1960s.

From 1965 to 1967, Ohlin served as associate director of the President's Commission on Law Enforcement and Administration of Justice. He accepted a position on the Harvard Law School faculty in 1967 and was one of the few nonlawyers there. Ohlin was also the research director of the Center for Criminal Justice at Harvard and held the Roscoe Pound Professorship of Criminology and, later, the Touroff-Glueck Emeritus Professorship of Criminal Justice. Ohlin was President of the American Society of Criminology in 1986, was honored as a Fellow in 1982, and received the Edwin Sutherland Award in 1967. He also received the Bruce Smith, Jr. Award from the Academy of Criminal Justice Sciences in 1992. After his retirement from Harvard Law School, in 1982 Ohlin continued work on several projects, including a study of the Massachusetts Juvenile Justice System. He consulted for the National Institute of Justice and other foundations, from his homes in Maine and California. Ohlin died December 6, 2008, in Santa Barbara, California, at the age of 90.

According to Cloward and Ohlin, more than one way exists for juveniles to reach their aspirations. In those urban, lower-class areas where very few legitimate opportunities are available, one can find opportunities of a different kind. Further, these opportunities are just as well established and access is just as limited as in the legitimate structure. Thus, position in society dictates the ability to participate in both conventional and criminal avenues of success.

Using the writings of Solomon Kobrin (1951) on integrated conventional and criminal activity in lower-class communities (Laub, 1983c), Cloward and Ohlin argued that the form of delinquent subculture depends on the degree of integration present in the community. Moreover, they suggested that in a community without a stable criminal structure, lower-class juveniles would have no greater opportunity to succeed in life through criminal avenues than they would through conventional means. There would be no criminal "business" to join and to work one's way up through the ranks, no way to learn properly a criminal trade, and no way to become a "professional." People who could work their way up through a criminal business, in contrast, could gain the wherewithal to enable them to slip over to legitimate business. In fact, this is exactly what Kobrin (1951, p. 657) meant by community integration: Leaders in legitimate and illegitimate businesses share the goal of profitability, membership in religious and social organizations, and participation in the political process. And, of course, they share the desire for safe streets in the neighborhood where they live.

Cloward and Ohlin proposed there would be three ideal types of delinquent gang subcultures: criminal, conflict, and retreatist. First, where communities are fully integrated, gangs would act almost as an apprenticeship group for adult, organized criminal concerns. In this criminal subculture, the primary focus would be on profit-making activities, and violence would be minimal. These subcultural gangs would practice the criminal "trades" under the loose supervision of organized crime. Gang members could participate in various gambling activities (e.g., "running numbers") or learn and participate in profit-making activities such as shoplifting, fencing, and extortion. A contemporary example of participation in illegal activities is drug distributors' use of underaged gang members as drug carriers and dealers. If caught with drugs, underage juveniles do not face the same penalties as adults.

Cloward and Ohlin also pointed out that criminal gangs exist where there is an integration of ages as well as legitimate and illegitimate groups. In this way, they stress the learning of roles and the effect of role models on the shaping of the subcultural activities. In other words, young juveniles learn by watching and associating with older youths, who in turn learn from the adults around them. As Cloward and Ohlin explained: "Just as the middle-class youth, as a consequence of intimate relationships with, say, a banker or a businessman, may aspire to become a banker or a businessman, so the lower-class youth may be associated with and aspire to become a 'policy king' " (the extortion racket) (1960, pp. 162–163). The influence of the Chicago School's symbolic interactionist perspective, especially Sutherland's differential association theory, is obvious here.

A nonintegrated community would not only lack a well-organized and ongoing illegitimate structure but, according to Kobrin (1951, p. 658), also exercise very weak community control over juveniles. Thus, any gang subculture that would develop in one of these communities would exhibit unrestrained behavior. As in Cohen's delinquent subculture, the primary focus would be on gaining "respect." Violence, property damage, and unpredictable behavior would become the hallmarks of such gangs. Cloward and Ohlin called this form the conflict subculture. These gangs would cause trouble equally for the community's adult criminal element as well as for law-abiding citizens. Fearful residents, reacting to the random nature of violence, would call the police more often, and likewise, older offenders would see the disruption of the status quo as attracting unwarranted law enforcement surveillance and intervention. In short, a socially disorganized community tends to create a gang subculture that is equally disorganized. Transient and unstable relationships in the community are reflected in juvenile interactions, and relationships and role models between youths of different ages would be difficult to sustain. Further, the illegitimate adult role models available to juveniles tend to be individuals who are not successful criminals (compared with those in organized crime). Interaction and learning in these areas reflect the nature of the community, and stable criminal learning environments cannot be developed.

In both integrated and nonintegrated communities, one can also find juveniles who have no access to either of the opportunity structures. These individuals, over time, develop what Cloward and Ohlin called a retreatist subculture. Their primary focus is on drugs, and their gang-related activities are designed to bring them the money for their own drug use. The term for these subcultural delinquents is "double failures," juveniles who for one reason or another cannot achieve sufficient success in either the legitimate or the illegitimate world. There are two possibilities for their retreat from the other two types of subcultures (Cloward & Ohlin, 1960, p. 181). First, they may simply have internalized prohibitions against violence or other criminal activity. Second, they may have failed to achieve status (or other forms of success) in a criminal or conflict gang. One possibility for this status failure is gangs are attributed different levels of "rep," or reputation, and these juveniles may have been previous members of gangs with little status. Not all "double failures" become drug users, but they are more susceptible than others. The interaction and learning involved in the retreatist subculture is derived from older drug users teaching new drug users how to find drug sources and how to use drugs.

In sum, differential opportunity theory extends the anomie theory of Merton and adds the community-based observations of the Chicago School. Additionally, it suggests that subcultural patterns determine the form of delinquent behavior. For that matter, Cloward and Ohlin seem to suggest the real problem of understanding deviance lies in explaining how different reactions (adaptations) to strain occur and defining the context in which those reactions appear (Cullen, 1984, pp. 39–49; 1988). Differential opportunity theory, then, assumes strain in the lower class as a given and attempts to explain the existence of various forms of delinquency as adaptations to strain, based on the stability of the community and the availability of adult role models. Because of this, the theory's major focus is on the learning mechanisms available to produce the ongoing forms of delinquent subculture.

Classification of the Theory

Differential opportunity theory is usually termed a "strain theory." But as with Cohen's theory, it has elements of both structure and process. In combining the strain of anomie theory and the process of the Chicago School and differential association theory (Cloward & Ohlin, 1960, p. x), differential opportunity theory leans more toward structure. Yet, even while emphasizing the effect of one's place in the social structure, it attempts to explain the process by which the content of criminal lifestyles is transmitted. In a similar vein, this one is a *bridging theory* that leans slightly toward the macrotheoretical level. Finally, the theory is both *positivistic* and *consensus oriented.* It attempts to explain how behavior is developed and transmitted, and it assumes, with Merton, a primary emphasis on reaching cultural goals.

Major Points of the Theory

1. Members of society share a common set of values that emphasize the desirability of certain life goals, especially that of success.
2. There are standard avenues—legitimate and illegitimate—for achieving these goals.
3. These two general avenues (opportunity structures) are not equally available to all groups and classes of society.
4. Members of the middle and upper classes have primary access to the legitimate opportunity structure (business, politics), while members of the lower class have primary access to the illegitimate opportunity structure (organized crime).
5. In any urban, lower-class area, the degree of integration of these two opportunity structures determines the social organization of the community. The less the integration, the more the community is disorganized.
6. Communities with well-organized and integrated illegal opportunity structures provide learning environments for organized criminal behavior. In such communities, the male delinquent subculture takes on either of two ideal forms that are dependent on the degree of access to the illegitimate structure:
   a. When an opportunity to participate successfully in the illegitimate structure is available to young males, the subcultural gang type most commonly found will be a criminal gang. This form of gang serves as a training ground for the form of illegitimate activity found in the community.
   b. When opportunities for joining the illegitimate structure are as limited as are those for joining the legitimate structure, the most common form of subcultural gang will be a retreatist gang. Here the gang members are basically withdrawn from the community (they are "double failures"), and they solve their problem of access to drugs.

7. Disorganized communities exert weak social controls and create disorganized gang subcultures. When young males are deprived of both legitimate and criminal opportunities, the common form of gang subculture will be a conflict gang. Such gangs engage in violence and destructive acts against both opportunity structures.

OTHER SUBCULTURE THEORIES

Miller's Lower-class Focal Concerns

After Cohen's work in 1955, Walter B. Miller (1958) examined lower-class areas in Boston and came to different conclusions.[4] As an anthropologist, Miller was familiar with ethnography, a research technique based on the direct observation of social groups in their natural settings. Using this approach, he concluded that middle-class values were less important to gang delinquency than Cohen and others thought. Thus, Miller's theoretical perspective stressed differences in social-class lifestyles to a greater degree than did the consensus models of Cohen and of Cloward and Ohlin.

Miller saw a society composed of different social groups or classes, each with a subculture resembling those of other groups in some respects and differing in others. Miller used the concept of focal concern rather than value to describe the things important to subcultures. Focal concerns are features or aspects of a subculture that require constant attention and care, as, for example, motherhood in the female subculture. Behavior related to focal concerns, such as the "trouble" concern in lower-class subculture, can be either valued or disvalued, depending on the situation and the people involved.

Walter Benson Miller (1920–2004)

Walter Miller was born in 1920 in Philadelphia, Pennsylvania. He went to the University of Chicago, ultimately receiving an M.A. in anthropology (Phi Beta Kappa) in 1950. His early fieldwork was a project studying the Fox Indians. The experience gave Miller a perspective on the cultural ways of smaller groups in larger societies that he used the rest of his life. He completed his Ph.D. in anthropology in 1954 at Harvard. His academic training in anthropology gave him a view of gangs, subcultures, and lower-class life that few others in the criminological field could attain.

Miller helped to start up the Roxbury Gang Delinquency Research Project for the National Institute of Mental Health in 1955 and served as its director from 1957 to 1964. Using ethnographic traditions he attempted to characterize the richness and complexities of the lifestyles of lower-class youth, particularly in the Boston communities where he worked. From 1974 to 1980, Miller directed the National Youth Gang Survey, which was sponsored by the Justice Department and Harvard University. In 1976, Miller conducted a study of the status of gangs in 12 major cities in the United States funded by the Law Enforcement Assistance Administration. His last major report, *The Growth of Youth Gang Problems in the United States: 1970–98,* was a comprehensive chronicle of 30 years of researching the American gang.

Prior to retirement, Miller was an active cyclist and in-line skater. His love of playing jazz and bluegrass, which had helped him connect with youth on the street, evolved in retirement into performing with a small jazz group around the New England area. He died in 2004 at the age of 84.

---

[4] Walter Miller reviewed and approved this summary for substantive accuracy.

The lower class, as an integral part of the larger society, shares many characteristics and concerns with other social classes. At the same time, the lower class also has distinctive features that differ significantly from those of the middle and upper classes. The legal system of the United States and the norms it incorporates conform more closely to the official standards of middle- and upper-class people than to those of lower-class people. As a result, certain common behaviors, viewed as entirely appropriate by some lower-class subcultures, routinely violate official moral or legal codes.

In common with other class subcultures, lower-class subcultures provide models for appropriate male and female behavior. They illustrate and teach those traits, skills, and characteristics needed for successful social and occupational performance in lower-class life. That is, they contribute necessary values and behaviors for a lifestyle in which low-skilled labor is common. Criminal behavior in lower-class communities, as in other communities, approximates the general characteristics of noncriminal behavior. For instance, legitimate financial and accounting skills that play a vital role in middle-class life equip people to engage in crimes such as embezzlement. Similarly, characteristics such as risk taking, physical courage, and the machismo ethic are not only important for many lower-class occupational roles but also prepare people to engage in violent crimes such as robbery and assault.

Miller tried to characterize the richness and complexity of lower-class subcultures in a shorthand fashion. He did this by describing a set of focal concerns that underlie the reasons and motivations for common forms of lower-class behavior. Most lower-class crime and delinquency result primarily from efforts to conform to lower-class subcultural standards rather than a deliberate flouting of middle-class standards (Cohen's perspective). Miller described six focal concerns characterizing the subcultures of low-skilled laboring populations in the United States: trouble, toughness, smartness, excitement, fate, and autonomy. Trouble represents a commitment to law-violating behavior or "being a problem" to other people. Toughness is "machismo" and being fearless, brave, and daring. Characteristics of smartness include being cunning, living by one's wits, and deceiving and "conning" others. Excitement means living for thrills, doing dangerous things, and taking risks. Fortune and luck are part of the focal concern of fate. Finally, autonomy signifies independence—not having to rely on others as well as rejecting authority.

These concerns play a role in the commission of activities that may be legal or illegal, depending on the circumstances. In lower-class subcultures, incentives for engaging in crime are generally stronger, and incentives for avoiding crime are weaker than in the other classes. However, while illegal forms of behavior are generally more common among lower-class youths than among youths in higher social classes, only a very small portion of behavior by lower-class youths is illegal.

In many lower-class households, Miller observes, children are raised by single mothers who often reside with other female family members of child bearing age. Miller used the term "serial monogamy" to indicate the mother's sequence of short-term relationships with men that does not allow the youth to develop significant relationships with a male acting in a father role. The absence of fathers creates a special problem for male children trying to learn appropriate adult male behavior. Youth gangs serve as one important device for accommodating this problem. Gangs provide a learning environment intensely focused on male qualities and abilities admired in lower-class communities: toughness, street-smartness, fighting ability, defeating rival groups by force and craft, earning respect by courage, and risk taking. Criminal activity often represents a highly effective means of achieving these goals. Gang membership also provides valuable psychological benefits, such as a sense of belonging and an opportunity to gain prestige and respect, which are difficult for lower-class youths to achieve in the context of family or school.

From Miller's viewpoint, then, the behavior of lower-class gang members is consistent with the special set of concerns, valued qualities, and life goals characteristic of many American lower-class communities. Miller (1958, p. 19) summarizes this by saying "the dominant component of the motivation of 'delinquent' behavior engaged in by members of lower class [street] corner groups involves a positive effort to achieve states, conditions, or qualities valued with the actor's most significant cultural milieu." Illegal practices, such as gang fighting and robbery, customarily undertaken by male gang members result in part from efforts to achieve qualities and conditions seen as appropriate adult male behavior in their own communities. However often such behavior violates the law, it is seldom seen as abnormal within this subcultural context.

Major Points of the Theory

1. Society is composed of different social classes whose lifestyles or subcultures have both common and differing features.
2. The subcultures of the lower, middle, and upper classes differ in significant respects from one another.
3. Because the dominant culture is the middle class, the existence of different values often brings the lower class into conflict with the dominant culture.
4. Lower-class values serve to create young male behaviors that are delinquent by middle-class standards but that are normal and useful in lower-class life.
5. Lower-class subcultures place special emphasis on a set of issues or "focal concerns" that influence customary behavior. These include trouble, toughness, smartness, excitement, fate, and autonomy.
6. Many lower-class males are raised in fatherless households. Learning behavior and attitudes appropriate to adult male roles thus poses special problems.
7. Youth gangs provide a context for learning important elements of adult male roles for many lower-class youth. Gangs also provide psychological benefits such as a sense of belonging, opportunities for gaining prestige, and enhanced self-esteem.
8. Gang crime that seriously victimizes the larger community is in part a by-product of efforts by lower-class youth to attain goals valued within their subcultural milieu.

Wolfgang and Ferracuti's Subculture of Violence

The last of the major subcultural theories was developed in 1967, by Marvin Wolfgang and Franco Ferracuti. Their work was substantively different from the other subculture theories, perhaps because it was developed almost a decade after delinquent-subculture theories and criminology had developed new concerns. Derived from Wolfgang's earlier study of homicide (1958), their subculture theory attempted to integrate a wide range of disciplinary approaches to understanding deviant behavior. As they expressly state, the idea of a subculture of violence was derived from a combination of theories (1967, p. 314). From the sociological perspective, they included culture conflict, differential association, and theories on culture, social, and personality systems. From psychology, they chose theories on learning, conditioning, developmental socialization, and differential identification. Finally, they also incorporated findings from research on criminal homicide and other assaultive crimes.

Their theory may be summarized as follows: Though members of a subculture hold values different from those of the central society, it is important to realize they are not totally different from or in total conflict with the greater society of which they are a part. Those in the subculture of violence learn a willingness to resort to violence and share a favorable attitude toward the use of violence. This attitude, though possible to hold at any age, is most common in groups ranging from late adolescence to middle age. Persons who commit violent crimes but are not identified by any link to a subculture are distinctly more pathological and display more guilt and anxiety about their behavior than do members of the subculture.

Studies of skinhead groups and militias (Hamm, 1993, 1997, 2001, 2007) detail many of the characteristics of a subculture of violence. Drug cartels, mercenaries, and terrorists all have informal codes and expectations about how problems are settled and what measures are acceptable for accomplishing group goals. Much of the research into these subcultures involves detailed interviews where subjects confirm their commitment to the values and attitudes of defending honor and eliminating potential enemies, often through the use of the many weapons they accumulate.

Summary

Along with anomie theory, subculture theories dominated criminology during the 1950s and the early 1960s. Interestingly, the primary authors Cohen, and Cloward and Ohlin had training in both the Chicago School tradition and Merton's anomie approach. Thus, the main approach was that of reconciling these two schools.

Even though these theorists focused on gang delinquency, the concept of subculture was the real problem to be explained. For Cohen, it was the question of how a subculture could develop; for Cloward and Ohlin it was the attempt to explain the form a subculture might take. In each case, they assumed Merton was correct, certain groups of people were disadvantaged in the great chase for success, and the problem was to explain resulting deviant behavior. Miller saw the same overall subculture picture as the other theorists but explained the delinquent subculture as a culture by itself, with its own lifestyles, values, and concerns. For Miller, there was no need to use strain to explain the creation of a set of values in opposition to the conventional ones. Wolfgang and Ferracuti were less interested in explaining the existence of subcultures than in outlining what those subcultures provide to their members. They assumed subcultures provide definitions for behavior that, once learned, result in their members' greater willingness to use violence.

Taken together, subculture theories provide explanations of how groups of individuals develop similar values and rationales for behavior. They differ in explaining the way in which the subcultures develop, but they all use the existence of subcultures to explain different forms of delinquency or crime. Moreover, they all locate the process of becoming delinquent or criminal in the subcultural environment.

Epilogue: Current Directions and Policy Implications

CURRENT DIRECTIONS

Except for the subculture of violence perspective, subculture theories are, at heart, based on a relationship between the lower class and delinquency or crime. Criticisms of the class–delinquency–crime connection emerged when self-report studies became popular in the early 1960s (these studies asked juveniles to "self-report" their own delinquent acts). Many of the studies found only weak class–delinquency relationships, but they also focused on less serious types of delinquency. Later, Charles Tittle, Wayne Villemez, and Douglas Smith (1978) reviewed the research literature and suggested that the class–crime relationship was a myth. Others, such as John Braithwaite (1981), disagreed, arguing that there was a "myth of classlessness." Of these criticisms, the self-report studies had the most impact because their popularity closely followed the dominant subcultural theories. In all probability, the issue of the class–delinquency relationship is not yet settled. But, as Steve Brown and David Brownfield have noted, not only are research measures of class and crime poorly constructed, but the critics fail to take into consideration that subculture theories do not necessarily predict high crime rates for the entire lower class. A part of the lower class is known as the "underclass." The underclass has even fewer opportunities and may be more involved in crime than the rest of the lower class. This group constitutes the real test of subculture theories.

Other modifications to subcultural theories have been presented. Gresham Sykes and David Matza (1957) critiqued Cohen's conception of lower-class gang values as the opposite of middle-class values. They argued that lower-class juveniles do not need opposite values to commit delinquent acts. All that is necessary is a series of rationalizations or "neutralizations" to overcome conventional values (see Chapter 11 on social control theory for more on the techniques of neutralization). Matza and Sykes (1961) also proposed that other respectable values, called "subterranean values," are present in the larger culture. It is not necessary one pursues the hard-working, always aspiring, set of dominant values. Subterranean values emphasize the worth of seeking fun or tolerating certain kinds of conflict or violence. Thus, juveniles at all class levels may share the alleged anti-middle-class values of Cohen's lower-class gang delinquents. Cohen, with James Short (1958), responded that the description of delinquency presented in *Delinquent Boys* was a "parent" delinquent subculture. By this they referred to a more extensive form of subculture, one with a general set of values and with behaviors that were not specialized. Other subcultures, specializing in various types of behaviors, were formed from this parent subculture. Short and his colleagues later demonstrated there was indeed evidence to suggest that a generic form of parent subculture existed and that more specialized forms of gangs and delinquent behaviors developed from it.

Where evidence for techniques of neutralization is concerned, the research results have been mixed. Shadd Maruna and Heith Copes (2005), in reviewing 50 years of research on techniques of neutralization, argued that the theory has been poorly tested and needed more explication. Further, they felt that it would be better used as an explanation of persistence of and desistance from crime rather than an explanation of initial deviance. In addition, they note obvious connections with cognitive psychology theories that have not been explored.

Other criminologists, such as Lewis Yablonsky (1959, 1962), have suggested that theories need to account for less cohesive groups and more poorly organized behavior than subcultural theories posit. Yablonsky proposed that, other than a central leader, other members might not be so strongly attached to the gang. He called these loosely formed gangs "near groups." He also theorized the leader was a psychotic type who instigated the others to engage in delinquent behavior.

The most widely known attempt to incorporate subculture concepts after the 1960s is referred to as the "Southernness hypothesis" (Gastil, 1971; Hackney, 1969). An extension of the subculture of violence thesis, the Southernness hypothesis reflects an effort to understand the distribution of homicide rates. The theory, which attempts to explain why the southern region of the United States has a higher homicide rate than other regions, argues that the region shares a subculture in which males are more ready to use violence to settle arguments. In short, the theory speculates as a part of their cultural background, those who live in the southern United States learn a willingness and readiness to use violence. Research on the issue has yet to come to a definitive conclusion, and some critics argue that no such subculture exists.

Another subcultural explanation for crime has been proposed by Claude Fischer (1975). Fischer's theory holds that the size of a place (the number of people living there) has a direct effect on participation in deviant behavior. The larger the place, the more deviant behavior is expected to occur. He links size with the variety, number, and intensity of subcultures and the presence of subcultures with deviant behavior. In one sense, Fischer's theory is related to the Chicago School's emphasis on cities and their attendant evils. However, he extends urbanness theory by suggesting that the size of the city operates through an increasing variety of subcultures to generate deviance.

POLICY IMPLICATIONS

Subculture theories proved to have important policy implications because they offered hope to a new generation of liberal-thinking people. The Kennedy and Johnson presidential administrations took to heart the subcultural theory promise of restructuring society and attempted to implement the major concepts of opportunity theory. They spent millions of dollars in the Great Society and War on Poverty efforts, most notably in such programs as the Peace Corps, the Job Corps, the Comprehensive Employee Training Act (CETA), and Project Head Start. Attorney General Robert Kennedy took the differential opportunity thesis and "adopted it as the blueprint for the federal response to crime during his brother's administration" (Brown, Esbensen, & Geis, 1991, p. 320). Lloyd Ohlin even served in a post at the Department of Health, Education, and Welfare with the job of redesigning federal delinquency prevention efforts.

The most famous of the 1960s subcultural projects was the Mobilization for Youth (MFY) Project in New York City, under the directorship of Richard Cloward. Designed to increase educational and job opportunities for youths in deprived communities, MFY had a $12 million budget. Part-time jobs and school books were provided, but providing better life opportunities was more difficult to accomplish. Recognizing this, MFY borrowed some of the ideas of the old Chicago Area Project and assisted in organizing the communities involved in the program. The main goal was to spur political action on behalf of the communities. MFY served as the central point for organizing strikes and protests, and for wielding the community's political power. Even today the political remnants of MFY exist in New York City, much to the chagrin of the city's political leaders. Unfortunately, however, even a project on the scope of MFY, with its large budget, was not enough to implement the theoretical concepts successfully. Restructuring society, even in small areas, proved to be too great a task. Critiques of the project are available, but there is no consensus on the extent of its success (Moynihan, 1969; Pfohl, 1985).

Several delinquency projects have also been grounded in the concepts of subculture theories. Two famous ones, the Silverlake and Provo experiments (Empey & Erickson, 1972; Empey & Lubeck, 1971), were based on the idea that groups of delinquents, under the guidance of an adult counselor, can assist each other to become more conventional. The usual term is "guided group interaction." These delinquency treatment projects attempt to change delinquents' subculture, or milieu, to make it more conducive to conventional definitions of behavior. These and other similar projects used peer pressure, staff guidance, and group meetings to facilitate nondelinquent values and goals.

School-based projects to alleviate the effects of lower-class subcultural environments are common. Many such programs have been created since the 1960s to help children do better and stay in school. Project Head Start is the most widely known of these programs. It was designed to reduce the difficulties encountered by underprivileged children entering school by offering them some of the same advantages given to middle-class children in private kindergartens and preschools. According to the subcultural thesis, a better-prepared child will do better in school, feel less deprivation, and be more likely to accept conventional values.

Today, there is some interest in attempting to identify and intervene with those who might be at risk to join a violence-prone subculture. Education programs attempt to cultivate antiviolence attitudes and values, build problem resolution skills in young children, and encourage communities to participate in gun "buy-back" programs to reduce the amount of weapons on the street. The labeling of extremist groups who favor violence to accomplish their political goals as terrorists, such as abortion clinic bombers, has allowed for more law enforcement resources being allocated to arresting these subcultural members.

Questions and Weblinks

Critical Thinking Questions

1. Are there subcultures of violence in our society today? Which ones? And what specific values do they hold that support the use of violence?
2. Critics of subculture theory argued that the work of this period singled out low-income families to blame for gangs. Do you think this criticism is valid? Why or why not?
3. Should crime prevention strategies specifically focus on gangs? Why or why not?

Practice Essay Questions

1. Discuss the role of illegitimate opportunities in a community including some of the advantages as well as disadvantages.
2. What were the basic characteristics of gangs according to the theorists of this time period? Do you think these features are similar to or different from gangs today, in what ways?
3. What would Cohen expect schools to do to offset the attractiveness of gangs and gang membership?

Related Websites

https://www.ncjrs.gov/pdffiles1/ojjdp/233581.pdf
http://www.nationalgangcenter.gov/

http://www.preventinghate.org
http://www.nw.org/network/index.asp

Bibliography

Bordua, D. J. (1960). *Sociological theories and their implications for juvenile delinquency: No. 2. Facts and facets.* Washington, DC: U.S. Government Printing Office.

Bordua, D. J. (1961). Delinquent subcultures: Sociological interpretations of gang delinquency. *Annals of the American Academy of Political and Social Science, 338,* 119–136.

Bordua, D. J. (1962). Some comments on theories of group delinquency. *Sociological Inquiry, 32,* 245–260.

Braithwaite, J. (1981). The myth of social class criminality reconsidered. *American Sociological Review, 46,* 37–57.

Brown, S. E., Esbensen, F.-A., & Geis, G. (1991). *Criminology: Explaining crime and its context.* Cincinnati, OH: Anderson.

Cloward, R. A. (1959). Illegitimate means, anomie, and deviant behavior. *American Sociological Review, 24,* 164–176.

Cloward, R. A., & Ohlin, L. E. (1960). *Delinquency and opportunity: A theory of delinquent gangs.* New York: Free Press.

Cohen, A. K. (1955). *Delinquent boys: The culture of the gang.* New York: Free Press.

Cohen, A. K., & Short, Jr., J. F. (1958). Research on delinquent subcultures. *Journal of Social Issues, 14,* 20–37.

Cullen, F. T. (1984). *Rethinking crime and deviance theory: The emergence of a structuring tradition.* Totowa, NJ: Rowman and Allanheld.

Cullen, F. T. (1988). Were Cloward and Ohlin strain theorists? *Journal of Research in Crime and Delinquency, 25,* 214–241.

Empey, L. T., & Erickson, M. L. (1972). *The Provo experiment: Evaluating community control of delinquency.* Lexington, MA: Lexington.

Empey, L. T., & Lubeck, S. G. (1971). *Explaining delinquency: Construction, test, and reformation of a sociological theory.* Lexington, MA: Heath Lexington Books.

Fischer, C. S. (1975). Toward a subcultural theory of urbanism. *American Journal of Sociology, 80,* 1309–1341.

Gastil, R. D. (1971). Homicide and a regional culture of violence. *American Sociological Review, 36,* 412–417.

Hackney, S. (1969). Southern violence. *American Historical Review, 74,* 906–925.

Hamm, M. S. (1993). *American skinheads: The criminology and control of hate crime.* Westport, CT: Praeger.

Hamm, M. S. (1997). *Apocalypse in Oklahoma: Waco and ruby ridge revenged.* Boston: Northeastern University Press.

Hamm, M. S. (2001). *In bad company: America's terrorist underground.* New York: New York University Press.

Hamm, M. S. (2007). *Terrorism as crime: From Oklahoma City to Al-Qaeda and beyond.* New York: New York University Press.

Kitsuse, J. I., & Dietrick, D. C. (1959). Delinquent boys: A critique. *American Sociological Review, 24,* 208–215.

Kobrin, S. (1951). The conflict of values in delinquency areas. *American Sociological Review, 16,* 653–661.

Laub, J. H. (1983a). Interview with Albert K. Cohen. In J. Laub, *Criminology in the making: An oral history* (pp. 182–203). Boston: Northeastern University Press.

Laub, J. H. (1983b). Interview with Solomon Kobrin. In J. Laub, *Criminology in the making: An oral history* (pp. 87–105). Boston: Northeastern University Press.

Laub, J. H. (1983c). Interview with Lloyd E. Ohlin. In J. Laub, *Criminology in the making: An oral History* (pp. 204–224). Boston: Northeastern University Press.

Lilly, J. R., Cullen, F. T., & Ball, R. A. (1989). *Criminological theory: Context and consequences.* Newbury Park, CA: Sage.

Maruna, S., & Copes, H. (2005). What have we learned from five decades of neutralization research? *Crime and Justice: A Review of Research, 32,* 221–320.

Matza, D., & Sykes, G. M. (1961). Juvenile delinquency and subterranean values. *American Sociological Review, 26,* 712–719.

Miller, W. B. (1958). Lower-class culture as a generating milieu of gang delinquency. *Journal of Social Issues, 14* (3), 5–19.

Moynihan, D. P. (1969). *Maximum feasible misunderstanding: Community action in the war on poverty.* New York: Free Press.

Murray, C. (1984). *Losing ground: American social policy, 1950–1980.* New York: Basic Books.

Pfohl, S. J. (1985). *Images of deviance and social control: A sociological history.* New York: McGraw-Hill.

Sykes, G. M., & Matza, D. (1957). Techniques of neutralization: A theory of delinquency. *American Sociological Review, 22,* 664–670.

Tittle, C. R., Villemez, W. J., & Smith, D. A. (1978). The myth of social class and criminality: An empirical assessment of the empirical evidence. *American Sociological Review, 43,* 643–656.

Wolfgang, M. E., & Ferracuti, F. (1967). *The subculture of violence: Towards an integrate theory in criminology.* London: Tavistock.

Yablonsky, L. (1959). The delinquent gang as near group. *Social Problems, 7,* 108–117.

Yablonsky, L. (1962). *The violent gang.* New York: Macmillan.

Research Bibliography

General Subculture (from 2000)

Barnes, J. C., Beaver, K. M., & Miller, J. (2010). Estimating the effect of gang membership on nonviolent and violent delinquency: A counterfactual analysis. *Aggressive Behavior, 36,* 437–451.

Bernburg, J. G., & Thorlindsson, T. T. (1999). Adolescent violence, social control, and the subculture of delinquency: Factors related to violent behavior and nonviolent delinquency. *Youth & Society, 30,* 445–460.

Cobbina, J. E., Like-Haislip, T. Z., & Miller, J. (2010). Gang fights versus cat fights: Urban young men's gendered narratives of violence. *Deviant Behavior, 31,* 596–624.

Finkenauer, J. O. (1992). Juvenile delinquency and youth subcultures in the former Soviet Union. *International Journal of Comparative and Applied Criminal Justice, 16*(1–2), 247–261.

Hagan, J., Boehnke, K., & Merkens, H. (2004). Gender differences in capitalization processes and the delinquency of siblings in Toronto and Berlin. *British Journal of Criminology, 44,* 659–676.

Jianhong, L. (2004). Subcultural values, crime, and negative social capital for Chinese offenders. *International Criminal Justice Review, 14,* 49–68.

Lane, J., & Meeker, J. W. (2000). Subcultural diversity and the fear of crime and gangs. *Crime & Delinquency, 46,* 497–521.

Lee, D. R., & Cohen, J. W. (2008). Examining strain in a school context. *Youth Violence & Juvenile Justice, 6,* 115–135.

Mackenzie, S. (2006). Psychosocial balance sheets: Illicit purchase decisions in the antiquities market. *Current Issues in Criminal Justice, 18,* 221–240.

Malakondaiah, M. M., & Murty, K. (2007). A study of urban adolescent street gangs in Guntur City. *Indian Journal of Criminology, 35–36*(1/2), 40–49.

Malsch, M., de Keijser, J. W., & Debets, S. C. (2011). Are stalkers recidivists? Repeated offending by convicted stalkers. *Violence & Victims, 26,* 3–15.

Ozer, M., & Engel, R. S. (2012). Revisiting the use of propensity score matching to understand the relationship between gang membership and violent victimization: A cautionary note. *Justice Quarterly*, *29*, 105–124.

Staff, J., & Kreager, D. A. (2008). Too cool for school? Violence, peer status and high school dropout. *Social Forces*, *87*, 445–471.

Zdun, S. (2007). Dynamic strategies to legitimize deviant behaviour of street culture youth. *Internet Journal of Criminology*, 1–20.

Subculture of Violence (from 2000)

Cohn, E. G., Rotton, J., Peterson, A. G., & Tarr, D. B. (2004). Temperature, city size, and the Southern subculture of violence: Support for social escape/avoidance (SEA) theory. *Journal of Applied Social Psychology*, *34*, 1652–1674.

D'Antonio-Del Rio, J. M., Doucet, J. M., & Chauvin, C. D. (2010). Violent and vindictive women: A re-analysis of the Southern subculture of violence. *Sociological Spectrum*, *30*, 484–503.

Hannon, L. (2004). Race, victim precipitated homicide, and the subculture of violence thesis. *Social Science Journal*, *41*, 115–121.

McGloin, J., Schreck, C. J., Stewart, E. A., & Ousey, G. C. (2011). Predicting the violent offender: The discriminant validity of the subculture of violence. *Criminology*, *49*, 767–794.

Labeling Theory

LEARNING OBJECTIVES

Objective 8.1: Explain what is meant by retrospective interpretation.

Objective 8.2: Describe labeling as both a conflict and a process theory.

Objective 8.3: Define the concept of master status and what it means for rehabilitation.

Objective 8.4: Distinguish between Lemert's view of primary and secondary deviance.

Objective 8.5: Discuss the link between societal reaction and labeling.

INTRODUCTION

In the early 1960s, a different approach to criminological theory was taken. Although it was an offshoot of older theories, labeling theory asked questions about crime and criminals from a new perspective, challenging previous definitions of deviance. Those associated with labeling argued earlier theories had placed too great a reliance on the individual deviant and neglected the variety of ways people could *react* to deviance. This message was important enough that the position became known as the *societal reaction school.*

By de-emphasizing the criminal, labeling came close to the old Classical School in its concern for the action of official agencies, as well as the making and application of law. The theory also spurred interest in the way these agencies operate, so for a while criminology was intensely interested in investigating the criminal justice process. Perhaps equally important, labeling sensitized criminology to the relativity of its subject matter and the middle-class values it had used to study criminals.

Labeling suggested criminologists had overemphasized the original deviant act as well as the character of the deviant. Noting definitions of crime change from time to time and from place to place, labeling theorists questioned the pervasive notion that because crime is bad, those who commit crime must also be bad and a criminal act is naturally bad. The same examples we gave for culture conflict apply to labeling. If something is not a crime in one country, but one commits that act in a second country in which that act is a crime, has the individual suddenly become "bad," or is a different criminal law the "cause" of the crime?

Some criminologists have debated the content of labeling theory, insisting it is not a theory but instead a sensitizing perspective. This point has considerable merit, especially since those most important in the development of the position do not refer to themselves as labeling theorists; in fact, there would appear to be no identifiable labeling theorists. Further, since it is an offshoot of symbolic interactionism, labeling may not be new. In truth, though, labeling has as much right to be called a theory as do most of the other approaches discussed in this book. Labeling makes logical causal statements and generates propositions for testing (see Wellford, 1975), which is perhaps more than some other criminological theories can claim. Whether it is a theory or perspective is not critical, because labeling has had a profound impact on criminology and on the study of deviance in general.

Finally, labeling has either one major part or two, depending on the differing perspectives of various scholars. Its original name was the "societal reaction school," and one camp argues that labeling is about the way in which people react to and label others. In this view, the focus is on the reactors, not the person labeled. The second camp argues that the effect of the label on the person labeled is also part of labeling theory. Thus, this perspective asks not only about the reactors but also about how the label affects the individual. Because the societal reaction school originally saw their purpose as a critique of existing criminological overemphasis on "the criminal" and the addition of an ignored side of the crime/criminal equation, the first camp would appear to be more historically correct.

THE HERITAGE OF THE THEORY

The Social Heritage

At the end of the 1950s, society was becoming conscious of racial inequality, segregation, and civil rights. The issue of underprivileged members of society became a real one. Civil rights protests and demonstrations were commonplace. African Americans protested their treatment in restaurants, theaters, buses, and college admission. Education itself became the center of much of the civil rights movement. While equality did not come quickly, white society grew more conscious of its treatment of minority groups. The umbrella of egalitarianism spread out over other special populations as women, the mentally ill, and the disabled became aware of the effects of a stigmatized, and thus marginalized, existence.

Social changes of this magnitude were bound to influence social thinkers. Educators began examining ways to create classless schools. The Supreme Court handed down several important civil rights decisions. New programs were instituted in the juvenile justice system with an avowed purpose of diverting juveniles before they were stigmatized with the label "delinquent." In short, the time was ripe for sociologists and criminologists to extend their theorizing about the effects of social class and minority status on those who came into contact with the criminal justice system.

The popularity of labeling theory, once it had been proposed, was enhanced by the social atmosphere promoted by the Kennedy and Johnson administrations: the Great Society where all would be equal. Social scientists embraced plans to make quality education more equally available to all, to increase opportunities, and to overcome the previous stigma associated with being a member of a minority group. Even as the country moved through the decade of the 1960s and became more critical of the prospect of government bringing equality to society, labeling seemed to be a natural answer to the question of why certain people were more frequently and negatively stereotyped. Indeed, with mistrust of government growing during the late 1960s and early 1970s, labeling was one way to critique and explain the abuses of power.

The Intellectual Heritage

The intellectual heritage of labeling reflected the Chicago School's symbolic interactionism. The teaching and writing of both George Herbert Mead and W. I. Thomas at the University of Chicago had influenced several creative people. Their students, some of whom returned to teach at Chicago, continued to spread the symbolic interactionist approach. A group of graduate students at Chicago during the late 1940s and early 1950s applied the approach to several areas of deviance. One of these students, Howard S. Becker, was to become the person most strongly identified with labeling.

In addition to the teachers of the Chicago School, their students and writings introduced others to the concept of symbolic interactionism. One of the first contributors to labeling, Edwin Lemert, took a symbolic interactionist approach and applied it to social pathologies, including stuttering among West Coast Indians. Lemert taught this approach to his students, some of whom would become important advocates of the new societal reaction school.

Bob Lilly, Frank Cullen, and Richard Ball (1989) suggest Robert Merton's (1968) concept of the "self-fulfilling prophecy" was also an important ingredient in the popularity of labeling. It was believed that many delinquents who may have started out as simply troubled youth felt that they might as well commit the offenses that they were going to be accused of. Living up to one's reputation becomes part of the adaptation of the teen who feels that he or she has few chances to become anything more. And, just by its presence, a false label can easily become the truth for those ready to believe it. As an example of this phenomenon, try to remember if you have ever been accused of something you didn't do. That you had not done anything didn't matter; what mattered was someone else reacted as if you had. Obviously, then, deviance is "in the eye of the beholder."

The late 1950s also precipitated a methodological innovation in the measurement of deviance with the rise of self-report studies (questionnaires and interviews with juveniles who reported on their own delinquent behavior). Although earlier researchers had asked young people about their delinquent acts, it was the systematic work of James Short and F. Ivan Nye (1958) that began the comparison of admitted delinquent activity with official statistics. Their work suggested that official statistics such as the *Uniform Crime Reports* and juvenile court records did not accurately portray those who commit delinquent acts. The differences in findings between self-report studies and official statistics suggested the portrait of an "official" delinquent might be, in part, a result of the kind of person who came to the attention of the authorities. This implied reaction by authorities rather than actual deviance might explain the disproportionate number of lower-class youths in the various delinquency statistics. The subsequent attempts to replicate the Short and Nye study also served to keep the topic current.

THE THEORETICAL PERSPECTIVE

Early Labeling Theory Literature

Many criminologists trace labeling theory to Frank Tannenbaum's 1938 book *Crime and the Community.* The "dramatization of evil," as Tannenbaum called it, suggested that deviant behavior was not so much a product of the deviant's lack of adjustment to society as it was the fact he or she

Howard Saul Becker (1928–)

Howard Becker was born in Chicago and educated in sociology at the University of Chicago (A.B., 1946; M.A., 1949; Ph.D., 1951), where he studied with Everett C. Hughes among others. He conducted research for the Chicago Area Project and did postdoctoral studies at the University of Illinois. He also pursued coursework in photography at the San Francisco Art Institute and played jazz piano most of his life. Becker taught sociology at the University of Chicago, Stanford University, Northwestern University, and the University of Washington, where he also taught in the music department. He was also the Project Director for Community Studies, Inc., in Kansas City from 1955 to 1962. He was editor of the journal *Social Problems* (1961–1964) and served as President of the Society for the Study of Social Problems (1965–1966). Although Becker's work has been extremely useful in the development of labeling approaches to crime, he was quick to acknowledge that he was not a criminologist. Becker viewed himself as an artist, musician, and a sociologist. He is retired and lives both in San Francisco and abroad.

had adjusted to a special group. Thus, criminal behavior is a product of "…the conflict between a group and the community at large" (1938, p. 8), where there are two opposing definitions of appropriate behavior. Tannenbaum wrote a "tag" becomes attached when a child is caught in delinquent activity. The tag identifies the child as a delinquent, may change the child's self-image, and causes people to react to the tag, not the child. Thus, his argument was that the process of tagging criminals or delinquents actually helps create delinquency and criminality (1938, pp. 19–20). Tannenbaum specifically outlined labeling as the process of defining, identifying, and segregating someone and then making them conscious and self-conscious of their faults and shortcomings.

Definition of Crime

Labeling theory required a different orientation to deviance than that of previous theories. Noting other definitions depend on statistical, pathological, or relativistic views of deviance, Becker pointed out that none of them does justice to the reality of deviance (1963, pp. 3–18). He saw that deviance can often be in the eye of the beholder because members of various groups have different conceptions of what is right and proper in certain situations.

Further, there must be a reaction to the act. That is, deviance must be discovered by some group that does not share a belief in the appropriateness of the behavior, and it must subsequently be called deviance. To the extent law reflects the values of that group, the behavior is labeled crime and the perpetrator a criminal. For advocates of labeling theory, this distinction is important because it emphasizes that those who engage in criminal behavior are not synonymous with those who are labeled criminal. Thus, the question of "Why do people become criminal?" becomes "How do people get reacted to as being deviant?" (Becker, in Debro, 1970, p. 167).

The resettlement of Hurricane Katrina evacuees in the Houston area is a good example of differential group definitions and reaction. The police, knowing that many offenders had been released during the crisis in New Orleans and that they as well as other ex-offenders were now in their area, took aggressive steps to exercise and maintain control over the population. As the needy and homeless stayed on in the area, tensions grew and public resentment allowed the group to be defined as a problem. In short time, newspapers and other media outlets went out of their way to cover more stories about the evacuees, and headlines identified all crime victims and perpetrators who were "Katrina-related," which became a euphemism for the city's "crime problem."

Studying the Reactors

Becker's interest in organizations and careers was in large part responsible for his defining deviance from outside the actor (those who are reacted to). The point he made was that, while sociologists ordinarily begin their study of other occupations by insisting the entire organization be examined, the study of crime focused only on the criminal. The remainder of the "crime organization" (the social audience and the criminal justice system) was ignored in favor of an isolated criminal. Becker noted he was merely following the occupational sociology approach: "I approached deviance as the study of people whose occupation, one might say, was either crime or catching criminals" (Becker, in Debro, 1970, p. 166).

This concern of labeling gained impetus through the influential work of John Kitsuse and Aaron Cicourel (1963). They questioned the way criminologists use official statistics, especially the *Uniform Crime Reports*, in determining the amount of criminality in society. Their point was official statistics may not represent levels of criminality as well as they reflect the behavior of those who take the reports of crime and compile the statistics. They suggested official statistics were a better measure of who the police, and others, react to by arresting and initiating the criminal process.

Labeling as a Result of Societal Reaction

The labeling approach to deviance can be broken down into two parts: the problem of explaining how and why certain individuals get labeled and the effect of the label on subsequent deviant behavior (Gove, 1975; Orcutt, 1973). The former view of labeling is really that of asking what causes the label; thus, the label is a dependent variable whose existence must be explained. The classic statement of this focus is Becker's:

> Social groups create deviance by making the rules whose infraction constitutes deviance, and by applying those rules to particular people and labeling them as outsiders. From this point of view, deviance is *not* a quality of the act the person commits, but rather a consequence of the application by others of rules and sanctions to an "offender." The deviant is one to whom that label has successfully been applied; deviant behavior is behavior that people so label [emphasis in original]. (1963, p. 9)

By the *creation* of deviance, Becker meant rules, circumstances, characteristics of the individual, and reactions of those in the "audience" serve to separate those acts that are "deviant" from those that are not, even though they may appear as identical behaviors. It is not even necessary the behavior exist; what is important is the reactors believe in its existence. Thus, it is the *reaction* to behavior that creates deviance. The problem is to explain how *outsiders*, as Becker referred to deviants, are chosen and labeled.

To explore this problem, Becker added to his discussion a typology of types of deviant behavior (1963, pp. 19–22). He considered whether a particular behavior was conforming or deviant and whether the reactors perceived the behavior as conforming or deviant. The resulting four types of deviant behavior were called falsely accused, pure deviant, conforming, and secret deviant. Falsely accused acts are those that either did not exist or were actually conforming, but the audience reacted as if the acts were deviant. Both pure deviant and conforming acts are those in which the perception matched the reality of the act. Finally, secret deviant acts are those in which deviance had indeed occurred but the audience either ignored the acts or had not reacted as if they were deviant. Becker believed secret deviant acts are quite common. As important as these four types of deviance are, even more critical is the possibility that characteristics of people have something to do with which of the types would be used.

Becker's Types of Deviant Behavior

	Obedient Behavior	Rule-breaking Behavior
Perceived as Deviant	Falsely Accused	Pure Deviant
Not Perceived as Deviant	Conforming	Secret Deviant

Source: Data derived from Howard S. Becker, *Outsiders: Studies in the Sociology of Deviance* (New York: Free Press, 1963, p. 20).

This approach to deviance meant several facts about criminals needed explaining in a completely new way. Those who were arrested were not equally distributed throughout our society, rather they were predominantly lower class, urban, young, and male. The new societal reaction school wanted to know why official agents reacted to these people more often than others. Their answers, exemplified by the earlier work of Garfinkel (1956), suggested some common factors are at work. The likelihood of reaction was greater if an individual were less socially powerful (age, social class), a member of a group with different values from the dominant group, or relatively isolated. Labeling theorists set about the process of determining how and why these types of people came to the attention of others.

Labeling as a Cause of Deviance

Labeling advocates were also concerned with the effect of labels on the person who is labeled. This aspect of labeling treats the label as an independent variable, a causal agent, which then creates deviant behavior. There are two ways in which this may take place: (1) The label may catch the attention of the labeling audience, causing the audience to watch and continue the labeling of the individual; and (2) the label may be internalized by the individual and lead to an acceptance of a deviant self-concept. Either of these processes may amplify the deviance (Wilkins, 1965) and create a *career deviant.*

Among the problems a label creates is a subsequent reaction. Individuals who have been labeled become more visible in the sense that people are more aware of them. This awareness often causes them to be watched more closely and, thus, a second and third discovery of deviant behavior is even more likely than the first time. Especially important is that those who are in deviance processing occupations (criminal justice agencies) closely watch individuals once they have come to the attention of their agency. In a sense, those labeled are the clientele of the criminal justice system, and, like any other good business, the system keeps close tabs on its customers. It is difficult for those once labeled, such as probationers, parolees, or ex-offenders, to escape the attention of this audience, and subsequent behavior is likely to be identified and relabeled.

When the original label is more likely to be distributed among those with lower-class characteristics, this attention serves to reinforce the image of those individuals as deviants. People who are identified as "deviants" then have fewer chances to make good in the conventional world.

This means conventional avenues to success are often cut off, and illegal means may become the only way left open. Thus, labeling advocates argue the lower class bears the brunt of the labeling process and is kept deviant through relabeling.

Labeling theorists were also concerned with the way deviant labels were applied to youth who associated with delinquent peers even if they had not themselves committed any offenses. This *courtesy stigma*, as Goffman (1963) referred to it, meant that youth were cautioned to avoid this youth or that one because of the implied negative inferences from associating with someone who had already acquired a delinquent reputation. When your range of new associates is restricted this way, it is hard to change or readjust your priorities, which is something stressed in rehabilitative programming, particularly those that emphasize reintegration into the community.

As an example, it appears one reason some people commit crime is because they have very few legitimate opportunities available to them to get a job, make money, and buy the things advertised on television. Young African American males in many central cities of the United States have unemployment rates of 40 to 50%. There are few jobs, and no one will hire them. After being previously caught for committing a couple of thefts, one individual is arrested again and receives a prison sentence. In the overcrowded prison, there is little to do except work in the license plate factory. After being released, the individual's opportunities for legitimate work have certainly not increased and have probably decreased. Employers who would not hire the individual before are even less likely to do so now. In short, there may be little for the individual to turn to except crime.

A study by Richard Schwartz and Jerome Skolnick (1962) illustrates the criminogenic effect of a criminal label. They conducted a field experiment to examine the effect of a criminal court record on the employability of an unskilled worker. Four employment folders were constructed with identical applications except for a record of criminal involvement. As Schwartz and Skolnick explain it:

> The four folders differed only in the applicant's reported record of criminal court involvement. The first folder indicated the applicant had been convicted and sentenced for assault; the second, he had been tried for assault and acquitted; the third, also tried for assault and acquitted, but with a letter from the judge certifying the finding of not guilty and reaffirming the legal presumption of innocence. The fourth folder made no mention of any criminal record. (1962, p. 134)

Twenty-five copies of each of the folders were created. These folders were presented by an employment agent to one hundred people hiring for resort hotel jobs in the Catskills. Reactions by the hotel employers were placed in one of two categories: a willingness to consider the applicant in any way and those who made no response or refused to consider the applicant. The results were only one employer expressed further interest in the convicted folder, three in the tried-but-acquitted folder, six in the tried-and-acquitted-with-letter folder, and nine in the no-criminal-record folder. While there are problems with the study, the labeling implications are clear: Not only does a criminal record help reduce employment opportunities but any suggestion of criminal involvement may have a similar effect.

At this point, we should add labeling is not all negative. The discussions of labeling in criminology are about negative effects because of the subject matter—crime and delinquency. Positive labeling also exists. Indeed, positive labels are actively pursued by all of us. Right now you are pursuing a number of positive labels, and one is probably a college degree. In other words, you are seeking a college degree for the status it provides and the image it projects to other people. Indeed, life is designed around labels.

Edwin McCarty Lemert (1912–1996)

Edwin Lemert was born to working-class parents in Cincinnati in 1912. He had a firsthand experience with deviant lifestyles when he ran away from home as a young teenager and, for a brief while, joined a traveling circus. Although his father did well enough in the insurance business, he regretted that he was a high school dropout and pushed his sons to earn professional degrees. Lemert's grandfather had been president of a law school so it is not surprising that Lemert studied political science, majored in Spanish, and planned on going to law school before becoming interested in sociology. He received his A.B. from Miami University of Ohio in 1934 and graduated from Ohio State University with a Ph.D. in sociology and anthropology in 1939. Lemert then taught at Kent State University, Western Michigan University, and the University of California at Los Angeles. In 1953, he went to the University of California at Davis, where he founded the sociology department and taught there until his death in 1996. Lemert served as president of the Society for the Study of Social Problems (1972) and later received the American Society of Criminology's prestigious Edwin Sutherland Award for lifetime achievement.

Lemert's Secondary Deviance

The second form of labeling effect, reflected in the work of Edwin Lemert (1951, 1967), suggests that, in addition to audience reaction, there is the possibility an individual will react to the societally imposed label. According to Lemert, in any population there is differentiation—there are people who deviate from the normal behavior and characteristics of the general society. This may be very noticeable or individuals may attempt to hide their behaviors. However, it is the societal or audience reaction to those deviations in some circumstances, while not in others that determines whether a person will be identified as a deviant. Because everyone is unique, individual responses to the society reaction will vary in sensitivity and vulnerability. This individuation, or personalized response, determines whether the internalization and adoption of that deviant role later occurs. This process is called secondary deviance.[1] In this instance, Lemert assumes the individual does not identify the initial act (primary deviance) as an important part of his or her self-image. If the original self-image is not strong enough, the labeled person may come to accept the image offered by others and change his or her self-image accordingly. The more often a person is labeled, the more likely it is this change will take place.

Feedback is important to the process by which a new self-concept is internalized. Lemert describes the road to secondary deviance as follows:

(1) primary deviation; (2) societal penalties; (3) further primary deviation; (4) stronger penalties and rejections; (5) further deviation, perhaps with hostilities and resentments beginning to focus upon those doing the penalizing; (6) crisis reached in the tolerance quotient, expressed in formal action by the community stigmatizing of the deviant; (7) strengthening of the deviant conduct as a reaction to the stigmatizing and penalties; (8) ultimate acceptance of deviant social status and efforts of adjustment on the basis of the associated role. (1951, p. 77)

In a sense, then, secondary deviance is gained through a trading back and forth until the labeled person finally accepts the label as a real identity. This often results in the person's joining

---

[1] Edwin Lemert, prior to his death, reviewed this material for substantive accuracy.

a deviant subculture with further deviance being the product of the subcultural lifestyle. That is, future forms of deviant behavior are a product of the new role itself. Deviance in its secondary form is quite literally *created* by the labeling process.

A good example of secondary deviance is the case of a nursing student who was under tremendous pressure from her family who were paying her way to succeed in school. When she received a DWI (the primary deviation), her father threw her out of the house and told her she was on her own. Depressed by the familial rejection, she attempted suicide by cutting her wrists in the middle of a mall buffet restaurant (further deviance). The chain eatery pressed charges against the girl, and she was again arrested and placed in jail, under suicide watch. Her father came to the jail to get her out but she was afraid of his condemnation and angry at his betrayal, so she told the officer that if she was to be released to her father she would assault a staff member to remain incarcerated. As she was taken to the visitor/release area, she struck the officer until she was diverted into a psychiatric hold (secondary deviance). After serving time in a treatment facility, she was released, whereupon she committed suicide (further secondary deviance).

In this case, it is easy to see that if it had not been for the DWI, and her family's reaction to that label or status, this young woman might not have changed her self-concept and engaged in the behaviors that are secondary to the primary offense. Labeling theorists argue this secondary deviance would not have occurred had it not been for the labeling process. Therefore, some criminologists (Schur, 1973) have suggested the best approach to reducing juvenile delinquency, and subsequent criminal behavior, is to do nothing when delinquent acts are discovered. This doesn't mean that you do not charge someone with DWI, or respond to the suicide attempt at the mall. However, it does mean that less drastic reactions might help lessen the secondary effects on someone who is emotionally traumatized and get them the help that they need in a less stigmatizing fashion.

Master Status and Retrospective Interpretation

Two other important labeling concepts are those of master status and retrospective interpretation. Master status, as developed by Everett Hughes (1945) and Becker (1963), conveys the notion that there are central traits to people's identities blinding us to their other characteristics. These traits can be separated into those statuses that are almost always the prime characteristics (master status) of a person and those that are important but secondary (auxiliary status) traits. Examples of common master statuses are one's sex, jobs (as priest, as physician), and some forms of deviance (homosexuality). Where deviance is concerned, "criminal" is usually a master status. This makes it difficult for a person once labeled a criminal to be perceived as someone who may be trustworthy, even though the criminal act may have been an isolated one in the person's life.

A classic study of the mentally ill in institutions (Rosenhan, 1973) demonstrates master status concept. Several researchers had themselves committed to a mental institution by pretending to have some symptoms of schizophrenia. Thereafter, they acted normally. Interestingly, only the inmates detected that there was nothing "wrong" with the researchers. All of the researchers were released but with diagnoses of "schizophrenia in remission." Apparently, the master status of being mentally ill is so powerful that it never goes away and is always lurking in the background.

It is always easy to test examples of the effect of master status. Just ask your friends what they think of when they hear the name Michael Vick. Chances are, his criminal convictions related to dogfighting have superceded his accomplishments as a star NFL quarterback and he will forever be remembered as the "animal abusing" football player. Despite their talent and career successes, Britney Spears and Lindsay Lohan may be recalled as troubled rehabilitation failures. An even more recent example of master status is Penn State's once-legendary football coach Joe Paterno. After the Sandusky sex abuse scandal, when it came to light that Paterno knew about the reports and seemingly looked the other way, the "sex abuse" master status was broad enough to encompass both Paterno and the Penn State University President, who were fired. The university went so far as to remove a statue of Paterno from the campus. His legendary football coaching career will be tarnished and supplanted by his new master status.

Unfortunately, victims can also inherit the effects of a "master status." A Texas teen who was violently beaten and sodomized with PVC piping and left to die by a couple of young men he associated with took months to recover before testifying before Congress about hate crime laws. The youth recalled being humiliated about news coverage calling him the degrading "pipe assault victim." Although he is said to have "rejected the victim tag," he also admitted that "everyone knows that I'm the kid" (Hewitt & Murphy, 2007). Within a year, the young man would commit suicide by jumping from a cruise ship.

Retrospective interpretation provides us with an idea of how identities can be reconstructed to fit a new label. Because the term "criminal" conveys a master status, it is difficult for people to understand how such a central fact about a person's character was not there before the criminal act and the labeling. To resolve this inconsistency, a process of reexamination takes place, and past events and behavior are reinterpreted to fit the new identity. Thus, we think back to the past and see a criminal was there all the time. Retrospective interpretation not only applies to people around the labeled person, but also to an official agency's reinterpretation of the person's records.

We practice retrospective interpretation all the time. When the media reports of a college campus shooting spree, we dig through the past of the offender to find what may have indicated that a potential serial killer was there all along. Neighbors and former teachers recall that the youth seemed "troubled" or "depressed." This raises doubts as to whether the gunman's past really evidenced those behaviors or that the person recalling them has been influenced by the new knowledge that they now have about the violent rampage. Thus, the audience sifts through all their past information and memories to find images and pieces that they feel will fit the new label. A recent shooting rampage at an Aurora, Colorado, theater playing a Batman movie exemplifies the process. At first, the media expressed frustration that those who knew the young gunman found his actions inexplicable. Then, some acquaintances remembered some small past "issues" and the reinterpretation process unfolded as usual.

CLASSIFICATION OF THE THEORY

Because labeling can be viewed as both an effect and a cause (societal reaction and secondary deviance), there are two forms of labeling. Perhaps nowhere is the lack of a coherent theory more noticeable than in the attempt to classify labeling. Thus, we first provide a classification for the main thrust of labeling and then note any variation for other parts of the theory.

Labeling theory is predominantly a *processual* theory because of its concern with the way labeling takes place. It does, however, have some elements of structure in its discussion of the types of individuals most likely to be labeled. Similarly, labeling is largely a *classical* theory in its emphasis on crime, law, and processing rather than on criminal behavior. While it is true that classical theory is normally a structural approach, labeling clearly is less interested in the criminal act than in the rules and guidelines for reaction to that act. The individual comes into focus only when attention turns to the effects of the labeling process. Lemert's version of secondary deviance suggests a return to positivist concepts with his explanation of how the labeling process causes subsequent deviant behavior. Here, the focus is once more on the individual actor.

Other classifications are more straightforward. Labeling is clearly a variation of *conflict* assumptions rather than being consensus oriented. From its refusal to treat definitions of crime as universal to its approach to explaining how reactions are distributed in society, the theory embodies cultural pluralism and value conflict. Finally, labeling is a *microtheory*. It focuses on the effects of societal reaction to the individual's behavior. Even when there is discussion of the way in which authorities react to deviance, the emphasis is on the process of labeling individuals instead of on explaining how social structure creates labels.

Summary

Labeling theory is a combination of several theoretical threads. With its heritage in symbolic interactionism and a divergent group of theorists, the core essence of labeling is hard to find. At least two main thrusts are present. First, there is the concept of societal reaction. This component treats the problem of differences in reaction to deviance and focuses on the meaning of deviance to the audience. Second, there is the issue of secondary deviance, the problem of what a label means, and does, to the person labeled. Both of these thrusts are compatible, yet they seem to suggest entirely different theoretical approaches.

The effect of labeling theory on criminology has been substantial. Perhaps most important, it caused criminologists to question the middle-class values they were using in their descriptions of deviance and criminality. Researchers began a critical examination of criminal justice agencies and the way in which those agencies process individuals. The need to study deviant subjects *as part of humanity* rather than as mere objects (Matza, 1969), also began to impress itself on criminologists. Even such criminal justice movements as diversion owe a direct debt to the work of those involved in the labeling movement. Finally, labeling was the precursor of conflict theories and, thus, in one fashion or another, occupied criminology for more than a decade.

MAJOR POINTS OF THE THEORY

1. Society is characterized by multiple values with differing degrees of overlap.
2. The quality of any individual behavior is determined only by the application of values. The identification of a behavior as deviant occurs through a reaction to that behavior.
3. Deviance is a quality of the reaction and is not intrinsic to the behavior itself. If there is no reaction, there is no deviance.
4. Once behavior is perceived by a social audience and labeled deviant, the individual who engaged in that behavior is also labeled deviant.
5. The process of reacting and labeling is more likely when those labeled are less socially powerful than their audience is. Thus, deviance is more commonly ascribed to the less powerful in society.
6. Reactors (individuals, social groups, law enforcement agencies) tend to observe more closely those whom they have identified as deviants and therefore find even more deviance in those persons. Subsequent acts are reacted to more quickly and the label more firmly affixed.
7. The audience views an individual, once labeled, as being what the label says he or she is. A person labeled as a criminal is perceived to be first and foremost a criminal; other attributes that are not covered by the label may be ignored.
8. In addition to "becoming" a deviant for the audience, an individual may begin to accept the label as a self-identity. Acceptance of the label depends on the strength of the individual's original self-concept and the force of the labeling process.
9. A change in self-concept results in an internalization of the deviant character, with all its attributes.
10. Further deviant behavior (secondary deviance) is a product of living and acting within the role of the deviant label, often as a part of a deviant subculture.

Epilogue: Current Directions and Policy Implications

CURRENT DIRECTIONS

Labeling ideas have been incorporated into criminology as standard observations. Even so, additions and clarifications have been made to the earlier literature. Edwin Schur (1971), for instance, points out there are three "audiences" who react to deviance. First, the *significant-other* audience is a very important informal group because its members are those whom the individual is most likely to feel are influential. These people have substantial informal labeling power. Second, the *social-control-agency* audience is primarily made up of authorities. Not only do these people have formal labeling power, but they can also adversely affect the life of the individual. The final group is the *society-at-large* audience. These people are primarily important as a group with the ability to define good and bad and to stir the authorities into action. Schur adds each of these groups can have subgroups that have particular interests and, therefore, may be more important to some labeling processes than to others. Another source of labeling Schur might have added to the list is self-labeling. Some individuals are so socialized that their "conscience" provides an important source of their own labels. To a varying degree, probably all of us are capable of self-labeling.

We should also note labeling has been heavily criticized, and some criminologists have suggested it has little evidence to back it up. These critiques are primarily based on the adequacy of research on labeling theory, and as with other theories we have discussed, there is some question whether the research has adequately tested labeling. Other criminologists have criticized labeling for being too simplistic. In truth, there has been no complete statement of labeling, and the lists of propositions and statements are mostly derived from sketches put together by the critics themselves. Labeling is potentially quite complex once one realizes it was meant as only one side of the deviance coin, the other side being the factors that go into creating the original act. Societal reaction by itself is exceedingly complex, and we have not yet fully introduced its intricacies into our studies of labeling.

One of the best arguments for labeling is that the concept of labeling (not just negative labeling) is an important part of our lives. Another way to view labels is to call them "categories." By using categories for things, we do not have to deal with individual objects or events; instead, we can treat them as a type of object or event and react accordingly. Imagine the problems that would occur if you had to treat each chair, food, or person you encountered as a specific and separate object. Our brains (and those of other organisms) are probably designed to identify objects as members of categories to reduce the strain that would otherwise result. Labeling seems to come naturally—the question is *how* we categorize people and events and *what effect* that categorization process has on the way we view and act toward people.

Some theorists have been working on more complex versions of labeling theory. Responding to the problem that the theory does not handle *mala in se* crimes (naturally bad behavior) very well, Gary LaFree (1981) has attempted to update labeling in this direction. Larry Sherman (1993) has tied labeling to criminal sanctions by using the concept of defiance. Dina Rose and Todd Clear (1998) have attempted an expansion of labeling from individual effects to community effects. Others (Braithwaite, 1989a; Grasmick, Bursik, & Arneklev, 1993; Grasmick, Bursik, & Kinsey, 1991; Scheff, 1988) focused on shaming, an obvious extension of labeling. While also found in the deterrence literature, shaming reflects the effect of self-labeling (or self-stigmatizing) or the effect of labeling-stigmatizing by others. The concept of shaming is quite old, having been the basis of many older forms of punishment (the stocks, the "scarlet letter").

REINTEGRATIVE SHAMING

The most elaborate of these perspectives is that proposed by John Braithwaite (1989a). He incorporates opportunity, subcultural, control, learning, and labeling theories to produce a theory that relies on the notion of differential shaming. Beginning with opportunity theory, Braithwaite notes that there are aspirations and means, both legitimate and illegitimate. For criminality or delinquency to occur, blocked legitimate opportunities must be replaced by available illegitimate ones. With this background, Braithwaite borrows from subcultural theories the concept of organization for learning and transmission of lawbreaking values. Here, he notes the contrast with social control theory (see Chapter 11). Social control creates conformity with the law, whereas differential learning and value transmission create conformity with the subculture and nonconformity with the law. However, the direction an individual takes is not explained by these concepts; a "tipping point" is needed.

Differential shaming is posited as that tipping point. Many forms of shaming are available both to conventional and subcultural groups. To the extent that an offender is exposed to shaming or anticipates shaming, a tipping point is reached. Two forms of shaming are presented: disintegrative shaming and integrative shaming. The former fails to reunite a shamed offender with the community or subgroup, thus resulting in an outcast status and greater deviance. The latter returns a shamed offender to the group with conciliatory gestures and separates the evil act from the character of the offender. The obvious policy implications are that acts can be strongly sanctioned, but a reformed offender can be treated in a forgiving fashion. Since subcultures have power to shame (as does the conventional moral order), the theoretical problem is to overcome the subcultural effect by a network of communities operating under a reintegrative shaming modality. Braithwaite's article on organizational crime (1989b) makes just such an attempt. Braithwaite's approach has been popular enough to produce research and commentary since its development.

GROUNDED LABELING

Another extension of labeling has been suggested by Dario Melossi (1985) in what he refers to as a "grounded labeling theory." Heeding a major criticism of critical theories, that there are no usable (or likely) policies to be generated from them, Melossi suggested that critical theorists return to their roots in labeling. In so doing, he proposed an integrated approach in which the motivation of an actor had to be set in the historical context of a society. The combination attempts to explain an act taking place for specific reasons and a reaction based on the audience's contemporary understanding of both the actor and his or her place in society. Further, the audience's place in society is also crucial. To illustrate, lower-class individuals might commit acts out of frustration with their lack of ability to succeed in society. The reaction to their acts is governed by the degree of threat to existing society represented by both the acts and the actors, and the necessity at that particular time and place to do something about the situation. If threat and situation necessity are high, the audience will react strongly to the individual.

LABELING AND SOCIAL ORDER

Finally, Joseph Gusfield (1981) has attempted to integrate labeling as a force in the maintenance of existing social order. Using four types of labels, he examined each for its effect on social order. The first label, sick deviants, is given to those who are believed to have no control over their behavior and whose acts are so deviant that no normal person would have done them (such as mass murderers). Gusfield views this label as reinforcing social order by emphasizing the true abnormality of such behavior. This was seen in the media coverage of the grisly cannibalistic murders committed by Jeffrey Dahmer. The second label, repentant deviants, also reinforces social order. People so labeled are those who have been defined as deviant and are now apologetic for their actions. Such persons are characterized by their volunteer work with other deviants and by membership in such organizations as Alcoholics Anonymous. Social order is reinforced by their public and obvious remorse over their previous behavior. Cynical deviants constitute the third label. These people exhibit an awareness of the deviant nature of their behavior but don't care and exhibit no remorse. Common criminals are frequently seen as this type. Cynical deviants are a threat to the social order precisely because they flout rules and laws. The last label is enemy deviants. These people not only believe nothing is wrong with their behavior, but they also believe the rules of society are incorrect. Their obvious threat to social order is based on a combination of their flouting the rules and their attempts to convert others to their beliefs.

What we do to people as we react to their deviance, then, depends on the type of label we give them.

WHERE NOW?

While no great resurrection of labeling theory is likely to occur, it is evident the concepts and ideas of labeling are being revived in a number of ways. Several theorists have used labeling concepts in integrated theories and labeling suggestions about who gets processed by the criminal justice system and the harshness of sanctions have never really been out of fashion. Researchers have consistently examined these "extra legal" variables to explain differences in arrests, prosecutions, and sentencing. Of all these ideas, and based on reception by other criminologists, the most promising appears to be Braithwaite's reintegrative shaming.

POLICY IMPLICATIONS

As was the case with strain theories, it is easy to produce policy statements from labeling theory. Indeed, concepts from labeling theory were used to create major changes in policy, especially in the juvenile justice system. Policy implications fall within four general areas: diversion, due process, decriminalization, and deinstitutionalization (Empey, 1982, p. 409; Lilly, Cullen, & Ball, 1989, pp. 131–135).

The first policy area, *diversion*, is a direct product of labeling's contention that labels can cause future problems; therefore, they should be avoided if at all possible (Lemert, 1971, 1981). If stigma is assigned to children because they are processed by the juvenile justice system, the obvious answer is to avoid processing them. In other words, divert them from the system. During the 1970s, diversion programs sprang up everywhere, perhaps because of overcrowding in the system's facilities. Children who would have been brought into the juvenile system were placed into informal programs outside of the system. The idea was to avoid records, stigmatizing labels such as "juvenile delinquent," and making the children seem different. If it worked, the diversion movement would reduce future delinquencies and adult criminality. Most of the diversions were for less serious acts of delinquency, and rarely were they used for delinquents who were persistent offenders.

Unfortunately, most of the evidence indicates diversion did not reduce labeling (the children simply received a different label), and the use of diversion seemed to increase the number of children brought into the control network (Austin & Krisberg, 1981; Blomberg, 1980; Dunford, 1977). Indeed, the diversion programs were said to have created a "net-widening" effect—a larger net was being cast over undesirable juvenile behavior. Children who would have been dismissed from the system were now being placed in diversion. Some studies, however, found diversion was being honestly practiced, removing children who really would have been processed by the system. Nonetheless, as Arnold Binder and Gilbert Geis (1984) observed, regardless of the honesty of diversion, the system cannot now do without the programs because it cannot otherwise absorb the cost and numbers of juveniles currently being diverted. In point of fact, diversion programs now *are* part of the official system of juvenile justice.

Due process, or the problem of differential processing, is another by-product of labeling. Because labeling was concerned that characteristics of individuals might create different reactions, it was obvious those characteristics might influence formal processing. Critics of the juvenile justice system of the 1960s charged that the justice being dispensed "in the best interests of the child" resulted in unpredictable and discriminatory practices. Thus, they wanted the same legal protections in juvenile systems that were found in adult criminal systems. Due process became a rallying cry, and by the mid-1970s most juvenile court proceedings were governed by due process considerations.

Where decriminalization is concerned, juveniles were not the only focus. The early *decriminalization* movements centered on status offenders (juveniles who committed an act that, had they been an adult, would not have been illegal). Status offenders were brought before the juvenile court for offenses such as running away, staying out too late, and engaging in sexual behaviors. By bringing these children into the juvenile system, even into detention facilities, criminologists argued the children were not only being stigmatized but were learning truly delinquent behavior from those with whom they were placed. In the resulting "correction" of the system, status offenders were generally removed from the juvenile justice system and handed over to social agencies.

Juveniles were not the only ones affected by the decriminalization movement, however. Some criminologists, particularly Edwin Schur (1965), argued victimless crimes should not be a part of the criminal justice system. Some forms of so-called victimless crimes were indeed removed. By the mid-1970s, most jurisdictions had begun to place drunken and disorderly offenders in alcohol treatment facilities rather than in jail. Another example can be found in drug offenses. For instance, marijuana use has been the focus of a decriminalization movement for more than 20 years. This doesn't mean the advocates of this position all want to legalize marijuana use; decriminalization literally means to remove it from the criminal law. Advocates argue that other forms of social sanctions may serve just as well to control drug use.

Finally, labeling was behind *deinstitutionalization* policies (Scull, 1977). The prolonged warehousing of the mentally ill was declared inhumane during the late 1960s. Except for the most serious of cases, mental patients were released from institutions and placed in community outpatient facilities. There was no great upsurge of mental health problems, and the idea is a standard one today. Concerning the juvenile justice system, an even grander experiment was undertaken in Massachusetts. Jerome Miller (1991),

the director of the juvenile institutions, decided the institutions were doing more harm to their wards than good. As a result, he ordered all the juvenile institutions closed. The predictions of dire results, as with the release of mental patients, again were unfounded.

Labeling theory has clearly been quite popular at the policy level. Those in today's criminal justice system, and particularly those in the juvenile justice system, routinely worry about the implications of labeling. Some criminologists have even suggested that just as labeling is a critical component of punishment, delabeling should also be undertaken. That is, we need a "coming-out ceremony" in which the previous bad label is exchanged for a new, good one (or at least a neutral one). Along these lines, John Braithwaite's reintegrative labeling approach contains theoretical notions that assist the process of returning an offender to the community. In this way, we might be able use a label to assist in punishment, yet diminish the problems associated with reaction to the label once punishment is over. Moreover, we have still to explore the policy implications of the emerging emphasis on shaming. A relatively similar approach, restorative justice, has become popular recently and evidence is currently being gathered on the various restorative justice programs sponsored by the federal government.

Questions and Weblinks

Critical Thinking Questions

1. Why is the definition of crime important to labeling theorists?
2. How have changes in society views toward certain types of crimes changed the amount of negative labeling that is associated with them? Cite some examples.
3. Discuss any recent event where a celebrity has been relabeled after a crime and why social views of that person changed.

Practice Essay Questions

1. Explain Becker's typology of deviant behavior types and how they are dependent on how behavior is perceived.
2. Distinguish between primary and secondary deviance using examples of each.
3. What types of social policies and criminal justice system changes took place after labeling theorists drew attention to the negative aspects of stigma?

Related Websites

http://criminology.fsu.edu/crimtheory/becker.htm
http://www.bullying.org/public/frameset.cfm

http://www.antibullying.net/
https://www.ncjrs.gov/pdffiles1/ojjdp/220595.pdf

Bibliography

Austin, J., & Krisberg, B. (1981). Wider, stronger, and different nets: The dialectics of criminal justice reform. *Journal of Research in Crime and Delinquency, 18,* 165–196.

Becker, H. S. (1963). *Outsiders: Studies in the sociology of deviance.* New York: Free Press.

Binder, A., & Geis, G. (1984). Ad populum argumentation in criminology: Juvenile diversion as rhetoric. *Crime and Delinquency, 30,* 624–647.

Blomberg, T. G. (1980). Widening the net: An anomaly in the evaluation of diversion programs. In M. W. Klein & K. S. Teilman (Eds.), *Handbook of criminal justice evaluation* (pp. 572–595). Beverly Hills, CA: Sage.

Braithwaite, J. (1989a). *Crime, shame, and reintegration.* Cambridge, UK: Cambridge University Press.

Braithwaite, J. (1989b). Criminological theory and organizational crime. *Justice Quarterly, 6,* 333–358.

Debro, J. (1970). Dialogue with Howard S. Becker. *Issues in Criminology, 5,* 159–179.

Dunford, F. W. (1977). Police diversion: An illusion. *Criminology, 15,* 335–352.

Empey, L. T. (1982). *American delinquency.* Chicago: Dorsey Press.

Garfinkel, H. (1956). Conditions of successful degradation ceremonies. *American Journal of Sociology, 61,* 420–424.

Goffman, E. (1963). *Stigma: Notes on the management of spoiled identity.* Englewood Cliffs, NJ: Prentice Hall.

Gove, W. R. (Ed.). (1975). *The labelling of deviance: Evaluating a perspective.* New York: Halsted.

Grasmick, H. G., Bursik, Jr., R. J., & Arneklev, B. J. (1993). Reduction in drunk driving as a response to increased threats of shame, embarrassment, and legal sanctions. *Criminology, 31,* 41–67.

Grasmick, H. G., Bursik, Jr., R. J., & Kinsey, K. A. (1991). Shame and embarrassment as deterrents to noncompliance with the law: The case of an antilittering campaign. *Environment and Behavior, 23,* 233–251.

Gusfield, J. (1981). *The culture of public problems: Drinking, driving, and the symbolic order.* Chicago: University of Chicago Press.

Hewitt, P., & Murphy, B. (2007, April 17). Moving on, and trying to shed 'victim' label. *Houston Chronicle,* pp. B1, B4.

Hughes, E. C. (1945). Dilemmas and contradictions of status. *American Journal of Sociology, 50,* 353–359.

Kitsuse, J., & Cicourel, A. V. (1963). A note on the use of official statistics. *Social Problems, 11,* 131–139.

LaFree, G. D. (1981). Official reactions to social problems: Police decisions in sexual assault cases. *Social Problems, 28,* 582–594.

Lemert, E. M. (1951). *Social pathology: A systematic approach to the theory of sociopathic behavior.* New York: McGraw-Hill.

Lemert, E. M. (1967). *Human deviance, social problems and social control.* Englewood Cliffs, NJ: Prentice Hall.

Lemert, E. M. (1971). *Instead of court: Diversion in juvenile justice.* National Institute of Mental Health. Center for Studies of Crime and Delinquency, Public Health Service Publication No. 2127. Washington, DC: U.S. Government Printing Office.

Lemert, E. M. (1981). Diversion in juvenile justice: What hath been wrought. *Journal of Research in Crime and Delinquency, 18,* 34–46.

Lilly, J. R., Cullen, F. T., & Ball, R. A. (1989). *Criminological theory: Context and consequences.* Newbury Park, CA: Sage.

Matza, D. (1969). *Becoming deviant.* New York: Prentice Hall.

Melossi, D. (1985). Overcoming the crisis in critical criminology: Toward a grounded labeling theory. *Criminology, 23,* 193–208.

Merton, R. K. (1968). *Social theory and social structure* (Rev. ed.). New York: Free Press.

Miller, J. G. (1991). *Last one over the wall: The Massachusetts experiment in closing reform schools.* Columbus: Ohio State University Press.

Orcutt, J. D. (1973). Societal reaction and the response to deviation in small groups. *Social Forces, 52,* 259–267.

Rose, D., & Clear, T. (1998). Incarceration, social capital, and crime: Implications for social disorganization theory. *Criminology, 36,* 441–479.

Rosenhan, D. L. (1973). On being sane in insane places. *Science, 179,* 250–258.

Scheff, T. J. (1988). Shame and conformity: The deference-emotion system. *American Sociological Review, 53,* 395–406.

Schur, E. M. (1965). *Crimes without victims.* Englewood Cliffs, NJ: Prentice Hall.

Schur, E. M. (1971). *Labeling deviant behavior: Its sociological implications.* New York: Harper and Row.

Schur, E. M. (1973). *Radical non-intervention: Rethinking the delinquency problem.* Englewood Cliffs, NJ: Prentice Hall.

Schwartz, R. D., & Skolnick, J. H. (1962). Two studies of legal stigma. *Social Problems, 10,* 133–138.

Scull, A. T. (1977). *Decarceration: Community treatment and the deviant: A radical view.* Englewood Cliffs, NJ: Prentice Hall.

Sherman, L. (1993). Defiance, deterrence, and irrelevance: A theory of the criminal sanction. *Journal of Research in Crime and Delinquency, 30,* 445–473.

Short, J. F., Jr., & Nye, F. I. (1958). Extent of unrecorded juvenile delinquency: Tentative conclusions. *Journal of Criminal Law, Criminology, and Police Science, 49,* 296–302.

Tannenbaum, F. (1938). *Crime and the community.* Boston: Ginn.

Wellford, C. F. (1975). Labelling theory and criminology: An assessment. *Social Problems, 22,* 332–345.

Wilkins, L. T. (1965). *Social deviance: Social policy, action, and research.* Englewood Cliffs, NJ: Prentice Hall.

Research Bibliography (from 1990)

Adams, M. S., Robertson, C. T., Gray-Ray, P., & Ray, M. C. (2003). Labeling and delinquency. *Adolescence, 38*(149), 171–186.

Albonetti, C. A. (1992). Charge reduction: An analysis of prosecutorial discretion in burglary and robbery cases. *Journal of Quantitative Criminology, 8,* 317–333.

Al-Talib, N. I., & Griffin, C. (1994). Labelling effect on adolescents' self-concept. *International Journal of Offender Therapy and Comparative Criminology, 38,* 47–57.

Asencio, E. K., & Burke, P. J. (2011). Does incarceration change the criminal identity? A systhesis of labeling and identity theory perspectives on identity change. *Sociological Perspectives, 54,* 163–182.

Bankston, C. L., III, & Caldas, S. J. (1996). Adolescents and deviance in a Vietnamese American community: A theoretical synthesis. *Deviant Behavior, 17,* 159–181.

Bartusch, D. J., & Matsueda, R. L. (1996). Gender, reflected appraisals, and labeling: A cross-group test of an interactionist theory of delinquency. *Social Forces, 75,* 145–176.

Bernburg, J. G., & Krohn, M. D. (2003). Labeling, life chances, and adult crime: The direct and indirect effects of intervention in adolescence on crime in early adulthood. *Criminology, 41,* 1287–1318.

Benburg, J. G., Krohn, M. D., & Rivera, C. J. (2006). Official labeling, criminal embeddedness, and subsequent delinquency: A longitudinal test of labeling theory. *Journal of Research in Crime and Delinquency, 43,* 67–88.

Brezina, T., & Aragones, A. A. (2004). Devils in disguise: The contribution of positive labeling to "sneaky thrills" delinquency. *Deviant Behavior, 25,* 513–535.

Brown, W. K. (1990). Juvenile probation department experiences compared by adult outcome. *Journal of Offender Counseling, Services and Rehabilitation, 15,* 109–116.

Brownfield, D., & Thompson, K. (2008). Correlates of delinquent identity: Testing interactionist, labeling, and control theory. *International Journal of Criminal Justice Sciences, 3,* 44–53.

Chen, H-T. (1991). Dropping in and dropping out: Judicial decisionmaking in the disposition of felony arrests. *Journal of Criminal Justice, 19,* 1–18.

Cheung, N., & Cheung, Y. (2008). Self-control, social factors, and delinquency: A test of the general theory of crime among adolescents in Hong Kong. *Journal of Youth & Adolescence, 7,* 412–430.

Downs, W. R., & Robertson, J. (1990). Referral for treatment among adolescent alcohol and drug abusers. *Journal of Research in Crime and Delinquency, 27,* 190–209.

Downs, W. R., & Robertson, J. (2000). The conditional effect of peer groups on the relationship between parental labeling and youth delinquency. *Sociological Perspectives, 43,* 499–515.

Hagan, J., & Palloni, A. (1990). The social reproduction of a criminal class in working-class London, circa 1950–1980. *American Journal of Sociology, 96,* 265–299.

Heckert, A., & Heckert, D. (2010). Differential labeling theory. *Sociological Imagination, 46*(2), 24–40.

Kaplan, H. B., & Damphousse, K. R. (1997). Negative social sanctions, self-derogation, and deviant behavior: Main and interactive effects in longitudinal perspective. *Deviant Behavior, 18,* 1–26.

Kaplan, H. B., & Johnson, R. J. (1991). Negative social sanctions and juvenile delinquency: Effects of labeling in a model of deviant behavior. *Social Science Quarterly, 71,* 98–122.

Kenney, J. (2002). Victims of crime and labeling theory: A parallel process? *Deviant Behavior, 23,* 235–265.

Liu, X. (2000). The conditional effect of peer groups on the relationship between parental labeling and youth delinquency. *Sociological Perspectives, 43,* 499–514.

Lopes, G., Krohn, M. D., Lizotte, A. J., Schmidt, N. M., Vásquez, B., & Bernburg, J. (2012). Labeling and cumulative disadvantage: The impact of formal police intervention on life chances and crime during emerging adulthood. *Crime & Delinquency, 58,* 456–488.

Lotz, R., & Lee, L. (1999). Sociability, school experience, and delinquency. *Youth and Society, 31,* 199–224.

Margolin, L. (1992). Deviance on record: Techniques for labeling child abusers in official documents. *Social Problems, 39,* 58–70.

Matsueda, R. L. (1992). Reflected appraisals, parental labeling, and delinquency: Specifying a symbolic interactionist theory. *American Journal of Sociology, 97,* 1577–1611.

McAra, L., & McVie, S. (2007). Youth justice?: The impact of system contact on patterns of desistance from offending. *European Journal of Criminology, 4,* 315–345.

McBarnet, D. (1991). Whiter than white collar crime: Tax, fraud insurance and the management of stigma. *British Journal of Sociology, 42,* 323–344.

Mingus, W., & Burchfield, K. B. (2012). From prison to integration: Applying modified labeling theory to sex offenders. *Criminal Justice Studies, 25,* 97–109.

Poynting, S., Noble, G., & Tabar, P. (2001). Middle Eastern appearances: "Ethnic gangs," moral panic and media framing. *Australian & New Zealand Journal of Criminology (Australian Academic Press), 34,* 67–90.

Sherman, L. W., & Smith, D. A. (1992). Crime, punishment, and stake in conformity: Legal and informal control of domestic violence. *American Sociological Review, 57,* 680–690.

Siennick, S. E. (2007). The timing and mechanisms of the offending-depression link. *Criminology, 45,* 583–615.

Smith, D. A., & Brame, R. (1994). On the initiation and continuation of delinquency. *Criminology, 32,* 607–629.

Smith, D. A., & Paternoster, R. (1990). Formal processing and future delinquency: Deviance amplification as selection artifact. *Law and Society Review, 24,* 1109–1132.

Smith, E., Wolf, A., Cantillon, D., Thomas, O., & Davidson, W. (2004). The Adolescent Diversion Project. *Journal of Prevention & Intervention in the Community, 27*(2), 29–47.

Sommers, I., & Baskin, D. (1990). The prescription of psychiatric medications in prison: Psychiatric versus labeling perspectives. *Justice Quarterly, 7,* 739–755.

Stewart, E. A., Simons, R. L., Conger, R. D., & Scaramella, L. V. (2002). Beyond the interactional relationship between delinquency and parenting practices: The contribution of legal sanctions. *Journal of Research in Crime and Delinquency, 39,* 36–59.

Stiles, B. L., & Kaplan, H. B. (1996). Stigma, deviance and negative social sanctions. *Social Science Quarterly, 77,* 685–696.

Tapia, M. (2011). U.S. juvenile arrests: Gang membership, social class, and labeling effects. *Youth and Society, 43,* 1407–1432.

Triplett, R. A. (1993). The conflict perspective, symbolic interactionism, and the status characteristics hypothesis. *Justice Quarterly, 10,* 541–558.

Triplett, R. A. & Jarjoura, G. R. (1994). Theoretical and empirical specification of a model of informal labeling. *Journal of Quantitative Criminology, 10,* 241–276.

Vanderwood, P. J. (1993). 'Indios, fanaticos, bandidos': Labeling the millenarium movement at Tomochic, Mexico. *Criminal Justice History: An International Annual, 13,* 161–189.

Walsh, A. (1990). Twice labeled: The effect of psychiatric labeling on the sentencing of sex offenders. *Social Problems, 37,* 375–389.

Wodarski, J., Feldman, R., & Pedi, S. J. (1994). Peers' rejection as a possible consequence of official reaction to delinquency in Chinese society. *Criminal Justice and Behavior, 21,* 387–402.

Zhang, L. (1997). Informal reactions and delinquency. *Criminal Justice and Behavior, 24,* 129–150.

Zhang, L. (2003). Official offense status and self-esteem among Chinese youths. *Journal of Criminal Justice, 31,* 99–105.

Zhang, L., & Messner, S. F. (1994). The severity of official punishment for delinquency and change in interpersonal relations in Chinese society. *Journal of Research in Crime and Delinquency, 31,* 416–433.

9

Conflict Theory

LEARNING OBJECTIVES

Objective 9.1: Describe the role of law and power in conflict theory.

Objective 9.2: Explain what Quinney means by the social reality of crime.

Objective 9.3: Discuss the roles that race and economics play in conflict in our society.

Objective 9.4: Summarize the views of Marxist criminologists and their contributions to understanding conflict today.

Objective 9.5: Describe the social policies that might be used to reduce crime and conflict in American society today.

INTRODUCTION

Criminological conflict theories emerged on the heels of labeling theory. Similar in some ways to labeling, conflict theories focus on the political nature of crime and examine the creation and application of criminal law. Although conflict theorist George Vold (1958) was writing at the same time as the early labeling theorists, his work attracted only mild interest. Perhaps because labeling was less politically oriented and therefore more acceptable to conservative criminologists, it was more popular than conflict theory until the 1970s.

Conflict theories share one fundamental assumption: Societies are more appropriately characterized by conflict rather than by consensus. This assumption allows several varieties of conflict theory to be viewed as if they were on a continuum. At one end, pluralist versions suggest society is composed of a myriad of groups, varying in size, and often temporary, all of which are struggling to see their interests are maintained in any of a number of issues. At the other end, class-conflict versions argue two classes are present in a society, both of which are attempting to dominate that society.

Regardless of their position on this continuum of the number of groups and amount of power sought, conflict theorists view consensus as an aberration. That is, they see consensus as a temporary state of affairs that either will return to conflict or will have to be maintained at great expense. It is the use of power to create and maintain an image of consensus, then, that represents the problem to be studied. Conflict theorists are less concerned with individual behavior than with the making and enforcement of law. Further, they are rarely concerned with the behavior of the offender.

THE HERITAGE OF THE THEORY

The Social Heritage

The decade from 1965 to 1975 was a time of unrest in American society. After a period of optimism in the late 1950s and early 1960s, many people in the United States became disenchanted with their society. The success of the civil rights movement gave incentive to other "powerless" groups, such as women and homosexuals, who marched for recognition and for equality in social opportunities. Even students protested their treatment at the hands of college administrators.

The number of demonstrations against the Vietnam War grew in the years between 1965 and 1968. Though protest had been viewed as a political tool for students and African Americans, it was soon adopted by others, including teachers, physicians, and members of the clergy. Despite its growing popularity as a means of expression, demonstration was still not seen as acceptable behavior; polls at the time showed some 40% of the public believed citizens have no right to demonstrate even peacefully (National Commission on the Causes and Prevention of Violence, 1969, p. 23). The shooting of protestors at Kent State University epitomized the ambivalent attitudes held by many people toward protest.

All these events were part of a mood among younger people that questioned the middle-class values of the United States. They often rejected the conventional lifestyles of their parents as being hypocritical and morally corrupt. As David Greenberg (1981, p. 4) points out, even criminal law was seen as a product of "the relative power of groups determined to use the criminal law to advance their own special interests or to impose their moral preferences on others." People were discussing decriminalization of "victimless" crimes at the same time police were arresting civil rights workers. Finally, the political scandal of Watergate cast a shadow of doubt and cynicism on the morality and integrity of all aspects of American government. No longer did it seem there were merely a few corrupt individuals running a fundamentally sound government structure; instead, it appeared the structure of government itself might be flawed. With a U.S. president implicated in governmental crimes, conflict theories seemed to be an obvious candidate for serious criminological consideration.

The Intellectual Heritage

Conflict theories developed, in a sense, as an offshoot of labeling. While they had their own intellectual roots in a variety of German social theories (those of Hegel, Marx, Simmel, and Weber, for example), it took labeling to prepare the way. Reacting to the events of the time, social scientists began asking questions about social and legal structures that labeling had largely ignored. The early statements of both Austin Turk (1964) and Richard Quinney (1965), for example, were directed to the notion of societal reaction.

Even though conflict had not been popular, a smattering of conflict-oriented writing had appeared in sociology proper, and a Dutch theorist, Wilhem Bonger (1916), created an early theory of criminality by combining Marxist and psychoanalytic approaches. The most important impetus for the development of pluralist (i.e., oriented toward multiple groups) forms of conflict theory was the work of two sociologists, Lewis Coser (1956) and Ralf Dahrendorf (1958, 1959), who were the first to espouse conflict ideas as the McCarthy-era witch hunt for "communists" ended. Their writings spurred sociological interest in conflict and enlarged the perspective in the 1960s. Meanwhile, the rising radicalization of academia in general revived interest in the earlier work of Marx, and some scholars began to apply Marxist theory to crime and legal structures.

THE THEORETICAL PERSPECTIVE

There are many forms of conflict theory bound together only by the assumption that conflict is natural to society. Just as the theories of anomie, subculture, and differential opportunity could be grouped under consensus theory even though there are obvious differences among them, conflict theory contains at least as many different approaches. Here, however, they are treated as one of two general forms: pluralist or critical-radical. This would seem to be a common approach since others have made a similar distinction (Farrell & Swigert, 1982; Gibbons, 1979; Sykes, 1974; Vold, Bernard, & Snipes, 2001).

The Pluralist Conflict Perspective

The central concept of pluralist conflict theories is that of power and its use. These theories assume conflict emerges between groups (thus the term "pluralist") attempting to exercise control over particular situations or events. Thus, the conflict approach views social issues almost as though they were fields of combat with opposing armies fighting to see who will prevail and rule the land. As with armies, the matter of resources is a crucial one. It is the control of resources (money, land, political power) that provides the ability to successfully "fight" and to emerge victorious on a particular issue.

These social issues may arise out of problems of everyday life, because of lobbying by some group, or through the regular business and political process. In each, decisions are made to take one course of action or another. Since several groups may have vested interests in the outcome of a decision, each will attempt to exert influence on its own behalf. Further, the amount of influence each group will have is a product of the resources the group has available. Power to affect decisions is, therefore, synonymous with having resources.

An excellent example of power and vested interests can be seen whenever a state or federal legislative session opens. Different groups who would like laws passed, or who oppose the passage of certain laws, hire people to lobby the lawmakers. These lobbyists attempt by persuasion, and sometimes bribery, to influence legislation. When decisions are made on the floor of the legislature, the vested-interest groups usually have had much more say in the making of a law than the citizens each legislator represents.

Because power can be equated with resources, it seems evident that those who are higher up in the social class structure will be the more powerful members of society. Their influence in the making of social decisions, and their ability to impose values, will also be greater than those of the lower social classes. For conflict theorists, this explains the presence of a dominant middle-class value system in society. Similarly, the important statements of a society—its laws, for example—are bound up in middle-class values. This is so because, historically, the merchant class helped create the form of society we have today. We may now begin to ask whether the middle class has reached its peak of influence and some higher class is beginning to exert more control in society.

Law itself represents a resource. If a group's values are embodied in law, it can use that law, and its enforcement, to its benefit. The agents of law, in their enforcement efforts, perpetuate the values embodied in law and thus help keep in power those who already have power. Further, those who have values, or interests, opposing those of the "winners" find themselves in the position of being the most likely targets of enforcement agents. At this point, labeling theory dovetails with conflict theory to produce an explanation of the reaction process by which the less powerful come to the attention of law enforcement agents. For example, the less powerful (or the "losers") are stigmatized by the more powerful because of their opposition. Laws are then created or modified to enhance official reaction to the less powerful.

A final point is implied in the relationship between the use of power and the creation of law. Since law embodies the values of those who create it, law is also more likely to criminalize the actions of those outside the power group. Put another way, people rarely object to their own way of doing things; thus, any objections are going to be to the behavior of others. Why should a group expend resources to have its values upheld if the results will be detrimental to the group? Obviously, then, power not only helps a group to create law in its own interest, but also serves to reduce the chances members of the group will be criminalized. When power is essentially equal between two groups, a give-and-take relationship can develop. The abortion issue provides an excellent illustration of this phenomenon. As the groups involved have gained or lost power, laws have been passed to restrict the activities of the other side. Thus, we have seen laws that prohibit blocking the entrance of an abortion clinic, and a Florida law made it unlawful for a pregnant woman to take drugs and thereby addict an unborn child. Three illustrative theories, characteristic of this form of conflict, are covered here.

George Vold (1958) produced a theory emphasizing the group nature of society and the various competing interests of those groups. He saw that "groups come into conflict with one another as the interests and purposes they serve tend to overlap, encroach on one another, and become competitive" (Vold & Bernard, 1986, p. 272). Moreover, group members become more loyal and tightly knit as conflict escalates. Vold argued groups had to be watchful of their interests and ever ready to defend them. Thus, a group is always engaged in a continuous struggle to maintain and improve its standing vis-à-vis other groups. The election struggles between the Republican and Democratic parties characterize this process. Another good example is each presidential administration's attempt to control the interpretation of law by appointing members to the Supreme Court who share the president's ideology.

From this viewpoint, Vold went on to discuss the presence of conflict in criminal law, writing that "the whole process of lawmaking, lawbreaking, and law enforcement directly reflects deep-seated and fundamental conflicts between group interests and the more general struggles among groups for control of the police power of the state" (Vold & Bernard, 1986, p. 274). Finally, Vold observed that since minority groups lack the ability to strongly influence the legislative process, their behavior would most often be legislated as criminal. This criminalization then legitimates the use of the authorities on behalf of the more powerful group. In the 1920s and 1930s, for example, the Federal Bureau of Investigation was used on behalf of large companies to help control labor unions.

Austin Turk is another conflict theorist who saw social order as a product of powerful groups attempting to control society.[1] This control is exerted by putting values into law and then by having the authorities enforce that law. Turk began his conflict work with an article in which he called for the study of criminality as opposed to criminal behavior (1964). Suggesting the only explanation for criminality would be found in the criminal law, he proposed the examination of

---

[1] We would like to express appreciation to Austin Turk for his review and comments on this summary of his work.

criminal law and its relationship to a definition of criminal status. His original concerns were to specify the conditions under which an individual would be defined as a criminal in an authority–subject relationship. He said crime is a status given to norm resisters whose perception of social norms and reality is inadequate to anticipate the result of their actions (1966). In other words, the less sophisticated the subjects are, the more likely their interaction with authorities will be characterized by conflict. Juveniles, for instance, have a higher probability of running afoul of authorities than adults do.

This concept of authority–subject relationships remains important in Turk's writings (1969, 1976). He sees as a fact of life that authorities must be dealt with, usually requiring a permanent adjustment of the subordinate to the powerful. There are, according to Turk, two major ways in which control can be exerted over a society. The first is coercion, or physical force. The more a population must be forced by the authorities to obey the law, the more difficult it will be to control that society. Thus, a delicate consensus–coercion balance has to be maintained by the powerful members of society.

The second form of control is much more subtle. This type is represented by the control of legal images and living time. The law itself can come to be seen as something that is more important than people. Further, there are two forms of law: the official list of undesirable forms of behavior and their associated punishments, and the established rules for processing people through the law enforcement system. A legal process that is fashioned in favor of the powerful provides a degree of subtle control. Control of living time, on the other hand, is a later concept developed by Turk (1976, 1982). He notes that after a period of coercion, a society will adjust itself to new rules. As time goes on, the generation of people who were part of the old society will die out. The remaining people have experience only with the new society and thus are less likely to compare the new social order with the old one. When this happens, there will be little questioning of the rules of the new social order or, as Turk would put it, the relationship between authorities and the population (subjects).

These comments lead to a variety of propositions about criminality. Higher crime rates can be expected when physical coercion is more common than subtle forms of control. Similarly, the greater the power of the controlling groups, the higher will be the rate of criminalization for the less powerful. Finally, if the less powerful are organized, then likelihood of conflict with the authorities will be greater, with commensurately higher crime rates.

Richard Quinney, another of the major conflict theorists of the late 1960s and 1970s, began to question the definitions of crime and the legal process being offered by authorities. In a widely quoted book, Quinney (1970) presented his theory of the social reality of crime in six propositions. While he was later to become a Marxist criminologist, this first conflict approach was of the pluralist variety and reflected on Vold's conflict theory as well as social interactionist theories. In truth, the theory was an integrative one that also incorporated concepts from differential association, social learning, and labeling. At the same time, Quinney began rejecting traditional ideas of science, particularly the idea that scientific researchers worked with data representing the real world. His argument was that reality is merely what we perceive it to be (this is also called "philosophical idealism").

Quinney viewed crime, as did labeling theorists, as the product of reaction. The reaction of most importance, though, is that of the legitimate authorities. These authorities not only react to behavior but also impose definitions of the types of behavior that can be defined as criminal. They do so by using political power to create and place into criminal law those behaviors to which they object. Those in lower-class positions are more likely to engage in objectionable behavior and, indeed, learn such behaviors from those around them.

Earl Richard Quinney (1934–)

Richard Quinney was born in the midst of the Great Depression in 1934. He grew up in rural Wisconsin and attended a one-room schoolhouse. He graduated with a B.A. from Carroll College in 1956 with a dual degree in sociology and psychology. Almost drawn into an ill-suited career in hospital administration, Quinney finished his master's and Ph.D. in Sociology. He taught at St. Lawrence University, the University of Kentucky, the University of New York, Brown University, Boston College, University of Wisconsin, and, finally, Northern Illinois University, where he spent the largest portion of his career. His use of media imagery and challenges to the "Lone Ranger" mentality of American values assured his place in the popular radical conflict perspectives of his time. Quinney was awarded the American Society of Criminology's prestigious Sutherland Award in 1984.

Crime, then, is the product of legal definitions constructed through the exercise of political power. But crime alone is not the entire picture. Just as crime is socially constructed, so is noncrime. That is, actions that are strikingly similar to illegal behavior are allowed through political definitions as desirable behavior. Both crime and noncrime definitions are spread through the media. With their pervasive effect, the media construct a social reality that certain actions are naturally crime and certain actions are naturally noncrime. Therefore, citizens tend not to think about the fact that definitions have been constructed for them.

As an example of socially constructed reality, Quinney used the Lone Ranger radio program (1973). The ingredients of an outnumbered "hero" who always prevails, the pure silver bullets with which he brings down evil, and the moralistic tone of the broadcast are all illustrations of a media construction of good guys and bad guys. Similarly, we go from televised athletic events sponsored by beer (alcohol) companies to news programs decrying drunken drivers and drug-related crime. Quinney was attempting to paint these kind of images with the brush of a socially constructed reality to demonstrate crime is part of a society controlled by the powerful and, in turn, is used by the powerful as a method of controlling people in that society. Others have used Lone Ranger examples as well. Williams (1997), for instance, used the Lone Ranger example to point out the controlled social reality of criminological research as well.

A final perspective that falls under a pluralist conflict approach is one originally developed by Hubert Blalock (1956, 1957, 1967) as "power-threat" theory. Rather than argue the usual conflict point that wealth and class are the crucial ingredients in the making of criminal laws, Blalock suggested that it is race and national origin that are important. Noting the fact that whites are in political and economic control of the nation, he posed that challenges to white dominance would be met with political control and/or violence. This challenge, or threat to power, arises when a minority group becomes an increasing percentage of the local population. The group in power responds in three ways: by restricting the political rights of the minority group, by increasing symbolic forms of segregation, and by creating a threat-oriented ideological system. In short, discrimination increases as power-threat increases. Forms of discrimination involve disenfranchisement (restriction of voting rights), criminal laws, and ordinances aimed at the minority group, and ideological values encouraging violence against members of the group. Darnell Hawkins (1987) revised Blalock's original position by including the concept of *perception of threat*, thus removing the requirement that a group is actually increasing in percentage of the local population. The simple perception that this is so should be sufficient to initiate action by the power group.

The Radical Conflict Perspective

Even more difficult than capturing pluralist conflict positions with a broad stroke of the pen is a summary of the work of radical conflict theorists of the 1970s–1990s. Their positions range from political anarchism (Ferrell, 1993; Tifft, 1979) through Marxism (Chambliss, 1975; Platt, 1982; Quinney, 1977; Spitzer, 1975) and economic materialism (Gordon, 1973) to value diversity (Pepinsky & Jesilow, 1985) and left realism (Young & Matthews, 1992). It is even difficult to determine exactly what to call these different approaches. Regardless of this variety, though, most of the current radical versions of conflict theory can be traced to the writings of Karl Marx.

A preliminary version of radical conflict theories is characterized by the work of William Chambliss in the late 1960s and early 1970s. Chambliss became interested in the making of law and the process by which it was applied. His examination of the vagrancy laws in England (1964) exemplified the historical form of research the Marxist theories would use as evidence for their position. Documenting that the creation and changes in the vagrancy laws served to benefit the ruling classes, Chambliss focused on the importance of labor, resources, and control for the existing social order. Indeed, these were all themes he touched on in a 1969 statement of an interest-group, rather than a Marxist-oriented, theory.

In a 1971 publication entitled *Law, Order and Power*, with Robert Seidman, Chambliss began a Marxist analysis of the American criminal justice system. Chambliss and Seidman argued the ruling class controls the resources of society and uses law as a means of control. This class exercises control in two ways: By creating laws emphasizing the behaviors of the lower classes, the lower classes are criminalized, and by encouraging a myth that law serves the interests of everyone, the lower classes join in their own control. Chambliss and Seidman present their theory in a series of propositions that ultimately discuss the fact that each point of the criminal justice process favors the more powerful at the expense of the powerless. This statement served as a springboard for many analyses and conflict perspectives that followed. By 1975, Chambliss had turned his own theoretical commentary and analysis in a deeply Marxist direction.

Marxist Criminology

While Marx said very little about crime and criminals, many radical criminologists have adapted his general model of society to their explanations of crime. Marx saw conflict in society as being due to a scarcity of resources and a historical inequality in the distribution of those resources, notably power. This inequality creates a conflict of interest between those with and those without power. By the dawn of the Industrial Age, conflict had developed between two economic classes of society, the proletariat (the working class) and the dominant bourgeoisie (the nonworking owners of wealth).

The main theme in this conflict of classes was that of control of the mode of production (the owning and controlling of productive private property). As the controlling class exploited the labor of the working class, a struggle developed. Because Marx felt a group's position in society shaped its consciousness of that society, the working class was led to believe the capitalist structure of society was in their interest (false consciousness). As members of the exploited class became aware of their true position and common interests, they would gradually join forces and initiate overt conflict against the dominant class. This conflict would take the form of a revolution that would overthrow the ruling class and allow a classless society to exist in a socialist world without economic exploitation.

Marxist criminologists, largely working during the 1970s, assumed that class struggle affects crime on three fronts. First, they have argued that the *law itself is a tool of the ruling class*. The definitions of crime found in the law are a reflection of the interests of the ruling class and serve to perpetuate existing concepts of property, which is the foundation of capitalism. At the same time, the behavior of the ruling class is generally *not* placed under the rule of criminal law (Michalowski & Bohlander, 1976) and, instead, if placed into law at all, is found under administrative and regulatory laws. A belief in the validity of law deflects questions about its purpose and application and results in members of the working class policing themselves. Marxist criminologists prefer to speak of law as a violation of more general human rights (Platt, 1974; Schwendinger & Schwendinger, 1970, 1972, 1977).

The second major position of Marxist criminologists is they *view all crime (in capitalist nations) as the product of a class struggle* producing individualism and competition. The emphasis on accumulation of wealth and property leads to conflict between classes and even within classes. Thus, the chase to get ahead "manifests itself in the pursuit, criminal or otherwise, of property wealth and economic self-aggrandizement" (Bohm, 1982, p. 570). Even violent crime is pictured as the result of the "brutal" conditions under which the working class must live (Quinney, 1977, pp. 53–54). For the working classes, then, it is their exclusion from the mode of production that creates a social structure conducive to criminal behavior. Not all Marxist criminologists have been comfortable with this position, however. Greenberg (1975) and others have declared that explaining all crime as a product of the capitalist system is too unidimensional.

Third, Marxist criminologists must deal with *relationships to the mode of production as an explanation for crime*. Richard Quinney (1977) and Steven Spitzer (1975) have discussed the problem of surplus labor in capitalist societies. Surplus labor guarantees wages will be low, but too large a surplus of labor may also cause problems. Spitzer (1975) lists five types of "problem populations": (1) the poor stealing from the rich, (2) those who refuse to work, (3) those who retreat to drugs, (4) those who refuse schooling or do not believe in the benefits of family life, and (5) those who actively propose a noncapitalist society. As long as the problem group is relatively quiet and poses no immediate threat to the ruling class, there is little need to expend scarce resources on their control. Skid-row alcoholics are a typical group of this type, and Spitzer calls them "social junk." If, however, the group is active, then it poses a threat to the ruling class, and controlling its members becomes important. These groups (political activists, criminals, and revolutionaries) are called "social dynamite" by Spitzer and they draw a disproportionate share of the control agents' resources.

Major Concepts in Radical Explanations of Crime

Other than the elements already noted, radical and Marxist forms of criminological theory focus on five major concepts: social class and stratification, political economy, family disorganization, economic conditions, and surplus value. Social class is perhaps the most widespread concept, and it is found or implied in every other criminological theory as well. For radicals, social class is not simply one's position in the social order but a part of the internal working of capitalism. The two classes (proletariat and bourgeoisie) are created by capitalism largely because they are critical to a capitalist economy. The primary ingredients of class are wealth, power, and prestige, and are important because they affect the life chances and socialization of individuals in society. Political economy uses the concept of class but widens the meaning to take in the entire economic structure. This includes economic institutions and economic structures, or the ways in which corporations, monetary systems, and Wall Street are set up and arranged for the benefit of the bourgeoisie. By creating economic inequalities, these structures contribute to social inequalities that, in turn, affect the relationships between individuals. For instance, Ray Michalowski says "inequality tends to increase crime by weakening the social bond" (1985, p. 410).

Family disorganization is one of the products of inequality. Mark Colvin and John Pauly (1983) propose that inequality and social relations in the workplace produce varying attitudes toward authority. When workplace control is authoritarian, hostility and alienation develop. These workplace experiences are reproduced in other social relations, such as the family, the school, and the peer group. Negative workplace experiences generate disorganized families and undesirable environments for children. This happens because lower-class workers tend to be employed in organizations depending on control techniques that are utilitarian (use material rewards), inconsistent, and coercive (erratic and stressful). As parents, such workers learn the same patterns of control and pass them on to their children. In such surroundings, children are more likely to engage in delinquency, particularly serious and sustained delinquency.

Economic conditions are also critical to many radical theories. Unemployment is among the most common of the factors assumed to be associated with crime. Quinney (1977, p. 149) expresses the relationship nicely: "Unemployment simultaneously makes necessary various actions of survival by the unemployed surplus population and requires the state to control that population in some way." During periods of economic depression and recession, industry must reconcile a threat to its survival with downsizing its labor force. Such a move creates more control over those workers who are retained but also creates a surplus group of unemployed workers. To keep these workers from becoming a problem for the capitalist economy, control is given over to the criminal justice system and prisons are used to warehouse those most threatening to the social order. In Spitzer's terms, the problem is some of those unemployed will become social dynamite. The same problem holds true for workers displaced by technological innovation. Bob Bohm (1985) views the situation not as one of economic crises causing crime but of the capitalist system creating competition over scarce resources and promoting self-interest. The irony is that the saving of labor costs by using the criminal justice system to control surplus labor also results in the expenditure of scarce resources. Certainly, the corporate world is concerned about the high cost and amount of crime. Less costly approaches to the problem are continually being sought.

Finally, surplus value is the capitalist exploitation of the difference between the cost of production and the value of the product. If workers can be made to work longer for the same amount of money, or if they can be replaced by more cost-effective machines, the amount of surplus value increases. Not only does such a condition create unemployment, but it also creates underemployment, and many people barely manage to earn a living. Meanwhile, the value of the product increases. The combination of increasing marginal populations and increasing product value makes conditions particularly conducive to property crime.

Left Realism

After criticisms that much of the Marxist and radical theories were too simplistic, a new form of radical criminology emerged in the 1980s, characterized by the writings of Jock Young in Britain and Walter Dekeseredy in the United States. The British version seems to have been the product of radicals' disenchantment with their ability to change and reform society and the exceedingly conservative direction of the ruling British Labour Party (see Young, 1992). This version takes to heart the problem of translating radical ideas into realistic social policy (thus the term "realism") and is similar to the grounded labeling theory proposed by Dario Melossi, briefly reviewed in the previous chapter. As the British version of left realism was coming together, Tony Platt (1985) was echoing similar thoughts in the United States, where opposition to the "get tough" policies and emphasis on crime control led to a search for alternatives. The central task of a realist criminology is to make the perspective of practical use to policymakers without losing its critical edge. Indeed, realists feel the best contribution criminology can make is to concern itself with specific analyses of crime and crime policies. In so doing, they must take crime as a social problem seriously in a way that most radical criminology has failed to do.

For the left realist, the "lethal combination" of relative economic deprivation and a market that encourages individual success creates not only a sense of unfairness and injustice (Young, 1999) but also the tendency for those trapped in inner-city poverty to prey upon each other (Dekeseredy, 2003; Dekeseredy & MacLean, 1991). This position represents a deviation from the Marxist view that all crime is a product of the capitalist system as realists recognize the presence of crime in socialist countries and posit crime is a real problem for all. Indeed, crime constitutes a net loss in the quality of life for all classes, and the most common victims of crime are the working class. Thus, they embrace the idea that crime is a problem and work to assist victims.

Rather than maintain the radical argument that the causes of crime are unemployment and poverty, a more complex explanation is offered. Trevor Jones, Brian MacLean, and Jock Young (1986) take pieces from both radical and traditional criminological theories and present four variables (the "square of crime") in their explanation of crime: the victim, the offender, the state, and the community. Further, the explanation combines both macrotheory and microtheory in an effort to demonstrate the effect of structural variables on processes that affect individuals.

Realists also believe crime control should be taken seriously, else the "right" will monopolize crime definitions and the criminal justice system. For instance, one realist proposal is to cede most control of local police to the community being policed. Realists have also embraced some traditional forms of research and policy. They have used surveys on victimization and fear of crime and have even examined local perceptions of the police. Proposals for policy initiatives have included community participation in the formulation of crime prevention schemes and various forms of short-term gains related to crime, such as increases in minimum wage, job training programs, and housing assistance. Finally, left realists have one major goal: to emphasize "social justice as a way of achieving a fair and orderly society" (Matthews & Young, 1992, p. 6).

Anarchist Criminology

As a radical theory, anarchism is different from Marxist thought. Anarchists are opposed to hierarchies in all their forms. That is, anarchist criminology views authorities as agents of domination, serving one or several groups at the expense of others. Anarchists, then, defy all forms of domination, whether political, patriarchal, religious, or other. While the history of anarchy is much older, Larry Tifft (1979) created the first modern anarchist viewpoint within criminology and argued for a face-to-face form of justice. Few others wrote in this area until the publication of Jeff Ferrell's *Crimes of Style* (1993).

Ferrell argues domination is accomplished not merely through coercion but also through structures of knowledge, perception, and understanding. By this he means domination is the ability to control the way in which we define something, come to view that thing, and understand how it exists. To the extent our reality is defined for us by others, anarchists believe we should oppose those others. As Ferrell says (1993, p. 161):

> Anarchism attacks these hierarchies of credibility, and seeks to dismantle the mythologies of certainty and truth on which they are built. It undercuts the taken-for-grantedness of the world, the reality which systems of authoritarian knowledge construct.

An anarchist criminology, then, seeks to "demythologize" the concepts behind the criminal justice system and the legal order on which it is based. In its place, anarchists prefer a pluralist set of ideas and rationales. Indeed, they prefer *ambiguity,* a world in which things are somewhat uncertain and without concrete meanings and purposes. How then does society exist under anarchy? The answer lies in the reconstruction of a society that appreciates diversity and tolerance. Such a society is decentralized and based on collective negotiations of the way people relate to and live with each other. Problems are solved and control is exercised by agreements between people and the groups of which they are a part. Finally, anarchism itself must avoid becoming an accepted formula for social order. To do this, thought and action are deemed of equal priority, and humor is used to overcome seriousness and emerging authority. An anarchist criminology is a criminology in which people are responsible for living with other people, negotiating flexible agreements about how they are to behave, and collectively administering control measures. Existing social structure and authority are deemed too rigid and harmful to the quality of human life.

CLASSIFICATION OF THE THEORY

First of all, conflict theories obviously assume that society is conflict oriented rather than consensus oriented. They also tend to focus on the political structure of society, especially the making and enforcement of law. Therefore, conflict theories represent a break with a positivist tradition of explaining criminality and, instead, return to many of the concerns of the original Classical School. Conflict theories are more *classical* and emphasize crime rather than criminals. Yet at the same time, most criminological conflict theories share the positivist concern with explaining crime. They simply prefer that explanation be focused on the political and economic conditions of life.

macro

Because of their emphasis on political and economic *structure,* conflict theories rarely engage in discussions of the process by which criminal behavior is produced. This leads to a classification of the conflict approach to crime as a *macrotheory.* Clearly, it is the nature of society and its subsequent effect on social institutions rather than behavior that is to be explained. Where conflict theories approach processual issues, their concerns are similar to those of strain theories—how to shift the macrolevel effects of social structural to the individual level.

Summary

The conflict perspective, whether pluralist or radical, has changed the nature of criminological theorizing over the last two decades. Most criminologists now acknowledge the presence of conflict in American society, although they reserve judgment about the extent to which it affects crime.

While it is difficult to characterize conflict theories because of their diversity (doing so is similar to discussing all consensus theories as if they were one theory), there are certain commonalities. First, of course, is the assumption that conflict is natural to society (Marxists actually argue conflict is unnatural but that it has almost always been with us). Second, resources are assumed to be scarce, or otherwise limited, and possession of these resources conveys power over others. Third, competition for resources always exists. Fourth, it is in this competition and use of power that law and law enforcement become tools to gain and maintain position in society. If a particular group gains control over enough resources and is able to maintain its position long enough, the conflict may result in a class system, with a ruling class and a subjugated class.

Marxist theorists assume these basic points but add that modern capitalist society creates conditions of life conducive to crime. Indeed, it is this divergence from conflict theories in general that characterizes the Marxist position. Richard Quinney and John Wildeman, in the third edition of their work *The Problem of Crime* (1991, p. 78), provide an excellent summary of the Marxist conflict perspective. They locate four propositions as the essence of Marxist criminology: (1) crime is best understood under the Marxist perspective, (2) crime constitutes more than the state definition of crime, (3) the state version of crime and other social harms are a product of the class struggle, and (4) crime represents the alienation of individuals by capitalist social structures and institutions.

MAJOR POINTS OF THE THEORY

1. Conflict is a fact of life; society is most appropriately characterized by conflict.
2. Resources, both physical and social, are scarce and therefore in demand. It is the attempt to control these resources that generates the major portion of conflict in society.
3. Control of resources creates power, and that power is used to maintain and expand the resource base of one group at the expense of others.
4. Once a group achieves dominance over others, it seeks to use available societal mechanisms for its benefit to assure it remains dominant.
5. Law is a societal mechanism that provides the group in power with strong means of control over other, less powerful groups.
6. Laws are formulated so that they express the values and interests of the dominant group, and to restrict behavior common to less powerful groups.
7. The application and enforcement of law leads to a focus on the behavior of less powerful groups, thus disproportionately "criminalizing" the members of those groups.
8. And for Marxist versions of conflict theory, the conditions generated under the capitalist political economy are the primary cause of political and economic actions that generate crime.

Epilogue: Current Directions and Policy Implications

CURRENT DIRECTIONS

Contemporary conflict theory is pursuing two generic avenues. First, the *basic conflict propositions dealing with power differentials between groups and discriminatory processing* have been the target of much research. Discrimination research has produced a large number of studies and at this point, the evidence is somewhat questionable. Some studies have found support for class, race, or gender discrimination and others have not. Indeed, depending on which studies one examines and the critical way in which they are assessed, a case can be made for either side of the issue.

Actually, two considerations are relevant to the argument and may help resolve some of the problems. First, the form of research design and mode of analysis are inextricably tied to the results and conclusions drawn from the various studies. If researchers use official data gathered by agencies in criminal justice system, there may be some question that these data represent the actual behaviors of those who process offenders. Also, if the important variables are poorly measured, potential discrimination may be difficult to find regardless of the sophistication of the analysis (this was, and is, the case with much of the data available for racial profiling). Second, many conflict theorists might even argue the issue of discrimination is spurious, that the making of laws is the important issue. If laws are made that have a discriminatory focus on certain groups in society, then those individuals can be arrested in large numbers and yet still be processed by criminal justice agencies without discrimination. Under this scenario, discrimination is still taking place, but not on the processing level. Regardless of these concerns, though, there is no evidence that the issue is about to be resolved.

The second general avenue being pursued is a group of related theoretical concerns that Jim Thomas and Aogan O'Maolchatha (1989) first characterized as a *transcending of dominant social control ideas.* They listed four areas in which radical and Marxist criminologists were making contributions. First, there is realist criminology. Second, a peacemaking criminology has developed and been implemented in the criminal justice arena as restorative justice. Third, feminist scholars have developed a new form of radical criminology based on gender. Fourth, a postmodernist (or deconstructionist) criminology has emerged from European philosophical and linguistic positions. Ray Michalowski echoes these sentiments while categorizing the various critical efforts differently. He sees critical criminology as working within broad social theories (feminism, political economy, poststructuralism, and postmodernism) and within "hybrid" theories such as anarchist criminology, constitutive criminology, cultural criminology, newsmaking criminology, peacemaking criminology, and left realist criminology.

Other contemporary areas for conflict research include analysis of police strength, funding and actions in predominantly minority communities, perceptions and stereotypes of crime-prone or dangerous areas, as well as civil rights and privacy intrusions by the government in the wake of perceived terrorist threats. Research on racial profiling, disproportionate minority confinement, felony disenfranchisement, three strikes, immigration, and capital punishment attempts to illustrate how poor, minority, and powerless groups are more likely to be subject to the most extreme forms of law enforcement and punishment. Further, government has a vested interest in not being perceived as making mistakes in the sentencing of those judged guilty even after evidence to the contrary is uncovered (Edelman, 2006; Gumbhir, 2007; Hipp, Tita, & Bobbess, 2009; Kieso, 2005; Markert, 2010; Miller, 2006; Noble, 2005). In short, all these areas are exploring different ways of examining the problem of crime, but at the same time all are attempting to develop conceptions that do not rely on traditional analyses of crime. Those who want to know more about conflict theory today will find that most of it now uses the "postmodernist" label (see Chapter 15).

POLICY IMPLICATIONS

While radical theories appear to have had little effect on contemporary law and policy, conflict theories in general have at least contributed to a greater concern with equality in the criminal justice system. Earlier proposals for policy changes generally followed a scheme for greater due process and the removal of barriers toward greater sharing in governance across race and gender lines. Today, however, radical criminologists are much more sensitive to the practical nature of policy. Two scholars frequently identified with the conflict perspective, Austin Turk and Elliot Currie have noted several policy changes that have been, or might be suggested, by radicals. These generally involve two general approaches: resolving economic inequality and resolving social inequality. For instance, increasing the minimum wage, providing free education, and changing income tax to a progressive version would all presumably reduce economic inequality and thereby reduce crime. Elimination of race, gender, or age discrimination, or increased civil rights would presumably reduce social inequality. Some of the programmatic ideas from these two generic approaches include Head Start being made available to all children who are at risk of growing up uneducated and health services (and mental health services as well) being provided to all children at risk of disease and emotional trauma (a central point of national health care laws). Family support programs should have a greater governmental commitment—particularly in the areas of domestic violence and child abuse. Programs to fight drug use should be reevaluated, and a greater share of resources given to treatment-oriented, nonpunitive models. Finally, Currie specifically suggests all forms of services needed by young children should be enhanced and greater efforts made to provide them.

Randall Amster (2004) uses a conflict perspective to help explain how the homeless and street people of Tempe, Arizona, are marginalized and criminalized by laws and regulations in support of business and wealthier segments of the urban population. In his estimation, protests and activist campaigns against the restrictions levied on the homeless have been successful in calling attention to the disproportionate use of social control resources toward a relatively minor social problem. He also demonstrates how the average citizen, including those who are occupying public spaces, is left out of the discussion of how to use and regulate those spaces. Theorists such as Amster want students to go beyond a focus on how laws, like a ban on sitting or loitering on sidewalks, affect the homeless and appear to protect businesses. They point out that attention should be paid to how that same law might be used to restrict protesters and activists who want to call attention to causes in a public forum. In the same way, Jeff Ferrell (2006), researching the underground trade of "dumpster diving, trash picking, and street scavenging," would argue that ordinances and aggressive enforcement of laws against such activities fit a conflict interpretation of capitalist interests. The entire notion of recycling and living off yard sale and discarded items is a threat to the throwaway model of consumerism promoted by and crucial to the U.S. economy.

Concerning white-collar crime, policies supported by conflict theorists would include allocation of more resources to regulatory agencies fighting corporate and occupational crime, requirements for codes of ethics in corporations, and the teaching of ethics courses in business schools. One of the policy successes of conflict theory from the 1980s to around 2000 was the initiation of programs for investigating and prosecuting white-collar crimes. As a corollary of this attention, businesses paid more attention to ethics issues. It is worth noting here that the rise of Homeland Security and the shift of attention and funds to security issues almost wiped out the FBI's white-collar crime program. Similarly, after 9–11 the financial industry apparently focused on security issues but somehow lost track of ethical concerns, resulting in the painful economy created by the recent Great Recession.

On a broader scale, conflict theorists would also encourage a redefinition of crime to include most cases of harm inflicted on society. Radical criminologists have proposed programs to eliminate racism and sexism in the criminal justice system and in society at large. They have argued for increased employment opportunities and enhanced skills training for large sectors of the population, as well as reductions in social stratification and inequality.

Policy directions, then, are available under conflict and radical theories, and some of these theorists are quite sensitive to practical application. The emergence of the left realist movement, for example, was expressly tied to a concern for application of theory at the local and neighborhood levels.

Questions and Weblinks

Critical Thinking Questions

1. Is conflict normal in society and, therefore, is crime a natural and expected product of our way of life in America?
2. Discuss some of the laws that appear to be differentially enforced by the criminal justice system today. Why do you think this occurs?
3. How do vested-interest groups operate? Do you think their influence is positive or negative? Why?

Practice Essay Questions

1. Discuss how the conflict aspects of earlier theories led up to the conflict theory of the 1960s.
2. What are some of the concepts and ideas used in contemporary criminological theory that have been borrowed from the work of Karl Marx?
3. Describe what Spitzer calls "problem populations" and the methods that are currently used to control them.

Related Websites

http://www.spartacus.schoolnet.co.uk/TUmarx.htm
http://critcrim.org/

http://www.nationalaffairs.com/doclib/20060406_issue_079_article_1.pdf

Bibliography

Amster, R. (2004). *Street people and the contested realms of public space.* New York: LFB Scholarly Publishing.

Blalock, H. M., Jr. (1956). Economic discrimination and Negro increase. *American Sociological Review, 21,* 584–588.

Blalock, H. M., Jr. (1957). Percent non-white and discrimination in the south. *American Sociological Review, 22,* 677–682.

Blalock, H. M., Jr. (1967). *Toward a theory of minority-group relations.* New York: John Wiley.

Bohm, R. M. (1982). Radical criminology: An explication. *Criminology, 19,* 565–589.

Bohm, R. M. (1985). Beyond unemployment: Toward a radical solution to the crime problem. *Crime and Social Justice, 21,* 213–222.

Bonger, W. A. (1916). *Criminality and economic conditions* (H. P. Horton, Trans.). Boston: Little, Brown.

Chambliss, W. B. (1964). A sociological analysis of the law of vagrancy. *Social Problems, 12,* 67–77.

Chambliss, W. B. (1975). Toward a political economy of crime. *Theory and Society, 2,* 152–153.

Chambliss, W. B., & Seidman, R. B. (1971). *Law, order and power.* Reading, MA: Addison-Wesley.

Colvin, M., & Pauly, J. (1983). A critique of criminology: Toward an integrated structural-Marxist theory of delinquency production. *American Journal of Sociology, 89,* 513–551.

Coser, L. (1956). *The functions of social conflict.* New York: Macmillan.

Dahrendorf, R. (1958). Out of Utopia: Toward a reconstruction of sociological analysis. *American Journal of Sociology, 67,* 115–127.

Dahrendorf, R. (1959). *Class and class conflict in an industrial society.* London: Routledge and Kegan Paul.

Dekeseredy, W. S. (2003). Left realism on inner-city crime. In M. D. Schwartz & S. E. Hatty (Eds.), *Controversies in critical criminology* (pp. 29–42). Anderson: Cincinnati.

Dekeseredy, W. S., & MacLean, B. (1991). Exploring the gender, race and class dimensions of victimization: A left realist critique of the Canadian Urban Victimization Survey. *International Journal of Offender Therapy and Comparative Criminology, 35,* 143–161.

Edelman, B. (2006). *Racial prejudice, juror empathy, and sentencing in death penalty cases.* New York: LFB Scholarly Publishing.

Farrell, R. A., & Swigert, V. L. (1982). *Deviance and social control.* Glenview, IL: Scott, Foresman.

Ferrell, J. (1993). *Crimes of style: Urban graffiti and the politics of criminality.* New York: Garland.

Ferrell, J. (2006). *Empire of scrounge: Inside the urban underground of dumpster diving, trash picking, and street scavenging.* New York: New York University Press.

Gibbons, D. C. (1979). *The criminological enterprise: Theories and perspectives.* Englewood Cliffs, NJ: Prentice Hall.

Gordon, D. M. (1973). Capitalism, class and crime in America. *Crime and Delinquency, 19,* 163–186.

Greenberg, D. F. (1975). On one-dimensional Marxist criminology. *Theory and Society, 3,* 610–621.

Greenberg, D. F. (1981). Introduction. In D. F. Greenberg (Ed.) *Crime & capitalism: Readings in Marxist criminology* (pp. 1–35) Palo Alto: Mayfield.

Greenberg, D. F. (Ed.) (1993). *Crime & capitalism: Readings in Marxist criminology* (Expanded and updated ed.). Philadelphia: Temple University Press.

Gumbhir, V. K. (2007). *But is it racial profiling? Policing, pretext stops, and the color of suspicion.* New York: LFB Scholarly Publishing.

Hawkins, D. F. (1987). Beyond anomalies: Rethinking the conflict perspective on race and capital punishment. *Social Forces, 65,* 719–745.

Hipp, J. R., Tita, G. E., & Bobbess, L. N. (2009). Intergroup and intragroup violence: Is violent crime an expression of group conflict or social disorganization? *Criminology, 47,* 521–564.

Jones, T., MacLean, B., & Young, J. (1986). *The Islington crime survey.* Aldershot, England: Gower.

Kieso, D. (2005). *Unjust sentencing and the California three strikes law.* New York: LFB Scholarly Publishing.

Markert, J. (2010). The changing face of racial discrimination: Hispanics as the dominant minority in the USA—A new application of power-threat theory. *Critical Sociology, 36,* 307–327.

Matthews, R., & Young, J. (1992). Reflections on realism. In J. Young & R. Matthews (Eds.), *Rethinking criminology: The realist debate* (pp. 1–23). Newbury Park, CA: Sage.

Michalowski, R. J. (1985). *Order, law and crime: An introduction to criminology.* New York: Random House.

Michalowski, R. J., & Bohlander, E. W. (1976). Repression and criminal justice in capitalist America. *Sociological Inquiry, 46,* 95–106.

Miller, K. S. (2006). *Wrongful capital convictions and the legitimacy of the death penalty.* New York: LFB Scholarly Publishing.

National Commission on the Causes and Prevention of Violence (1969). *The Politics of protest: Task force report on violent aspects of protest and confrontation.* New York: Simon and Schuster.

Noble, R. L. (2005). *Black rage in the American prison system.* New York: LFB Scholarly Publishing.

Pepinsky, H. E., & Jesilow, P. (1985). *Myths that cause crime* (2nd ed., annotated). Cabin John, MD: Seven Locks Press.

Platt, T. (1974). Prospects for a radical criminology in the United States. *Crime and Social Justice, 1,* 2–6.

Platt, T. (1982). Crime and punishment in the United States: Immediate and long-term reforms from a Marxist perspective. *Crime and Social Justice, 18,* 38–45.

Platt, T. (1985). Criminology in the 1980s: Progressive alternatives to law and order. *Crime and Social Justice, 21,* 191–199.

Quinney, R. (1965). Is criminal behaviour deviant behaviour? *British Journal of Criminology, 5,* 132–142.

Quinney, R. (1970). *The social reality of crime.* Boston: Little, Brown.

Quinney, R. (1973). There's a lot of folks grateful to the Lone Ranger: Some notes on the rise and fall of American criminology. *Insurgent Sociologist, 4,* 56–64.

Quinney, R. (1977). *Class, state and crime: On the theory and practice of criminal justice.* New York: McKay.

Quinney, R., & Wildeman, J. (1991). *The problem of crime: A peace and social justice perspective* (3rd ed.). Mountain View, CA: Mayfield.

Schwendinger, H., & Schwendinger, J. (1970). Defenders of order or guardians of human rights? *Issues in Criminology, 5,* 113–146.

Schwendinger, H., & Schwendinger, J. (1972). The continuing debate on the legalistic approach to the definition of crime. *Issues in Criminology, 7,* 71–81.

Schwendinger, H., & Schwendinger, J. (1977). Social class and the definition of crime. *Crime and Social Justice, 7,* 4–13.

Spitzer, S. (1975). Towards a Marxian theory of deviance. *Social Problems, 22,* 638–651.

Sykes, G. M. (1974). The rise of critical criminology. *Journal of Criminal Law and Criminology, 65,* 206–213.

Thomas, J., & O'Maolchatha, A. (1989). Reassessing the critical metaphor: An optimistic revisionist view. *Justice Quarterly, 6,* 143–171.

Tifft, L. L. (1979). The coming redefinitions of crime: An anarchist perspective. *Social Problems, 26,* 392–402.

Turk, A. T. (1964). Prospects for theories of criminal behavior. *Journal of Criminal Law, Criminology and Police Science, 55,* 454–461.

Turk, A. T. (1966). Conflict and criminality. *American Sociological Review, 31,* 338–352.

Turk, A. T. (1969). *Criminality and legal order.* Chicago: Rand McNally.

Turk, A. T. (1976). Law as a weapon in social conflict. *Social Problems, 23,* 276–291.

Turk, A. T. (1982). *Political criminality: The defiance and defense of authority.* Beverly Hills, CA: Sage.

Vold, G. B. (1958). *Theoretical criminology.* New York: Oxford University Press.

Vold, G. B., & Bernard, T. J. (1986). *Theoretical criminology* (3rd ed.). New York: Oxford University Press.

Vold, G. B., Bernard, T. J., & Snipes, J. B. (2001). *Theoretical criminology* (5th ed.). New York: Oxford University Press.

Williams, F. P., III. (1997). There's still a lot of folks grateful to the Lone Ranger. *Social Pathology, 3,* 16–23.

Young, J. (1992). Ten points of realism. In J. Young & R. Matthews (Eds.), *Rethinking criminology: The realist debate* (pp. 24–68). Newbury Park, CA: Sage.

Young, J. (1999). *The exclusive society.* London: Sage.

Young, J., & Matthews, R. (Eds.) (1992). *Rethinking criminology: The realist debate.* Newbury Park, CA: Sage.

Research Bibliography

General Conflict Theory (from 1990)

Antonaccio, O., & Tittle, C. R. (2007). A Cross-national test of Bonger's theory of criminality and economic conditions. *Criminology, 45,* 925–958.

Abril, J. C. (2007). Cultural conflict and crime: Violations of native American Indian cultural values. *International Journal of Criminal Justice Sciences, 2,* 44–62.

Arsovska, J., & Verduyn, P. (2008). Globalization, conduct norms, and 'culture conflict': Perceptions of violence and crime in an ethnic Albanian context. *British Journal of Criminology, 48,* 226–246.

Balkwell, J. (1990). Ethnic inequality and the rate of homicide. *Social Forces, 69,* 53–70.

Barlow, D. E., Barlow, M. H., & Chiricos, T. G. (1993). Long economic cycles and the criminal justice system in the U.S. *Crime Law and Social Change, 19,* 143–169.

Beckett, K., Nrop, K., & Pfingst, L. (2006). Race, drugs, and policing: Understanding disparities in drug delivery arrests. *Criminology, 44,* 105–137.

Brown, M. C., & Warner, B. (1992). Immigrants, urban politics, and policing in 1990. *American Sociological Review, 57,* 293–305.

Brownsberger, W. (2000). Race matters: Disproportionality of incarceration for drug dealing in Massachusetts. *Journal of Drug Issues, 30,* 345–374.

Butcher, K., & Piehl, A. (1998). Evidence on the relationship between immigration and crime. *Journal of Policy Analysis and Management, 17,* 457–493.

Chamlin, M. (1990). Determinants of police expenditures in Chicago, 1904–1958. *Sociological Quarterly, 31,* 485–494.

Chamlin, M. B. (2009). Threat to whom? Conflict, consensus, and social control. *Deviant Behavior, 30,* 539–559.

Chamlin, M., & Myer, A. (2009). Disentangling the crime-arrest relationship: The influence of social context. *Journal of Quantitative Criminology, 25,* 371–389.

Chiricos, T. G., & Delone, M. (1992). Labor surplus and punishment: A review and assessment of theory and evidence. *Social Problems, 39,* 421–446.

Chiricos, T. G., Welch, K., & Gertz, M. (2004). Racial typification of crime and support for punitive measures. *Criminology, 42,* 359–389.

Denq, F., Lee, L. J., & Vaughn, M. S. (1996). Drug crime in Taiwan: A time-series analysis from 1965 to 1994. *Deviant Behavior, 17,* 347–368.

Gabbidon, S. (2003). Racial profiling by store clerks and security personnel in retail establishments. *Journal of Contemporary Criminal Justice, 19,* 345–364.

Gorton, J., & Boies, J. L. (1999). Sentencing guidelines and racial disparity across time: Pennsylvania prison sentences in 1977, 1983, 1992 and 1993. *Social Science Quarterly, 80,* 37–54.

Greenleaf, R. G., & Lanza-Kaduce, L. (1995). Sophistication, organization, and authority-suspect conflict: Rediscovering and unraveling Turk's theory of norm resistance. *Criminology, 33,* 565–586.

Hipp, J. R., Tita, G. E., & Bobbess, L. N. (2009). Intergroup and intragroup violence: Is violent crime an expression of group conflict or social disorganization? *Criminology, 47,* 521–564.

Holmes, M. D. (2003). Ethnicity, concentrated minority disadvantage, and perceived risk of victimization. *Journal of Ethnicity and Criminal Justice, 1*(3/4), 1–20.

Holmes, M. D., Hosch, H. M., Daudistel, H. C., Perez, D. A., & Graves, J. B. (1996). Ethnicity, legal resources, and felony dispositions in two Southwestern jurisdictions. *Justice Quarterly, 13,* 11–30.

Howard, G. J., Newman, G., & Freilich, J. D. (2002). Further evidence on the relationship between population diversity and violent crime. *International Journal of Comparative & Applied Criminal Justice, 26,* 203–229.

LaFree, G., & Tseloni, A. (2006). Democracy and Crime: A Multilevel Analysis of Homicide Trends in Forty-Four Countries, 1950–2000. *Annals of the American Academy of Political & Social Science, 605,* 26–49.

Lanza-Kaduce, L., & Greenleaf, R. G. (1994). Police-citizen encounters: Turk on norm resistance. *Justice Quarterly, 11,* 605–623.

Lawrence, R. G. (1996). Accidents, icons, and indexing: The dynamics of news coverage of police use of force. *Political Communication, 13,* 437–454.

Lee, M., Martinez, R., & Rosenfeld, R. (2001). Does immigration increase homicide? Negative evidence from three border cities. *Sociological Quarterly, 42,* 559–580.

Lee, N. (1995). Culture conflict and crime in Alaskan native villages. *Journal of Criminal Justice, 23,* 177–189.

Leiber, M. J. (1995). Toward clarification of the concept of 'minority' status and decision-making in juvenile court proceedings. *Journal of Crime and Justice, 18,* 79–108.

Leiber, M. J., & Jamieson, K. M. (1995). Race and decision making within juvenile justice: The importance of context. *Journal of Quantitative Criminology, 11,* 363–388.

Lynch, A. M. (2008). Hating the neighbors: The role of hate crime in the perpetuation of black residential segregation. *International Journal of Conflict & Violence, 2,* 6–27.

Lynch, M. J., Groves, W. B., & Lizotte, A. (1994). The rate of surplus value and crime. A theoretical and empirical examination of Marxian economic theory and criminology. *Crime, Law, and Social Change, 21,* 15–48.

MacLean, B. D. (1993). Left realism, local crime surveys and policing of racial minorities: A further analysis of data from the first sweep of the Islington Crime Survey. *Crime, Law, and Social Change, 19,* 51–86.

Maguire, B. (1990). The police in the 1800s: A three city analysis. *Journal of Crime and Justice, 13,* 103–132.

Messner, S. F., & Krohn, M. D. (1990). Class, compliance structures, and delinquency: Assessing integrated structural Marxist theory. *American Journal of Sociology, 96,* 300–328.

Mitchell, B. C., & Beth A. S. (2010). Macro social determinants of black police force size: Political mobilization and crime control. *Policing, 33*, 607–620.

Petrocelli, M., Piquero, A., & Smith, M. (2003). Conflict theory and racial profiling: An empirical analysis of police traffic stop data. *Journal of Criminal Justice, 31*, 1–11.

Quillian, L., & Pager, D. (2001). Black neighbors, higher crime? The role of racial stereotypes in evaluations of neighborhood crime. *American Journal of Sociology, 107*, 717–767.

Sampson, R., & Lauritsen, J. (1997). Racial and ethnic disparities in crime and criminal justice in the United States. *Crime and Justice, 21*, 311–374.

Smith, B. L., & Damphouse, K. R. (1996). Punishing political offenders: The effect of political motive on federal sentencing decisions. *Criminology, 34*, 289–321.

Weidner, R., & Terrill, W. (2005). A test of Turk's theory of norm resistance using observational data on police-suspect encounters. *Journal of Research in Crime and Delinquency, 42*, 84–109.

Weitzer, R. (1996). Racial discrimination in the criminal justice system: Findings and problems in the literature. *Journal of Criminal Justice, 24*, 309–322.

Williams, J. J. (1991). Predicting decisions rendered in criminal appeals. *Journal of Criminal Justice, 19*, 463–469.

Power Threat Theory (from 1990)

Bodapati, M., Anderson, J. F., & Brinson, T. E. (2008). Revisiting Hubert Blalock's power threat theory to determine its effect on court workgroup behavior as it concerns structured sentencing. *Criminal Justice Studies, 21*, 109–134.

Chiricos, T.G., McEntire, R., & Gertz, M. (2001). Perceived racial and ethnic composition of neighborhood and perceived risk of crime. *Social Problems, 48*(3), 322–340.

Crawford, C., Chiricos, T., & Kleck, G. (1998). Race, racial threat, and sentencing of habitual offenders. *Criminology, 36*, 481–512.

Eitle, D., D'Alessio, S. J., & Stolzenberg, L. (2002). Racial threat and social control: A test of the political, economic, and threat of black crime hypothesis. *Social Forces, 80*, 557–576.

Holmes, M. D. (2000). Minority threat and police brutality: Determinants of civil rights criminal complaints in U.S. municipalities. *Criminology, 38*, 343–368.

Holmes, M. D., Smith, B., Freng, A., & Munoz, E. (2008). Minority threat, crime control, and police resource allocation in the southwestern United States. *Crime & Delinquency, 54*, 128–152.

Kent, S. L., & Jacobs, D. (2005). Minority threat and police strength from 1980 to 2000: A fixed-effects analysis of nonlinear and interactive effects in large cities. *Criminology, 43*, 731–760.

Liu, B. (2001). Racial context and white interest: Beyond black threat and racial tolerance. *Political Behavior, 23*(2), 157–180.

Markert, J. (2010). The changing face of racial discrimination: Hispanics as the dominant minority in the USA—A new application of power-threat theory. *Critical Sociology, 36*, 307–327.

Myers, M. (1990a). Black threat and incarceration in postbellum Georgia. *Social Forces, 69*, 373–393.

Myers, M. (1990b). Economic threat and racial disparities in incarceration: The case of postbellum Georgia. *Criminology, 28*, 627–656.

Myers, M. (1991). Economic conditions and punishment in postbellum Georgia. *Journal of Quantitative Criminology 7*, 99–121.

Parker, K., Stults, B., & Rice, S. (2005). Racial threat, concentrated disadvantage and social control: Considering the macro-level sources of variation in arrests. *Criminology, 43*, 1111–1134.

Rouhana, N. N., & Fiske, S. T. (1995). Perception of power, threat, and conflict intensity in asymmetric intergroup conflict: Arab and Jewish citizens of Israel. *Journal of Conflict Resolution, 39*, 49–81.

Smith, B. W., & Holmes, M. D. (2003). Community accountability, minority threat, and police brutality: An examination of civil rights criminal complaints. *Criminology, 41*, 1035–1063.

Taylor, M. (1998). Local racial/ethnic proportions and white attitudes: Numbers count, *American Sociological Review, 63*, 512–35.

Tolnay, S. E., Deane, G., & Beck, E. M. (1996). Vicarious violence: Spatial effects on Southern lynchings, 1890–1919. *American Journal of Sociology, 102*, 788–815.

Gender-based Theories

LEARNING OBJECTIVES

Objective 10.1: Discuss why feminist theories are also considered conflict theories.

Objective 10.2: Define the social feminist concepts of paternalism, sexism, and chivalry and explain how each is used in the theories of this section.

Objective 10.3: Explain how parenting roles influence delinquency according to Hagan's power-control theory.

Objective 10.4: Discuss the concept of economic marginalization and why it is central to most feminist perspectives.

Objective 10.5: Describe how theorists can argue that because of women's liberation crime might increase or decrease.

INTRODUCTION

The gender theories comprise a diverse group of perspectives that specify gender as a critical variable in understanding crime. On the whole, they are designed to sensitize scholars to the relative "invisibility" of women in the field (in terms of offenders, workers, victims, and scholars). The perspective is largely based on a view of a patriarchal (male-based) society that empowers males in virtually all social interaction that matters. Males dominate government, make rules, define gender roles, and set the patterns for power in society. In short, males are dominant and females are subordinated. The most important point for virtually all feminist perspectives is males fail to understand the importance of gender and sex roles in society. Thus, critique of traditional male-based theoretical positions is an essential part of feminist criminology.

There are goals other than sensitizing. One is to produce a distinctly feminist perspective on society. Some feminist scholars (see Daly & Chesney-Lind, 1988) strongly feel that existing criminological knowledge is a product of "men's experiences" and therefore is a biased and power-centered view of the world. By analyzing and evaluating through female perspectives, it is assumed a different view will emerge of personal conflict, crime, and crime prevention. Indeed, many feminist criminologists focus on the intersection of social class, race, ethnicity, and sexual orientation with gender in an attempt to understand and highlight gender differences in crime.

THE HERITAGE OF THE THEORY

The Social Heritage

Although we have previously discussed the cultural and social climate of the 1960s and 1970s, there are a few things still worth mentioning in the context of feminist theory. The civil rights movement did more than sensitize some of the public to discriminatory practices affecting minorities; people began to realize females were also being treated unequally. One's gender became the subject of equal opportunity discussions and females ultimately fell under the equal opportunity statutes. The women's liberation movement was instrumental in bringing feminist issues to the surface and "women's lib" became a commonplace term. New magazines were devoted to the topic (e.g., *Cosmopolitan*) and many of society's cultural elite bandied the topic around. Television news shows and commentaries often reported "women's lib" issues. At the same time, criticism of government policies and emergent radical discussions served to highlight an overall sense of who was in power and who was being dominated. As minority groups began to get their discrimination message across, feminist concerns joined in the fray. A constitutional amendment guaranteeing equal rights ("ERA") was passed by Congress and just failed in ratification by the states. By the beginning of the 1990s, female themes had become so prevalent that catering to "the female vote" was intrinsic to national political campaigns.

The Intellectual Heritage

With the social turmoil, conflict-based theories became popular in academic circles. Because of their emphasis of power relationships, it was merely a matter of time before conflict theory discussions turned to the issue of gender. Indeed, the first gender-based article in criminology (Klein, 1973) was born out of a radical orientation. Even as late as the 1980s, a general mood of critique (and some degree of uneasiness about the dominant positivist model) in the social sciences contributed to, and was reflected in, feminist theorizing. In the 1980s, women's studies programs began to grow in universities and by the end of the decade had become commonplace. Feminist issues became part of the academic landscape. With that base, treatment of gender issues flourished and gender scholarship moved into virtually all academic disciplines. And this, perhaps more than anything, is the core intellectual heritage of feminist theory—it is not based in the traditional academic disciplines but is truly interdisciplinary.

THE THEORETICAL PERSPECTIVE

Many sources point to females as the forgotten population in criminology and criminal justice. Even when females have been included in theories of crime and delinquency, their behavior is explained by simple concepts and motives (Klein, 1973). There is, of course, no reason to suppose females are less complex in their behavior than males. A number of theorists have also found it unusual that, as a whole, females remain relatively noncriminal, yet gender is one of the least explored areas of criminology (Leonard, 1982). How, for instance, do we explain that criminality is 80% male? Gender-based theories have attempted to do just that.

Although we are oversimplifying here for convenience, the gender perspective has two basic functions. One serves to criticize traditional male, *androcentric* (male-centered) approaches to studying crime and the traditional operations of the criminal justice system. The second function is the development of gender-sensitive interpretations of deviance and a consideration of the nature of female criminality. Among these interpretations are a number of major works making up what is characterized as feminist theory.

Social Traits and Feminism

A feminist perspective on crime developed in criminology the same way the feminist view came to literature, art, politics, and science: one writer, one artist, one senator, and one astronaut at a time. Books such as Henrik Ibsen's *A Doll's House*, Kate Chopin's *The Awakening*, and Virginia Woolfe's *A Room of One's Own* highlighted the struggle of women coming of age in a society rooted in paternalism, chivalry, and sexism. These social traits have become the cornerstones of several different approaches to studying female criminality.

PATERNALISM   Patriarchal (male-based) power relations are central to understanding the way we define and study crime. The roots of patriarchal power in our social system are dominant enough to explain why women are more likely to be victimized in the home, and by friends and intimates, than outside the home and by strangers. Paternalism suggests females need to be protected for their own good. A paternalistic society is organized around independence for males and dependence for females. A good example can be found in *Turner v. Safley*, in which the U.S. Supreme Court criticized the Missouri Department of Corrections for its paternalistic policies regarding the marriage of female inmates. While the marriages of male inmates were all routinely approved, the requests of females were carefully scrutinized and only rarely granted. It seems Missouri wardens were "protecting" their female inmates. The major impetus in granting a marriage request for a female prisoner was the presence of a child born out of wedlock. Calling the arbitrary policy unconstitutional, the court chastised the wardens for their discriminatory control of First Amendment rights. Meda Chesney-Lind (1981, 1987, 1988a, 1988b) argues paternalism is the major reason female juveniles are detained much more frequently for status offenses. The court was "protecting girls for their own good."

A number of researchers have argued that women as caregivers seem to benefit from the court's paternal reluctance to separate children from their mothers (Kaukinen, 1995; Kramer & Ulmer, 1996). Examining sentencing guidelines, Koons-Witt (2002) found that women with dependent children received more community alternative sentences than women without dependent children.

CHIVALRY   The notion of chivalry is tied up with old conceptions of men doing things for women and, of course, is one way in which paternalism can be practiced. A classic example of chivalry is a man rushing ahead to open a door for a woman. Chivalry implies attitudes toward female offenders may account for differential processing in the criminal justice system. At each discretionary step from arrest to sentencing, women may benefit from the belief that males "just don't treat ladies badly" and thereby receive lenient dispositions. If police routinely chose not to arrest women, then female crime rates would appear to be quite low. If the system were to reduce its practice of chivalry, there would be a false perception that female criminality is increasing.

There is evidence chivalry does, indeed, exist within the criminal justice system, although the practice of chivalry appears to be complex. In form, it often involves stereotypical expectations that only some female offenders may appear to meet. As Mallicoat (2007) found, girls were less likely to be considered criminally dangerous, which may account for less serious outcomes in the process although they also had poorer relationships with their family, and they were more likely to have run away, which may influence the decision to place them in detention facilities. Visher (1983), Saulters-Tubbs (1993), Spohn, Gruhl, and Welch (1987), and Albonetti (1986) all found evidence of chivalry in either police encounters, district attorney charging decisions, or charge reduction decisions. On the other hand, Curran (1983) failed to find support for chivalry at any decision point other than sentencing. In her research, judges seemed to be more lenient toward women when issuing sentences, whereas MacDonald and Chesney-Lind (2001) found that girls received harsher treatment in the later stages of court processing than did their counterpart males.

Analyzing data from 1948 to 1976, Marvin Krohn, James Curry, and Shirley Nelson-Kilger (1983) found evidence of gender bias in the processing of juvenile status offenses. While girls were as likely to be referred to probation as boys who had committed misdemeanors (paternalism), they were still less likely to be referred for both misdemeanors and felonies (chivalry). Daly (1989a, 1989b, 1994a, 1994b) reports that there is substantial evidence females are treated more leniently than males by the criminal justice system. However, as the most current studies have indicated, race, socioeconomic status, family, and work circumstances as well as perceptions of parenting suitability may interact with gender to influence disposition decisions.

SEXISM   Sexism refers to attitudes or practices having the effect of producing inequality between the sexes. Over 70 years ago, a St. Louis official lamented that sexism created problems in the way illegitimate births were handled (Mangold, 1926). He claimed social service agencies were confronted with the prejudices of judges and prosecutors, as well as of the public, who believed that (1) illegitimate babies should not be kept with their mothers but taken from them as soon as possible, (2) the parents of an illegitimate child should marry as soon as possible, (3) married men who father illegitimate children should not be exposed, and (4) the mothers of illegitimate children should wear the "scarlet letter." Much of the literature on the early juvenile justice system demonstrates the court's preoccupation with status offenses, particularly in sanctioning the sex-related behaviors of girls. Although girls were less likely than boys to be apprehended and adjudicated, they were more likely to be detained and institutionalized for status offenses (Chesney-Lind, 1977; Chesney-Lind & Shelden, 1992). This was true even though self-report studies showed males as likely, if not more likely, to be involved in status offenses (Canter, 1982). Obviously, the juvenile courts were practicing a double standard for acceptable behavior.

Contemporary Theories of Female Criminality

The first of the modern gender-based perspectives on crime attempted to explain female criminality rather than offer a gender-sensitive approach to crime in general. Because of a lack of explanations of female crime, these perspectives were received with interest. With the advent of the feminist movement in the late 1960s, social observers began following changes in the role of women in society. By the mid-1970s, it appeared substantial changes were under way, and two criminologists, Freda Adler and Rita James Simon, proposed new theories of female criminality.

LIBERATION AND OPPORTUNITY   Liberation/masculinity perspectives argue that as the gender gap narrows, the behavior, both legitimate and illegitimate, of women and men will become more alike. In *Sisters in Crime* (1975), Freda Adler developed the idea that changes

Freda Alder (1934–)

Freda Adler was born in 1934 and received her bachelor's, master's, and Ph.D. in sociology at the University of Pennsylvania. Adler taught for many years at Rutgers University, where she helped to launch one of the first schools of criminal justice. She was elected President of the American Society of Criminology (ASC) in 1995 and was named a Fellow in the ASC. She was also a faculty member of the National Judicial College and a Visiting Fellow at Yale University. In 2007, she received the Founders Award from the Academy of Criminal Justice Sciences (ACJS), and in 2010, she was named a Fellow in that organization (ACJS). She is currently a Visiting Professor in Criminology at the University of Pennsylvania and Professor Emeritus, School of Criminal Justice, Rutgers.

in female criminality are the product of changes in the social roles of women in our society. This is an explanation of female crime based on the women's liberation movement. American society has grown progressively more receptive to women in the work force, and women have gained greater freedom. According to Adler, as women assume more assertive positions in society and adopt more traditionally "male" roles and statuses, they will experience a masculinizing of their own behaviors. This process will result in women committing more traditional male crimes, such as violent crimes and white-collar crimes. The rate of female crime will also increase (Adler, 1981).

While Adler's ideas are logical and intriguing, research has yet to find much support for her position (Radosh, 1990; Steffensmeier & Steffensmeier, 1980). For example, Stephen Cernkovich and Peggy Giordano (1979a, 1979b) looked at delinquent activity and attitudes supporting "women's liberation" and failed to find a relationship. Instead, they found juveniles with the most liberated attitudes were less delinquent.

Rita James Simon (1975) presented a variation on this approach that focuses on opportunities available to females. She argued that the nature of female criminality has been molded by the social, familial, and occupational structures of the lives of women. Consequently, changes in the traditional roles of women are also a key to the hypothesis that, over time, women will be involved in more employment-related crimes. Instead of focusing on changes in the personal roles of women in society or on the consideration of behaviors as either feminine or masculine, however, this perspective simply looks at the opportunities women have available to participate in crime. Simon argues, in the past, limited participation in the labor force blocked women's access to opportunities to commit crimes such as fraud, embezzlement, and grand larceny. For example, as clerks and tellers, women in business and banking were too closely supervised to steal successfully. As women move into the ranks of executives, managers, and accountants, however, it is expected that they will gain greater access to more covert theft opportunities. Indeed, several of the targeted executives of the ENRON fraud network were women.

The opportunities for women in illegitimate markets may expand over time as well. As an example, in 1993, Italian police captured a key figure of one of the major branches of organized crime, Rosetta Cutolo. Although her prominent place in the organization was initiated by her brother, the founder of the gang, she was allegedly responsible for arranging the murder of a prison warden and the car bombing of a rival. The newspaper pointed out that seven of thirty-two leaders arrested from this organized crime gang have been women, and that the Camorra gang has "offered more equal opportunities for women than the Cosa Nostra, its Sicilian cousin" (Montalbano, 1993). Likewise, Anderson (2005) argues that women perform a number of functions central to the drug economy. The arrest of a female drug lord in Mexico received considerable attention as tales of her rise to power with seduction and deception generated folk legends, a YouTube video, and a massive federal investigation. Sandra Avila Beltran, officials say, was head of a family-run drug cartel, united Columbian and Mexican traffickers, and romanced a number of kingpins (Rodriguez, 2007) until her capture. Still, she managed to elude authorities much longer than many of her male relatives who were also leading drug smugglers in the area.

As with masculinity or liberation approaches, there is little evidence of any significant impact on female criminality generated by changing opportunity structures apart from some anecdotal accounts as described above. It appears that the lower-class females who are most likely to engage in crime have had very little increase in opportunities. In a sense, Simon's theory could be called a theory of middle-class female criminality, and there is some question whether substantially greater opportunities exist or, if they do, whether female participation in white-collar crime has increased.

ECONOMIC MARGINALIZATION Clarice Feinman (1979, 1986) and Ngaire Naffine (1987, 1994) have added a twist to the opportunity approach. In contrast to that approach, their economic marginalization theory argues that it is the *absence of real meaningful opportunities* for women that leads to increases in crime. Despite the strides made by some women in some areas of the business market, the majority of women remain underemployed and underpaid. This is supported by statistics showing that the bulk of female offenders are either unemployed or concentrated in a "pink-collar ghetto" where pay is low and work is unrewarding. Other evidence of economic marginalization can be found in figures that show female offenses are mostly oriented toward petty property crimes. Such crimes seem to indicate a rational response to the poverty and economic insecurity of the lower class. And, if race and depressed earnings are in any way correlated, then minority women will be overrepresented in the marginalized and incarcerated population, as Gilbert (1999) found in her study of African American women.

Examining both part-time employment and poverty, Parker and Reckdenwald (2008) found that where there were increases in the percentages of women working part time, there was an increase in female property crime arrests. Where there were increases in the percentage of women who lived below the poverty level, there were increases in violent crime arrests for women. Similar results have been found in studies where economic marginalization is correlated with women committing homicide as well as robbery and aggravated assault (DeWees & Parker, 2003; Steffensmeier & Haynie, 2000; Whaley & Messner, 2002).

Gender-based Theories of Criminality

Unlike theories explaining only female criminality, gender-based theories use the role of gender in explaining criminal and delinquent behavior of both males and females. John Hagan's power-control theory, while not a feminist theory, is an integrated theory that is feminist informed. We include it here because gender is the most critical component of the theory. Feminist theories are also incorporated in this section. For two reasons, we doubt justice can be done to the perspective. First, too little space can be devoted to it, and second, there is still little agreement on the various directions of feminist criminological theory. We discuss this in greater detail in the next sections. (For those interested in reading about feminist criminology in greater detail, we suggest four excellent sources: Daly, 1997; Daly & Chesney-Lind, 1988; Miller & Mullins, 2006; and Schram & Koons-Witt, 2004.)

POWER-CONTROL THEORY   The work of John Hagan (1989a, 1989b) and colleagues in *Structural Criminology* (1989b) brings together a conflict-oriented theory with social control versions of family relationships to present a "power-control" theory of gender and delinquency. Hagan argues power relationships in larger society, especially in the workplace, are reflected in the family. In short, the relationships one learns in the work world, the methods of establishing authority and dominance over others, are carried home to the family. Members of different social classes experience different power relationships and therefore construct different family relationships. Similarly, because workplace relationships vary by gender, males and females experience different roles, expectations, and values. The combination of social class and gender experiences creates structured family relationships that help explain the social distribution of delinquency. As Hagan puts it (1991, p. 130):

> The social reproduction of gender relations refers to the activities, institutions, and relationships that are involved in the maintenance and renewal of gender roles, in the family and elsewhere. These activities include the parenting involved in caring for, protecting and socializing children for the roles they will occupy as adults. According to power-control theory, family class structure shapes the social reproduction of gender relations, and in turn the social distribution of delinquency.

The critical components of gender relations in the patriarchal family, as they relate to delinquent behavior, include the way in which delinquency is defined, the amount and type of control parents exercise over children, and gender preferences for risk taking. First, delinquency (and criminality) reflects activities that are potentially fun, exciting, and pleasurable. All these are stratified by gender in the larger society such that males have greater access. Therefore, females are not as free to search out ways that lead to behaviors associated with delinquency. Second, reflecting the gender differences in the work world, males are less controlled and dominated than females are. This control is reproduced in the family, and females receive greater control than do males. Control can be achieved through close parental relations and domination, both of which are applied more thoroughly to females. Third, the form of control exercised over juveniles affects their preferences toward risk taking. Males are allowed greater freedom in both pleasure-seeking activity and in parental control; thus, they develop more taste for risk taking. Finally, because delinquency is allied with risk taking, delinquent behavior is stratified along gender lines, with males being more likely to commit delinquent acts.

Power-control theory then predicts the more patriarchal the family structure, the greater is the gender gap in delinquent behavior between sons and daughters. On the other hand, a more egalitarian family will reproduce relations that lead to sons and daughters participating more equally in delinquency. A final note from power-control theory is worthwhile. Because the gender roles in delinquency are shaped in the family by reflection from the workplace, power-control theory offers a potential explanation of the effect of the changing occupational roles of women. Clearly, as women gain more employment opportunities, or opportunities of a different nature, we should expect the gender distribution of delinquent behaviors to shift.

BROADER CONSTRUCTIONS OF POWER   In contrast to Hagan's emphasis on parents as power "brokers," others interpret power relationships more broadly to include a wider variety of social practices, motivations, and needs that define gender including surviving tragedy and hardship, making friends, and experiencing sexual intimacy (Bottcher, 2001). Another power-oriented theory, this one proposed by James Messerschmidt (1986, 1987, 1993, 1997, 2004), views sex, race, and class as created by social structure. By this, Messerschmidt means that a social structure defines the ways in which sex, race, and class are perceived and socially constructed. Once those perceptions are created, the next issue is how people *do* those categories—that is, how people in those roles act and interact according to their defined category. The social structure in a capitalist society helps determine these roles through economic competition and the validation of a white, male-dominated, patriarchal system. Typical "street" criminality, then, is a product of powerlessness for females and lower-class, nonwhite males. On the other hand, male power is also implicated in white-collar and corporate crime and sex crime. Messerschmidt is aware power can vary by role. For instance a male may exercise power as a husband, while being powerless as a factory worker (1997, p. 9). Thus, he views masculinity and femininity as a fluid construct and *crime as "structured action."*

THE FEMINIST AGENDA: FIVE PERSPECTIVES FOR CRIMINOLOGISTS   Over the last 20 years, a growing body of literature has accumulated that represents feminist perspectives on crime and criminology. There is, however, no single feminist criminology. Approaches vary in how to develop a gender-sensitive perception of the problems and solutions for studying crime and justice. Perhaps mirroring the evolution of traditional criminological theory, feminist theorists have now developed a typology of specialized perspectives (liberal, radical, Marxist, socialist feminism, and postmodern). This development has been applied to criminology, and attempts have been made to summarize existing criminological work into these perspectives (Daly & Chesney-Lind, 1988; Danner, 1989; Moe, 2007; Radosh, 1990; Simpson, 1989, 1991). An examination of this literature is important because of the growing popularity of both gender-based work and work that incorporates feminist conceptions of gender.

Despite early enthusiasm for the hypothesis that there is a link between liberation and crime, as we have noted, meaningful research support never materialized. Sally Simpson (1989) speculates the quest may have even distracted researchers from examining more productive variables such as economics, class, and opportunities. While Simpson believes the earlier liberal (quantitative and mainstream academic) contributions are now being answered with more radical critiques, she looks forward to work that emphasizes qualitative, historical, and more subjective approaches. In the face of debate about the precise role of the feminist perspective, writers such as Kathleen Daly and Meda Chesney-Lind (1988) call for integration of feminist thought in all areas of criminology. Mona Danner (1989) believes socialist feminism in particular, with its emphasis on the overlapping effects of class, race, and gender, will serve to strengthen critical criminological thought. In a recent article, Kathleen Daly (1997) identifies three major movements in contemporary gender scholarship as "class-race-gender," "doing gender," and "sexed bodies." She notes they critique each other and believes the discourse to be healthy. Finally, there is debate on whether to incorporate feminist thought into existing criminological theories or to throw out the old theories and begin fresh.

Liberal Feminism   Perhaps the first feminist perspective in criminology, liberal feminism focused on gender discrimination (Chapman, 1980; Datesman & Scarpitti, 1980; Feinman, 1986) and women's liberation. The general notion was that females deserve equal treatment in the criminal justice system. Concepts of paternalism and chivalry were the mainstay of liberal analyses. Gender-based laws were questioned, and criminal justice processing was examined for discriminatory and harmful practices. Perhaps as much as anything, liberal feminists challenged the prevailing assumptions that males and females have different roles in society. Females were said to have power in the domestic or private world and males to have power in the public world. Liberal feminists denounced the private/public division and demanded public power as well. This led to challenges of personnel policies and hiring in the various system agencies. The presumption was that, as females were more fully integrated into the work force, justice would be more evenly dispensed and discrimination would decrease. In addition, the work of Adler and Simon on liberation and opportunities characterizes liberal feminist criminology (Daly & Chesney-Lind, 1988, p. 507).

Radical Feminism   While not exclusively so, the rise of radical feminist criminology is a product of two factors: the emergent radical criminology and a critique of liberal feminism. Its primary focus is on the way in which power is constructed and dominated by males in society (Brownmiller, 1975; Dobash & Dobash, 1979; Griffin, 1971; Smart, 1976, 1979, 1990, 1995). Rather than focus on roles, radical feminism deals with the way in which the capitalist economic system fosters crime through the creation of a patriarchal and sexist society. Patriarchy defines women as subjects, with men having the right of control. Sexism defines the value of women in terms of the family (unpaid housework as natural) and gives men control over reproduction. Thus, men generate legal concepts, such as marriage, that define women as property and de-emphasize the significance of assault on women (marital rape, domestic violence). Obviously, the radical feminist agenda include changes in legal definitions of crime and the introduction of more gender-sensitive laws. Even more important, however, is the ability of women to exercise control over their own bodies and the restructuring of family relationships to eliminate male domination. And, as do the liberal feminists, radical feminists also want to eliminate the private/public division in gender roles.

Unlike some liberal feminists, however, radical feminists do not believe women's liberation will increase female crime rates. Dorie Klein and June Kress (1979, p. 89) claim "if the women's movement develops a class analysis of women's oppression, and a program around which working class women can be organized, then we may witness a decrease in women's individualism, self-destruction, competitiveness and crime." Radical feminist theories of crime, then, suggest liberation can result in lower crime rates for women and should even precipitate a decrease in male violence against women.

Marxist Feminism   Ironically, early radical and Marxist theorists (including Marx himself) never addressed female criminality. Indeed, in many cases, crimes committed by females have been expressly excluded. In keeping with the general Marxist position, Marxist feminists see the capitalist system as exploiting subordinate groups (often based on race and gender) for capital production (profit). The emphasis on production and labor in Marxist thought results in a feminist focus on the sexual division of labor, which is literally a caste rather than a class (Radosh, 1990). Females are relegated to labor positions with little value and low occupational status. Further, acquisition and disbursement of capital is primarily restricted to males, with only token female participation. As a result, Polly Radosh (1990, p. 113) describes the sexual division of labor as "the epitome of economic inequality." Crime, then, for women has two primary sources: a threat to the current distribution of property or a threat to the sexual division of labor. Under Marxist feminism, this explains why women are most frequently arrested for property crimes and sexually oriented offenses.

Another primary focus is on the status of women in the work force (Daly & Chesney-Lind, 1988). Females are viewed as secondary sources of labor, or as a surplus work force. This marginalization of their worth results in women being heavily dependent on males, or in the absence of a male in the family, dependent on welfare. The anger and frustration of such a position is another cause of crime. In fact, Radosh (1990, p. 126) succinctly summarizes the Marxist feminist position when she says:

> Women's behavior is often labeled as criminal according to the moral implications of capitalism, but real criminal perpetration among women reflects the class differential of the economic system. Certain women occupy inter-generational positions outside of the legitimate system of rewards, which assures that a perpetual underclass, within the caste of women, suffers from alienation and frustration. This factor, more than any other social, psychological or physical characteristic, produces female crime.

As should be evident, the theories produced by Marxist feminists follow the radical and Marxist conflict approaches discussed in Chapter 9 and differ primarily in their inclusion of gender issues. Gender, however, is secondary to the concept of class in Marxist feminist analyses.

Socialist Feminism   Uniting radical and Marxist principles, socialist feminism identifies the oppression of women as a symptom of the patriarchal capitalist system (Danner, 1989). It considers criminality to be a product of the class-based system, and its discussions of female criminality are usually confined to property crimes. The social distribution of crime is derived from relationship to both the production domain and the reproductive, or family, domain. Both domains are equally important. Patriarchal, capitalist society creates groups with different positions and opportunities in society. Females are exploited by the capitalist patriarchal system both for their labor and for their sexuality. James Messerschmidt (1986) notes crimes by powerless people reflect their resistance and accommodation to their position in society. Because of the way social organization is structured by gender, males commit crimes reflecting resistance and females commit crimes characterized by accommodation. In other words, males are most likely to commit violent street crime, whereas females are most likely to commit property and vice crimes.

Postmodern Feminism   The most recent of the feminist perspectives, postmodernism shares with other nonfeminist versions an examination of meanings, in this case of gender within the criminological framework (D'Unger, 2005). For these scholars, gender is the critical issue and crime is a secondary problem. Perhaps an alternative title for this work is more telling: *gendered lives*. The argument is that gender (not biological sex) is the single most important variable in the way humans react to each other (see Bottcher, 2001, for a discussion of the gendering of social practices). By situating illegality in the daily lives of women, the relativist nature of that illegality is explored along with the relative nature of the different gender roles. Postmodernists argue that there is no absolute and objective truth, so the meaning of illegality will vary with their different roles (child, wife, worker, mother, etc.) (Wonders, 1999). Moreover, the nature of gender and crime shifts along with ethnicity, social status, and age. Prior life experiences also have an effect in determining the meaning and motivation of women's behavior, particularly when those experiences are of a negative form, such as racism, molestation, or rape. Thus, postmodern feminists are sensitive to the complexity of women's lives and the situated meanings of illegality for them.

CLASSIFICATION OF THE PERSPECTIVE

Because there are so many variations of gender theory, there is no accurate classification system. For the same reason, we have not prepared a list of the major points of the theory; it would contain so many caveats as to be useless. Some generalities, however, may be drawn.

On the whole, gender theories may be considered *structural* theories because they attempt to explain differences in rates of female crime or differences between the crimes of males and females. We can also, with reasonable accuracy, classify gender-based theories as *conflict oriented*. Most of these theories have also attempted to explain crime from a determinist perspective, but conflict-oriented theorists resist the idea that conflict theories have anything in common with positivist theories. However, newer versions of feminist thought tend to share with postmodernism a rejection of the positivist approach.

POLICY IMPLICATIONS

Many of the changes that gender-based theories would introduce into crime control policy are not directly focused on crime. The general assumption is that reform of society to eliminate patriarchal domination would result in improved conditions for all, and that crime would lessen as a by-product of those improvements. Therefore, policies designed to equalize relationships between the genders are critical. Under the various feminist perspectives, this means increasing the role of women in most spheres of life, particularly the public ones. Feminists would provide greater access to educational opportunities, modify economic structures perhaps by strengthening and enforcing child-support measures, address teen pregnancy, socialize (or elevate the importance of) child care, eliminate or modify marriage laws, and emphasize the importance of gender relations in general. They expect the results of such changes to reduce social images of competition with and ownership of others, decrease aggressive behavior, and bolster self-esteem. Crime would then be affected in smaller numbers of female property and sexual offenses and a lessening of violence among males. Under power-control theory, policies would focus on relationships in the family (much as with low self-control theory), and children would be socialized in a more egalitarian fashion.

Unfortunately, the overlapping problems of race, class, and gender that affect young women in the criminal justice system seem to propel them into complex cycles of victimization and offending. Researchers often argue for interventions that would allow more restorative approaches to justice and more therapeutically oriented resources. Alternative homes and residential treatment centers appear to be suggested by findings that not only do young women express relief at being removed from turbulent or abusive homes (Gaarder & Belknap, 2002) but also parents are more likely to seek out-of-home placement for delinquent girls than boys (Krause & McShane, 1994).

Overall, gender-based theorists seek to sensitize males and females to the biases and stereotypes underlying gender roles in society. Such agendas are often found in rape crisis centers, domestic abuse shelters, the multicultural/gender diversity programs found in educational institutions and in business seminars on sexual harassment. And, perhaps as important as any of the programmatic efforts, the victims' rights movement reflects many gender concerns and is the most extensive policy direction in criminal justice today.

Questions and Weblinks

Critical Thinking Questions

1. What issues seem to define the feminist agenda and what advances and changes in society have contributed to successful achievements in these areas?

2. Do you think that greater participation in the workplace and more economic equality for women will increase or decrease their participation in crime? Explain your answer.

3. Why do you think that crime theories in the past have ignored or minimalized the role of women in crime?

Practice Essay Questions

1. Describe some of the ways feminist theories differ from traditional criminological theories.
2. Explain how the concepts of sexism, paternalism, and chivalry might be evident in the criminal justice system.
3. Briefly define what is meant by economic marginalism and how it is related to crime in feminist-based theories.

Related Weblinks

National Organization for Women
www.now.org
National Women's History Project
www.nwhp.org
Women in the Criminal Justice System
www.sentencingproject.org/doc/publications/womenincj_
    total.pdf

www.aclu.org/women-and-criminal-justice-system
Girls and Delinquency
www.ncjrs.gov/pdffiles1/ojjdp/226358.pdf

Bibliography

Adler, F. (1975). *Sisters in crime: The rise of the new female criminal.* New York: McGraw-Hill.

Adler, F. (1981). *The incidence of female criminality in the contemporary world.* New York: New York University Press.

Albonetti, C. A. (1986). Criminality, prosecutorial screening, and uncertainty: Toward a theory of discretionary decision making in felony case processing. *Criminology, 24,* 623–645.

Anderson, T. (2005). Dimensions of women's power in the illicit drug economy. *Theoretical Criminology, 9*(4), 371–400.

Bottcher, J. (2001). Social practices of gender: How gender relates to delinquency in the everyday lives of high-risk youths. *Criminology, 39,* 893–931.

Brownmiller, S. (1975). *Against our will: Men, women and rape.* New York: Simon and Schuster.

Canter, R. J. (1982). Sex differences in self-report delinquency. *Criminology, 20,* 373–393.

Cernkovich, S., & Giordano, P. C. (1979a). A comparative analysis of male and female delinquency. *Sociological Quarterly, 20,* 131–145.

Cernkovich, S., & Giordano, P. C. (1979b). Delinquency, opportunity and gender. *Journal of Criminal Law and Criminology, 70,* 145–151.

Chapman, J. R. (1980). *Economic realities and the female offender.* Lexington, MA: Lexington.

Chesney-Lind, M. (1977). Judicial paternalism and the female status offender: Training women to know their place. *Crime and Delinquency, 23,* 121–130.

Chesney-Lind, M. (1981). Girls, crime and women's place: Towards a feminist model of female delinquency. *Crime and Delinquency, 35,* 5–29.

Chesney-Lind, M. (1987). Girls and violence: An exploration of the gender gap in serious delinquent behavior. In D. Crowell, I. Evans, & C. O'Donnell (Eds.), *Childhood aggression and violence: Sources of influence, prevention, and control* (pp. 207–229). New York: Plenum Press.

Chesney-Lind, M. (1988a). Doing feminist criminology. *Criminologist, 13*(4), 1, 3, 16–17.

Chesney-Lind, M. (1988b). Girls and status offenses: Is juvenile justice still sexist? *Criminal Justice Abstracts, 20,* 144–165.

Chesney-Lind, M., & Shelden, R. G. (1992). *Girls, delinquency and juvenile justice.* Belmont, CA: Wadsworth.

Curran, D. (1983). Judicial discretion and defendant's sex. *Criminology, 21,* 41–58.

Daly, K. (1989a). Criminal justice ideologies and practices in different voices: Some feminist questions about justice. *International Journal of the Sociology of Law, 17,* 1–18.

Daly, K. (1989b). Neither conflict nor labeling nor paternalism will suffice: Intersections of race, ethnicity, gender and family in criminal court decisions. *Crime and Delinquency, 35,* 136–168.

Daly, K. (1994a). Criminal law and justice system practices as racist, white and racialized. *Washington and Lee Law Review, 51,* 431–464.

Daly, K. (1994b). *Gender, crime and punishment.* New Haven, CT: Yale University Press.

Daly, K. (1997). Different ways of conceptualizing sex/gender in feminist theory and their implications for criminology. *Theoretical Criminology, 1,* 25–51.

Daly, K., & Chesney-Lind, M. (1988). Feminism and criminology. *Justice Quarterly, 5,* 497–538.

Danner, M. (1989). Socialist feminism: A brief introduction. *Critical Criminologist, 1,* 1–2.

Datesman, S., & Scarpitti, F. R. (1980). *Women, crime and justice.* New York: Oxford University Press.

Dewees, M. A., & Parker, K. F. (2003). Women, region, and types of homicide: Are there regional differences in the structural status of women and homicide offending? *Homicide Studies, 7,* 368–393.

Dobash, R. E., & Dobash, R. P. (1979). *Violence against wives: The case against patriarchy.* New York: Free Press.

D'Unger, A. V. (2005). Feminist theories of criminal behavior. In R. A. Wright & J. M. Miller (Eds.), *Encyclopedia of criminology* (Vol. 1, pp. 559–565). New York: Routledge.

Feinman, C. (1979). Sex role stereotypes and justice for women. *Crime and Delinquency, 25,* 87–94.

Feinman, C. (1986). *Women in the criminal justice system.* New York: Praeger.

Gaarder, E., & Belknap, J. (2002). Tenuous borders: Girls transferred to adult court. *Criminology, 40,* 481–517.

Gilbert, E. (1999). Crime, sex, and justice: African-American women in U.S. prisons. In S. Cook & S. Davies (Eds.), *Harsh punishment: International experiences of women's imprisonment.* Boston: Northeastern University Press.

Griffin, S. (1971). Rape: The all-American crime. *Ramparts, 10*(3), 26–35.

Hagan, J. (1989a). Micro- and macro-structures of delinquency causation and a power-control theory of gender and delinquency. In S. F. Messner, M. D. Krohn, & A. E. Liska (Eds.), *Theoretical integration in the study of deviance and crime: Problems and prospects* (pp. 213–227). Albany: State University of New York Press.

Hagan, J. (1989b). *Structural criminology.* New Brunswick, NJ: Rutgers University Press.

Hagan, J. (1991). A power-control theory of gender and delinquency. In R. Silverman, J. Teevan, & V. Sacco (Eds.), *Crime in Canadian society* (4th ed., pp. 130–136). Toronto: Butterworths.

Kaukinen, C. (1995). *Women lawbreakers constructed in terms of traditional definitions of femininity: The sentencing of women in conflict with the law.* Unpublished master's thesis, University of Windsor, Ontario, Canada.

Klein, D. (1973). The etiology of female crime: A review of the literature. *Issues in Criminology, 8,* 3–30.

Klein, D., & Kress, J. (1979). Any woman's blues: A critical overview of women, crime, and the criminal justice system. In F. Adler & R. Simon (Eds.), *Criminality of deviant women* (pp. 82–90). Boston: Houghton Mifflin.

Koons-Witt, B. A. (2002). The effect of gender on the decision to incarcerate before and after the introduction of sentencing guidelines. *Criminology, 40,* 297–327.

Kramer, J. & Ulmer, J. (1996). Sentencing disparity and departures from guidelines. *Justice Quarterly, 13,* 81–106.

Krause, W., & McShane, M. (1994). A deinstitutionalization retrospective: Relabeling the status offender. *Journal of Crime and Justice, 17,* 45–67.

Krohn, M., Curry, J. P. & Nelson-Kilger, S. (1983). Is chivalry dead? An analysis of changes in police dispositions of males and females. *Criminology, 21,* 417–437.

Leonard, E. (1982). *Women, crime and society: A critique of theoretical criminology.* New York: Longman.

MacDonald, J. M., & Chesney-Lind, M. (2001). Gender bias and juvenile justice revisited: A multiyear analysis. *Crime & Delinquency, 47,* 173–195.

Mallicoat, S. L. (2007). Gendered justice. *Feminist Criminology, 2*(1), 4–30.

Mangold, G. (1926). Illegitimacy in St. Louis. *Annals of the American Academy of Political and Social Science, 125,* 63–67.

Messerschmidt, J. (1986). *Capitalism, patriarchy and crime: Toward a socialist feminist criminology.* Totowa, NJ: Rowan and Littlefield.

Messerschmidt, J. (1987). Feminism, criminology and the rise of the female sex 'delinquent,' 1880–1930. *Contemporary Crises, 11,* 243–264.

Messerschmidt, J. (1993). *Masculinities and crime: Critique and reconceptualization of theory.* Lanham, MD: Rowman and Littlefield.

Messerschmidt, J. (1997). *Crime as structured action: Gender, race, class, and crime in the making.* Thousand Oaks, CA: Sage.

Messerschmidt, J. (2004). *Flesh and blood: Adolescent gender diversity and violence.* Lanham, MD: Rowman and Littlefield.

Miller, J., & Mullins, C. W. (2006). The status of feminist theories in criminology. *Advances in Criminological Theory, 15,* 217–249.

Moe, A. M. (2007). Feminist criminology. In G. Ritzer (Ed.), *Blackwell Encyclopedia of Sociology* (pp. 1693–1696). Oxford, UK: Blackwell.

Montalbano, W. (1993, February 9). Italy jails top female gang leader. *Houston Chronicle,* p. A8.

Naffine, N. (1987). *Female crime: The construction of women in criminology.* Boston: Allen and Unwin.

Naffine, N. (1994). *Gender, crime and feminism.* Brookfield, VT: Dartmouth.

Parker, K. F., & Reckdenwald, A. (2008). Women and crime in context: Examining the linkages between patriarchy and female offending across space. *Feminist Criminology, 3*(1), 5–24.

Radosh, P. (1990). Women and crime in the United States: A Marxian explanation. *Sociological Spectrum, 10,* 105–131.

Rodriguez, O. (2007, October 5). Arrest of alleged 'diva' drug lord proves as scintillating as a telenovela. *Houston Chronicle,* p. A15.

Saulters-Tubbs, C. (1993). Prosecutorial and judicial treatment of female offenders. *Federal Probation, 57,* 37–42.

Schram, P. J., & Koons-Witt, B. (2004). *Gendered (in)justice: Theory and practice in feminist criminology.* Long Grove, IL: Waveland.

Simon, R. J. (1975). *Women and crime.* Lexington, MA: Lexington Books.

Simpson, S. S. (1989). Feminist theory, crime and justice. *Criminology, 27,* 605–632.

Simpson, S. S. (1991). Caste, class, and violent crime: Explaining differences in female offending. *Criminology, 29,* 115–136.

Smart, C. (1976). *Women, crime and criminology: A feminist critique.* Boston: Routledge and Kegan Paul.

Smart, C. (1979). The new female criminality: Reality or myth? *British Journal of Criminology, 19,* 50–59.

Smart, C. (1990). Feminist approaches to criminology: Postmodern woman meets atavistic man. In A. Morris & L. Gelsthorpe (Eds.), *Feminist perspectives in criminology* (pp. 71–84). London, UK: Routledge and Kegan Paul.

Smart, C. (1995). *Law, crime and sexuality: Essays in feminism.* London, UK: Sage.

Spohn, C., Gruhl, J., & Welch, S. (1987). The impact of the ethnicity and gender of defendants on the decision to reject or dismiss felony charges. *Criminology, 25,* 175–191.

Steffensmeier, D., & Haynie, D. (2000). Gender, structural disadvantage, and urban crime: Do macro-social variables also explain female offending rates? *Criminology, 38,* 403–438.

Steffensmeier, D., & Steffensmeier, R. H. (1980). Trends in female delinquency. *Criminology, 18,* 62–85.

Visher, C. A. (1983). Gender, police arrest decisions, and notions of chivalry. *Criminology, 21,* 5–28.

Whaley, R. B., & Messner, S. F. (2002). Gender equality and gendered homicides. *Homicide Studies, 6,* 188–210.

Wonders, N. (1999). Postmodern feminist criminology and social justice. In B. A. Arrigo (Ed.), *Social justice/criminal justice: The maturation of criminal theory in law, crime, and deviance* (pp. 111–128). Belmont, CA: Wadsworth.

Research Bibliography (from 2000)

Anderson, T. (2005). Dimensions of women's power in the illicit drug economy. *Theoretical Criminology, 9*(4), 371–400.

Becker, S., & McCorkel, J. A. (2011). The gender of criminal opportunity: The impact of male co-offenders on women's crime. *Feminist Criminology, 6,* 79–110.

Blackwell, B., & Piquero, A. (2005). On the relationship between gender, power control, self-control, and crime. *Journal of Criminal Justice, 33,* 1–17.

Block, C. R., Blokland, A. A. J., van der Werff, C., van Os, R., & Nieuwbeerta, P. (2010). Long-term patterns of offending in women. *Feminist Criminology, 5,* 73–107.

Bottcher, J. (2001). Social practices of gender: How gender relates to delinquency in the everyday lives of high-risk youths. *Criminology, 39,* 893–931.

Bright, C. L., Ward, S. K., & Negi, N. J. (2011). "The chain has to be broken": A qualitative investigation of the experiences of young women following juvenile court involvement. *Feminist Criminology, 6,* 32–53.

Cecil, D. K. (2007). Looking beyond caged heat: Media images of women in prison. *Feminist Criminology, 2*(4), 304–326.

Dennis, J. P. (2012). Girls will be girls: Childhood gender polarization and delinquency. *Feminist Criminology, 7,* 220–233.

Embry, R., & Lyons, P. M., Jr. (2012). Sex-based sentencing: Sentencing discrepancies between male and female sex offenders. *Feminist Criminology, 7,* 146–162.

Estrada, F., & Nilsson, A. (2012). Does it cost more to be a female offender? A life-course study of childhood circumstances, crime, drug abuse, and living conditions. *Feminist Criminology, 7,* 196–219.

Fontaine, N., Carbonneau, R., Vitaro, F., Barker, E. D., & Tremblay, R. E. (2009). Research review: A critical review of studies on the developmental trajectories of antisocial behavior in females. *Journal of Child Psychology and Psychiatry, 50,* 363–385.

Frieburger, T. L., & Burke, A. S. (2011). Status offenders in the juvenile court: The effects of gender, race, and ethnicity on the adjudication decision. *Youth Violence and Juvenile Justice, 9,* 352–365.

Hagan, J., McCarthy, B., & Foster, H. (2002). A gendered theory of delinquency and despair in the life course. *Acta Sociologica, 45,* 37–46.

Heide, K. M., Solomon, E. P., Sellers, B. G., & Chan, H. C. (2011). Male and female juvenile homicide offenders: An empirical analysis of U.S. arrests by offender age. *Feminist Criminology, 6,* 3–31.

Jennings, W. G., Maldonado-Molina, M. M., Piquero, A. R., Odgers, C. L., Bird, H., & Canino, G. (2010). Sex differences in trajectories of offending among Puerto Rican youth. *Crime and Delinquency, 56,* 327–357.

Johansson, P., & Kempf-Leonard, K. (2009). A gender-specific pathway to serious, violent, and chronic offending? Exploring Howell's risk factors for serious delinquency. *Crime & Delinquency, 55,* 216–240.

Karstedt, S. (2000). Emancipation, crime and problem behavior of women: A perspective from Germany. *Gender Issues, 18,* 21–59.

Kempf-Leonard, K., & Sample, L. (2000). Disparity based on sex: Is gender-specific treatment warranted? *Justice Quarterly, 17,* 89–128.

Kerpelman, J., & Smith-Adcock, S. (2005). Female adolescents' delinquent activity: The intersection of bonds to parents and reputation enhancement. *Youth & Society, 37*(2), 176–200.

Koons-Witt, B. A. (2002). The effect of gender on the decision to incarcerate before and after the introduction of sentencing guidelines. *Criminology, 40,* 297–327.

Leiber, M. J., Brubaker, S. J., & Fox, K. C. (2009). A closer look at the individual and joint effects of gender and race on juvenile justice decision making. *Feminist Criminology, 4,* 333–358.

Moore, L. D., & Padavic, I. (2010). Racial and ethnic disparities in girls' sentencing in the juvenile justice system. *Feminist Criminology, 5,* 263–285.

Mustard, D. B. (2001). Racial, ethnic, and gender disparities in sentencing: Evidence from the U.S. Federal Courts. *Journal of Law and Economics, 44,* 285–314.

Nofziger, S. (2010). A gendered perspective on the relationship between self-control and deviance. *Feminist Criminology, 5,* 29–50.

Peralta, R. L., Steele, J. L., Nofziger, S., & Rickles, M. (2010). The impact of gender on binge drinking behavior among U.S. college students attending a midwestern university: An analysis of two gender measures. *Feminist Criminology, 5,* 355–379.

Pizarro, J. M., DeJong, C., & McGarrell, E. F. (2010). An examination of the covariates of female homicide victimization and offending. *Feminist Criminology, 5,* 51–72.

Pollock, J. M., & Davis, S. M. (2005). The continuing myth of the violent female offender. *Criminal Justice Review, 30,* 5–29.

Rodriguez, S. F., Curry, T. R., & Lee, G. (2006). Gender differences in criminal sentencing: Do effects vary across violent, property, and drug offenses? *Social Science Quarterly, 87,* 318–339.

Sanchez, L. (2001). Gender troubles: The entrapment of agency, violence, and law in the lives of women in prostitution. In C. Renzetti & L. Goodstein (Eds.), *Women, Crime, and Criminal Justice* (pp. 60–76). Los Angeles: Roxbury.

Spohn, C., & Beichner, D. (2000). Is preferential treatment of female offenders a thing of the past? A multisite study of gender, race, and imprisonment. *Criminal Justice Policy Review, 11,* 149–184.

Spohn, C., & Spears, J. W. (2000). Gender and sentencing of drug offenders: Is chivalry dead? *Criminal Justice Policy Review, 9,* 365–399.

Steffensmeier, D., Zhong, H., Ackerman, J., Schwartz, J., & Agha, S. (2006). Gender gap trends for violent crimes, 1980 to 2003: A UCR-NCVS comparison. *Feminist Criminology, 1,* 72–98.

Thompson, M., & Petrovic, M. (2009). Gendered transitions: Within-person changes in employment, family, and illicit drug use. *Journal of Research in Crime and Delinquency, 46,* 377–408.

Vandiver, D. M., & Teske, R. (2006). Juvenile female and male sex offenders: A comparison of offender, victim, and judicial processing characteristics. *International Journal of Offender Therapy and Comparative Criminology, 50,* 148–165.

Zimmerman, G. M., & Messner, S. F. (2010). Neighborhood context and the gender gap in adolescent violent crime. *American Sociological Review, 75,* 958–980.

Social Control Theory

LEARNING OBJECTIVES

Objective 11.1: Explain why delinquents use techniques of neutralization and how they work.

Objective 11.2: Describe policy changes and programs that would be supported by social control theories.

Objective 11.3: Summarize the various bonds that Hirschi felt operated to provide social control.

Objective 11.4: Discuss Durkheim's view of social control.

Objective 11.5: Compare and contrast the concepts of inner and outer containment and how they work to prevent deviance.

INTRODUCTION

As the popularity of labeling theory began to wane and conflict theory moved toward more radical perspectives, control theory began to appeal to conservative criminologists. Although certainly not new, the term "control theory" refers to any perspective that discusses the control of human behavior (Empey, 1978). Among their various forms, such theories include explanations based on genetics, neurochemistry, sociobiology, personality, and environmental design. *Social* control theories attribute crime and delinquency to the usual sociological variables (family structures, education, and peer groups, for example), thus their approach is different from other control theories.

Despite differences in the way social control theorists explain criminal behavior, they all share one basic thought. Rather than asking the typical criminological question, "What makes people criminal?" these theorists share a conviction that deviant behavior is to be expected. What must be explained, they say, is "why people obey rules" (Hirschi, 1969, p. 10). As a result, some social control theories demonstrate a view of human nature that reflects the beliefs of Thomas Hobbes, a seventeenth-century English philosopher who was convinced humans are basically evil. This view is not particularly crucial for the creation of social control theories, but they must at least assume a neutral human nature. The critical component of all social control theories, then, is their attempt to explain factors keeping people from committing criminal or delinquent behavior.

Another way to look at social control theory is to call it socialization theory. Since unsocialized humans—babies, for example—will simply act out their desires, it is the presence of other people that necessitates those behaviors be controlled. The most important way we exercise control is through the process of socialization. We teach the "right" way to do things (rules, norms), both informally, as in the family, and formally, as in school. In fact, much of our early upbringing is designed to socialize us so we can function in society. Social control theories emphasize the quality of this process.

THE HERITAGE OF THE THEORY

The Social Heritage

Because control theory has wide-ranging perspectives and spans a number of years, a discussion of the heritage of this approach has more to do with an explanation of its recent popularity than with its origins. Therefore, the discussion here focuses on explaining the theory's current acceptance.

While the 1960s brought about a questioning of social values and traditional institutions, there were also those who defended the status quo. Our previous characterizations of the decade should not be taken to mean that all, or even a majority, were protesting and voicing their opinions about change in America. Within any period, the dominant group is a relatively conservative one ("conservative" essentially means to stick with the status quo). Thus, life for most people continued with relatively little change. In addition, the energy and promise of the 1960s, and in particular the social programs designed to create greater equality and opportunity, were brought up short with the assassinations of Martin Luther King and Robert Kennedy. While liberals carried on the ideals of the period, the steam seemed to be taken out of the movement, leaving less resistance to conservative demands.

Some of the subtle changes taking place in society, however, would affect those who were more conservative. Religion became more important for many, and the "born-again" movement grew throughout the 1970s. A cynicism about government, fostered by Watergate, further disillusioned those who had thought the United States could become a "Great Society." Even the skyrocketing prices of gasoline in the mid-1970s heightened economic concerns. Finally, the taking of American hostages in Iran seemed to act as a catalyst for a politically conservative movement. As opposed to the liberal climate of the mid- to late 1960s, the mood of the following decade could be more accurately characterized as increasingly conservative. While conservatism enhanced the popularity of control theories, however, the theories themselves are not inherently conservative. The neutralization theory of Gresham Sykes and David Matza was not particularly conservative, nor was the drift theory subsequently proposed by Matza.

The Intellectual Heritage

The intellectual heritage of social control theories is difficult to ascertain. It may, however, be accurate to say the modern versions were originally developed as alternatives or reactions to strain theories. Clearly, this is the case for the 1950s theories of Albert Reiss (1951), Walter Reckless (1955), Sykes and Matza (1957), and F. Ivan Nye (1958). For later theories, especially those of Matza (1964) and Travis Hirschi (1969), the same may be inferred from their critical discussions of anomie and subculture theories. Even the usual identification of Emile Durkheim as the father of social control theory suggests there is a connection with strain theories.

Chicago School ideas were also critical to the development of social control theories. Arguably, many of the Chicago School's ideas may be viewed as emergent social control theory. This is particularly true of the social disorganization concept, which posits that a socially disorganized area frees juveniles to engage in delinquent acts. Solomon Kobrin's notion of nonintegrated neighborhoods lacking control over their youths is a direct product of the Chicago School. Among the first of the modern social control theorists, Reiss and Reckless were students at Chicago, and Nye was closely affiliated with the school.

The rise in popularity of social control theory did not occur until the mid-1970s, suggesting the blossoming of the theory may have been a result of three distinct trends within criminology. The first was a reaction to the labeling and conflict orientation and a return to the examination of criminal behavior. Conservative criminologists had little interest in the "new" criminology and wanted to return to the field's traditional subject matter, the criminal. Second, the rise of the study of criminal justice as a discipline helped move criminology in a more pragmatic and system-oriented direction. The increase in the government's interest and funding for criminal justice projects and crime fighting served to enhance the pragmatic nature of the movement. As a result, criminology was relatively free of theoretical work and until about 1990 was left with its final theoretical inventions from the 1960s (Williams, 1984). The theory meeting nearly everyone's personal explanation for criminal behavior was Hirschi's version of social control theory.

Finally, social control theories were linked with a new research technique for locating delinquent behavior, the self-report survey. By the time 1960s versions of social control theory were proposed, self-report studies had become the dominant form of criminological evidence. Surveys of juveniles, asking about their behaviors, were so in vogue they became a new paradigm for criminology. The theory proposed by Hirschi was the first one to be expressly rooted in the self-report tradition and was the result of a survey of a 1965 school survey in Contra Costa County, California. As a result, social control theories gave criminologists theoretical puzzles to solve with the new methodology.

THE THEORETICAL PERSPECTIVE

Durkheim's Social Control Theory

Theories of social control all rely on social factors to explain how people are restrained from acting in ways harmful to others. The earliest explanation of this approach was that of Durkheim (1895). He said a society will always have a certain number of deviants and deviance is really a *normal* phenomenon. By examining various societies around the world, Durkheim concluded every society has crime. If that is so, then crime must serve a function in society. Any society without crime and deviance is, by definition, abnormal. Further, deviance assists in maintaining social order because there are vague moral "boundaries" that define which acts are allowed and which are disapproved. These boundaries specify the various degrees of disapproval for various acts, ranging from mild displeasure to legal sanctions and imprisonment. Since the actual boundary lines are not clear, it is the social reaction to someone else's deviant act that helps people determine what they should not do. Thus, Durkheim argued behavior is controlled by social reaction (displeasure, punishment).

To illustrate the issue that crime serves a boundary maintenance function, Durkheim gave an example of a "society of saints." In this society, there would be no crime as we know it. Indeed, most behavior we believe to be harmful would not occur. Yet crime would still be present. Crimes in such a society would represent behavior we do not think twice about but for the saints would be repulsive and harmful. Imagine a new crime of failing to say a blessing before a meal, or of using the Lord's name in vain. If crime represents harm to society, such behavior for the saints could threaten their social order. Controls, then, are necessary for order to exist and for people to understand the boundaries of accepted behavior.

Durkheim also related anomie to the existence of controls. A normal (nonanomic) society is one in which social relationships are working well and social norms (regulations) are clearly specified. When relationships and norms begin to break down, the controls they create begin to deteriorate. Durkheim noted a breakdown of those controls leads to crime and suicide. He was particularly concerned with situations in which uncontrolled rising aspirations lead to suicide. Whenever anomie exists in society, controls begin to disappear.

Personality-oriented Social Control Theories

In the 1950s, several theorists presented social control explanations of delinquency. These theories set the stage for the contemporary approach to explaining crime and delinquency. Since Durkheim's time, the notion of social control had gone through several adaptations. The concepts of personality and socialization had become commonplace, and one or the other was being used in most of the sociological work on deviance. In addition, there had been several decades of research and writing on the ability of the family environment, religious institutions, schools, proper friends and associates, and community organizations to control delinquency.

Albert J. Reiss, Jr. (1951) combined concepts of personality and socialization with the work of the Chicago School to produce a social control theory that anticipated most of the later work. Although Reiss used psychoanalytic theory and wrote at length on the importance of personality, his theory suggested that three components of social control explained delinquency (1951, p. 196). He said delinquency would result from any or all of the following: (1) a lack of proper internal controls developed during childhood; (2) a breakdown of those internal controls; and/ or (3) an absence of, or conflict in, social rules provided by important social groups (the family, close others, the school). These three factors have been used, in whole or in part, by almost every social control theorist writing since then. The first point is the essential ingredient in what is probably today's most popular theory, low self-control, by Gottfredson and Hirschi (1990). The second point is used by a wide range of social control theorists (and others) who discuss the personal result of pressures and strains on people. The third one is essentially the entire position of Hirschi's 1969 social control theory. Given that so much is repeated from Reiss's statement, it may well represent the best summary of social control theory.

Containment Theory

The next popularly received approach was developed by Walter Reckless around 1955 to 1956, with subsequent work in collaboration with a colleague, Simon Dinitz (Reckless & Dinitz, 1967). This theory, referred to as containment theory, explains delinquency as the interplay between two forms of control: internal (inner) and external (outer). Reckless expressly saw his theory as an explanation of both conformity and deviance (1961, p. 42). At the same time, he did not claim containment theory explained all forms of deviance; indeed, following the example of Robert Merton, he referred to it as a "middle-range" theory. He excluded behavior resulting from inner pushes (psychoses, personality disorders, compulsions, organic brain disorders, and neuroses) and from the playing of expected roles (subcultural dictates, certain forms of culture conflict, and organized crime). However, this middle range of behavior is very large.

Inner containment, while never clearly specified by Reckless, was presented as components of the "self." A laundry list of these components (Reckless, 1961, p. 44) includes self-control, good self-concept, ego strength, well-developed superego, high frustration tolerance, high resistance to diversions, high sense of responsibility, goal orientation, and ability to find substitute satisfactions. Outer containment was viewed as the social environment. Examples of outer containment are family and school reinforcement of social norms and values, effective supervision and discipline, reasonable opportunities for social activity, availability of alternatives to deviance, and "opportunities for acceptance, identity, and belongingness."

Emphasizing inner containment, Reckless said a self-concept exists in people and is formed when they are quite young. This self-concept provides either a "good" or a "bad" image of the self and acts as a buffer to outside influences. He also stressed that there are a variety of "pushes and pulls" toward deviant behavior that all individuals experience. The effect of these inducements to commit delinquent acts depends on the strength of an individual's inner and outer containments. If the self-concept were bad, outer social controls would have little effect on the individual and delinquency would be more likely to result. On the other hand, an individual with a good self-concept could withstand weak external social control and resist committing delinquent acts. While Reckless discussed both external and internal forms of containment, it is clear he perceived the internal to be the more important of the two.

Social Bonding Theories

The concept of external social controls came into prominence with the work of David Matza. His first writing on the subject, coauthored with Gresham Sykes (1957), was a critique of Albert Cohen's subculture theory. In that critique, however, was the notion that everyone, even the lower-class gang delinquent, is bound to the dominant value system of society. Sykes and Matza proposed that one becomes "free" for delinquent acts through the use of techniques of neutralization. These techniques allow individuals to neutralize and temporarily suspend their commitment to societal values, thus providing the freedom to commit delinquent acts. Sykes and Matza listed five forms of neutralization, which they called *denial of responsibility, denial of injury, denial of the victim, condemnation of the condemners,* and *appeal to higher*

Gresham M'Cready Sykes (1922–2010)

Gresham Sykes was born in Plainfield, New Jersey, in 1922. From 1942 to 1946 he served in the U.S. Army Corps of Engineers, earning the rank of Captain. He married Carla Adelt, who would become his lifelong partner. Sykes received his Ph.D. in sociology from Northwestern University in 1953 and returned to teach at Princeton University, where he had obtained his A.B. degree. Early in his career he published what has become a classic in the field of corrections, *The Society of Captives: A Study of the Maximum Security Prison*. He later taught at Northwestern, Dartmouth, the University of Denver, and the University of Houston, before chairing the department at the University of Virginia. Sykes also served as the first Executive Officer for the American Sociological Association from 1963 to 1964, which was also the year the organization moved into a designated office space in Washington, DC. In 1980, the American Society of Criminology honored Sykes with the prestigious Edwin H. Sutherland Award in criminology. He retired in 1988 and devoted himself to artwork in his Virginia studio.

loyalties. They argued that these neutralizations are available not just to lower-class youth but also generally throughout society. They further explain that such rationalizations or justifications are particularly useful during celebrations and holidays, when a certain amount of deviance or law violation may be viewed by many as expected and fun. This would include shooting off fireworks that may be banned or restricted, firing weapons into the air on New Year's, drinking excessively and driving home from Christmas parties at work, tearing down goal posts at football victories, and public intoxication on Saint Patrick's day. Even those with normally conservative social values may overlook some celebratory behavior and "neutralize it" as acceptable on this one particular day.

Matza's subsequent work on subterranean values (Matza, 1961), in particular his work on drift (1964), included an explicit use of the term "bond" to the moral order, by which he meant the tie that exists between individuals and the dominant values of society. The problem for criminology is to explain how this bond could be either strengthened or weakened. Matza used neutralizations to explain how a person might be available for deviant behavior. Once neutralizations were used, he said, the individual was in a state of limbo or drift that made deviant acts permissible. From this point, it was possible either to reenter conformity or to commit a deviant act.

The thrust or impetus for action is centered around the *will* to do something. The will has two activating conditions: preparation, which provides for the repetition of old behavior, and desperation, which precipitates new behavior. These two theoretical components pull an individual out of drift and allow behavior to take place. Whether the behavior is conforming or deviant, however, depends on the situation and on the form of the neutralizations.

David Matza (1930–)

David Matza was born on May 1, 1930, in New York. His bachelor's degree was awarded in 1953 from the City of New York College. He went on to obtain his master's and doctorate degrees from Princeton University from the Department of Economics and Sociology. In addition he completed a postdoctoral program at the University of Chicago's law school in behavioral science and the law. Matza spent his entire career teaching at the University of California, Berkeley, where he is now Professor Emeritus. His book *Delinquency and Drift* won the prestigious C. Wright Mills Award in 1966, and he was awarded a Guggenheim Fellowship in 1967.

In 1973, Richard Ball developed a scale to assess a person's acceptance of neutralizations that has been revised and reformulated over the years in a number of research studies. Early tests of the techniques of neutralization found that delinquents tended to use more neutralizations than nondelinquents, that boys and girls were equally likely to accept the use of these techniques, and that the use of neutralizations might vary as a person ages or matures. In fact, recent research seems to indicate that more serious or seasoned offenders may be less inclined to use neutralizations as they may have become more accepting of their own behavior and feel less pressure to justify it (Cechaviciute & Kenny, 2007).

Techniques of neutralization continue to be examined across a wide variety of juvenile and adult subpopulations (Khoo & Oakes, 2000; Topalli, 2006) as well as a broad array of offenses. Studies have looked at the way pedophiles used techniques of neutralization (Malesky & Ennis, 2004), while others have looked at fireworks (Buzzell, 2005), sex trafficking (Antonopoulos & Winterdyk, 2005), topless dancing (Thompson, Harred & Burks, 2003), marijuana smoking (Peretti-Watel, 2003), and music piracy (Ingram & Hinduja, 2008). Therapists and counselors believe that understanding how offenders think about their criminal behavior may help them confront and address it in correctional and rehabilitation settings, so there is a connection to cognitive skills programming.

Other theorizing by James Short and Fred Strodtbeck (1965), while not directed to Matza's theory, emphasized the importance of attachment to peers and the rewards provided by those peers in strengthening or weakening bonds to society. Finally, Scott Briar and Irving Piliavin (1965), elaborating on an earlier work by Jackson Toby (1957), introduced the concept of commitments to conformity. By this they referred to the investment one makes in conventional images and appearances (student government president, for example). Those with the greater investments have correspondingly greater potential losses from being discovered to be deviant. Great potential losses mean not only material deprivation and punishment but also social deprivation. If one extends the idea of investments to material things, such as property, business, and wealth, then Briar and Piliavin's theory can be viewed as a direct precursor to contemporary social control theory.

Sykes and Matza's Techniques of Neutralization

Denial of Responsibility

Acts are the product of forces beyond the control of the delinquent. The delinquent has a "billiard ball" conception of self where he or she is continually pulled/pushed into situations beyond his or her control. "I didn't mean it."

Denial of Injury

Acts do not really cause any harm. The victim can easily afford the damage or loss. "I didn't really hurt anybody."

Denial of the Victim

Acts, given the circumstances, were not really wrong. The offender is actually retaliating for a previous act of the victim. The victim deserves the injury. Or, there is no real victim. "They had it coming to them."

Condemnation of the Condemners

The motives and behaviors of those who disapprove of the act are suspect. The condemners are hypocrites or are reacting out of personal spite. "Everybody's picking on me."

Appeal to Higher Loyalties

Societal rules have to take a "back seat" to the demands of loyalty to important others or groups. You always help a buddy and never squeal on a friend. "I didn't do it for myself."

Travis Hirschi (1935–)

Travis Hirschi was born in Rockville, Utah, and obtained both his bachelor's and his master's from the University of Utah. His Ph.D. in sociology is from the University of California, Berkeley. He taught at the University of Washington, the University of California, Davis, and the State University of New York at Albany before moving to the University of Arizona, where he spent the next 18 years. Hirschi served as President of the American Society of Criminology in 1983 and was given that organization's Sutherland Award in 1986. He retired as Professor Emeritus in 1997.

Hirschi's Social Control Theory

The most popular version of social control theory during the 1970s and 1980s was the one presented by Travis Hirschi (1969). Synthesizing and elaborating on the work of other social control theorists, Hirschi provided a clearer picture of what was meant by a social bond. Indeed, some criminologists refer to the theory as "social bonding" theory. Rather than seeing individuals as deviant or conforming, Hirschi, like Durkheim, believed behavior reflects varying degrees of morality. He argued that the power of internalized norms, conscience, and the desire for approval encourage conventional behavior. As did Sykes and Matza, Hirschi saw that a person becomes "free" to engage in delinquency. Instead of using neutralizing techniques, however, he blamed broken or weakened bonds to society. While not all social control theorists have done so, Hirschi expressly rejected the idea that any motivation is necessary for deviant behavior to occur. Actually, he viewed individuals as self-interested and therefore ready to act in a fashion that provides the greatest benefits. Society serves as a restraint on that behavior, and, if the restraints are loosened, self-interested behavior will emerge.

Hirschi has acknowledged some of the hidden theoretical threads from which his theory was woven. In an interview with Clemens Bartollas (1985, p. 190), he noted that the Chicago School's social disorganization theory is at the root of his approach. At the time he proposed his social control theory, however, social disorganization was in disrepute, and he avoided making references to it. The entire issue of weakened controls (disorganization) was at the heart of the Chicago School's treatment of deviance. In a major divergence with the Chicago School, however, Hirschi refused to give credence to the possibility that deviant behavior is relative. Where the Chicago School saw a variety of situations with their own conforming definitions, Hirschi saw only one legitimate definition of behavior: the common value system of society at large. As a result, no behavior can be defined as conforming simply because it follows the norms and rules of a smaller group or subculture. If the rules or opinions of the majority in society define that behavior as deviant, it is simply deviant. In short, "conventional" society governs the perspective from which the behavior is to be viewed.[1]

---

[1] Hirschi also intended his research and subsequent theory to show that Sutherland's differential association theory and Cloward and Ohlin's differential association theory were invalid. In order to do this, he made use of two categories of theory, constructed by Ruth Kornhauser in an unpublished paper, to "reconceive" the critical elements of those two approaches. These were called "cultural deviance theory" (differential association) and "strain theory" (differential opportunity). In part, then, his social control theory was specifically designed to be in opposition to both popular theories, and he has referred elsewhere to this as "oppositional theory construction" (Hirschi, 1989). It is worth noting that both of the contested theories allow for behavior derived from relative moral orders, rather than a single absolute one.

Hirschi's Elements of the Bond

Element	Examples
Attachment	Identification with peers or parents, emotional bond between child and parent, concern and respect for parents' or peers' opinions, engaging in activities with peers, supervision by parents, intimate communications with parents, attitudes toward school, concern for teachers' opinions, and general sensitivity to the opinions of others
Involvement	Time-consuming activity (work, sports, recreation, hobbies, etc.), time spent on homework, lack of boredom, amount of nonactive leisure time, and time spent talking with friends
Commitment	Investment in society (education, career, family, etc.), academic competence, educational aspirations and expectations, achievement orientation, expected occupation, and importance of reputation
Belief	Respect for authorities, importance of and respect for law, and absence of neutralizations

Hirschi characterized the social bond as having four elements or dimensions (1969, pp. 16–34): attachment, involvement, commitment, and belief. The most important element is attachment. The strength of the attachments, or ties, one has to significant others (parents, friends, role models) or to institutions (schools, clubs) can inhibit deviance. Attachment is important for creating conformity even when those others are deviant themselves. Second, involvement means the degree of activity (the time and energy) available for conventional or unconventional behavior. Those most occupied by conventional activities simply have less time to be involved in deviance. Thus, participation in clubs, recreational activities, and other extracurricular activities serves to increase levels of conformity.

Commitment represents the investment one has already built up in conventional society. This investment may take such forms as the amount of education, a good reputation, or the establishment of a business. Those with these forms of commitment to conventional society also have more to lose if they are caught engaging in deviant behavior. College students, for instance, have already built up a strong degree of investment in education. Clearly, to engage in crime and get caught would represent a potential loss of that investment. The last element, belief, constitutes the acknowledgment of society's rules as being fair. That is, one has a respect for those rules and norms and feels a moral obligation to obey them. The critical component here is a respect for the common value system. In a sense, the more one believes in "behaving properly," the more likely one is to be conforming.

These four elements all affect the bond between an individual and society. Because all individuals exhibit some bonding to society, the question before criminologists is how much these bonds need to be weakened before deviance results. As any of the four elements are weakened, the freedom to engage in deviant behavior increases. What is less clear is the extent to which a weakening or absence of any one component of the bond affects the other elements. For instance, does the strong presence of three elements, and the absence of a fourth, mean deviance will result? The elements also, obviously, interact with each other to produce varying degrees of effect. While Hirschi did discuss some of the relationships among the elements, he saw this as an empirical question (an issue for research to answer) and preferred to keep the question open. With Hirschi's main contribution to social control theory being the aggregation and synthesis of the elements of the bond, a lack of information about their relationship with each other is a serious deficiency.

A final point should be made about Hirschi's and others' versions of social control theory: they all rely on a specialized methodology of discovering crime and criminality—self-report studies—for their evidence. Other methodologies, such as the use of official crime report statistics or victimization data, do not particularly lend themselves to the social control approach. When those other methodologies are used to produce evidence, social control theory suffers. In a real sense, then, social control theories are somewhat methodologically bound.

CLASSIFICATION OF THE THEORY

Social control theories are *positivist* theories in that they endeavor to explain behavior, albeit conforming behavior. Moreover, they imply (and in some cases overtly declare) criminal behavior should be treated by increasing the influence of the family, schools, churches, and law-abiding peers. They also concentrate on the *process* by which the social bond is weakened rather than on the structural reasons for the existence of that bond.

The issue of whether social control theories are consensus or conflict oriented is more difficult. They are based on the assumption that human nature is either neutral or, in the Hobbesian view, evil; therefore, conflict seems inevitable. However, it is the assumption of the existence of a dominant moral order that orients social control theories toward a *consensus* view of society. Uniformly, social control theories posit the existence of a common value system in society and deny the validity of subcultural or other group values in a diverse society. Finally, these theories are in the *microtheoretical* range. Clearly, they focus on etiological issues rather than on explaining social structure. In fact, other than assuming a moral order exists, they state little about social structure itself. Instead, they set forth at length how the weakening of the effect of various social institutions allows for an increase in deviant behavior among individuals.

Summary

Social control theory, for all its recent popularity, is not new. Moreover, it is probably the one theoretical approach most closely matching the public's conception of why people become criminals. Whether one believes a person becomes criminal because of associating with the wrong friends, an improper family upbringing, a lack of religion, or a lack of education, social control theory can be seen to reflect that belief. Further, for criminologists themselves, this theory contains bits and pieces of the theories of social disorganization, differential association, and anomie, making it especially attractive to those criminologists who have been reluctant to embrace conflict theories.

In sum, social control theory takes a view of human nature that assumes deviance is natural (which makes this theory similar to labeling in this regard). Conformity, then, is the real question worthy of explanation. Positing a moral order, or a conventional framework in society, social control theory finds common social institutions that strengthen the bond. When these institutions are weakened, whatever the cause, the bond that ties individuals to the moral order is also weakened. This weakened bond automatically permits a greater degree of deviance to occur.

MAJOR POINTS OF THE GENERAL SOCIAL CONTROL THEORY APPROACH

1. Self-preservation and gratification are characteristic of human nature; therefore, human behavior tends to be "self-interested."

2. Human behavior must be restrained and regulated for the benefit of all.
3. The rules and regulations for living in a society constitute a moral order.
4. Humans are bound to the moral order beginning with childhood socialization and later through the institutions of society.
5. The bond to the moral order is composed of elements that maintain and strengthen conformity.
6. The elements of the bond include attachment to important others and institutions, commitment to or investment in conventional society, involvement in conventional activities, and belief in societal values.
7. These elements are present in varying degrees. To the extent they may become weak, or are absent, individuals have more freedom to pursue self-interested and deviant behavior.

Epilogue: Current Directions and Policy Implications

CURRENT DIRECTIONS

Criminological researchers have spent many hours testing social control theories, primarily Hirschi's version. In fact, social control theory is probably the most tested theory in criminology, largely because Hirschi himself presented the theory in conjunction with his research results. The points of the theory are relatively straightforward and testable, except for the relationships between elements of the bond. While the research results are not totally clear, several issues have emerged.

TESTING THE THEORY

Social control theory may be best for explaining less serious forms of delinquency. Because of its grounding in self-report studies, which traditionally have focused on less serious forms of behavior, it makes sense that social control theory works best for minor to moderate delinquency. Another problem centers on the relationship of the attachment element to delinquency. The predicted relationship says any attachment to others should result in a reduction of delinquency. Hirschi's own research found a positive relationship for delinquents and friends; that is, delinquents were more attached to delinquent peers rather than conforming peers (this would support Sutherland rather than Hirschi). Finally, a reanalysis of Hirschi's own original data by David Greenberg (1999) found that the general explanatory power of the theory was rather weak.

DATA-SPECIFIC RESULTS

The theory also does best when tested with cross-sectional data. Causal order (what comes first) is difficult to determine in cross-sectional data because they are collected at only one point in time. As a result, we do not know whether attachment or commitment occurred before or after delinquency. When longitudinal data are used (data collected at more than one point in time), the theory does not fare as well. In particular, longitudinal research tends to show that peer attachments affect delinquency and delinquency, in turn, affects other attachments. In other words, a weakening of the social bond may be a result of delinquency rather than a cause. Of course, the same problem applies to most of the other theories we have discussed.

GENERIC EXPLANATION OF CRIME

Social control theory appears to have promise as an explanation for a wide variety of behavior. Because it is not based on assumptions about the criminal propensities of different social classes, social control theory should be able to explain lower-, middle-, and upper-class crime and delinquency equally well. In fact, Travis Hirschi, with Michael Gottfredson (1987), has used it as an explanation of white-collar crime. Others have examined middle-class delinquency from the perspective of control theory.

MATURING OUT OF CRIME

Another important use of social control theory is as an explanation of the long-observed fact that most delinquents grow out of delinquency. That is, they seem to quit engaging in delinquent acts without any intervention on the part of others. Indeed, this "aging-out" phenomenon is the origin of the labeling theory suggestion that we simply leave delinquents alone (Edwin Schur's "radical nonintervention"). In an early commentary on the effect of commitment, Larry Karacki and Jackson Toby (1962) suggested an adolescent's "stakes in conformity" increase with age. Hirschi's version similarly posits commitment to conventional activity is an important piece of the social bond. If juveniles and youths continue to increase their levels of commitment as they grow older (go to work, increase their education, perhaps get married), then the result is a maturing out of delinquency and crime. Thomas Bernard (1987) has argued commitment is the primary element of the social bond, influencing all other elements. If he is correct, the maturation hypothesis is an important part of social control theory. In addition, adolescence in our culture has long been regarded as a period characterized by leisure time. As we get older, leisure time decreases in favor of the work world (see lifestyle theory in Chapter 13 for another explanation of the relationship between crime, age, and leisure).

INTEGRATION WITH OTHER THEORIES

Several criminologists have suggested integration of social control theory concepts with other theories. Ron Akers, the prime architect of social learning theory, has agreed his theory is most compatible with social control (1985, p. 67). Actually, just about every attempt to integrate theories has incorporated social control theory (see, for example, the discussion of integrated theories in Chapter 15). However, Hirschi (1979) rejects attempts at integration of his social control theory with other theoretical concepts or models. He believes the theory is substantially changed by these additions. A preferable approach, he believes, is to create a new theory with a logically coherent set of assumptions. One might argue that is exactly what he and Gottfredson (1990) did with self-control theory (see Chapter 14). Hirschi himself, until he wrote an essay in 2004, made no comments on the direct connections between his earlier social control theory and the current one. In fact, it initially appeared in his 1990 work with Gottfredson as if he was arguing that most elements of the bond constitute a false relationship with delinquency and that both bonds and delinquency are created by early parenting relationships. In the 2004 essay (pp. 543–544), he redefined self-control as "inhibitions carried with one wherever one happens to go" and added the statement that differences in social control were stable over time. These inhibitions seem to be the same as elements of the bond.

POLICY IMPLICATIONS

Social control theories suggest a group of commonsense policies for crime and delinquency control. Perhaps it is for this reason they have been popular; yet very few policies or programs seem to have been expressly created from social control concepts. Nonetheless, the theoretical perspective has allowed criminologists to approve of projects that in the popular mind "just make good sense."

Examples of such projects are school-based programs to keep children busy. The more conventional activities they engage in, the less time is available for delinquent activities. Thus, recreational programs, social groups, and athletic events are all designed from the viewpoint of involvement. Social clubs, 4-H clubs, Boy Scouts, Girl Scouts, and Little League baseball are classic examples of programs designed to assist children in learning conventional values (becoming committed) and being involved in conventional activities. Of course, schools are not the only source of these programs. Religious groups generate their share, especially those focusing on the values important to the group. YMCA and YWCA programs are commonplace in larger cities. Both actor Denzel Washington and singer-actress Jennifer Lopez recall how their neighborhood Boys & Girls clubs were places where important mentoring took place. Washington explains that his first public performance was winning a talent show at the club (Relin, 2006).

Over the past two decades, social policy to help juveniles in danger of becoming delinquent has consistently championed strategies like the Big Brother/ Big Sister programs. These programs couple a role model with conventional activities for children. In addition, strategies to increase the stability of families have been developed, among them parenting programs. Finally, any approach that emphasizes social activities, keeping children in school, or improving scholastic skills, or one that stresses the values of the "American Way" is compatible with social control theories.

Questions and Weblinks

Critical Thinking Questions

1. What is the basis of human nature according to social control theorists? Do you agree? Why or why not?
2. Discuss your experiences with any of the delinquency prevention programs implicated by social control theory—do you think they are successful? Why or why not?
3. While differential association theory would stress the influence of peers, social control theories would emphasize the role of parents, teachers, and coaches. How do you see these two competing models in terms of predicting delinquency?

Practice Essay Questions

1. Compare and contrast the various elements of the social bonds as they were imagined by Travis Hirschi.
2. What are the techniques of neutralization and how are they used?
3. How do outer and inner containment function and what are the benefits and deficits of each as a form of social control?
4. What factors contribute to delinquency according to Albert Reiss and how would you categorize his theoretical views?

Related Weblinks

https://www.ncjrs.gov/pdffiles1/nij/grants/188263.pdf

Big Brothers Big Sisters of America

http://www.bbbs.org/site/c.diJKKYPLJvH/b.1539751/k. BDB6/Home.htm

Boys and Girls Clubs of America

http://www.bgca.org/

National Center for School Engagement

http://www.schoolengagement.org/

Bibliography

Akers, R. L. (1985). *Deviant behavior: A social learning approach* (3rd ed.). Belmont, CA: Wadsworth.

Antonopoulos, G. A., & Winterdyk, J. A. (2005). Techniques of neutralizing the trafficking of women: A case study of an active trafficker in Greece. *European Journal of Crime, Criminal Law & Criminal Justice, 13*, 136–147.

Ball, R. (1973). Ball's neutralization scale. In W. C. Reckless (Ed.), *American criminology* (pp. 26–36). Englewood Cliffs, NJ: Prentice Hall.

Bartollas, C. (1985). *Juvenile delinquency*. New York: Macmillan.

Bernard, T. J. (1987). Structure and control: Reconsidering Hirschi's concept of commitment. *Justice Quarterly, 4,* 409–424.

Briar, S., & Piliavin, I. (1965). Delinquency, situational inducements, and commitment to conformity. *Social Problems, 13,* 35–45.

Buzzell, T. (2005). Holiday revelry and legal control of fireworks: A study of neutralization in two normative contexts. *Western Criminology Review, 6*(1), 30–42.

Cechaviciute, I., & Kenny, D. T. (2007). The relationship between neutralizations and perceived delinquent labeling on criminal history in young offenders serving community orders. *Criminal Justice and Behavior, 34*(6), 816–829.

Durkheim, E. (1895). *The rules of the sociological method* (S. A. Solovay & J. H. Mueller, Trans.). New York: Free Press (Reprinted 1965).

Empey, L. T. (1978). *American delinquency: Its meaning and construction.* Homewood, IL: Dorsey.

Gottfredson, M., & Hirschi, T. (1990). *A general theory of crime.* Stanford, CA: Stanford University Press.

Greenberg, D. F. (1999). The weak strength of social control theory. *Crime and Delinquency, 45,* 66–82.

Hirschi, T. (1969). *Causes of delinquency.* Berkeley: University of California Press.

Hirschi, T. (1979). Separate and unequal is better. *Journal of Research in Crime and Delinquency, 16,* 34–38.

Hirschi, T. (1989). Exploring alternatives to integrated theory. In S.E. Messner, M. D. Krohn, & A. E. Liska (Eds.), *Theoretical integration in the study of deviance and crime: Problems and perspectives* (pp. 37–49). Albany, NY: State University of New York Press.

Hirschi, T. (2004). Self-control and crime. In R. F. Baumeister & K. D. Vohs (Eds.), *Everyday problems with self-regulation* (pp. 537–552). New York: Guilford.

Hirschi, T., & Gottfredson, M. (1987). Causes of white-collar crime. *Criminology, 25,* 949–974.

Ingram, J. R., & Hinduja, S. (2008). Neutralizing music piracy: An empirical examination. *Deviant Behavior, 29,* 334–366.

Karacki, L., & Toby, J. (1962). The uncommitted adolescent: Candidate for gang socialization. *Sociological Inquiry, 32,* 203–215.

Khoo, A. C. E., & Oakes, P. J. (2000). The variability of the delinquent self: Anti-authority attitudes and endorsements of neutralization techniques among incarcerated delinquents in Singapore. *Asian Journal of Social Psychology, 2,* 125–132.

Malesky, L. A., Jr., & Ennis, L. (2004). Supportive distortions: An analysis of posts on a pedophile internet message board. *Journal of Addictions and Offender Counseling, 24,* 92–100.

Matza, D. (1961). Juvenile delinquency and subterranean beliefs. *American Sociological Review, 26,* 713–719.

Matza, D. (1964). *Delinquency and drift.* New York: Wiley.

Nye, F. I. (1958). *Family relationships and delinquent behavior.* New York: Wiley.

Peretti-Watel, P. (2003). Neutralization theory and the denial of risk: Some evidence from cannabis use among French adolescents. *British Journal of Sociology, 54,* 21–42.

Reckless, W. C. (1955). *The crime problem.* New York: Appleton-Century-Crofts.

Reckless, W. C. (1961). A new theory of delinquency and crime. *Federal Probation, 25,* 42–46.

Reckless, W. C., & Dinitz, S. (1967). Pioneering with self-concept as a vulnerability factor in delinquency. *Journal of Criminal Law, Criminology and Police Science, 58,* 515–523.

Reiss, A. J., Jr. (1951). Delinquency as the failure of personal and social controls. *American Sociological Review, 16,* 196–207.

Relin, D. O. (2006, March 26). It only takes one. *Sunday Parade,* p. 4.

Sampson, R. J., & Laub, J. (1990). Crime and deviance over the life course: The salience of adult social bonds. *American Sociological Review, 55,* 609–627.

Short, J. F., Jr., & Strodtbeck, F. L. (1965). *Group process and gang delinquency.* Chicago: University of Chicago Press.

Sykes, G. M., & Matza, D. (1957). Techniques of neutralization: A theory of delinquency. *American Sociological Review, 22,* 664–670.

Thompson, W. E., Harred, J. L., & Burks, B. E. (2003). Managing the stigma of topless dancing: A decade later. *Deviant Behavior, 24,* 551–570.

Toby, J. (1957). Social disorganization and stake in conformity: Complimentary factors in the predatory behavior of hoodlums. *Journal of Criminal Law, Criminology and Police Science, 48,* 12–17.

Topalli, V. (2006). The seductive nature of autotelic crime: How neutralization theory serves as a boundary condition for understanding hardcore street offending. *Sociological Inquiry, 76,* 475–501.

Williams, F. P., III. (1984). The demise of the criminological imagination: A critique of recent criminology. *Justice Quarterly, 1,* 91–106.

Research Bibliography

Containment Theory (from 1980)

Brownfield, D., & Thompson, K. (2005). Self-concept and delinquency: The effects of reflected appraisals by parent and peers. *Western Criminology Review, 6*(1), 22–29.

Dinitz, S., & Pfau-Vicent, B. A. (1982). Self-concept and juvenile delinquency. *Youth and Society, 14*, 133–158.

Dodder, R. A., & Long, J. R. (1980). Containment theory re-evaluated: An empirical explanation. *Criminal Justice Review, 5*, 74–84.

Eyo, I. E. (1981). British delinquents and nondelinquents on seven domains of the self-concept. *Journal of Psychology, 109*, 137–145.

McCarthy, J. D., & Hoge, D. R. (1984). The dynamics of self-esteem and delinquency. *American Journal of Sociology, 90*, 396–410.

Roberts, J., Gunes, I., & Seward, R. (2011). The impact of self esteem, family rituals, religiosity, and participation in conforming activities upon delinquency: A comparison of young adults in Turkey and the United States. *Journal of Comparative Family Studies, 42*, 59-76.

Thompson, W. E., & Dodder, R. A. (1983). Juvenile delinquency explained? A test of containment theory. *Youth and Society, 15*, 171–194.

Thompson, W. E., & Dodder, R. A. (1986). Containment theory and juvenile delinquency: A reevaluation through factor analysis. *Adolescence, 21*, 365–376.

Bonding Theory (from 2000)

Alarid, L. F., Burton, V. S., Jr., & Cullen, F. T. (2000). Gender and crime among felony offenders: Assessing the generality of social control and differential association theories. *Journal of Research in Crime and Delinquency, 37*, 171–201.

Baay, P., Liem, M., & Nieuwbeerta, P. (2012). Ex-imprisoned homicide offenders: Once bitten, twice shy?" The effect of the length of imprisonment on recidivism for homicide offenders. *Homicide Studies, 16*, 259–279.

Booth, J. A., Farrell, A., & Varano, S. P. (2008). Social control, Serious delinquency, and risky behavior: A gendered analysis. *Crime & Delinquency, 54*, 423–456.

Bouffard, J. A., & Rice, S. K. (2011). The influence of the social bond on self-control at the moment of decision: Testing Hirschi's redefinition of self-control. *American Journal of Criminal Justice, 36*, 138–157.

Cernkovich, S. A., Giordano, P., & Rudolph, J. L. (2000). Race, crime, and the American dream. *Journal of Research in Crime and Delinquency, 37*, 131–169.

Chapple, C. L., Hope, T. L., & Whiteford, S. W. (2005). The direct and indirect effects of parental bonds, parental drug use, and self-control on adolescent substance use. *Journal of Child & Adolescent Substance Abuse, 14*(3), 17–38.

Chapple, C. L., McQuillan, J. A., & Berdahi, T. A. (2005). Gender, social bonds, and delinquency: A comparison of boys' and girls' models. *Social Science Research, 34*, 357–383.

Chui, W., & Chan, H. (2011). Social bonds and male juvenile delinquency while on probation: An exploratory test in Hong Kong. *Children & Youth Services Review, 33*, 2329–2334.

Cretacci, M. A. (2003). Religion and social control: An application of a modified social boind on violence. *Criminal Justice Review, 28*, 254–277.

Cretacci, M. A., Rivera, C. J., & Ding, F. (2009). Self-control and Chinese deviance: A look behind the bamboo curtain. *International Journal of Criminal Justice Sciences, 4*, 131–143.

De Li, S. (2004). The impacts of self-control and social bonds on juvenile delinquency in a national sample of midadolescents. *Deviant Behavior, 25*, 351–373.

Doherty, E. E. (2006). Self-control, social bonds, and desistance: A test of life-course interdependence. *Criminology, 44*, 807–834.

Dornbusch, S. M., Erickson, K. G., Laird, J. L., & Wong, C. A. (2001). The relation of family and school attachment to adolescent deviance in diverse groups and communities. *Journal of Adolescent Research, 16*, 396–423.

Erickson, K. G., Crosnoe, R., & Dornbusch, S. M. (2000). A social process model of adolescent deviance: Combining social control and differential association perspectives. *Journal of Youth and Adolescence, 29*, 395–425.

Giordano, P. C., Lonardo, R. A., Manning, W. D., & Longmore, M. A. (2010). Adolescent romance and delinquency: A further exploration of Hirschi's 'cold and brittle' relationships hypothesis. *Criminology, 48*, 919–946.

Hay, C., Stults, B., & Restivo, E. (2012). Suppressing the harmful effects of key risk factors: Results from the Children at Risk Experimental Intervention. *Criminal Justice and Behavior, 39*, 1088–1106.

Huebner, A. J., & Betts, S. C. (2002). Exploring the utility of social control theory for youth development: Issues of attachment, involvement, and gender. *Youth & Society, 34*, 123–145.

Kerpelman, J., & Smith-Adcock, S. (2005). Female adolescents' delinquent activity: The intersection of bonds to parents and reputation enhancement. *Youth & Society, 37*, 176–200.

Mack, K. Y., Leiber, M. J., Featherstone, R. A., & Monserud, M. A. (2007). Reassessing the family-delinquency association: Do family type, family processes, and economic factors make a difference? *Journal of Criminal Justice, 35*, 51–67.

Morris, R. G., Gerber, J., & Menard, S. (2011). Social bonds, self-control, and adult criminality. *Criminal Justice & Behavior, 38*, 584–599.

Nakhaie, M., Silverman, R. A., & LaGrange, T. C. (2000). Self-control and social control: An examination of gender, ethnicity, class and delinquency. *Canadian Journal of Sociology, 25*, 35–59.

Ozbay, O., & Ozcan, Y. Z. (2008). A test of Hirschi's social bonding theory: A comparison of male and female delinquency. *International Journal of Offender Therapy and Comparative Criminology, 52*, 134–157.

Ozbay, O., & Ziya-Ozcan, Y. (2006). A test of Hirschi's social bonding theory. *International Journal of Offender Therapy & Comparative Criminology, 50*, 711–726.

Popp, A. M., & Peguero, A. A. (2012). Social bonds and the role of school-based victimization. *Journal of Interpersonal Violence, 27*(17), 3366–3388.

Ryan, J. P., Testa, M. F., & Fuhua, Z. (2008). African American males in foster care and the risk of delinquency: The value of social bonds and permanence. *Child Welfare, 87*, 115–140.

Sims, R. (2002). Ethical rule breaking by employees: A test of social bonding theory. *Journal of Business Ethics, 40*, 101–109.

Veenstra, R., Lindenberg, S., Tinga, F., & Ormel, J. (2010). Truancy in late elementary and early secondary education: The influence of social bonds and self-control—The TRAILS study. *International Journal of Behavioral Development, 34*, 302–310.

Wadsworth, T. (2000). Labor markets, delinquency, and social control theory: An empirical assessment of the mediating process. *Social Forces, 78*, 1024–1067.

Weerman, F. M., & Hoeve, M. (2012). Peers and delinquency among girls and boys: Are sex differences in delinquency explained by peer factors? *European Journal of Criminology, 9*, 228–244.

Windlin, B., & Kuntsche, E. (2012). Differences in the impact of the frequency and enjoyment of joint family activities on adolescent substance use and violence. *Journal of Health Psychology, 17*, 509–519.

Neutralization Theory (from 2000)

Antonopoulos, G. A., & Winterdyk, J. A. (2005). Techniques of neutralizing the trafficking of women: A case study of an active trafficker in Greece. *European Journal of Crime, Criminal Law & Criminal Justice, 13*, 136–147.

Buzzell, T. (2005). Holiday revelry and legal control of fireworks: A study of neutralization in two normative contexts. *Western Criminology Review, 6*(1), 30–42.

Christensen, T. (2010). Presumed guilty: Constructing deviance and deviants through techniques of neutralization. *Deviant Behavior, 31*, 552–577.

Copes, H. (2003). Societal attachments, offending frequency, and techniques of neutralization. *Deviant Behavior, 24*, 101–127.

Costello, B. J. (2000). Techniques of neutralization and self-esteem: A critical test of social control and neutralization theory. *Deviant Behavior, 21*, 307–329.

Cromwell, P., & Thurman, Q. (2003). The devil made me do it: Use of neutralizations by shoplifters. *Deviant Behavior, 24*(6), 535–550.

Crosswhite, J. M., & Kerpelman, J. L. (2009). Coercion theory, self-control, and social information processing: Understanding potential mediators for how parents influence deviant behaviors. *Deviant Behavior, 30*, 611–646.

Fritsche, I. (2005). Predicting deviant behavior by neutralization: Myths and findings. *Deviant Behavior, 26*, 483–510.

Gauthier, D. K. (2001). Professional lapses: Occupational deviance and neutralization techniques in veterinary medical practice. *Deviant Behavior, 22*, 467–490.

Ingram, J. R., & Hinduja, S. (2008). Neutralizing music piracy: An empirical examination. *Deviant Behavior, 29*, 334–366.

Kreager, D. A. (2007). When it's good to be "bad": Violence and adolescent peer acceptance. *Criminology, 45*, 893–923.

Marcum, C. D., Higgins, G. E., Wolfe, S. E., & Ricketts, M. L. (2011). Examining the intersection of self-control, peer association and neutralization in explaining digital piracy. *Western Criminology Review, 12*(3), 60–74.

Morris, R. G., & Higgins, G. E. (2009). Neutralizing potential and self-reported digital piracy: A multitheoretical exploration among college undergraduates. *Criminal Justice Review, 34*, 173–195.

Peretti-Watel, P. (2003). Neutralization theory and the denial of risk: Some evidence from cannabis use among French adolescents. *British Journal of Sociology, 54*, 21–42.

Piquero, N., Tibbetts, S. G., & Blankenship, M. B. (2005). Examining the role of differential association and techniques of neutralization in explaining corporate crime. *Deviant Behavior, 26*, 159–188.

Thompson, W. E., Harred, J. L., & Burks, B. E. (2003). Managing the stigma of topless dancing: A decade later. *Deviant Behavior, 24*, 551–570.

Topalli, V. (2005). When being good is bad: An expansion of neutralization theory. *Criminology, 43*, 797–836.

Topalli, V. (2006). The seductive nature of autotelic crime: How neutralization theory serves as a boundary condition for understanding hardcore street offending. *Sociological Inquiry, 76*, 475–501.

Ulsperger, J. S., Hodges, S. H., & Paul, J. (2010). Pirates on the plank: Neutralization theory and the criminal downloading of music among Generation Y in the era of late modernity. *Journal of Criminal Justice & Popular Culture, 17*, 124–151.

van San, M. (2007). Petty thieves and muggers: How Curacaoan youths in the Netherlands justify criminal behaviour. *Caribbean Journal of Criminology & Social Psychology, 12*(1/2), 86–113.

12

Social Learning Theory

LEARNING OBJECTIVES

Objective 12.1: Discuss the different elements involved in crime according to Lifestyle theory.

Objective 12.2: Explain the various factors that interact for crime to occur according to Routine Activities theory.

Objective 12.3: Describe what is meant by routine activities and how these have changed over time in our society.

Objective 12.4: Outline the process of decision making in committing a crime according to the Rational Choice perspective.

Objective 12.5: Describe the policies and programs that are suggested by rational theories.

INTRODUCTION

Even though social learning theory was developed a short time (1965–1966) before Hirschi's social control theory, it is newer than the other versions of social control theory and has become popular since 1975. There are really two theories under this generic name. The first was developed by C. Ray Jeffery as a direct application of popular operant-based learning theories from psychology. The other, which has received greater acceptance by criminologists, is Ronald Akers's *social* learning theory. Akers's theory evolved from its 1966 origins, and the version popular today was developed mostly in the 1970s. In addition, social learning theory is primarily an extension of Edwin Sutherland's differential association theory. Had we not been attempting in this book to keep the theories in chronological order, social learning theory would best have been placed after the chapter on differential association.

Both these theories rely on behavioral psychology. There are two general types of psychological approaches: Skinnerian, or operant, theory and social learning theory. B. F. Skinner's original version of operant theory allows only for direct material sources of reinforcement and punishment. Social versions of learning, on the other hand, begin with Skinner's theory and add the concept of indirect social stimuli and cognitive processes. Jeffery uses the more straightforward Skinnerian approach, whereas Akers relies on the social learning variety.

THE HERITAGE OF THE THEORY

The Social Heritage

Behavioral theories in psychology rose to the peak of their popularity in the 1960s. The optimistic spirit of the early part of the decade led psychologists to believe that otherwise untreatable behavior problems could be successfully treated by using the newly developed behavioral therapies. The civil rights campaign had also spilled over into mental health issues. Recognition of the rights of mental patients gave them a right to treatment, rather than just being warehoused. Further, behavior modification, a branch of applied behavioral psychology, was especially suitable for training in life skills so that the patient could eventually be released from the institution.

As part of the Great Society concept, schools were experimenting with new and better ways of learning. Education began championing behavior modification and adapting it to the classroom setting. By the 1970s, people felt so convinced that behavioral psychologies were the answer to behavior problems that Skinner made the bestseller list with two popular books, *Beyond Freedom and Dignity* and *Walden II*. One controversial movie, *A Clockwork Orange*, even featured the use of a punishment-oriented version of behavior modification.

An optimistic philosophy had also developed in corrections and the juvenile justice system, with state and federal governments funding several experimental programs. Among those programs, behavior modification appeared to have the most promise, largely because it seemed to work within institutions, if not outside them. Even at the end of the decade, when people had become cynical about treatment programs, behavior modification programs were still in use (those versions based on punishment were, however, beginning to come under fire). Ultimately, however, futuristic books and films that emphasized the possible abuses of behavior programming and mind control as well as suspicions about government abuses of power that developed with the Watergate scandal probably all contributed to public concerns about behavioral psychology and created a strong reaction against the behavior modification movement. Radicals, in particular, objected to the use of behavior modification, claiming it was an elite plan to brainwash those who threatened the state.

The Intellectual Heritage

The most obvious intellectual source of social learning theory is behavioristic psychology. Ray Jeffery adopted the approach as a faculty member at Arizona State University, where two prominent psychologists, Arthur and Carolyn Staats, were making strides in the new field of behavior modification. In addition, Jeffery was involved in the Washington, DC, Dropout Project, a program that attempted to apply the principles of behavior modification to delinquent youth. Ron Akers, on the other hand, developed his theory as the result of interaction with another young faculty member, Robert Burgess, in the sociology department at the University of Washington (Akers, 1985). Burgess had studied behavioral psychology and convinced Akers it could profitably be applied to criminology. Burgess was later to employ learning theory in several environmental programs, including an antilittering program for a park system.

Perhaps as important as psychology is the heritage gained from differential association. Both Jeffery and Akers published their original learning theory articles as an explanation of Sutherland's statement, "Criminal behavior is learned." Jeffery was, in fact, one of the last of Sutherland's students. Akers, who earned his doctoral degree under Richard Quinney, was intimately familiar with Sutherland's work, especially since Quinney was working on a reformulation of differential association theory (DeFleur & Quinney, 1966). Indeed, many criminologists today see social learning theory as an extension and modernization of differential association theory.

THE THEORETICAL PERSPECTIVE

Operant and General Social Learning Theories

Before one can appreciate criminological learning theories, a basic understanding of operant-based learning theory is necessary. Operant learning theory is concerned with the effect an individual's behavior has on the environment and, subsequently, the consequences of that effect on the individual. As Skinner (1971, p. 16) relates, behavior is shaped and maintained by its consequences. Therefore, behavior is a product of present and past events in the life of the individual. The contingencies of reinforcement and punishment (aversive stimuli) determine whether the frequency of any particular behavior is increased or diminished.

We discuss here six basic principles: positive reinforcement, negative reinforcement, positive punishment, negative punishment, discriminative stimuli, and schedules. Reinforcement may be described as any event that follows the occurrence of behavior and that alters and increases the frequency of the behavior. Some events directly increase the frequency of behavior they follow. These are *positive* reinforcers, or rewards. A mother who gives her child a cookie for doing something good is providing positive reinforcement. Other events increase the frequency of behavior if they remove something undesirable following the behavior. These are called *negative* reinforcers. If a child does something bad and then says he is sorry, the mother may not punish the child. Perhaps the easiest way to distinguish between the two is positive reinforcement provides a reward and negative reinforcement removes some form of punishment.

Punishment, or aversive stimuli, is the opposite of reinforcement. That is, it reduces the frequency of any behavior it follows. The process of decreasing the emission of behavior through the presence of an aversive stimulus is called *positive* punishment. This is the typical reason for spanking a child. *Negative* punishment results in the removal of rewards that would ordinarily have been present after a behavior. In this case, the child does not get the cookie.

Discriminative stimuli, on the other hand, do not occur after behavior but are present either before or as the behavior occurs. Further, they can be used to control behavior because they indicate whether reinforcement or punishment is forthcoming. Thus, they function as *cues*, or signals, that help the individual determine those situations in which a particular behavior may be appropriate (likely to be reinforced). It is this form of stimulus that is crucial in social settings; almost all our social world is composed of discriminative stimuli. Advertising, for example, is primarily based on the use of discriminative stimuli to get us to associate a product with something we find rewarding.

A final concept is that of the schedule of consequences. This refers to the frequency with which, and probability that, a particular consequence will occur, as well as to the length of time it occurs after the behavior. Those consequences immediately following behavior and having a high probability of occurrence are the ones that have the strongest effect on the individual. This means some forms of behavior will be preferred over others because of their reinforcement schedule. Conversely, it means if we wait too long to punish someone for a crime, for example, the punishment will lose much of its effect.

Learning, then, takes place because of the consequences associated with behavior. If an individual is reinforced after doing something, that behavior will occur again: the behavior has been learned. On the other hand, if punishment occurs after certain behavior, the individual learns to avoid that kind of behavior. Since people do not all have the same reward and punishment experiences in their past, some people will have learned some behavior while others will not. Finally, any social environment contains several possible situations, each of which might provide different cues and consequences for a behavior. It is relatively easy to misinterpret a situation and assume previous learning will apply when in fact it will not.

Social learning theory also considers the concept of imitation, or modeling, to be central to the learning process (Bandura, 1969, pp. 118–203; 1977). This involves the process of learning by observing the behavior of others. If, for instance, some other person is rewarded for certain behavior, an individual watching that situation can also learn the behavior. In this way, the observer is "vicariously reinforced." Strict operant learning theory insists learning must be based on behavior and consequences applied to the individual, not some other person. Therefore, social learning theory is different in that it adds the social environment to the learning process. Under this approach, it is possible to learn not only from other people around us but also from television and movies.

Jeffery's Differential Reinforcement Theory

In 1965, Jeffery published the first article linking criminal behavior and operant learning theory.[1] His thesis was differential association is "not valid in its present form, though it is basically sound in asserting that criminal behavior is learned" (1965, p. 294). Sutherland's theory needed reformulation into modern learning theory, but Jeffery maintained that once that was done the theory no longer would be a theory of *social* reinforcement. It would be, he said, a more complete theory that could explain how "criminal behavior can be maintained without social approval" (1965, p. 296). In fact, Jeffery thought his new learning theory put differential association to rest by convincingly adding nonsocial explanations for behavior (personal communication, 1975).

Jeffery began his theory of differential reinforcement with a brief description of the six basic operant principles. He added one more set of concepts to his discussion: *satiation* and *deprivation*.

Clarence Ray Jeffery (1921–2007)

C. Ray Jeffery was born into a criminal justice–oriented family in Pocatello, Idaho. His father was both a prosecutor and a defense attorney, and his uncle was a police officer. He received his bachelor's in economics and philosophy and his master's in sociology. Because his major professor focused on issues of crime and law, Jeffery was identified as a "criminologist" as soon as he graduated. That being the case, he went to Indiana University to study with Edwin Sutherland, where he was one of Sutherland's last students. Although Jeffery took coursework in an interdisciplinary curriculum of law, sociology, and behavioral psychology, he received a Ph.D. in Sociology. Supported by his eclectic academic background, Jeffery pioneered several of the theoretical perspectives in criminology, including conflict theory, learning theory, environmental design, and sociobiology. He taught at Colby College, Arizona State University, and New York University (where he became editor of the American Society of Criminology's newsletter transitioning to journal, *Criminologica*, which then became *Criminology*) before moving to Florida State University's School of Criminology in 1970. Jeffery spent the remainder of his career there as a Professor of Criminology and Criminal Justice until 1995, when he was honored with Professor Emeritus status. Jeffery was President of the American Society of Criminology in 1978. He passed away after a lengthy illness in 2007.

---

[1] C. R. Jeffery, prior to his death, reviewed and approved this summary of his work.

It suggests a stimulus will be more or less reinforcing depending on the individual's current condition. For example, a person who already has wealth (satiated) will be less likely to find robbing someone of their money to be reinforcing, while the impoverished individual (deprived) will more likely see the money as a reinforcer. Such a concept of the condition of the individual allows for similar interpretations of the effect of social class and poverty as those we saw in the strain theories of Robert Merton, Albert Cohen, and Richard Cloward and Lloyd Ohlin.

A brief summary of the elements of differential reinforcement is as follows (Jeffery, 1965, p. 295): People do not have the same past experiences; therefore, their conditioning histories are different. The stimuli people experience daily also have distinct meanings that produce differing qualities of reinforcement. Among these stimuli are some that have previously affected criminal behavior. Thus, some people have been reinforced for criminal behavior and some have been punished. Since most consequences are relatively intermittent (rarely is anything rewarded or punished every time), criminal behavior is not reinforced or punished each time it occurs. Instead, past experience is sufficient to maintain the current criminal behavior.

Finally, Jeffery also insisted that the most important forms of reinforcers are material, such as money and cars. As a result, differential reinforcement maintains that one does not need associates to provide reinforcing consequences for criminal behavior, for the product of the crime itself can be the reinforcer. Other people are said to be important for their discriminative value; that is, they provide cues about the probability of being rewarded for a criminal act. This decreased emphasis on social reinforcement has continued to characterize Jeffery's work. His book, *Crime Prevention through Environmental Design* (1977), incorporates his work in sociobiology and states that the reinforcing quality of all behavior lies in the brain. By this Jeffery means that the brain contains pleasure and pain centers that mediate and interpret all stimuli. Thus, he now says social reinforcement is really a secondary form of reinforcement and is maintained only by a relationship with the more primary form of biological reinforcement (1977, p. 312).

Jeffery continued with his work on brain-mediated behavior and strongly argued for interdisciplinary work on the problem of criminal behavior. His final approach is that a general theory of crime should have three components: genetics, brain structure and function, and learning theory (1989b, p. 73). His perspective is that sociological, psychological, and biological characteristics should be seen as interacting together in a total system to produce criminal behavior. He posits that individuals are born with particular biological (genetic) and psychological characteristics that not only may predispose but may actually cause certain forms of behavior. This "nature" is independent of the socialization process present in the social environment. There is, however, a good deal of interplay between nature and socialization through physical environments and the feedback mechanisms existing in biochemical systems. For example, Jeffery notes poverty translates to a certain type of diet and exposure to pollutants. Both of these are transformed by the biochemical system into neurochemical compounds within the brain. Thus, poverty indirectly leads to behavioral differences (and, potentially, criminal behavior) through the interaction of individual and environment.

Jeffery clearly suggests that any theory of criminal behavior is incomplete without a consideration of all elements making up the human organism (1989a). In addition, he notes that the study of criminal behavior is not possible without an understanding and theory of criminal law. A summary of his overall approach combining both behavior and law is as follows: Humans are born with biological and psychological differences. These differences lead to direct conflict with other humans. To reduce this conflict, humans must be socialized into conformity, and, lacking this, control systems (the state and criminal law) must be created to restrict behavior. Criminal behavior is behavior restricted by these control systems.

Ronald Louis Akers (1939–)

Ron Akers was born in New Albany, Indiana, in 1939 and obtained his B.S. from Indiana State College in social studies (secondary education) in 1960. He began his lifelong commitment to sociology with a master's from Kent State in 1961 and a Ph.D. in Sociology from the University of Kentucky in 1966, under his mentor Richard Quinney. Over the years, he taught in sociology/criminology programs including those at the University of Washington, Florida State University, and the University of Iowa. He spent the largest and last portion of his career at the University of Florida, where he has served as Chair of the department, Associate Dean of the College of Arts and Sciences, and Director of the Center for Studies in Criminology and Law. Akers was President of the American Society of Criminology (ASC) in 1979, and in 1988 he won the distinguished Edwin Sutherland Award from that organization and was named an ASC Fellow. He also served as President of the Southern Sociological Society and as Chair of the Criminology Section of the American Sociological Association. He is perhaps as well known to many of his colleagues for his bluegrass band that has played each year for the last decade or so at the ASC meeting to raise money for minority scholarships.

Akers' Social Learning Theory

Akers and Burgess provided criminology with the second connection between psychological learning theory and differential association (Burgess & Akers, 1966).[2] After reading Jeffery's 1965 article, they decided a more detailed statement of learning theory would be beneficial and began the process of fully reformulating the propositions of differential association theory. The final version of seven propositions, which they labeled "differential association-reinforcement theory," was not originally intended as an alternative to Sutherland's theory. Of necessity, however, it became a "new, broader theory" (Akers, 1985, p. 41).

In contrast to Jeffery's approach, it is obvious Akers views the social environment as the most important source of reinforcement. He even suggests that most of the learning of deviant behavior is the result of social interaction (1985, p. 45). In fact, it is the presence of various subcultures in society that allows us to predict which stimuli are likely to be effective reinforcers for people. This approach leads to the presence of *definitions* as one of the crucial aspects of the theory.

Definitions of behavior, both for Sutherland and Akers, are the moral components of social interaction expressing whether something is right or wrong. Akers refers to these definitions as verbal behavior and notes they are learned just as any other behavior is learned. Once learned, however, definitions become a form of discriminative stimuli or cues about the consequences to be expected from other behavior. They can be general beliefs, applying to a range of behavior, or specifically focused on a single form of behavior. Those indicating approval of certain behavior are clearly positive in their action; that is, they denote the behavior is morally correct and will be rewarded (positive reinforcement). Others are neutralizing definitions, providing a way to avoid some (or all) of an expected punishment and justifying or excusing the behavior (negative reinforcement).

Akers has continued the development of the theory, most notably in his books *Deviant Behavior: A Social Learning Approach* (1985) and *Social Learning and Social Structure* (1998).

---

[2] We would like to express our appreciation to Ron Akers for reviewing and approving this summary of his work in an earlier edition of this book. This new version adds the social structure element and has not been reviewed.

The most recent version of social learning theory can be summarized as follows. First, behavior is learned through operant conditioning principles but with the addition of social learning principles such as imitation. Learning occurs both in nonsocial and social (the behavior of other persons) situations that either reinforce or offer discriminating cues for behavior. While nonsocial learning exists, it primarily takes place in social situations where groups provide the largest part of an individual's reinforcements. These groups present stimuli according to their structural position in society, including culture, subculture, class, gender, and economic position. This is the component of the theory where differential reinforcement is stressed— individuals have different social groups and situations available to them on a consistent basis, thus, different associations with others. Next, the learning of any behavior is a function of reinforcing stimuli and the contingencies for reinforcement provided by an individual's various social situations. It is important to note that an individual does not have to be directly reinforced because discriminating social cues offer an individual the possibility of imitating the reinforced behavior of others.

Depending on the social situation providing the reinforcers and their contingencies, an individual can receive either specific attitudes and techniques or more general social values. Thus, both very focused definitions for specific behaviors, including the techniques for these, and general cultural (or subcultural) values can be transmitted. Any individual learned behavior is governed by a combination of the immediate reinforcement provided to an individual and the conforming or deviant orientation of values and definitions from past reinforcement. These more general values and definitions (norms, rationalizations, neutralizations) increase the likelihood of certain behaviors (generally, deviant or conforming) in a particular situation by providing discriminative cues to an individual that those behaviors will be reinforced.

Finally, the frequency and duration of a behavior's occurrence depends on the amount, frequency, and probability of its reinforcement. Because these reinforcements (and discriminative cues) vary in different social situations and with different associates, it is an individual's structural position in society that primarily determines his or her patterns of values and definitions. It is this same social position that affects the associations available to an individual and subsequently the number and probability of deviant versus nondeviant reinforcements and definitions in the general social environment. To the extent that a subculture accepts and provides reinforcement for deviant definitions, an individual member of that group will exhibit more or less deviant behavior.

In the development and empirical testing of his theory, Akers has focused on the principal processes of differential association, definitions, differential reinforcement, and imitation. Social learning theory, then, states people learn both deviant behavior and the definitions that go along with it from others. The learning can be direct, as through conditioning, or indirect, as through imitation and modeling. The learned deviance can then be strengthened by reinforcement or weakened by punishment. Its continued maintenance depends not only on its own reinforcement but also on the quality of the reinforcement available for alternative behavior. If the definitions of deviant behavior are reinforcing and if alternative behaviors are not reinforced as strongly, an individual is likely to engage in deviant behavior. The structural component of the theory is complementary to the issue of differential association and states that learning opportunities are structured by one's location in society. That is, learning opportunities are affected by the values and definitions shared and transmitted by intimate groups whose members are situated within a family, neighborhood, subculture, or culture. Where deviant values and definitions are more likely to be espoused, rates of deviant behavior are likely to increase.

CLASSIFICATION OF THE THEORY

Social learning qualifies as a *positivist* theory. Compared with other theories, it focuses more directly on behavior and presents an obvious treatment or remedy for deviance. Similarly, because learning theory is focused on the individual, it is primarily classified as a *microtheory*. Even though the theoretical principles are general enough to apply to all behavior, its main focus is to explain how individuals come to engage in criminal behavior.

Social learning is also a *processual* theory. It explains the process by which criminal behavior takes place and tells us why that behavior occurs. The theory does have a structural component that places the individual in a particular location in society, with all that implies in terms of class, subculture, and so forth. However, this is essentially a statement that values and definitions are differentially available to individuals and that availability is structured. It is the process of learning that is still paramount for the theory.

The more difficult point of classification is that of consensus conflict. The theory itself does not require either orientation, so we must look to the theorists to determine which it is. We would infer Jeffery takes a consensus orientation to society. This appears to be the case because his work provides many applications to "treat" criminal behavior, yet he does not question the origin of those laws requiring that treatment. In fairness to Jeffery, however, he does state that a theory of the creation of law is necessary before one can discuss criminal behavior but once that law exists he seems not to question it. Akers, on the other hand, believes that there is a "core of consensual values" while "admitting the importance of power and conflict" (1985, p. 19). This, he says, is a pluralist conflict approach, which is made more evident in his discussion of the structural side to the theory. Since both these theorists seem to assume a core set of common social values, however, we will cautiously classify social learning theory as primarily a *consensus* theory.

Summary

Social learning theory developed from the combination of differential association theory with psychological learning theories. Though Jeffery's final version de-emphasizes the social aspects of learning, Akers's theory is still directly associated with Sutherland's perspective. They both, however, explain deviant behavior by emphasizing reinforcement and discriminative stimuli.

Behavior, whether deviant or not, can be expected to be maintained if it is reinforced in the social environment. Thus, the problem for behavioral criminologists is to determine where these reinforcements originate. Jeffery suggests reinforcement is biologically based in the pleasure–pain center of the brain (Jeffery, 1998). Preferring to keep his theory on a social level, Akers finds the origin of deviance reinforcement in common rationalizations and in the various groups and subcultures of society.

As has been the case for social control theory, the popularity of social learning theory has increased during the past two decades. However, some sociologically oriented criminologists remain skeptical of the approach because it is directly derived from psychology. Nonetheless, as a major theory not requiring an acceptance of the conflict position (though Akers leans a bit toward conflict), social learning theory has been steadily gaining in acceptance. It is now quite common to see commentary or research on the theory in the various criminological journals and recent surveys of criminologists have suggested that is now one of the most-favored theories. Several theorists even attempted to integrate social control and social learning theories, an effort Akers would encourage (1985, p. 67; 1989). Moreover, Akers has stated he views social learning theory as a major approach to integrating other deviance-oriented theories (1985, p. 70; 1998) and now regards it as a general theory of behavior, not just of deviance.

MAJOR POINTS OF THE THEORY

1. Human behavior is organized around the seeking of pleasure and the avoidance of pain.
2. The two concepts involved in the learning of behavior are reinforcement and punishment. Reinforcement increases the frequency of a behavior, whereas punishment decreases the frequency.
3. Criminal behavior is learned through both material and social reinforcements in the same way as is any other behavior. This learning process is a product of past and present experiences; therefore, all individuals have a different set of learned behaviors and expected consequences.
4. Social reinforcements serve as factors both in directly learning deviant behavior and in setting the values (definitions) that define behavior as good or bad, desirable or undesirable. The social environment also provides various behavior models that can be imitated.

5. Social definitions, which are originally learned in the same way as any other behavior, act as cues signaling whether a particular behavior will or will not be reinforced. In the case of values, definitions provide discriminative cues that certain behaviors espoused by those values will be reinforced.
6. Definitions assist in the learning of crime as direct signals that a reward is forthcoming or as rationalizations used to avoid punishment for criminal behavior.
7. Social structure acts to position individuals in roles that are differentially exposed to reinforcement and definitions conducive to criminal behavior.
8. Criminal behavior is behavior that has been differentially reinforced through social definitions and material rewards in the individual's structured environment.
9. Material reinforcements are often provided by crime itself. Therefore, when individuals are deprived, criminal behavior may be maintained by its own rewards.

Epilogue: Current Directions and Policy Implications

CURRENT DIRECTIONS

Social learning theories continue to be popular. Several criminologists have attempted to test the approach, particularly Akers's version of the theory. Indeed, Akers himself has led the way with several research projects, most of which have focused on drug use, including alcohol and cigarettes. In addition, studies using social learning theory have examined cheating and other forms of academic dishonesty, suicide, participation in gangs, and more recently, computer crime. In one analysis, both differential association and differential reinforcement were found in those most likely to engage in the illegal downloading of music (piracy) (Hinduja, 2006). Other tests of theories, have commonly found that social learning variables explain at least as much of deviant behavior as other theories do. Actually,

the findings usually are that social learning explains delinquency and deviance *better* than most other theories (Akers & Jensen, 2006; Pratt et al., 2010).

Other approaches to learning theory have also been developed, particularly with reference to personality traits (some as early as 1962). One of the more popular versions in criminology is an adaptation of differential association theory by Daniel Glaser. In his 1978 book, *Crime in Our Changing Society*, Glaser proposed a theory of differential anticipation. Drawing on his previous idea that identification with criminal roles is more important than one's associates, he incorporated social learning concepts and said expectations determine conduct. Indeed, he saw three sources of expectations: pro- and anticriminal social bonds, differential learning, and perceived opportunities. Individuals have different groups of people around them who may reward behavior according to different values. Therefore, people have different sources of behavior and values and thus learn differently. The process involves learning discriminative stimuli as a way of knowing what behavior will be rewarded and punished. Finally, opportunities for crime involve an assessment of risks and gains individuals expect to receive from committing a crime. Glaser's basic idea is that an individual will commit a crime when the expected (anticipated) gains outweigh the expected punishments. These expectations, of course, are all learned from one's social environment.

Social learning theory has also been a mainstay of attempts to integrate criminological theories. Most common is an attempt to combine it with social control, to which others have added labeling and/or strain. Akers has proposed relationships with each of the other major theories, explaining that social learning acts to explain the general process in which those theories translate to the behavior of individuals. Moreover, Akers has argued social learning concepts are compatible with, and even part of, rational choice models and deterrence (1990). His integrative approach is one of "conceptual absorption," which he defines as "subsuming concepts from one theory as special cases of the phenomena defined by the concepts of another" (Akers, 1997, p. 209). In other words, integration can be accomplished by joining theories together or by incorporating concepts from other theories into an existing theory. Akers has clearly identified concepts of social control theory as adaptable to integration, and the structural components of anomie and subculture theories can be used to demonstrate how groups produce differential learning experiences (see Akers & Sellers, 2008, for more on the general nature of social learning).

Akers more recently has called for more sophisticated modeling and testing of the relationship between social learning and social structure, a concept originating in Sutherland's differential social organization, and adopted in social learning's earliest assumptions. A number of theorists have responded, including some who have examined the ways that social learning might mediate the effects of social structure, including social disorganization, on crime and delinquency but so far the results have been mixed (see for example Chan, Heide, & Beauregard, 2011; Higgins, Mahoney,

& Ricketts, 2009; Holt, Burruss, & Bossier, 2010; Meneses & Akers, 2011; Morris & Blackburn, 2009; Orcutt & Schwabe, 2012; Verrill, 2008).

POLICY IMPLICATIONS

While crime policies have not been directly proposed from social learning theories, there are several examples of behavior modification projects involving inmates and delinquents. In most of these instances, the program has been set up to reward inmates or delinquents for correct behavior and to punish incorrect behavior. Often referred to as an "M&M" economy, after the popular candy, the treatment scheme is designed to move the individual through successive stages of behavior. Beginning with a simple behavioral change (e.g., doing nothing wrong for 10 minutes), the individual progresses through longer and more complex steps. At each stage, the individual is rewarded for doing something correctly and thereby "learns" the new behavior. The results of such programs, whether carried out in prison or some other controlled environment, have been uniformly positive. People can indeed learn to behave in more "correct" ways and to keep those behaviors in place. After they leave the controlled environment, the learned behaviors tend to disappear, however. In other words, they learn or relearn behaviors appropriate for the regular social environment. The problem for these treatment programs is to find ways of making the learned behaviors carry over to the outside environment.

Another policy implication of social learning theories involves environmental design. As Jeffery would have put it, the more difficult it is to commit a behavior, the less likely an individual will be to do that act. From the perspective of learning theory then, the behavior has little probability of being rewarded and thus will be extinguished. With this in mind, Jeffery helped to design neighborhood convenience stores so that committing a crime is more difficult, the rewards from crime are diminished, and the probability of being caught is greater. For instance, raising the clerk's counter and positioning it where it can be seen from outside the store (surveillance) and placing all large bills in a locked floor safe are part of the design. The federal government and many business corporations have embraced environmental design ideas.

Other potential policy ideas include teaching prosocial definitions in schools, encouraging religious training (morality), and emphasizing the important values present in law. Another central idea is providing school-based instruction that emphasizes the importance of current behavior for future life opportunities. Learning theories tell us behavior will be based on immediate rewards and punishment unless discriminative stimuli are developed to reinforce the presence of future rewards. In short, without a learning process (socialization, perhaps), teenage behavior will tend to be hedonistic and based on short-term rewards. The problems are how to teach juveniles the implications of those behaviors for long-term rewards and how to assess the long-term effects of their behavior. Clearly, such goals are difficult to achieve, yet the work of behavior modification specialists in such areas as mental illness has demonstrated a high degree of effectiveness. Social learning theories are quite useful at the policy level; we simply need to develop ideas for their use.

Questions and Weblinks

Critical Thinking Questions

1. What do you think criminology can draw from the field of psychology in trying to explain crime and deviance?
2. Consider the reasoning of a career criminal, a delinquent, and an average citizen. What would be the reinforcements, the rewards, and punishments that they consider in their activities each day?
3. How do you think material reinforcements compare to social rewards, for others as well as for you?

Practice Essay Questions

1. According to social learning theory, why do people commit crime?
2. Discuss Glaser's theory of differential anticipation and what it contributes to our knowledge of social learning.
3. Explain the similarities and differences between Akers' and Jeffery' views of social learning.

Related Websites

https://www.ncjrs.gov/pdffiles1/ojjdp/232790.pdf
http://psychology.about.com/od/behavioralpsychology/a/schedules.htm

Bibliography

Akers, R. L. (1985). *Deviant behavior: A social learning approach* (3rd ed.). Belmont, CA: Wadsworth.

Akers, R. L. (1989). A social behaviorist's perspective on integration of theories of crime and deviance. In S. F. Messner, M. D. Krohn, and A. E. Liska (Eds.), *Theoretical integration in the study of deviance and crime: Problems and prospects* (pp. 23–36), Albany: State University of New York Press.

Akers, R. L. (1990). Rational choice, deterrence, and social learning theory in criminology: The path not taken. *Journal of Criminal Law and Criminology, 81,* 653–676.

Akers, R. L. (1997). *Criminological theories: Introduction and evaluation* (2nd ed.). Los Angeles: Roxbury.

Akers, R. L. (1998). *Social learning and social structure: A general theory of crime and deviance.* Boston: Northeastern University Press.

Akers, R. L., & Jensen, G. F. (2006). The empirical status of social learning theory: Past, present, and future. *Advances in Criminological Theory, 15,* 37–76.

Akers, R. L., & Sellers, C. (2008). *Criminological theories: Introduction and evaluation* (5th ed.). New York: Oxford University Press.

Bandura, A. (1969). *Principles of behavior modification.* New York: Holt, Rinehart and Winston.

Bandura, A. (1977). *Social learning theory.* Englewood Cliffs, NJ: Prentice Hall.

Burgess, R. L., & Akers, R. L. (1966). A differential association-reinforcement theory of criminal behavior. *Social Problems, 14,* 128–147.

Chan, H. C., Heide, K. M., & Beauregard, E. (2011). What propels sexual murderers: A proposed integrated theory of social learning and routine activities theories. *International Journal of Offender Therapy & Comparative Criminology, 55,* 228–250.

DeFleur, M. L., & Quinney, R. (1966). A reformulation of Sutherland's differential association theory and a strategy for empirical verification. *Journal of Research in Crime and Delinquency, 3,* 1–22.

Glaser, D. (1978). *Crime in our changing society.* New York: Holt, Rinehart and Winston.

Higgins, G. E., Mahoney, M., & Ricketts, M. L. (2009). Nonsocial reinforcement of the nonmedical use of prescription drugs: A partial test of social learning and self-control theories. *Journal of Drug Issues, 39,* 949–963.

Hinduja, S. (2006). *Music piracy and crime theory.* New York: LFB Scholarly Publishing.

Holt, T. J., Burruss, G. W., & Bossier, A. M. (2010). Social learning and cyber-deviance: Examining the importance of a full social learning model in the virtual world. *Journal of Crime & Justice, 33,* 31–61.

Jeffery, C. R. (1965). Criminal behavior and learning theory. *Journal of Criminal Law, Criminology and Police Science, 56,* 294–300.

Jeffery, C. R. (1977). *Crime prevention through environmental design* (2nd ed.). Beverly Hills, CA: Sage.

Jeffery, C. R. (1989a). *Criminology: An interdisciplinary approach.* Englewood Cliffs, NJ: Prentice Hall.

Jeffery, C. R. (1989b). An interdisciplinary theory of criminal behavior. *Advances in Criminological Theory, 1,* 69–87.

Jeffery, C. R. (1998). Prevention of juvenile violence: A critical review of current scientific strategies. *Journal of Offender Rehabilitation, 28,* 1–28.

Meneses, R., & Akers, R. L. (2011). A comparison of four general theories of crime and deviance: Marijuana use among American and Bolivian university students. *International Criminal Justice Review, 21,* 333–352.

Morris, R. G., & Blackburn, A. G. (2009). Cracking the code: An empirical exploration of social learning theory and computer crime. *Journal of Crime & Justice, 32,* 1–34.

Orcutt, J. D., & Schwabe, A. M. (2012). Gender, race/ethnicity, and deviant drinking: A longitudinal application of social structure and social learning theory. *Sociological Spectrum, 32,* 20–36.

Pratt, T. C., Cullen, F. T., Sellers, C. S., Thomas Winfree, L. L., Madensen, T. D., Daigle, L. E., & Gau, J. M. (2010). The empirical status of social learning theory: A meta-analysis. *Justice Quarterly, 27,* 765–802.

Skinner, B. F. (1971). *Beyond freedom and dignity.* New York: Knopf.

Verrill, S. (2008). *Social structure-social learning and delinquency: Mediation or moderation?* NY: LFB Scholarly Publishing.

Research Bibliography (from 2000)

Akins, S., Smith, C. L., & Mosher, C. (2010). Pathways to adult alcohol abuse across racial/ethnic groups: An application of general strain and social learning theories. *Journal of Drug Issues, 40,* 321–351.

Alarid, L. F., Burton, V. S., Jr., & Cullen, F. T. (2000). Gender and crime among felony offenders: Assessing the generality of social control and differential association theories. *Journal of Research in Crime and Delinquency, 37,* 171–199.

Bao, W-N., Haas, A., Chen, X., & Pi, Y. (2012). Repeated strains, social control, social learning, and delinquency: Testing an integrated model of general strain theory in China. *Youth & Society, xx*(x), 1–23.

Beaver, K., Wright, J. P., & DeLisi, M. (2008). Delinquent peer group formation: Evidence of a gene X environment correlation. *Journal of Genetic Psychology, 169,* 227–244.

Bellair, P. E., Roscigno, V. J., & Velez, M. B. (2003). Occupational structure, social learning, and adolescent violence. *Advances in Criminological Theory, 11,* 197–226.

Benda, B. B., & Corwyn, R. F. (2002). The effect of abuse in childhood and in adolescence on violence among adolescents. *Youth and Society, 33,* 339–365.

Boman, J. H., & Gibson, C. L. (2011). Does the measurement of peer deviance change the relationship between self-control and deviant behavior? An analysis of friendship pairs. *Journal of Criminal Justice, 39*, 521–530.

Bottcher, J. (2001). Social practices of gender: How gender relates to delinquency in the everyday lives of high-risk youths. *Criminology, 39*, 893–932.

Brezina, T., & Piquero, A. R. (2003). Exploring the relationship between social and non-social reinforcement in the context of social learning theory. *Advances in Criminological Theory, 11*, 265–288.

Brownfield, D., & Thompson, K. (2002). Distinguishing the effects of peer delinquency and gang membership on self-reported delinquency. *Journal of Gang Research, 9*, 1–10.

Burruss, G. W, Bossler, A., & Holt, T. J. (2012). Assessing the mediation of a fuller social learning model on low self-control's influence on software piracy. Crime & Delinquency, *xx*(x), 1–28.

Chan, H. C., Heide, K. M., & Beauregard, E. (2011). What propels sexual murderers: A proposed integrated theory of social learning and routine activities theories. *International Journal of Offender Therapy & Comparative Criminology, 55*, 228–250.

Chappell, A. T., & Piquero, A. R. (2004). Applying social learning theory to police misconduct. *Deviant Behavior, 25*(2), 89–108.

Childs, K. K., Sullivan, C. J., & Gulledge, L. M. (2011). Delinquent behavior across adolescence: Investigating the shifting salience of key criminological predictors. *Deviant Behavior, 32*, 64–100.

Doherty, E., Green, K. M., & Ensminger, M. E. (2012). The impact of adolescent deviance on marital trajectories. *Deviant Behavior, 33*, 185–206.

Forrest, W., & Hay, C. (2011). Life-course transitions, self-control and desistance from crime. *Criminology & Criminal Justice: An International Journal, 11*, 487–513.

Haynie, D. L. (2002). Friendship networks and delinquency: The relative nature of peer delinquency. *Journal of Quantitative Criminology, 18*, 99–134.

Haynie, D. L., & Osgood, D. W. (2005). Reconsidering peers and delinquency: How do peers matter? *Social Forces, 84*, 1109–1130.

Higgins, G. E., Fell, B. D., & Wilson, A. L. (2007). Low self-control and social learning in understanding students' intentions to pirate movies in the United States. *Social Science Computer Review, 25*, 339–357.

Higgins, G. E., Mahoney, M., & Ricketts, M. L. (2009). Nonsocial reinforcement of the nonmedical use of prescription drugs: A partial test of social learning and self-control theories. *Journal of Drug Issues, 39*, 949–963.

Hoffman, J. P. (2002). A contextual analysis of differential association, social control, and strain theories of delinquency. *Social Forces, 81*, 753–785.

Holt, T. J., Burruss, G. W., & Bossier, A. M. (2010). Social learning and cyber-deviance: Examining the importance of a full social learning model in the virtual world. *Journal of Crime & Justice, 33*, 31–61.

Hwang, S., & Akers, R. L. (2003). Substance use by Korean adolescents: A Cross-Cultural test of social learning, social bonding, and self-control theories. *Advances in Criminological Theory, 11*, 39–64.

Kim, T. E., & Goto, S. G. (2000). Peer delinquency and parental social support as predictors of Asian American adolescent delinquency. *Deviant Behavior, 21*, 331–348.

Lance, L. M., & Ross, C. E. (2000). Views of violence in American sports: A study of college students. *College Student Journal, 34*, 191–200.

Lanza-Kaduce, L., & Capece, M. (2003). Social structure-social learning (SSSL) and binge drinking: A specific test of an integrated general theory. *Advances in Criminological Theory, 11*, 179–196.

Lanza-Kaduce, L., Capece, M., & Alden, H. (2006). Liquor is quicker: Gender and social learning among college students. *Criminal Justice Policy Review, 17*, 127–143.

Lee, G., Akers, R. L., & Borg, M. (2004). Social learning and structural factors in adolescent substance use. *Western Criminology Review, 5*(1), 17–34.

Liu, R. X. (2003). The moderating effects of internal and perceived external sanction threats on the relationship between deviant peer associations and criminal offending. *Western Criminology Review, 4*, 191–202.

Lo, C. C. (2000). The impact of first drinking and differential association on collegiate drinking. *Sociological Focus, 33*, 265–280.

Lonardo, R., Giordano, P., Longmore, M., & Manning, W. (2009). Parents, friends, and romantic partners: Enmeshment in deviant networks and adolescent delinquency involvement. *Journal of Youth & Adolescence, 38*, 367–383.

McGloin, J. (2009). Delinquency balance: Revisiting peer influence. *Criminology, 47*, 439–477.

Meneses, R., & Akers, R. L. (2011). A comparison of four general theories of crime and deviance: Marijuana use among American and Bolivian university students. *International Criminal Justice Review, 21*, 333–352.

Miller, H. V., Jennings, W. G., Alvarez-Rivera, L. L., & Miller, J. M. (2008). Explaining substance use among Puerto Rican adolescents: A partial test of social learning theory. *Journal of Drug Issues, 38*, 261–283.

Morris, R. G., & Blackburn, A. G. (2009). Cracking the code: An empirical exploration of social learning theory and computer crime. *Journal of Crime & Justice, 32,* 1–34.

Neff, J., & Waite, D. (2007). Male versus female substance abuse patterns among incarcerated juvenile offenders: Comparing strain and social learning variables. *Justice Quarterly, 24,* 106–132.

O'Donnell, P., Richards, M., Pearce, S., & Romero, E. (2012). Gender differences in monitoring and deviant peers as predictors of delinquent behavior among low-income urban African American youth. *Journal of Early Adolescence, 32,* 431–459.

Orcutt, J. D., & Schwabe, A. M. (2012). Gender, race/ethnicity, and deviant drinking: A longitudinal application of social structure and social learning theory. *Sociological Spectrum, 32,* 20–36.

Osgood, W. D., & Anderson, A. L. (2004). Unstructured socializing and rates of delinquency. *Criminology, 42,* 519–549.

Payne, A., & Salotti, S. (2007). A comparative analysis of social learning and social control theories in the prediction of college crime. *Deviant Behavior, 28,* 553–573.

Rader, N. E. & Haynes, S. H. (2011). Gendered fear of crime socialization: An extension of Aker's social learning theory. *Feminist Criminology, 6,* 291–307.

Rebellon, C. J. (2006). Do adolescents engage in delinquency to attract the social attention of peers? *Journal of Research in Crime & Delinquency, 43,* 387–411.

Singer, S. D., & Hensley, C. (2004). Applying social learning theory to childhood and adolescent firesetting: Can it lead to serial murder? *International Journal of Offender Therapy & Comparative Criminology, 48,* 461–476.

Sung Joon, J. (2002). Race, ethnicity, and deviance: A study of Asian and non-Asian adolescents in America. *Sociological Forum, 17,* 647–680.

Verrill, S. (2008). *Social structure-social learning and delinquency: Mediation or moderation?* NY: LFB Scholarly Publishing.

Walters, G. D. (2000). Outcome expectancies for crime: Their relationship to fear and the negative consequences of criminal involvement. *Legal & Criminological Psychology, 5,* 261–272.

Wang, S., & Jensen, G. F. (2003). Explaining delinquency in Taiwan: A test of social learning theory. *Advances in Criminological Theory, 11,* 65–84.

Wiesner, M., Capaldi, D. M., & Patterson, G. (2003). Development of antisocial behavior and crime across the life-span from a social interaction perspective: The coercion model. *Advances in Criminological Theory, 11,* 317–338.

Wilson, C., Parry, L., Nettelbeck, T., & Bell, J. (2003). Conflict resolution tactics and bullying: The influence of social learning. *Youth Violence and Juvenile Justice, 1,* 64–78.

Yarbrough, A., Jones, S., Sullivan, C., Sellers, C., & Cochran, J. (2012). Social learning and self-control: Assessing the moderating potential of criminal propensity. *International Journal of Offender Therapy & Comparative Criminology, 56,* 191–202.

13

Rational Theories

LEARNING OBJECTIVES

Objective 13.1: Discuss all of the different elements involved in crime according to lifestyle theory.

Objective 13.2: Explain the various factors that interact in order for crime to occur according to routine activities theory.

Objective 13.3: Describe what is meant by routine activities and how these have changed over time in our society.

Objective 13.4: Outline the process of decision making that takes place relative to committing a crime according to the rational choice perspective.

Objective 13.5: Describe the types of policies and programs that are suggested by theories based on a rational approach to crime.

INTRODUCTION

An entire group of contemporary theories is referred to as rational theories. Rational theories cover a range of psychological and sociological versions. The versions we cover in this chapter are sociological in orientation and are alternatively known as "lifestyle" or "routine activities" theories. One psychological variant, cognitive theory (Walters & White, 1989), was briefly examined in Chapter 3 on the Positive School. Another older perspective, deterrence, which is also directly associated with rationality and which has experienced a revival from the 1970s to the present, has already been discussed in Chapter 2 on the Classical School.

THE HERITAGE OF THE THEORY

The Social Heritage

The late 1970s and 1980s were a period of conservative thought, politics, and economic policies. Beginning with the oil crisis and Iranian hostage incident, Americans seemed to feel threatened, and they retreated to traditional values. Liberal policies were supplanted, and the term "liberal" even became an epithet to be used for political gain by conservatives. Reflecting the mood of the citizenry, politicians reinstated conservative governmental policies, increased defense budgets, removed restrictions on businesses, and attempted to trim welfare programs.

For criminal justice and crime, this was a time of crime control and punitive policies. Criminals were seen as people who were bad (Wilson, 1975) and who purposefully decided to commit criminal acts. They were to be punished because they "deserved it." Victims' rights were introduced into the criminal justice system, and victims were asked for their opinion about sentences. The country decided, as a whole, that more severe punishment would help to solve the crime problem. As a result, more prisons were built over a short period of time than ever before. The United States declared war on crime and shortly thereafter discovered the drug problem. The country then declared war on drugs and made drugs a problem to be handled by the criminal justice system. Drug users and sellers were targeted in a massive law enforcement effort, and the new prisons were soon filled to capacity.

All in all, the 1980s represented a time when U.S. society was punitively oriented and relatively intolerant. Several political and power groups emerged, each advocating their own position with little concern for others. Each group explained why others were not to be trusted, were doing bad things to the country, or had incorrect values. Indeed, all these things seemed to come together during the Republican Convention in 1992 and probably served as a major reason George Bush was not reelected. Against this backdrop, scholars were gaining ideas and reacting to popular positions.

The Intellectual Heritage

Throughout the 1980s, some criminologists observed that the field was growing theoretically stagnant (Braithwaite, 1989; Meier, 1985; Whitehead, 1986; Williams, 1984). The 1970s were criticized as unimaginative and lacking creativity for criminological theory. The lone exception seemed to be the progressive theorizing present in radical and critical theory (Chambliss, 1975; Gordon, 1973; Quinney, 1977; Spitzer, 1975; Tifft, 1979). As the 1980s progressed, however, a concern with theoretical criminology seemed to grow. That effort seemed to be balanced with popular, antitheoretical positions taken by some writers on crime (Wilson, 1975) and administrators in government criminal justice circles. Just as rehabilitation was pronounced dead in the 1970s, so was criminological theorizing pronounced a waste of money and effort in the 1980s. It would suffice, we were told, that evil people would be held responsible for their actions and punished. Our needs were simple: more efficient criminal justice systems, more prisons, and more police officers on the street.

If people are indeed evil or self-centered, the problem was not how to explain the background factors of criminality, but instead to explain how criminals think differently. The criminal personality theory of Samuel Yochelson and Stanton Samenow (1976) began the period, but criminologists were still sociologically oriented enough to want a more social perspective. Thus, scholars returned to some of the central ideas of the old Classical School: rational humans, deterrence, and punishment. In fact, much of the new criminology has been called "neoclassical theory" by some criminologists (Brown, Esbensen, & Geis, 2010).

Finally, just as self-report studies had created a new form of evidence for crime theories, the emergence of national victimization studies in 1972 provided yet another set of facts to be explained. By 1980, victimization statistics had become a mainstay of criminological evidence about crime and a variety of national victim data sets were now available for the more sophisticated computer analyses that researchers were developing. The *Uniform Crime Reports: Supplementary Homicide Reports* was one of these, and it provided insight into the complexity of victim–offender relationships. The field of victimology was growing with courses in most criminal justice programs and journals like *Victimology, Homicide Studies*, the *Journal of Interpersonal Violence,* and *Violence Against Women*. And, as was probably inevitable, these statistics and research provided the fuel for the new rationalist theories and a new paradigm for criminology.

THE THEORETICAL PERSPECTIVE

With the late 1970s emphasis on individual responsibility, criminologists realized no versions of theory contained an assumption of a rational, thinking individual. The closest theory to include such a criterion was David Matza's (1964) drift theory, which introduced the "will" as a predisposing factor in the decision to commit deviance. Matza did not mean to convey, however, that the individual had free will and made a calculated, rational decision to commit a delinquent act. Indeed, it is significant that Matza referred to the theory as "soft determinism" rather than as "soft free will." While sociologists were pondering how to introduce rationality, economists began discussing crime and, with their usual approach to behavior, assumed criminals make a rational decision to commit crime (Becker, 1974, 1976; Ehrlich, 1973). Borrowing from the economic approach, today's rational choice theorists talk in terms of opportunities, costs, and benefits when discussing offenders' decisions to commit crimes. In a sense, the economic approach brought us full circle to the 200-year-old classical position that individual behavior is a calculation of gain and pain. Indeed, rationalist theories seem to share a common belief that criminal rationality is hedonistic and certain background factors lead to such a result.

The beginnings of rational theory were sociological in orientation and relied on the new victimization statistics. Variously called lifestyle theory (Hindelang, Gottfredson, & Garofalo, 1978), routine activities theory (Cohen & Felson, 1979), opportunity perspective (Mayhew, Clarke, Sturman, & Hough, 1976), or the rational choice model (Cornish & Clarke, 1986), the idea was to describe the factors one would expect to find in aggregate decisions to commit crime. Those decisions were expected to reflect ease of committing crime, the availability of worthwhile targets, and the anticipated presence of witnesses.

Routine Activities Theory

The routine activities perspective advanced by Larry Cohen and Marcus Felson (1979), initially viewed as a very practical look at crime, gained popularity, and became a staple of the 1980s. One reason for its popularity was the easy connection with the burgeoning interest in victimology and a new ecological crime prevention approach. The major reason, however, was the resurgence of assumptions about the nature of humans as rational beings. Either way, routine activity theory clearly has been an important contribution to criminology.

Routine activity theory basically states that the volume of criminal offenses is related to the nature of everyday patterns of social interaction. As the pattern of social interaction changes, so does the number of crimes. Cohen and Felson drew heavily from the work of Amos Hawley (1950), who had sketched out a popular theory of human ecology. Hawley emphasized the nature of routine activities as an essential part of everyday life. Routine activity means any commonly occurring social activity providing for basic needs. Examples include formal work, leisure pursuits, obtaining shelter, child rearing, grocery shopping, and sleeping. As social change disrupts or changes routine activities, social disorganization can occur. In emphasizing both social disorganization and ecology, routine activities theory can be considered a continuation of the work of the Chicago School.

Cohen and Felson's theory has three major areas of focus for a predatory criminal event or, perhaps more appropriately, a victimization event. First, they said there must be a motivated offender. They were not particularly concerned with this factor, however. Existing criminological theories uniformly focus on the offender and the influences motivating him or her to an offense; Cohen and Felson wanted to examine the other pieces of the puzzle. Second, they speculated there must be a suitable target: that is, something worth stealing or taking, or that has the appearance of worth. Third, they said there must be an absence of a capable guardian: no one present who could prevent the occurrence of the crime.

In addition to these three elements, Cohen and Felson were concerned with changes in society, particularly those leading to social disorganization. As routine activities change, so does crime opportunity. In fact, they suggested that social changes since World War II led to routine activities taking place farther from the home, thus creating greater opportunities for crime. Indeed, under this reasoning, ecological and environmental factors suggest certain areas will be more prone to crime than others.

These ingredients come together as follows. Routine activities serve to bring offenders and victims into contact and create a convergence in time and space of motivated offenders, suitable targets, and absence of guardians. If one of these components is missing, crime is not likely to happen. However, if all components are present (and one element is even strengthened), the probability of crime increases. Because of routine activities, suitable victims (or targets) are found more frequently in some settings than in others. For example, work schedules present opportunities for burglary by presenting a suitable target (a house) with few guardians (people at home). Social changes such as an increased number of women in the work force have resulted in fewer people at home during work hours, thereby increasing the probability of a successful burglary. Moreover, Cohen and Felson argue that the changes that have taken place in American society have resulted in greater interaction with motivated offenders, more suitable targets, and a greater absence of guardians. Even if the number of motivated offenders does not increase, crime will be greater because of the increase in the latter two elements.

The theory can be used to explain rates of victimization for specific crimes. Based on differences in their routine activities, certain individuals will be more susceptible than others to robbery, burglary, rape, and homicide. Similarly, certain locations are more susceptible to crime because of the type of activities and the amount of social activity present. As areas gain a reputation for being crime "hot spots" (the most crime-ridden places in the city), feedback occurs, and fewer people go there at certain times. As a result, the absence of guardians is even greater, and offenders define more individuals in the area as suitable victims. Hot spots themselves can be determined empirically by finding their geographical centers and then mapping their boundaries.

Routine activity theory has also been extended to offenders in an attempt to explain what may facilitate crime. Marcus Felson has explored the implications of routine activities for offenders (1986, 1994, 2002, and with Boba, 2010), as have others. One of his additions involves the concept of "handlers," which he implies is a combination of an offender having social bonds (handles) and the availability of prosocial adult who can use those handles to restrain offending (Felson, 1986). This concept has since been elaborated by John Eck (2001, 2003; Tillyer & Eck, 2011). A number of recent studies have continued to work on the idea that unstructured and unsupervised socializing among young adults (a routine activity) can increase deviance. This happens because of an absence of authority figures, a reduction in social control responses, available unsupervised time, and an increase in the probability of reward for deviant behavior. The roles of alcohol, a sports environment, and fraternities on college campuses have also been examined (Gilbertson, 2006; Jackson, Gilliland, & Veneziano, 2006). Thus, the routine activities approach, which originally encompassed only victimization, is now a theory of offending as well and such concepts as target attractiveness, degree of exposure to deviant lifestyles and level of exposure to other offenders (Spano & Freilich, 2009).

Lifestyle Theory

The question of risk is central to the theoretical perspective developed by Michael Hindelang et al. (1978). In short, they wanted to know why certain groups of people are at greater risk of being victims of crime than others. Their answer is that patterned activities, or lifestyles, of individuals lead to differential victimization rates. These lifestyles are characterized by daily functions involving both work and leisure activities.

Lifestyles are influenced by three basic elements. First, the social roles played by people in society. Based on the expectations of others, people conduct themselves in certain ways and construct lifestyles more or less conducive to victimization. For this reason, young persons are more frequently victimized because they have social roles that require frequent social activities outside the home, particularly at night. The second element is position in the social structure. Generally, the higher one's position, the lower the risk of victimization—largely because of the kind of activities in which one engages and the places one frequents. The third element is a "rational component," in which decisions are made about which behaviors are desirable. Based on one's social role and structural position, decisions can be made to restrict routine behaviors to relatively safe ones or to accept risk. Young people tend to enhance their victimization probabilities by choosing to engage in activities in time and space with greater risk levels, such as going to nightclubs or attending sporting events.

When lifestyle variations are taken into account, victimization experiences and potential victimizations are relatively predictable. For those whose social and structural background creates greater interaction with offenders and places conducive to crime, there is indeed a greater risk of victimization. Similarly, individuals of higher social class engage in fewer routine activities (i.e., have a lifestyle) that involve crossing paths with fewer criminals (at least of the street-criminal variety). Such risks can be decreased, or increased, beyond the levels normally expected for one's group by the conscious decisions individuals make to engage in certain lifestyles.

The Rational Choice Perspective

A final approach to rational theory is a more generic one: rational choice theory. Identified most strongly with Derek Cornish and Ronald Clarke (1986, 1987), there are many criminologists who have embraced at least some part of the perspective, including Travis Hirschi (1986). Rational choice theory explains offender motivation to crime as an attempt to meet commonplace needs. Rationality is the decision-making process of determining the opportunities for meeting those needs, the potential costs of action, and the anticipated benefits. Full rationality is not required by the perspective, nor is the offender assumed to be sophisticated in his or her decision making. Adequate or accurate information is not even necessary. Thus, it is more precise to say the offender demonstrates limited rationality.

Rational choice theorists separate decision making into two different areas: involvement decisions and event decisions. *Involvement decisions* are those in which the choice is made to become involved in an offense, continue with an offense, or withdraw from an offense. These types of decisions are instrumental in the weighing of costs and benefits. Ken Tunnell (1992), for instance, found in his interviews with repetitive property offenders that money was the primary motivation for decisions to engage in crime. Indeed, other motivations were rare, leaving a quick and easy way to gain resources as the dominant force in the offenders' thinking. The other form of decision making, *event decisions*, is that in which the tactics of carrying out an offense (the demands placed on the offender) are determined. If the tactics are easy, the involvement decision gains potential benefits. If the tactics are difficult, the involvement decision loses potential benefits.

The tactics issue also suggests that there are crime-specific decisions to be made. Because the demands of committing an offense vary by the offense itself, one can assume rational choices are themselves crime specific. In addition, the needs of offenders vary—as do the needs offenses will meet. Therefore, rational choice theorists view the needs/demands choices as crime specific and focus on the prevention of individual crime types, rather than on a general approach to preventing crime (such as deterrence). Each form of crime offers different "choice-structuring properties" where a combination of availability and attractiveness can appeal to certain individuals at certain times.

Crime prevention under this model, then, is based on decreasing opportunity and attractiveness of specific crimes. Cornish and Clarke recommend drawing up lists of choice-structuring properties for various types of crime. Each list would be used to design greater cost into the offense and reduce its attractiveness. To build such lists, more information is needed about the ecological distribution of crimes and offenders' perceptions of opportunities, costs, and benefits. Because the theoretical perspective has obvious direct policy implications, rational choice theory has been popular within governmental circles, and particularly so within the criminological research centers of Great Britain.

CLASSIFICATION OF THE THEORY

As a whole, rational theories represent a return to some of the concerns of the old Classical School. They assume people have the capacity to make their own decisions, yet most of the theories also restrict those decisions by including the effects of the environment or social structure. Therefore, rational theories are primarily characterized by "soft free will" and are *classical*. They are also *consensus oriented* because they assume an individual who decides to commit a crime chooses to behave in opposition to the established order of society. In addition, the approach tends to be more *process oriented* and *microtheoretical*, with an emphasis on the individual making the decision. This is not always the case, however. Some versions are more concerned with the structural and environmental considerations that influence choices; thus, these are more macrotheoretical in character. In short, there are a number of variations within the general perspective of rational theory. As opposed to most earlier theories, however, the most distinctive feature of rational theory is the free-will, individualistic assumption.

MAJOR POINTS OF THE RATIONAL THEORY MODEL

1. Humans live in a world in which behavior is partially determined and partially free will.
2. Social structures and institutions create the conditions of life for individuals in society.
3. Conditions of life are the chief determinants of social interactions between people in society and the social activities in which those people engage.
4. Social interactions and activities create generalized lifestyles, or routine activities, for groups in society. Those lifestyles are more conducive to some pursuits, and less so to others.
5. To the extent crime occurs in society, lifestyles are a critical element in placing people at risk of victimization and in generating needs that offenders wish to satisfy.
6. As changes in society produce changes in lifestyles, the general risk of victimization and probability of offending changes accordingly.
7. Individuals may introduce variation into their general victimization risk through conscious decisions to follow or avoid certain activities and areas. Similarly, offenders may increase or decrease their opportunities and costs.
8. Those individuals who make lifestyle choices with increased exposure are increasing their risk of victimization by enhancing the cost-benefit gains of potential offenders.

Epilogue: Current Directions and Policy Implications

CURRENT DIRECTIONS

Rational theories are popular today, although in various versions, some of which have other theoretical elements. They combine elements from the old Chicago School, newer ways of looking at communities, concepts from environmental design, and even social learning and control theories. In one sense, they offer a promising approach to integrating knowledge and research findings on ecological areas with popular opinion stressing individual moral responsibility for one's actions. While we have introduced three different types of rational theories, the fact is most researchers and theorists have tended to combine both routine activities and lifestyle approaches into a generic rational choice model (see Ken Tunnell's *Choosing Crime* [1992] for one attempt to explain property crime). One of the results of this is to generate a victim/offender model that can be called a "criminal event." The advantage of this is to remind us that offender and victims should be explained separately.

Because much of the rational choice perspective is derived from an economic model assuming rationality of people, a recent rejection of this model by a substantial number of economists gives pause to a full acceptance of the criminological versions. Indeed, a Nobel Prize was awarded to an economist for demonstrating in part that people make somewhat irrational decisions under various circumstances. Some criminologists also have begun to question the validity of the perspective (see Moran, 1996; Mustaine & Tewksbury, 1998). While research on routine activity, in particular, has been popular, only one meta-analysis of the research has been done. In summarizing their analytical findings, Spano and Freilich (2009, p. 311) found the research results mixed and support was likely to be "more concentrated in samples of college students, adolescent or college age samples."

POLICY IMPLICATIONS

One of the major advantages to rational theories is they are practical and relevant to policy. First, they give permission for punishment of offenders, because offenders are responsible for their actions and make purposeful decisions to commit crime. This, then, is a politically popular approach to crime causation. Criminals can be punished because they deserve it and they should have known better. Second, rational theories emphasize victims. Victim assistance programs help prepare victims for the criminal justice process, introduce victim testimony to ensure just deserts for offenders, and increase the chances of conviction. They also place some responsibility on potential victims to recognize risk and take preventive measures to avoid being a target. This includes staying away from high-risk places, people, and activities, such as bars in "bad" neighborhoods or automated teller machines at night. Third, the concepts of capable guardians and suitable targets yield a number of environmental design options. Potential areas of change include increasing surveillance in neighborhoods (neighborhood watch programs, Guardian Angels, volunteer civilian patrols), target hardening with deadbolt locks and burglar bars, and placing more lights in poorly lit areas. Paul Brantingham and Patricia Brantingham (1981, 1991, 1993) and others have additionally espoused the connections between rational theories and crime opportunities related to place and developed a geospatial, environmental criminology to examine those connections. The findings and methodologies related to this criminology are adding to our knowledge of how both offenders and victims interact in their routine activities. From this, we can begin to design areas to reduce crime.

Questions and Weblinks

Critical Thinking Questions

1. According to theories discussed in this section, what can people do to prevent being victimized? Do we seem to blame victims who do not seem to do enough to avoid exposure to crime?
2. Certain people and places appear to be more likely to experience crime according to rational theories, can you think of some examples of this?

3. After reading the theories in this chapter, does it appear that offenders use rationality, particularly a cost-benefit type of analysis before they commit crimes? What examples in the news support or conflict with this idea?

Practice Essay Questions

1. Explain how crime theorists would describe a high-risk lifestyle.
2. What is meant by "soft" free will and how is this related to crime?

3. Describe the types of data that would be collected by routine activities theorists.
4. Discuss the three elements of an offense according to Cohen & Felson.

Related Weblinks

Hot Spots
https://www.ncjrs.gov/pdffiles1/ojjdp/231575.pdf

National Crime Prevention Council
http://www.ncpc.org/

Neighborhood Watch Program
http://www.usaonwatch.org/

Office of Community Oriented Policing Services
http://www.cops.usdoj.gov

Bibliography

Becker, G. S. (1974). Crime and punishment: An economic approach. In G. Becker & W. Landes (Eds.), *Essays in the economics of crime and punishment* (pp. 1–54). New York: Columbia University Press.

Becker, G. S. (1976). *The economic approach to human behavior.* Chicago: University of Chicago Press.

Braithwaite, J. (1989). The state of criminology: Theoretical decay or renaissance. *Australian and New Zealand Journal of Criminology, 22,* 129–135.

Brantingham, P. J., & Brantingham, P. L. (1981). *Environmental criminology.* Beverly Hills, CA: Sage.

Brantingham, P. L., & Brantingham, P. J. (Eds.) (1991). *Environmental criminology.* Prospect Heights, IL: Waveland.

Brantingham, P. L., & Brantingham, P. J. (1993). Environment, routine, and situation: Toward a pattern theory of crime. *Advances in Criminological Theory, 5,* 259–294.

Brown, S. E., Esbensen, F., & Geis, G. (2010). *Criminology: Explaining crime and its context* (7th ed.). Cincinnati, OH: Anderson.

Chambliss, W. J. (1975). Toward a political economy of crime. *Theory and Society, 2,* 149–169.

Cohen, L. E., & Felson, M. (1979). Social change and crime rate trends: A routine activities approach. *American Sociological Review, 44,* 588–607.

Cornish, D. B., & Clarke, R. V. (Eds.). (1986). *The reasoning criminal: Rational choice perspectives on offending.* New York: Springer-Verlag.

Cornish, D. B., & Clarke, R. V. (1987). Understanding crime displacement: An application of rational choice theory. *Criminology, 25,* 933–947.

Eck, J. E. (2001). Policing and crime event concentration. In R. F. Meier, L. W. Kennedy, & V. Sacco (Eds.), *The process and structure of crime: Criminal events and crime analysis, Theoretical advances in criminology* (pp. 249–276). Monsey, NY: Criminal Justice Press.

Eck, J. E. (2003). Police problems: The complexity of problem theory, research and evaluation. In J. Knutsson (Ed.), *Problem-oriented policing: From innovation to mainstream* (pp. 79–113). Monsey, NY: Criminal Justice Press.

Ehrlich, I. (1973). Participation in illegitimate activities: A theoretical and empirical investigation. *Journal of Political Economy, 81,* 521–565.

Felson, M. (1986). Linking criminal choices, routine activities, informal control, and criminal outcomes. In D. Cornish & R. Clarke (Eds.), *The reasoning criminal: Rational choice perspectives on offending* (pp. 119–128). New York: Springer-Verlag.

Felson, M. (1994). *Crime and everyday life: Insights and implications for society.* Thousand Oaks, CA: Pine Forge Press.

Felson, M. (2002). *Crime and everyday life* (3rd ed.). Thousand Oaks, CA: Sage.

Felson, M., & Boba, R. L. (2010). *Crime and everyday life* (4th ed.). Thousand Oaks, CA: Sage.

Gilbertson, T. A. (2006). Alcohol-related incident guardianship and undergraduate college parties: Enhancing the social norms marketing approach. *Journal of Drug Education, 36*(1), 73–90.

Gordon, D. M. (1973). Capitalism, class and crime in America. *Crime and Delinquency, 19,* 163–186.

Hawley, A. (1950). *Human ecology: A theory of community structure.* New York: Ronald.

Hindelang, M. J., Gottfredson, M., & Garofalo, J. (1978). *Victims of personal crime: An empirical foundation for a theory of personal victimization.* Cambridge, MA: Ballinger.

Hirschi, T. (1986). On the compatibility of rational choice and social control theories of crime. In D. Cornish & R. Clarke (Eds.), *The reasoning criminal: Rational choice perspectives on offending* (pp. 105–118). New York: Springer-Verlag.

Jackson, A., Gilliland, K., & Veneziano, L. (2006). Routine activity theory and sexual deviance among male college students. *Journal of Family Violence, 21,* 449–460.

Matza, D. (1964). *Delinquency and drift.* New York: John Wiley.

Mayhew, P. M., Clarke, R. V., Sturman, A., & Hough, J. M. (1976). *Crime as opportunity* (Home Office Research Study No. 24). London: H. M. Stationary Office.

Meier, R. F., (Ed.). (1985). *Theoretical methods in criminology.* Beverly Hills, CA: Sage.

Moran, R. (1996). Bringing rational choice theory back to reality. *Journal of Criminal Law and Criminology, 86,* 1147–1160.

Mustaine, E. E., & Tewksbury, R. (1998). Predicting risk of larceny theft victimization: A routine activity analysis using refined lifestyle measures. *Criminology, 36,* 829–857.

Quinney, R. (1977). *Class, state, and crime.* New York: Longman.

Spano, R., & Freilich, J. D. (2009). An assessment of the empirical validity and conceptualization of individual level multivariate studies of lifestyle/routine activities theory published from 1995 to 2005. *Journal of Criminal Justice, 37,* 305–314.

Spitzer, S. (1975). Toward a Marxian theory of deviance. *Social Problems, 22,* 638–651.

Tifft, L. (1979). The coming redefinitions of crime: An anarchist perspective. *Social Problems, 26,* 392–402.

Tillyer, M., & Eck, J. E. (2011). Getting a handle on crime: A further extension of routine activities theory. *Security Journal, 24,* 179–193.

Tunnell, K. D. (1992). *Choosing crime: The criminal calculus of property offenders.* Chicago: Nelson Hall.

Walters, G. D., & White, T. W. (1989). The thinking criminal: A cognitive model of lifestyle criminality. *Criminal Justice Research Bulletin, 4,* 1–10.

Whitehead, J. T. (1986). The criminological imagination: Another view. *Criminal Justice Review, 10,* 22–26.

Williams, F. P., III. (1984). The demise of the criminological imagination: A critique of recent criminology. *Justice Quarterly, 1,* 91–104.

Wilson, J. Q. (1975). *Thinking about crime.* New York: Basic Books.

Yochelson, S., & Samenow, S. E. (1976). *The criminal personality: A profile for change* (Vol. I). New York: Jason Aronson.

Research Bibliography

Routine Activities & Lifestyle Theory (from 2000)

Andresen, M. A. (2006). A spatial analysis of crime in Vancouver, British Columbia: A synthesis of social disorganization and routine activity theory. *Canadian Geographer, 50*(4), 487–502.

Averdijk, M. (2011). Reciprocal effects of victimization and routine activities. *Journal of Quantitative Criminology, 27,* 125–149.

Bernberg, J. G., & Thorlindsson, T. (2001). Routine activities in social context: A closer look at the role of opportunity in deviant behavior. *Justice Quarterly, 18,* 543–567.

Bossler, A. M., & Holt, T. J. (2009). On-line activities, guardianship, and malware infection: An examination of routine activities theory. *International Journal of Cyber Criminology, 3,* 400–420.

Boudreaux, M. C., Lord, W. D., & Javis, J. P. (2001). Behavioral perspectives on child homicide: The role of access, vulnerability, and routine activities theory. *Trauma, Violence and Abuse, 2,* 56–79.

Brunet, J. R. (2002). Discouragement of crime through civil remedies: An application of a reformulated routine activities theory. *Western Criminology Review, 4*(1), 68–79.

Cass, A. I. (2007). Routine activities and sexual assault: An analysis of individual- and school-level factors. *Violence & Victims, 22,* 350–366.

Chan, H. C., Heide, K. M., & Beauregard, E. (2011). What propels sexual murderers: A proposed integrated theory of social learning and routine activities theories. *International Journal of Offender Therapy & Comparative Criminology, 55,* 228–250.

Donovan, G. H., & Prestemon, J. P. (2012). The effect of trees on crime in Portland, Oregon. *Environment & Behavior, 44,* 3–30.

Eck, J. E. (2001). Policing and crime event concentration. In R. F. Meier, L. W. Kennedy, & V. Sacco (Eds.), *The process and structure of crime: Criminal events and crime analysis, Theoretical advances in criminology* (pp. 249–276). Monsey, NY: Criminal Justice Press.

Eck, J. E. (2003). Police problems: The complexity of problem theory, research and evaluation. In J. Knutsson (Ed.), *Problem-oriented policing: From innovation to mainstream* (pp. 79–113). Monsey, NY: Criminal Justice Press.

Eliason, S. L. (2012). Trophy poaching: A routine activities perspective. *Deviant Behavior, 33,* 72–87.

Fisher, B. S., Daigle, L. E., & Cullen, F. T. (2010). What distinguishes single from recurrent sexual victims? The role of lifestyle-routine activities and first-incident characteristics. *Justice Quarterly, 27,* 102–129.

Groff, E. (2007). Simulation for theory testing and experimentation: An example using routine activity theory and street robbery. *Journal of Quantitative Criminology, 23,* 75–103.

Groff, E. R. (2008). Adding the temporal and spatial aspects of routine activities: A further test of routine activity theory. *Security Journal, 21*(1/2), 95–116.

Guerette, R. T., & Santana, S. A. (2010). Explaining victim self-protective behavior effects on crime incident outcomes: A test of opportunity theory. *Crime & Delinquency, 56,* 198–226.

Guerette, R. T., Stenius, V., & McGloin, J. M. (2005). Understanding offense specialization and versatility: A reapplication of the rational choice perspective. *Journal of Criminal Justice, 33,* 77–87.

Henson, B., Wilcox, P., Reyns, B. W., & Cullen, F. T. (2010). Gender, adolescent lifestyles, and violent victimization: Implications for routine activity theory. *Victims & Offenders, 5,* 303–328.

Holt, T. J., & Bossler, A. M. (2009). Examining the applicability of lifestyle-routine activities theory for cybercrime victimization. *Deviant Behavior, 30,* 1–25.

Holtfreter, K., Reisig, M. D., & Pratt, T. C. (2008). Low self-control, routine activities, and fraud victimization. *Criminology, 46,* 189–220.

Hutchings, A., & Hayes, H. (2009). Routine activity theory and phishing victimisation: Who gets caught in the 'net'? *Current Issues in Criminal Justice, 20,* 433–451.

Jackson, A., Gilliland, K., & Veneziano, L. (2006). Routine activity theory and sexual deviance among male college students. *Journal of Family Violence, 21,* 449–460.

Johnson, B. R., Yalda, C. A., & Kierkus, C. A. (2010). Property crime at O'Hare International Airport: An examination of the routine activities approach. *Journal of Applied Security Research, 5*, 42–63.

Kuo, S., Cuvelier, S. J., Sheu, C., & Zhao, J. (2012). The concentration of criminal victimization and patterns of routine activities. *International Journal of Offender Therapy & Comparative Criminology, 56*, 573–598.

Landau, S. F., & Bendalak, Y. (2008). Personnel exposure to violence in hospital emergency wards: A routine activity approach. *Aggressive Behavior, 34*, 88–103.

Lutya, T. (2010). Lifestyles and routine activities of South African teenagers at risk of being trafficked for involuntary prostitution. *Journal of Child & Adolescent Mental Health, 22*, 91–110.

Marcum, C. D., Higgins, G. E., & Ricketts, M. L. (2010). Potential factors of online victimization of youth: An examination of adolescent online behaviors utilizing routine activity theory. *Deviant Behavior, 31*, 381–410.

Marcum, C. D., Ricketts, M. L., & Higgins, G. E. (2010). Assessing sex experiences of online victimization: An examination of adolescent online behaviors using routine activity theory. *Criminal Justice Review, 35*, 412–437.

Messner, S. F., Zhou, L., Lening, Z., & Jianhong, L. (2007). Risks of criminal victimization in contemporary urban China: An application of lifestyle/routine activities theory. *Justice Quarterly, 24*, 496–522.

Navarro, J. N., & Jasinski, J. L. (2012). Going cyber: Using routine activities theory to predict cyberbullying experiences. *Sociological Spectrum, 32*, 81–94.

Novak, K. B., & Crawford, L. A. (2010). Routine activities as determinants of gender differences in delinquency. *Journal of Criminal Justice, 38*(5), 913–920.

Payne, B. K., & Gainey, R. R. (2006). The criminal justice response to elder abuse in nursing homes: A routine activities perspective. *Western Criminology Review, 7*(3), 67–81.

Pizarro, J. M., Corsaro, N., & Sung-suk Violet, Y. (2007). Journey to crime and victimization: An application of routine activities theory and environmental criminology to homicide. *Victims & Offenders, 2*, 375–394.

Pollock, W., Joo, H., & Lawton, B. (2010). Juvenile arrest rates for burglary: A routine activities approach. *Journal of Criminal Justice, 38*, 572–579.

Popp, A., & Peguero, A. A. (2011). Routine activities and victimization at school: The significance of gender. *Journal of Interpersonal Violence, 26*, 2413–2436.

Pratt, T. C., Holtfreter, K., & Reisig, M. D. (2010). Routine online activity and internet fraud targeting: Extending the generality of routine activity theory. *Journal of Research in Crime & Delinquency, 47*, 267–296.

Rengifo, A. F., & Bolton, A. (2012). Routine activities and fear of crime: Specifying individual-level mechanisms. *European Journal of Criminology, 9*(2), 99–119.

Reyns, B. W., Henson, B., & Fisher, B. S. (2011). Being pursued online: Applying cyberlifestyle–routine activities theory to cyberstalking victimization. *Criminal Justice & Behavior, 38*, 1149–1169.

Schreck, C. J., & Fisher, B. S. (2004). Specifying the influence of family and peers on violent Victimization: Extending routine activities and lifestyles theories. *Journal of Interpersonal Violence 19*, 1021–1041.

Spano, R., Freilich, J. D., & Bolland, J. (2008). Gang membership, gun carrying, and employment: Applying routine activities theory to explain violent victimization among inner city, minority youth living in extreme poverty. *Justice Quarterly, 25*, 381–410.

Stein, R. E. (2009). Assault victimization: A comparative analysis of the United States, the Netherlands, and England & Wales. *International Journal of Criminal Justice Sciences, 4*, 44–59.

Svensson, R., & Oberwittler, D. (2010). It's not the time they spend, it's what they do: The interaction between delinquent friends and unstructured routine activity on delinquency: Findings from two countries. *Journal of Criminal Justice, 38*, 1006–1014.

Tewksbury, R. A. & Mustaine, E. E. (2001). Lifestyle factors associated with the sexual assault of men: A routine activity theory analysis. *Journal of Men's Studies, 9*, 153–182.

Tewksbury, R., Mustaine, E., & Stengel, K. M. (2008). Examining rates of sexual offenses from a routine activities perspective. *Victims & Offenders, 3*, 75–85.

Tillyer, M., & Eck, J. E. (2011). Getting a handle on crime: A further extension of routine activities theory. *Security Journal, 24*, 179–193.

Uludag, S., Colvin, M., Hussey, D., & Eng, A. L. (2009). Modernization, inequality, routine activities, and international variations in household property crimes. *International Journal of Criminal Justice Sciences, 4*, 23–43.

Vazsonyi, A., Pickering, L., Belliston, L. M., Hessing, D., & Junger, M. (2002). Routine activities and deviant behaviors: American, Dutch, Hungarian, and Swiss youth. *Journal of Quantitative Criminology, 18*, 397–422.

Waldner, L. K., & Berg, J. (2008). Explaining antigay violence using target congruence: An application of revised routine activities theory. *Violence & Victims, 23*, 267–287.

Wittebrood, K., & Nieuwbeerta, P. (2000). Criminal victimization during one's life course: The effects of previous victimization and patterns of routine activities. *Journal of Research in Crime and Delinquency, 37*, 91–123.

Rational Choice (from 2000)

Becker, R., & Mehlkop, G. (2006). Social class and delinquency: An empirical utilization of rational choice theory with cross-sectional data of the 1990 and 2000 German General Population surveys (ALLBUS). *Rationality & Society, 18*, 193–235.

Bouffard, J., Bry, J., Smith, S., & Bry, R. (2008). Beyond the "science of sophomores": Does the rational choice explanation of crime generalize from university students to an actual offender sample? *International Journal of Offender Therapy & Comparative Criminology, 52*, 698–721.

Cardone, C., & Hayes, R. (2012). Shoplifter perceptions of store environments: An analysis of how physical cues in the retail interior shape shoplifter behavior. *Journal of Applied Security Research, 7*, 22–58.

Kroneberg, C., Heintze, I., & Mehlkop, G. (2010). The interplay of moral norms and instrumental incentives in crime causation. *Criminology, 48*, 259–294.

Maimon, D., Antonaccio, O., & French, M. T. (2012). Severe sanctions, easy choice? Investigating the role of school sanctions in preventing adolescent violent offending. *Criminology, 50*, 495–524.

O'Grady, W., & Asbridge, M. (2000). Illegal tobacco sales to youth: A view from rational choice theory. *Canadian Journal of Criminology, 42,* 1–20.

Piquero, N., Exum, M., & Simpson, S. S. (2005). Integrating the desire–for–control and rational choice in a corporate crime context. *Justice Quarterly, 22*, 252–280.

Wright, B. E., Caspi, A., Moffitt, T. E., & Paternoster, R. (2004). Does the perceived risk of punishment deter criminally prone individuals? Rational choice, self-control, and crime. *Journal of Research in Crime & Delinquency, 41*, 180–213.

Opportunity (from 2000)

Albanese, J. S. (2000). The causes of organized crime: Do criminals organize around opportunities for crime or do criminal opportunities create new offenders? *Journal of Contemporary Criminal Justice, 16*, 409–423.

Alvi, S., Schwartz, M. D., Dekeseredy, W. S., & Maume, M. O. (2000). Women's fear of crime in Canadian public housing. *Violence Against Women, 7*, 638–662.

Bernasco, W. (2007). The usefulness of measuring spatial opportunity structures for tracking down offenders: A theoretical analysis of geographic offender profiling using simulation studies. *Psychology, Crime & Law, 13*, 155–171.

Bowers, K., Johnson, S., & Hirschfield, A. (2004). Closing off opportunities for crime: An evaluation of alley-gating. *European Journal on Criminal Policy & Research, 10*, 285–308.

Eck, J. E., & Eck, E. B. (2012). Crime place and pollution. *Criminology & Public Policy, 11*, 281–316.

Elffers, H., Reynald, D., Averdijk, M., Bernasco, W., & Block, R. (2008). Modelling crime flow between neighbourhoods in terms of distance and of intervening opportunities. *Crime Prevention & Community Safety, 10*(2), 85–96.

Farrell, G., Tilley, N., Tseloni, A., & Mailley, J. (2010). Explaining and sustaining the crime drop: Clarifying the role of opportunity-related theories. *Crime Prevention & Community Safety, 12*, 24–41.

Guerette, R. T., & Santana, S. A. (2010). Explaining victim self-protective behavior effects on crime incident outcomes: A test of opportunity theory. *Crime & Delinquency, 56*, 198–226.

Kleck, G., & Chiricos, T. (2002). Unemployment and property crime: A target-specific assessment of opportunity and motivation as mediating factors. *Criminology, 40*, 649–680.

Lee, M. R., & Alshalan, A. (2005). Geographic variation in property crime rates: A test of opportunity theory. *Journal of Crime & Justice, 28*, 101–127.

Mears, D. P., Scott, M. L., & Bhai, A. S. (2007). Opportunity theory and agricultural crime victimization. *Rural Sociology, 72*, 151–184.

O'Neill, L., & McGloin, J. (2007). Considering the efficacy of situational crime prevention in schools. *Journal of Criminal Justice, 35*, 511–523.

Reynald, D. M. (2011). Factors associated with the guardianship of places: Assessing the relative importance of the spatio-physical and sociodemographic contexts in generating opportunities for capable guardianship. *Journal of Research in Crime & Delinquency, 48*, 110–142.

Rotton, J., & Cohn, E. G. (2000). Weather, disorderly conduct, and assaults. *Environment and Behavior, 32*, 651–674.

Stitt, G., Giacopassi, D., & Vandiver, M. (2000). A minor concern? Underage casino gambling and the law. *Social Science Journal, 37*, 361–374.

Tillyer, M., Fisher, B. S., & Wilcox, P. (2011). The effects of school crime prevention on students' violent victimization, risk perception, and fear of crime: A multilevel opportunity perspective. *Justice Quarterly, 28*, 249–277.

14

Contemporary Theories of Process

LEARNING OBJECTIVES

Objective 14.1: Describe strain theory and how it is related to the concept of anomie studied earlier.

Objective 14.2: Explain the concept of social capital and its use in criminological theory.

Objective 14.3: Discuss developmental theories in general and the research evidence on them.

Objective 14.4: Highlight some of the anticrime policies that would be consistent with the theories described in this section.

Objective 14.5: Identify the major principles of low self-control theory and their implications for crime and delinquency.

INTRODUCTION

Previous chapters explored explanations of crime and criminality from the perspective of rational and feminist thought, and the adaptations of older theories have been noted at the end of each of their respective chapters. Contemporary theories, though, are more diverse than suggested by these reviews. Some of the recent (say from 1985 to the present) perspectives are quite complex and conceptually different from preceding work. In this chapter, then, we provide an overview of three theoretical directions that have proven popular among criminologists in the new century.

THE HERITAGE OF CONTEMPORARY THEORY

The 1980s and 1990s were socially a period of conservatism. Two generations of birth cohorts emerged during that time, the first called the "me generation" and the second called the "X generation." Both were products of a reaction to the exuberant 1960s and 1970s and their names were expressions of the concern with self that eventually culminated with a "lost" generation (one that was not paid much attention). The feeling during this period, as noted in the chapter on rational theories, was that individuals controlled their lives. The 1960s-based social perspectives were clearly being rejected. In fact, it was not unusual to find humor in cartoons with criminals explaining that "society made them do it." The emerging social and political conservatism fostered a feeling that individual responsibility and restraint were the crucial ingredients in resisting deviance. How one learned responsibility and restraint, however, needed to be explained. The general answer was that correct values, learned from one's parents, were the ticket to avoiding problems in life. Of course, the issues of whose values were to be learned was a critical one. Certain societal groups felt that their values were the correct ones and attempted to have those values placed into law in a process not dissimilar to that discussed earlier in the chapter on conflict theory.

Since around 2000, it appears that either the events assisting a creative period dissipated or criminology decided to sit back and take stock of its work. Regardless, the period of new theorizing seems to have tapered off. Indeed, a consensus appears to be building that three contemporary theoretical approaches, general strain theory, self-control theory, and developmental or life-course theory (along with an older one, social learning theory) are the new dominant perspectives. Of the three new ones, self-control theory appears to be the most popular. An intriguing element is that all are based on older theoretical models and evidence: general strain theory from anomie theory, self-control theory from social control, and life-course theory in both social control and data collected by Sheldon and Eleanor Glueck in the 1950s. Perhaps this means that we have returned to more "comfortable" theories or even that there is a dominant, mainstream force that governs the popularity of theory. Each one, though, adds substantial nuances to the original formulations.

There is another element in common among the three approaches in this chapter: the importance of factors in early life. General strain theory examines the effect of stress and frustration among school-age children, self-control theory focuses on early parenting, and life-course perspectives deal with child development (although they then argue that early developmental factors can be overcome later in life). In one sense, this attention to early childhood development and school reflects the social and political concerns of the 1980s that families had fallen apart and permissive parenting had led to children being raised without "proper" values. In the midst of this concern with children, it seems that mainstream criminology also became convinced that crime is a product of what happens to children, particularly at early ages.

MODERN STRAIN THEORY

Anomie, or strain, theory was originally a structural theory focusing on the effect of cultural change and inequality. Given the focus of more recent theories, it was perhaps predictable that criminologists would attempt to find ways to bring strain to the processual, or personal, level. Theories emerged during the 1980s and 1990s to do just that.

General Strain Theory

This best known of the contemporary versions of strain theory is the result of the work of Robert Agnew (1985, 1989, 1992, 2005). Agnew contends that traditional strain theories look at problems achieving positively valued goals, that is, the inability to achieve what one wants. But, he argues, just as an individual's goals can be blocked, so can the ability to avoid undesirable situations or stressful life events. Therefore, he adds another theoretical ingredient: the avoidance of painful (or negative) situations. These types of strains involve being faced with the loss of positively valued stimuli or with the presentation of negative stimuli, normally referred to as stressors. These negative relationships and the generation of anger, frustration, and other negative emotions can pressure one toward crime and delinquency. Individuals with the greatest access to coping mechanisms are more likely to be conforming. However, a lack of coping mechanisms opens the individual up to deviance. For instance, a juvenile may not be able to avoid a bad family situation or dropping out of school as a solution to poor grades, or even hiding from peer rejection. All these situations may yield levels of frustration and anger as high as those from blocked aspirations or immediate goals. The ability to cope with these negative situations is critical to the production of deviance. Coping mechanisms include skills one might have, as well as alternative avenues of behavior, and even intelligence.

When both positive blockage and negative avoidance are combined, the stress levels suggest that we can expect the highest rates of delinquency or deviance. Agnew (2007, p. 4782) says that stressful ingredients whose combination is most likely to lead to crime involve (1) events thought of as unjust, (2) stimuli strong in stress, (3) low social control, and (4) yielding to pressure to engage in criminal coping. As is obvious, the theory draws from factors producing low social control, rational thinking (calculating the damage from criminal coping), and personality features (in particular one's susceptibility to strong emotions).

General strain theory has thus far received support from a number of research studies (Agnew, Cullen, Burton, Evans, & Dunaway, 1996; Agnew & White, 1992; Broidy & Agnew, 1997; Hoffman & Su, 1997; Paternoster & Mazerolle, 1994). In one study, Garase (2006) found strain to be related to road rage; however, she also found that both females and minorities were less likely to participate in road rage. In another study, Piquero and Sealock (2004) attempted to distinguish gender differences in strain and found that although males and females may experience similar levels of strain, they seem to identify negative emotions differently (anger, depression) and may have different coping strategies for them including involvement with peers in delinquent activity. Overall, general strain theory has been of interest to criminologists who continue to feel there is value to the old anomie perspective.

MODERN SOCIAL CONTROL THEORY

Social control theory, specifically Travis Hirschi's version, has been the most popular of all criminological theories for the past 30 years. The most recent version of social control theory is Michael Gottfredson and Travis Hirschi's "general theory of crime" or, as it has been popularly called, "self-control theory" (an earlier version was entitled "propensity-event theory"). In three articles and one book (Gottfredson & Hirschi, 1989, 1990; Hirschi & Gottfredson, 1983, 1989), Gottfredson and Hirschi present a theory of crime based on an examination of both crime and criminality. Its key ingredients are underlying propensities (crime proneness) and the conditions under which these propensities translate into crime.

First, Gottfredson and Hirschi redefine the concept of crime to allow more latitude in capturing various forms of criminality. They did this primarily because white-collar crimes are not normally recognized by most existing theories. Their new definition of crime is *"acts of force or fraud undertaken in the pursuit of self-interest"* (1990, p. 15, emphasis added). While apparently broader than some legal definitions of crime, this definition may not capture some forms of crime, such as crimes of accident or negligence. However, the definition does serve a broader theoretical interest and provides focus to what Gottfredson and Hirschi mean to explain. Further, the definition is compatible with Hirschi's social control assumption that people are, by nature, self-interested (see the discussion in Chapter 11). The authors further state that crimes are exciting for the offender particularly because of the involvement of risk or thrills, and most acts require little planning or skill and involve few long-lasting or substantial benefit.

Hedonism

Second, Gottfredson and Hirschi reject the traditional core concepts of other criminological theories, particularly class and race. Indeed, they maintain that these concepts are ambiguous enough to be relatively useless. The concepts are still with us, the authors claim, because they are at the very core of sociology. Better, however, is to view crime by its common characteristics: immediate gratification; easy or simple gratification; exciting, risky, or thrilling; few or meager long-term benefits; little skill or planning; and pain and discomfort for the victim (1990, p. 89). These characteristics convinced Gottfredson and Hirschi that crime is basically a problem of low "self-control." This new core concept, "self-control," is essentially derived from Hirschi's earlier social control theory but is more focused on the individual rather than on external sources of control. Self-control is defined as "the idea that people also differ in the extent to which they are vulnerable to the temptations of the moment" (1990, p. 87) or, in other words, their ability to restrain themselves. Hirschi (2004, pp. 543–544) has redefined self-control (as we noted in Chapter 11) to make it more compatible with social control concepts. The new definition is that self-control is the presence of inhibitions derived from the elements of the bond (in social control theory) and carried with the individual. Because elements of the bond are provided through the external process of social control, this could make an inherent trait of impulsivity a questionable measure of the theory.

Commensurate with Hirschi's assumptions behind social control theory, the new theory also presumes criminals have no special motivations (or needs and desires). All individuals have access to the same motivations. The real problem is self-control. Low self-control yields a higher probability that an individual will engage in crime, whereas high self-control yields a low probability for criminal behavior (1990, p. 89).

The general theory of crime declares individuals have certain traits, among them impulsivity, insensitivity, self-centeredness, and lower-than-average intelligence. These traits affect low social control mainly by affecting an individual's ability to accurately calculate the consequences of an action (1990, p. 95). Gottfredson and Hirschi argue that these traits are established early (by age eight) and persist throughout life. They view child-rearing practices as the major influence on the formation of certain propensities (1990, p. 97). Child-rearing is primarily the parents' responsibility but may include other caregivers, as for example teachers, relatives, and good friends. Inadequate child-rearing practices affect traits in ways that are conducive to criminality. These traits are often associated with particular social settings and thus are difficult to separate from those settings. The relationship of these traits with crime is less than perfect because they are not necessary conditions for crime and, in fact, will reveal themselves in noncriminal activities as well. Those other activities, though, may share some of the characteristics of crime (e.g., alcohol or drug use). In short, Gottfredson and Hirschi assume criminality traits are naturally present and "in the absence of socialization the child will tend to be high on crime potential" (1989, p. 61).

Crime, on the other hand, is viewed by Gottfredson and Hirschi as an event in time and space, and several factors may need to be present for a crime to occur. This aspect of self-control theory is derived from Gottfredson's (Hindelang, Gottfredson, Garofalo, 1978) earlier foray into opportunity or routine activity theories, a form of rational theory (Gottfredson, 2007, p. 4164). As a result, the concept of opportunity plays an important part in self-control theory. Crime has an attractiveness to those with propensities toward it, thus the crime-propensity affinity entices individuals and promises pleasure. The rationalist perspective of the theory proposes that the crime event must be capable of gratifying the offender, and the consequences (perceived or real) must not overcome the pleasure to be gained from the event. Of course, the event requires certain conditions, namely that there be some potential target and that the situation suggest a lack of undesirable consequences. There may also be internal conditions (strength, speed, presence of alcohol) assisting in the evaluation of the event. The presence of opportunity for crime, as a unique feature of the theory, has been rejected by Gottfredson and Hirschi (2003) because they claim that crime's simplistic nature means that opportunities for crime are literally always present.

For example, in an illegal drag race that resulted in the death of two teens, the driver admitted he was cheered and jeered into the activity by others in the crowd. He also perceived that it was the responsibility of others to have stopped him, saying he felt that somebody should have stopped him or taken his keys. Another youth charged with stealing a car and joyriding until crashing into a parked train killing all four passengers had methamphetamines, marijuana, and other drugs in his system at the time of the crash. His defense strategy seemed to include blaming the train that had no reflective material and the railroad crossing that had no flashing lights or crossing arms. His grandmother argued that "kids get in trouble no matter how close you watch them," an attitude that may have condoned, if not encouraged, his actions. This would be particularly true if no consequences were anticipated (George, 2007).

Finally, Gottfredson and Hirschi note that their theory does not require an individual with low self-control to commit a crime. In fact, low self-control results in a wide variety of behaviors, only one of which is crime. Because of this, they believe any action taken to raise self-control will not only affect crime but also decrease other undesirable social behaviors (for instance, truancy, runaway, aggression, auto accidents, and alcohol abuse). Thus, there is no displacement effect to other forms of deviance when crime is lowered.

The combination of propensity and event within one theory shows promise. It accepts psychological, and even biological, evidence about individual differences, while highlighting the social setting that provides for patterns of both child-rearing practices and structured events. Thus, the theory tolerates variation from a variety of sources and even maintains that other, similarly pleasurable, behavioral events may substitute for crime. This, however, may also be one of the theory's greatest problems: the prediction of crime requires the identification and prediction of other outcome events as well, such as drug use, aggression, and truancy.

Some criminologists have identified other problems. Jason Kissner (2008), for example, analyzes the theory and finds logical inconsistencies in the precipitating factors of rational judgment and parental management as specified by the theory. Others, such as Kenneth Polk (1991) and Charles Tittle (1991), find fault with the evidence used by Gottfredson and Hirschi. He claims they have conveniently overlooked evidence that would be damaging to their theory and declared evidence on their side as "good" evidence. He and Ron Akers (1991) also feel the definition of crime is too restrictive and there are non–self-interested crimes that lie outside the purview of the theory. Akers believes Gottfredson and Hirschi have overstated the view that

Major Points of Low Self-control Theory

1. Humans naturally act in a self-interested fashion.
2. Socialization and training are necessary to restrict human self-interest and create self-control.
3. Improper or inadequate child-rearing practices result in traits that lend themselves to low levels of self-control and poor social bonding.
4. Low levels of self-control result in high frequencies of short-term, pleasure-seeking behaviors.
5. Crime is among the various self-interested behaviors.
6. Increasing self-control results in lower levels of crime and other allied behaviors.

their theory opposes all other contemporary crime theories. In fact, Akers views much of the general theory as compatible with his own social learning theory (Akers, 1998). In addition, Gil Geis (2000, 2008) has also issued stinging critiques of the theory ranging from challenging the main concepts to questioning the motives behind the "explaining away of inconvenient research."

Research on Low Self-Control

Overall, data on crime support the idea that offenders are predominantly young and impulsive and that most offenses, while discomforting to victims, are less dramatic than sensationalized media accounts convey. To date, research on self-control theory has been supportive, though frequently the researchers tend to add other factors to the theory (Beaver, DeLisi, Vaughn, & Wright, 2010; Cretacci, 2008; Hensley, Tung, Xu, Gray-Ray, & Ray, 1999; Pratt & Cullen, 2000; Wai Ting Cheung, & Che`ung, 2010). Grasmick, Tittle, Bursik, and Arneklev (1993) developed a scale that measures low self-control using six dimensions identified in the theory: impulsivity, desire for simple tasks, preference for physical activity, self-centeredness, risk seeking, and temper. This scale has been widely used in testing the theory. One of the problems is that Hirschi (2004) has suggested that such scales do not accurately measure the self-control concept and has offered his own scale based on his previous social control work and a redefined version of self-control. At present, there are few studies using this new approach (but see Cretacci, 2009; Cretacci, Rivera, & Ding, 2009; Piquero & Bouffard, 2007). Still, research using previous versions of self-control measurements continues to support the theory.

Self-control is, according to the theory, a relatively stable characteristic over the life of the individual. Thus, research indicating that offenders do not specialize as much as believed would support low self-control. For example, sex offenders have been found to commit a wide range of offenses, many in relation to low self-control (Buzzel, Foss, & Middleton, 2006; Cleary, 2004). Still, the stability of self-control as the product of child-rearing is the one point about which research seems uncertain. For instance, Beaver, Wright, and DeLisi (2007) found that self-control was stable in a sample of adolescents, but the stability appeared to be due to genetic factors rather than child-rearing and their further research (Beaver, DeLisi, Vaughn, & Wright, 2010) appears to confirm this. There are also theoretical alternatives to the stability position. Robert Sampson and John Laub (1993, 1995) have produced a theory of developmental change over the life course (see the discussion below) based on contrary evidence to the self-control position.

Another major point of the theory is that it is a "general" theory; thus, it explains any behavior falling within its range. Benson and Moore (1992) have examined white-collar offenders and present evidence they may be different from other offenders (particularly "typical" street-crime offenders) (see also Reed & Yeager, 1996). David Friedrichs and Martin Schwartz (2008) also see a paradox in explaining what they view as high-self-control white-collar offenders as having low self-control. Others have questioned the theory's utility for explaining drug use (Goode, 2008) and violence (Felson & Osgood, 2008). Thus, the "general" claim may still be questionable.

Self-Control Theory and Policy

In contrast to many other theoretical presentations, Gottfredson and Hirschi (1990, pp. 255–275) expressly treat policy implications. First, they believe that from the perspective of the theory certain existing policies are useless. Short-term changes in arrest rates or length of sentences do not substantially affect estimates of consequences. Second, programs that attack assumed causes of delinquency, such as truancy, will not reduce crime because both truancy and delinquency are symptoms of low self-control. Third, attacking crime by reducing poverty or other social ills assumed to drive people into crime will have no effect because these things do not result in "overwhelming impulses to commit crime" (1990, p. 256).

Policies that low self-control theory would advocate include programs to properly socialize children within the first six to eight years of life. Indeed, Gottfredson and Hirschi explicitly state "policies directed toward enhancement of the ability of familial institutions to socialize children are the only realistic long-term state policies with potential for substantial crime reduction" (1990, pp. 272–273). By familial institutions, however, they do not necessarily mean the traditional family itself. Potential program emphases include training in parenting, instilling discipline in children, and teaching responsibility. Gottfredson, for instance, sees "considerable promise" in providing childcare resources for high-risk groups (2007, p. 4165). Another policy direction of reducing the attractiveness of criminal events would be more difficult to accomplish. Perhaps the best direction here can be found in environmental design concepts, with changes that make crime more difficult to commit.

MODERN DEVELOPMENTAL THEORIES

In contrast to Gottfredson and Hirschi's position that offenders have a stable propensity for offending, developmental theories argue that an individual's likelihood of offending changes across time. Proponents of this approach note that important good or bad life events, such as experiencing family violence, employment and unemployment, and marriage and divorce, can affect propensity for offending. Exactly what these life events are, and the factors associated with them, vary among developmental theorists. Gerald Patterson, Barbara DeBaryshe, and Elizabeth Ramsey (1989), for instance, agree with Gottfredson and Hirschi that poor early-childhood parenting (dysfunctional families) is critical for developing antisocial personalities and conduct. However, they reject the social control model and view social learning (proper parental interaction and discipline) as a mechanism for reforming antisocial behavior. On the whole developmental theories focus on the way individuals change throughout life and the risk factors found at various life stages.

Life-Course Theory

Perhaps the most important of modern integrative theories, life-course theory is derived from social control, ecology, and a new perspective on an old dataset that has been developed by Robert Sampson and John Laub (1990, 1992, 1993, 2003). Based on an analysis of the Glueck & Glueck (1950) early data on a thousand juveniles followed until age 32 (and later until age 70), Sampson and Laub found that traditional delinquency experiences predicted criminality in adult life. Thus, they conclude change over time is a critical component in explaining crime: the criminal experience is a dynamic one.

Central to the life-course perspective is the idea that one's life changes in two ways: trajectories and transitions. Trajectories refer to the different roles one assumes with aging: going from being a sibling to perhaps a fraternity brother, professional colleague, spouse, father, and grandfather. Coinciding with these role shifts, transitions represent significant life events precipitating role changes, such as graduation, entering the military service, marriage, experiencing the birth of children, and being diagnosed with a life-threatening illness (Phillipson, 2007).

For life-course theorists, informal social control also seems to have an effect on the likelihood of delinquent experiences. Events after becoming an adult, such as job stability, were important in decreasing adult criminality. In other words, various forms of social bonds (particularly work, education, and the family) change the life trajectory of crime (Sampson & Laub, 1990, p. 618) and at different points in life have different effects. Just as they serve to reduce criminal activity, these bonds can also be broken and then act as a destabilizing force over the affected portion of the life course. These events are referred to as turning points and they, as well as influential forms of social control, vary systematically across age groups throughout life.

Sampson and Laub also enlarge Hirschi's concept of the bond into what they call "social capital," which is the notion that the quality of interpersonal relationships among people produces resources for an individual to draw upon. The greater the resources, the greater is the importance of conformity because of what can be lost. The focus on a dynamic approach to life events is crucial to the theory (particularly the effects of social and biological aging, stability and change, human agency, cohort, and historical period). Some research has also examined the effect of spirituality and the influence of religion on commitments to desistence (Giordano, Longmore, Schroeder, & Seffrin, 2008), as well as the effects of levels of employment on teen delinquency (Wright, Cullen, & Williams, 2002).

In addition to the social factors, Sampson and Laub recognize the presence of individual differences in children that will influence those (primarily the family) attempting to exercise control. As opposed to Gottfredson and Hirschi's position, they argue that social control can modify individual propensities to antisocial behavior and shape behavior into conformity. A good example is a 32-year-old man interviewed about his past as a militant extremist working on explosives in Afghanistan. He had first taken up fighting at age 19 with energy, restlessness, and high religious principles, optimistic about his abilities to defend fellow Muslims. Years later, and after serving time at the U.S. prison at Guantanamo Bay, he felt that organizations like al-Qaeda had strayed into terrorism from the original goals that he had originally believed in. Married and working in a traditional job, he is now satisfied with a comfortable, conforming routine (Ambah, 2008). As a related policy issue, although theory and research tell us that individuals will age out of crime, it is still doubtful whether policies such as three-strikes, life sentence without parole, and capital punishment will be adjusted so that offenders who have matured past the point of continued risk can resume their lives.

There are several criminologists now working within the life-course perspective and helping to elaborate its concepts. David Farrington is at this point one of the most prolific contributors, although his interests seem to lie more in the risk-factor and treatment aspects of the theory (see for instance his ASC Sutherland Award speech, 2003). Others, including Alex Piquero and colleagues (2010), have tied developmental theory to criminal careers.

Life-Course-Persistent Offending

Terrie Moffitt (1990, 1993, 1997), another developmental theorist, believes that there is a small group of relatively persistent offenders and a much larger group of offenders who change across time. The first group begins antisocial behaviors in childhood and continues into adulthood. These offenders are likely to be the result of what Moffitt calls "neurological deficits"—neural development somehow obstructed at prenatal to childhood ages—and its effect on the psychological development of the individual. Even here, though, there is an important environmental feedback or reaction to the offenders' behavior, which further reduces their opportunities for learning prosocial skills. Most delinquents, however, are in the second group and do not continue with offending into adulthood. These, Moffitt argues, are merely acting as a result of common early adolescent development in which children want to take on adult roles but are largely prevented from doing so. Delinquency among these individuals is a product of social learning (modeling) from older youth and serves to demonstrate "maturity" and independence. Once these otherwise psychologically healthy youths age out of adolescence, society accepts their adulthood and their offending disappears. A small number, though, are caught in the negative circumstances common to persistent offenders and get trapped in continuing criminal behavior.

Moffitt's research includes analysis of genes that regulate levels of serotonin in the brain. She has attempted to ascertain how genetics may interface with environmental circumstances such as abuse, antisocial personality, and criminality. While Moffitt does not support the concept of genetic determinism, she argues that some youth may be more vulnerable to personality disturbances. Such findings may be helpful in explaining why some abused children become violent and abusive as adults, while others, experiencing similar levels of mistreatment, do not. Building on this, research has also examined the way that cognitive abilities may influence the persistence of criminality.

Interactional Theory

Terence Thornberry (1987, 1996, 1997, 2005; Thornberry, Krohn, Lizotte, Smith, & Tobin, 2003) is another theorist who has suggested that a developmental perspective of criminality works best. Using social control theory's core concept of attachment to parents, Thornberry argues that childhood is a time when attachment to parents is particularly important. Successful parental attachment results in the remainder of the social control elements (commitment, involvement, and belief) and helps the child to avoid deviance. If unsuccessful, the child is open to other, deviant alternatives. These children develop delinquent friends and, according to the mechanisms of social learning theory, begin to learn values and behaviors conducive to delinquency. This process is influenced by both neighborhood characteristics and personal characteristics (race, ethnicity, gender, and social class).

Of interest to this explanation is that Thornberry posits that the social control and learning mechanisms are part of a two-way street (called "interaction")—conventional values and behaviors are reinforcing to further conventionality and the development of stronger bonds, while deviant values and behaviors are reinforcing to deviance and weaker bonds. Thus, involvement in delinquency essentially feeds on itself. These effects vary across stages in life and major sources of bonds change. Continuation in delinquency, or deviance, is then affected by the new bonds, and many individuals react by dropping out of delinquent behavior. The problem is that the results of previous behaviors and attitudes can lock an individual into deviant roles.

Of note is the fact that Thornberry (2005, pp. 230–231) takes great pains to point out that interactional theory is not an integrated theory. His term is "elaborated" theory. The difference is that elaboration borrows from theories without requiring the use of their assumptions or even a majority of their elements. This is important because the final theory comprises a set of propositions that stand alone because of the *set*, rather than the uniqueness of the individual propositions. It also allows Thornberry to modify interactional theory as evidence points the way.

Summary

Sampson and Laub's life-course theory has already gained popularity as a way of arguing for dynamic theory and longitudinal research. And, as we noted earlier, the theory is the primary competitor for Gottfredson and Hirschi's popular self-control theory. Perhaps the critical ingredient in the debate between the two is the contrasting beliefs of dynamic versus static behavior. Sampson and Laub see the propensity for criminal behavior as changing over time in response to various social control conditions. Gottfredson and Hirschi view criminal propensity as fixed at an early age.

Research so far has not strongly supported either view of static or dynamic natures, although there is some evidence for both positions. For example, O'Connell (2006) found that although criminal propensity predicted recidivism and relapse in a group of drug offenders released from prison (Hirschi & Gottfredson's position), employment seemed to significantly decrease the likelihood of going back to prison (Sampson & Laub's perspective), while marriage and children seemed to have no effect. Robert Agnew's general strain theory also has empirical support and is more popular among criminologists who lean toward structural explanations.

At this point, the differences between the theories, and their research support, may be more the result of how one views reality and the methodologies used in testing than any real difference in how delinquency and criminality occur. In the next chapter, we will introduce some theories that argue this very point by discussing either the way we view criminality or the way we tend to overlook the complexity of life.

Questions and Weblinks

Critical Thinking Questions

1. Do certain people have a "propensity" to commit crime? If so, how much can society do to control incidents that may or may not occur?
2. How is rehabilitation implicated in each of the theories covered in this chapter?
3. What types of events do you think are most influential in reducing the occurrence of criminality over the life course?
4. Can you think of some examples of how low self-control may be related to specific types of crimes? How do you think low self-control could best be addressed in treatment?

Practice Essay Questions

1. What is meant by institutional strain and how can it be reduced in American communities today?
2. What do developmental perspectives contribute to explanations of crime and delinquency?
3. Discuss how child-rearing practices may be related to later law-abiding behavior according to theories in this chapter.
4. Explain the role of static and dynamic factors in influencing the criminal activity of a person over time.

Related Website

https://www.ncjrs.gov/app/Search/Abstracts.aspx?id=192543

Bibliography

Agnew, R. (1985). A revised strain theory of delinquency. *Social Forces, 64,* 151–167.

Agnew, R. (1989). A longitudinal test of the revised strain theory. *Journal of Quantitative Criminology, 5,* 373–387.

Agnew, R. (1992). Foundation for a general strain theory of crime and delinquency. *Criminology, 30,* 47–66.

Agnew, R. (2005). *Pressured into crime: An overview of general strain theory.* New York: Oxford University Press.

Agnew, R. (2007). Strain theories. In G. Ritzer (Ed.), *The Blackwell Encyclopedia of Sociology* (pp. 4781–4782). Malden, MA: Blackwell.

Agnew, R., Cullen, F. T., Burton, V. S., Jr., Evans, T. D., & Dunaway, R. G. (1996). A new test of classic strain theory. *Justice Quarterly, 13,* 681–704.

Agnew, R., & White, H. R. (1992). An empirical test of general strain theory. *Criminology, 30,* 475–499.

Akers, R. (1991). Self-control as a general theory of crime. *Journal of Quantitative Criminology, 7,* 201–211.

Akers, R. (1998). *Social learning and social structure: A general theory of crime and deviance.* Boston: Northwestern University Press.

Ambah, F. S. (2008, March 28). Released from Gitmo, disillusioned with bin Laden. *Houston Chronicle,* p. A19.

Beaver, K. M., DeLisi, M., Vaughn, M. G., & Wright, J. (2010). The intersection of genes and neuropsychological deficits in the prediction of adolescent delinquency and low self-control. *International Journal of Offender Therapy & Comparative Criminology, 54,* 22–42.

Beaver, K. M., Wright, J. P., & Delisi, M. (2007, November). *Genetic influences on the stability of low self-control: Results from a longitudinal sample of twins.* Paper presented at the annual meeting of the American Society of Criminology, Atlanta, Georgia.

Benson, M. L., & Moore, E. (1992). Are white-collar and common offenders the same? An empirical and theoretical critique of a recently proposed general theory of crime. *Journal of Research in Crime & Delinquency, 29,* 251–272.

Broidy, L., & Agnew, R. (1997). Gender and crime: A general strain theory perspective. *Journal of Research in Crime and Delinquency, 34,* 275–307.

Buzzell, T., Foss, D., & Middleton, Z. (2006). Explaining use of online pornography: A test of self-control theory and opportunities for deviance. *Journal of Criminal Justice and Popular Culture, 13*(2), 96–116.

Cleary, S. (2004). *Sex offenders and self-control: Examining sexual violence.* New York: LFB Scholarly Publishing.

Cretacci, M. A. (2008). A general test of self control theory. Has its importance been exaggerated? *International Journal of Offender Therapy and Comparative Criminology, 52,* 538–553.

Cretacci, M. A. (2009). Which came first, the bond or self-control? A test of Hirschi's revision of low self-control. *Critical Issues in Justice and Politics, 2,* 71–85.

Cretacci, M. A., Rivera, C. J., & Ding, F. (2009). Self-control and Chinese deviance: A look behind the bamboo curtain. *International Journal of Criminal Justice Sciences, 4,* 131–143.

Farrington, D. (2003). Developmental and life-course criminology: Key theoretical and empirical issues—the 2002 Sutherland Award address. *Criminology, 41,* 221–255.

Felson, M., & Osgood, D. D. (2008). Violent crime. In E. Goode (Ed.), *Out of control* (pp. 160–172). Stanford, CA: Stanford University Press.

Friedrichs, D. O., & Schwartz, M. D. (2008). Low-self control and high organization control: The paradoxes of white-collar crime. In E. Goode (Ed.), *Out of control* (pp. 145–159). Stanford, CA: Stanford University Press.

Garase, M. (2006). *Road rage.* New York: LFB Scholarly Publishing.

Geis, G. (2000). On the absence of self-control as the basis for a general theory of crime. *Theoretical Criminology, 4,* 35–53.

Geis, G. (2008). Self-control. A hypercritical assessment. In E. Goode (Ed.), *Out of control* (pp. 203–216). Stanford, CA: Stanford University Press.

George, C. (2007, September 8). Baytown train tragedy. *Houston Chronicle,* p. B1.

Giordano, P. C., Longmore, M. A., Schroeder, R. D., & Seffrin, P. M. (2008). A life-course perspective on spirituality and desistance from crime. *Criminology, 46,* 99–132.

Glueck, S., & Glueck, E. (1950). *Unraveling juvenile delinquency.* New York: The Commonwealth Fund.

Goode, E. (2008). Drug use and criminal behavior. In E. Goode (Ed.), *Out of control* (pp. 185–201). Stanford, CA: Stanford University Press.

Gottfredson, M. (2007). Self-control theory. In G. Ritzer (Ed.), *Encyclopedia of Sociology* (pp. 4163–4166). New York: Blackwell.

Gottfredson, M., & Hirschi, T. (1989). A propensity-event theory of crime. *Advances in criminological theory, 1,* 57–67.

Gottfredson, M., & Hirschi, T. (1990). *A general theory of crime.* Stanford, CA: Stanford University Press.

Gottfredson, M. R., & Hirschi, T. (2003). Self-control and opportunity. In C. L. Britt & M. R. Gottfredson (Eds.), *Control theories of crime and delinquency* (pp. 5–39). New Brunswick, NJ: Transaction.

Grasmick, H. G., Tittle, C. R., Bursik, R. J., Jr., & Arneklev, B. K. (1993). Testing the core empirical implications of Gottfredson and Hirschi's general theory of crime. *Journal of Research in Crime & Delinquency, 30,* 5–29.

Hensley, C., Tung, Y-K., Xu, X., Gray-Ray, P., & Ray, M. C. (1999). A racial comparison of Mississippi's juvenile violent and property crime: A test of self-control and subculture of violence theories. *Journal of African American Studies, 4*(3), 21–44.

Hindelang, M. J., Gottfredson, M., & Garofalo, J. (1978). *Victims of personal crime: An empirical foundation for a theory of personal victimization.* Cambridge, MA: Ballinger.

Hirschi, T. (2004). Self-control and crime. In R. F. Baumeister & K. D. Vohs (Eds.), *Everyday problems with self-regulation* (pp. 537–552). New York: Guilford.

Hirschi, T., & Gottfredson, M. R. (1983). Age and the explanation of crime. *American Journal of Sociology, 89,* 522–584.

Hirschi, T., & Gottfredson, M. R. (1989). The significance of white-collar crime for a general theory of crime. *Criminology, 27,* 359–371.

Hoffman, J. P., & Su, S. S. (1997). The conditional effects of stress on delinquency and drug use: A strain theory assessment of sex. *Journal of Research in Crime & Delinquency, 34,* 46–79.

Kissner, J. (2008). On the identification of a logical inconsistency in the general theory of crime. *Journal of Crime and Justice, 31*(2), 1–25.

Moffitt, T. E. (1990). Juvenile delinquency and attention deficit disorder: Boys' developmental trajectories from age 3 to 15. *Child Development, 61,* 893–910.

Moffitt, T. E. (1993). Adolescence-limited and life-course-persistent antisocial behavior: A developmental taxonomy. *Psychological Review, 100,* 674–701.

Moffitt, T. E. (1997). Adolescence-limited and life-course-persistent offending: A complementary pair of developmental theories. *Advances in Criminological Theory, 7,* 11–54.

O'Connell, D. (2006). *Prisoner reentry and the life course: The role of race and drugs.* New York: LFB Scholarly Publishing.

Paternoster, R., & Mazerolle, P. (1994). General strain theory and delinquency: A replication and extension. *Journal of Research in Crime & Delinquency, 31,* 235–263.

Patterson, G. R., DeBaryshe, B. D., & Ramsey, E. (1989). A developmental perspective on antisocial behavior. *American Psychologist, 44,* 329–335.

Phillipson, C. (2007). Life course and family. In G. Ritzer (Ed.) *Blackwell encyclopedia of sociology* (pp. 2632–2634). Malden, MA: Blackwell.

Piquero, A. R., & Bouffard, J. (2007). Something old, something new: A preliminary investigation of Hirschi's redefined self-control. *Justice Quarterly, 24,* 1–27.

Piquero, A., Jennings, W. G., & Reingle, J. (2010). Criminal careers. In F. Cullen & P. Wilcox (Eds.), *Encyclopedia of criminological theory.* Thousand Oaks: Sage.

Piquero, A., & White, N. A. (2003). On the relationship between cognitive abilities and life-course persistent offending among a sample of African Americans: A longitudinal test of Moffitt's hypothesis. *Journal of Criminal Justice, 31,* 399–410.

Piquero, N., & Sealock, M. D. (2004). Gender and general strain theory: A preliminary test of Broidy and Agnew's Gender/GST Hypothesis. *Justice Quarterly, 21,* 125–158.

Polk, K. (1991). Book review of "A general theory of crime." *Crime & Delinquency, 37,* 275–279.

Pratt, T. C., & Cullen, F. T. (2000). The empirical status of Gottfredson and Hirschi's general theory of crime: A meta-analysis. *Criminology, 38,* 931–960.

Reed, G. E., & Yeager, P. C. (1996). Organizational offending and neoclassical criminology: Challenging the reach of a general theory of crime. *Criminology, 34,* 357–382.

Sampson, R. J., & Laub, J. H. (1990). Crime and deviance over the life course: The salience of adult social bonds. *American Sociological Review, 55,* 609–627.

Sampson, R. J., & Laub, J. H. (1992). Crime and deviance in the life course. *Annual Review of Sociology, 58,* 63–84.

Sampson, R. J., & Laub, J. H. (1993). *Crime in the making: Pathways and turning points through life.* Cambridge, MA: Harvard University Press.

Sampson, R. J., & Laub, J. H. (1995). Understanding variability in lives through time: Contributions of life-course criminology. *Studies on Crime and Crime Prevention, 4,* 143–158.

Sampson, R. J., & Laub, J. H. (2003). Life course desisters? Trajectories of crime among delinquent boys followed to age 70. *Criminology, 41,* 555–592.

Thornberry, T. P. (1987). Toward an interactional theory of delinquency. *Criminology, 25,* 863–891.

Thornberry, T. P. (1996). Empirical support for interactional theory: A review of the literature. In J. D. Hawkins (Ed.), *Delinquency and crime: Current theories* (pp. 198–235). New York: Cambridge University Press.

Thornberry, T. P. (1997). Introduction: Some advantages of developmental and life-course perspectives for the study of crime and delinquency. *Advances in Criminological Theory, 7,* 1–10.

Thornberry, T. P. (2005). Explaining multiple patterns of offending across the life course and across generations. *The ANNALS of the American Academy of Political and Social Science, 602* (1), 156–195.

Thornberry, T. P., Krohn, M. D., Lizotte, A. J., Smith, C. A., & Tobin, K. (2003). *Gangs and delinquency in developmental perspective.* New York: Cambridge University Press.

Tittle, C. R. (1991). Book review. *American Journal of Sociology*, 96, 1609–1611.

Wright, J. P., Cullen, F. T., & Williams, N. (2002). The embeddedness of adolescent employment and participation in delinquency: A life course perspective. *Western Criminology Review, 4*(1), 1–19.

Research Bibliography

General Strain Theory (from 2000)

Agnew, R., Brezina, T., Wright, J. P., & Cullen, F. T. (2002). Strain, personality traits, and delinquency: Extending general strain theory. *Criminology, 40*, 43–70.

Amato, P. R., & Sobolewski, J. M. (2001). The effects of divorce and marital discord on adult children's psychological well-being. *American Sociological Review, 66*, 900–921.

Baron, S. W. (2003). Self-Control, social consequences, and criminal behavior: Street youth and the general theory of crime. *Journal of Research in Crime & Delinquency, 40*, 403–425.

Baumer, E. P., & Gustafson, R. (2007). Social organization and instrumental crime: Assessing the empirical validity of classic and contemporary anomie theories. *Criminology, 45*, 617–663.

Capowich, G. E., Mazerolle, P., & Piquero, A. R. (2001). General strain theory, situational anger, and social networks: An assessment of conditioning influences. *Journal of Criminal Justice, 29*, 445–461.

Eitle, D., & Turner, R. J. (2003). Stress Exposure, Race, and Young Adult Male Crime. *Sociological Quarterly, 44*, 243–269.

Ellwanger, S. (2007). Strain, attribution, and traffic delinquency among young drivers. *Crime & Delinquency, 53*, 523–551.

Mazzerolle, P., & Maahs, J. (2000). General strain theory and delinquency: An alternative examination of conditioning influences. *Justice Quarterly, 17*, 753–778.

Mazerolle, P., Burton, V. S., Jr., Cullen, F. T., Evans, T. D., & Payne, G. L. (2000). Strain, anger, and delinquency adaptations: Specifying general strain theory. *Journal of Criminal Justice, 28*, 89–101.

Ostrowsky, M., & Messner, S. F. (2005). Explaining crime for a young adult population: An application of general strain theory. *Journal of Criminal Justice, 33*, 463–476.

Piquero, A. R., & Sealock, M. D. (2000). Generalizing general strain theory: An examination of an offending population. *Justice Quarterly, 17*, 449–484.

Piquero, A. R., & Sealock, M. D. (2004). Gender and general strain theory: A preliminary test of Broidy and Agnew's gender/GST hypothesis. *Justice Quarterly, 21*, 125–158.

Wai Ting Cheung, N., & Cheung, Y. W. (2010). Strain, self-control, and gender differences in delinquency among Chinese adolescents: Extending general strain theory. *Sociological Perspectives, 53*, 321–345.

Wallace, L. H., Patchin, J., & May, J. D. (2005). Reactions to victimized youth: Strain as an explanation of school delinquency. *Western Criminological Review, 6*(1), 104–116.

Wareham, J., Cochran, J. K., Dembo, R., & Sellers, C. (2005). Community, strain, and delinquency: A test of a multi-level model of general strain theory. *Western Criminology Review, 6*(1), 117–133.

Warner, B. D., & Fowler, S. K. (2003). Strain and violence: Testing a general strain theory of community violence. *Journal of Criminal Justice, 31*, 511–521.

Self-Control Theory (from 2000)

Armstrong, T. (2005). Evaluating the competing assumptions of Gottfredson and Hirschi's (1990) "A General Theory of Crime" and psychological explanations of aggression. *Western Criminological Review, 6*(1), 12–21.

Baker, J. O. (2010). The expression of low self-control as problematic drinking in adolescents: An integrated control perspective. *Journal of Criminal Justice, 38*, 237–244.

Baumeister, R. F., Boone, A. L., & Tangne, J. P. (2004). High self control predicts good adjustment, less pathology, better grades, and interpersonal success. *Journal of Personality, 72*, 271–324.

Beaver, K. M., DeLisi, M., Vaughn, M. G., & Wright, J. (2010). The intersection of genes and neuropsychological deficits in the prediction of adolescent delinquency and low self-control. *International Journal of Offender Therapy & Comparative Criminology, 54*, 22–42.

Beaver, K. M., DeLisi, M., Wright, J., & Vaughn, M. G. (2009). Gene-environment interplay and delinquent involvement: Evidence of direct, indirect, and interactive effects. *Journal of Adolescent Research, 24,* 147–168.

Benda, B. B. (2005). The robustness of self-control in relation to form of delinquency *Youth & Society, 36,* 418–444.

Boisvert, D., Vaske, J., Taylor, J., & Wright, J. P. (2012). The effects of differential parenting on sibling differences in self-control and delinquency among brother–sister pairs. *Criminal Justice Review, 37,* 5–23.

Boman, J. H., & Gibson, C. L. (2011). Does the measurement of peer deviance change the relationship between self-control and deviant behavior? An analysis of friendship pairs. *Journal of Criminal Justice, 39,* 521–530.

Booth, J. A., Farrell, A., & Varano, S. P. (2008). Social control, serious, delinquency and risky behavior. *Crime & Delinquency, 54,* 423–456.

Brame, R., Mulvey, E. P., & Piquero, A. R. (2001). On the development of different kinds of criminal activity. *Sociological Methods and Research, 29,* 319–341.

Brannigan, A., Gremmel, W., Pevalin, D. J., & Wade, T. J. (2002). Self-control and social control in childhood misconduct and aggression: The role of the family structure, hyperactivity, and host parenting. *Canadian Journal of Criminology, 44,* 119–142.

Buzzell, T., Foss, D., & Middleton, Z. (2006). Explaining use of online pornography: A test of self-control theory and opportunities for deviance. *Journal of Criminal Justice and Popular Culture, 13*(2), 96–116.

Chapple, C. L. (2005). Self-control, peer relations, and delinquency. *Justice Quarterly, 22,* 89–106.

Cheung, N., & Cheung, Y. (2008). Self-control, social factors, and delinquency: A test of the general theory of crime among adolescents in Hong Kong. *Journal of Youth & Adolescence, 37,* 412–430.

Cretacci, M. A. (2009). Which came first, the bond or self-control? A test of Hirschi's revision of low self-control. *Critical Issues in Justice and Politics, 2,* 71–85.

Cretacci, M. A., Rivera, C. J., & Ding, F. (2009). Self-control and Chinese deviance: A look behind the bamboo curtain. *International Journal of Criminal Justice Sciences, 4,* 131–143.

de Kemp, R. T., Vermulst, A. A., Finkenauer, C., Scholte, R. J., Overbeek, G., Rommes, E. M., & Engels, R. E. (2009). Self-control and early adolescent antisocial behavior: A longitudinal analysis. *Journal of Early Adolescence, 29,* 497–517.

De Li, S. (2004). The impacts of self-control and social bonds on juvenile delinquency in a national sample of midadolescents. *Deviant Behavior, 25,* 351–373.

DeLisi, M., Hochstetler, A., Higgins, G. E., Beaver, K. M., & Graeve, C. M. (2008). Toward a general theory of criminal justice. Low self-control and offender noncompliance. *Criminal Justice Review, 33,* 141–158.

Doherty, E. E. (2006). Self-control, social bonds, and desistance: A test of life-course interdependence. *Criminology, 44,* 807–834.

Eisner, M. (2001). Modernization, self-control and lethal violence. *British Journal of Criminology, 41,* 618–638.

Ezinga, M. J., Weerman, F. M., Westenberg, P. M., & Bijleveld, C. H. (2008). Early adolescence and delinquency: Levels of psychosocial development and self-control as an explanation of misbehaviour and delinquency. *Psychology, Crime & Law, 14,* 339–356.

Gibson, C. L., Schreck, C., & Miller, J. M. (2004). Binge drinking and negative alcohol-related behaviors: A test of self-control theory. *Journal of Criminal Justice, 32,* 411–420.

Gibson, C. L., & Wright, J. P. (2001). Low self-control and worker delinquency: A research note. *Journal of Criminal Justice, 29,* 483–492.

Gibson, C. L., Wright, J. P., & Tibbetts, S. G. (2000). An empirical assessment of the generality of the general theory of crime: The effects of low self-control on social development. *Journal of Crime and Justice, 23,* 109–134.

Hay, C. (2001). Parenting, self-control, and delinquency: A test of self-control theory. *Criminology, 39,* 707–736.

Hay, C., & Forrest, W. (2008). Self-control theory and the concept of opportunity: The case for a more systematic union. *Criminology, 46,* 1039–1072.

Higgins, G. E. (2005). Can low self-control help with the understanding of the software piracy problem? *Deviant Behavior, 26,* 1–24.

Higgins, G. E. (2009). Parental criminality and low self-control: an examination of delinquency. *Criminal Justice Studies, 22,* 141–152.

Higgins, G. E., & Ricketts, M. L. (2004). Motivation or opportunity: Which serves as the best mediator in self-control theory? *Western Criminological Review, 5*(2), 77–96.

Higgins, G. E., & Ricketts, M. L. (2005). Self-control theory, race, and delinquency. *Journal of Ethnicity in Criminal Justice, 3*(3), 5–22.

Higgins, G. E., & Tewksbury, R. (2006). Sex and self-control theory: The measures and causal model may be different. *Youth & Society, 37,* 479–503.

Intravia, J., Jones, S., & Piquero, A. R. (2011). The roles of social bonds, personality, and perceived costs: An empirical investigation into Hirschi's 'new' control theory. *International Journal of Offender Therapy and Comparative Criminology, 55*(8), 1–19.

Jeong, S., & Eamon, M. (2009). A model of family background, family process, youth self-control, and delinquent behavior in two-parent families. *Journal of Family Social Work, 12*, 323–339.

Jones, S., Lynam, D., & Piquero, A. R. (2011). Substance use, personality, and inhibitors: Testing Hirschi's predictions about the reconceptualization of self control. *Crime & Delinquency, 57*(6), 1–21.

Kissner, J., & Pyrooz, D. C. (2009). Self-control, differential association, and gang membership: A theoretical and empirical extension of the literature. *Journal of Criminal Justice, 37*, 478–487.

Lavikainen, H., Salmi, V., Aaltonen, M., & Lintonen, T. (2011). Alcohol-related harms and risk behaviours among adolescents: Does drinking style matter. *Journal of Substance Use, 16*, 243–255.

Longshore, D., Chang, E., Hsieh, E., & Messing, N. (2004). Self-control and social bonds: A combined control perspective on deviance. *Crime & Delinquency, 50*, 542–564.

Lynskey, D. P., Peterson, D., Winfree, L. T., Jr., Esbensen, F., & Clason, D. L. (2000). Linking gender, minority group status and family matters to self-control theory: A multivariate analysis of key self-control concepts in a youth-gang context. *Juvenile and Family Court Journal, 51*, 1–19.

Mason, W. A., & Windle, M. (2002). Gender, self-control, and informal social control in adolescence: A test of three models of the continuity of delinquent behavior. *Youth & Society, 33*, 479–514.

McCartan, L. M., & Gunnison, E. (2007). Examining the origins and influence of low self-control. *Journal of Crime & Justice, 30*, 35–62.

McGloin, J., & Shermer, L. (2009). Self-control and deviant peer network structure. *Journal of Research in Crime & Delinquency, 46*, 35–72.

Meldrum, R. C., Young, J. N., & Weerman, F. M. (2009). Reconsidering the effect of self-control and delinquent peers: Implications of measurement for theoretical significance. *Journal of Research in Crime & Delinquency, 46*, 353–376.

Morris, G. D., Wood, P. B., & Dunaway, R. (2007). Testing the cultural invariance of parenting and self-control as predictors of American Indian delinquency. *Western Criminology Review, 8*(1), 32–47.

Morris, R., Gerber, J., & Menard, S. (2011). Social bonds, self-control, and adult criminality: A nationally representative assessment of Hirschi's revised self-control theory. *Criminal Justice and Behavior, 38*, 584–599.

Nakhaie, M. R., Silverman, R. A., & Lagrange, T. C. (2000a). Self-control and resistance to school. *Canadian Review of Sociology and Anthropology, 37*, 443–461.

Nakhaie, M. R., Silverman, R. A., & Lagrange, T. C. (2000b). Self-control and social control: An examination of gender ethnicity, class and delinquency. *Canadian Journal of Sociology, 25*, 35–59.

Nelson, M. S., & Boisvert, D. (2011). Testing the effects of delinquent peers and self-control on disruptive behaviors in the college classroom. *Criminal Justice Studies, 24*, 165–181.

Ousey, G., & Wilcox, P. (2007). The interaction of antisocial propensity and life-course varying predictors of delinquent behavior: Differences by method of estimation and implications for theory. *Criminology, 45*, 313–353.

Paternoster, R., & Brame, R. (2000). On the association among self-control, crime, and analogous behaviors. *Criminology, 38*, 971–982.

Pauwels, L., & Svensson, R. (2010). Informal controls and the explanation of propensity to offend: A test in two urban samples. *European Journal on Criminal Policy & Research, 16*, 15–27.

Perone, D., Sullivan, C. J., Pratt, T. C., & Margaryan, S. (2004). Parental efficacy, self-control, and delinquency: A test of a general theory of crime on a nationally representative sample of youth. *International Journal of Offender Therapy and Comparative Criminology, 48*, 298–312.

Phythian, K., Keane, C., & Krull, C. (2008). Family structure and parental behavior: Identifying the sources of adolescent self-control. *Western Criminology Review, 9*, 73–87.

Piquero, A. R., & Bouffard, J. (2007). Something old, something new: A preliminary investigation of Hirschi's redefined self-control. *Justice Quarterly, 24*, 1–27.

Pratt, T., & Cullen, F. T. (2000). The empirical status of Gottfredson and Hirschi's general theory of crime: A meta-analysis. *Criminology, 38*, 931–964.

Rebellon, C. J., Manasse, M. E., Van Gundy, K. T., & Cohn, E. S. (2012). Perceived injustice and delinquency: A test of general strain theory. *Journal of Criminal Justice, 40*, 230–237.

Romero, E., Gomez-Fraguela, J. A., Luengo, M. A., & Sobral, J. (2003). The self-control construct in the general theory of crime: An investigation in terms of personality psychology. *Psychology, Crime, and Law, 9*, 61–86.

Stewart, E. A., Elifson, K. W., & Sterk, C. (2004). Integrating the general theory of crime into an explanation of violent victimization among female offenders. *Justice Quarterly, 21*(1), 159–181.

Title, C., Ward, D., & Grasmick, H. (2003). Gender, age, and crime/deviance: A challenge to self-control theory. *Journal of Research in Crime & Delinquency, 40*, 426–453.

Turner, M. G., & Piquero, A. R. (2002). The stability of self-control. *Journal of Criminal Justice, 30*, 457–471.

Turner, M. G., Piquero, A. R., & Pratt, T. (2005). The school context as a source of self-control. *Journal of Criminal Justice, 33,* 327–339.

Vazonyi, A., & Belliston, L. M. (2007). The family flow self control deviance: The general theory of crime across contexts. *Criminal Justice and Behavior, 34,* 505–530.

Vazonyi, A., Pickering, L., Junger, M., & Hessing, D. (2001). An empirical test of a general theory of crime: A four nation comparative study of self-control and the prediction of deviance. *Journal of Research in Crime & Delinquency, 38,* 91–131.

Wai Ting Cheung, N., & Cheung, Y. W. (2010). Strain, self-control, and gender differences in delinquency among Chinese adolescents: Extending general strain theory. *Sociological Perspectives, 53,* 321–345.

Wiebe, R. P. (2006). Using an expanded measure of self-control to predict delinquency. *Psychology, Crime & Law, 12,* 519–536.

Williams, J. M., & Dunlop, L. C. (1999). Pubertal timing and self-reported delinquency among male adolescents. *Journal of Adolescence, 22,* 157–171.

Wright, J., & Beaver, K. (2005). Do parents matter in creating self-control in their children? A genetically informed test of Gottfredson and Hirschi's theory of low self-control. *Criminology, 43,* 1169–1202.

Wright, J., Beaver, K., Delisi, M., & Vaughn, M. (2008). Evidence of negligible parenting influences on self-control, delinquent peers, and delinquency in a sample of twins. *Justice Quarterly, 25,* 544–569.

Young, J. (2011). How do they 'end up together'? A social network analysis of self-control, homophily, and adolescent relationships. *Journal of Quantitative Criminology, 27,* 251–273.

Young, J. N., Barnes, J. C., Meldrum, R. C., & Weerman, F. M. (2011). Assessing and explaining misperceptions of peer delinquency. *Criminology, 49,* 599–630.

Developmental Theory (from 2000)

Bender, K. (2012). The mediating effect of school engagement in the relationship between youth maltreatment and juvenile delinquency. *Children & Schools, 34,* 37–48.

Beyers, J. M., & Loeber, R. (2003). Untangling developmental relations between depressed mood and delinquency in male adolescents. *Journal of Abnormal Child Psychology, 31,* 247–266.

Brook, D. W., Brook, J. S., Rubenstone, E., Zhang, C., & Saar, N. S. (2011). Developmental associations between externalizing behaviors, peer delinquency, drug use, perceived neighborhood crime, and violent behavior in urban communities. *Aggressive Behavior, 37,* 349–361.

Bushway, S. D., Piquero, A. R., Broidy, L. M., Cauffman, E., & Mazerolle, P. (2001). An empirical framework for studying desistance as a process. *Criminology, 39,* 491–515.

Cernkovich, S. A., & Giordano, P. C. (2001). Stability and change in antisocial behavior: The transition from adolescence to early adulthood. *Criminology, 39,* 371–410.

Crosnoe, R. (2000). Friendship in childhood and adolescence: The life course and new direction. *Social Psychology Quarterly, 63,* 377–392.

Doherty, E. (2006). Self-control, social bonds, and desistance: A test of life-course interdependence. *Criminology, 44,* 807–833.

El-Sheikh, M., Hinnant, J., & Erath, S. (2011). Developmental trajectories of delinquency symptoms in childhood: The role of marital conflict and autonomic nervous system activity. *Journal of Abnormal Psychology, 120,* 16–32.

Enter-Wright, B. R., Caspi, A., Moffitt, T. E., & Silva, P. A. (2001). The effects of social ties on crime vary by criminal propensity: A life-course model of interdependence. *Criminology, 39,* 321–351.

Fleming, C. B., Catalano, R. F., Oxford, M. L., & Harachi, T. W. (2002). A test of generalizability of the social development model across gender and income groups with longitudinal data from the elementary school developmental period. *Journal of Quantitative Criminology, 18,* 423–439.

Ford, J. A. (2005). Substance use, the social bond, and delinquency. *Sociological Inquiry, 75,* 109–128.

Gunnison, E., & McCartan, L. M. (2010). Persistent versus late onset among female offenders: A test of state dependent and population heterogeneity interpretations. *Western Criminology Review, 11*(3), 45–62.

Hagan, J., & Foster, H. (2003). S/He's a rebel: Toward a sequential stress theory of delinquency and gendered pathways to disadvantage in emerging adulthood. *Social Forces, 82,* 53–86.

Hagan, J., McCarthy, B., & Foster, H. (2002). A gendered theory of delinquency and despair in the life course. *Acta Sociologica, 45,* 37–46.

Hanson, R. K. (2002). Recidivism and age: Follow-up data from 4,673 sexual offenders. *Journal of Interpersonal Violence, 17,* 1046–1062.

Hoffmann, J. P. (2010). A life-course perspective on stress, delinquency, and young adult crime. *American Journal of Criminal Justice, 35*(3), 105–120.

Johnson, M. C., & Menard, S. (2012). A longitudinal study of delinquency abstention: Differences between life-course abstainers and offenders from adolescence into adulthood. *Youth Violence & Juvenile Justice, 10,* 278–291.

Katz, R. S. (2000). Explaining girls' and women's crime and desistance in the context of their victimization experiences: A developmental test of revised strain theory and the life course perspective. *Violence Against Women, 6*, 633–661.

Lee, J., Bell, N. J., & Watson, W. (2007). Situating alcohol use and delinquency within developmental and societal context: The case of Korean youth. *Journal of Adolescence, 30*, 835–851.

Lynne-Landsman, S. D., Graber, J. A., Nichols, T. R., & Botvin, G. J. (2011). Trajectories of aggression, delinquency, and substance use across middle school among urban, minority adolescents. *Aggressive Behavior, 37*, 161–176.

Matjasko, J., Needham, B., Grunden, L., & Farb, A. (2010). Violent victimization and perpetration during adolescence: Developmental stage dependent ecological models. *Journal of Youth & Adolescence, 39*, 1053–1066.

Meeus, W. W., Branje, S. S., & Overbeek, G. J. (2004). Parents and partners in crime: a six-year longitudinal study on changes in supportive relationships and delinquency in adolescence and young adulthood. *Journal of Child Psychology & Psychiatry, 45*, 1288–1298.

Mendez, V. (2011). Does missing the maturity gap predict drug abstention among adolescents?: An analysis of Moffitt's developmental taxonomy. *Southwest Journal of Criminal Justice, 7*(3), 341–367.

Miller, S., Malone, P. S., & Dodge, K. A. (2010). Developmental trajectories of boys' and girls' delinquency: Sex differences and links to later adolescent outcomes. *Journal of Abnormal Child Psychology, 38*, 1021–1032.

Murray, J., & Farrington, D. P. (2005). Parental imprisonment: Effects on boys' antisocial behaviour and delinquency through the life-course. *Journal of Child Psychology & Psychiatry, 46*, 1269–1278.

Murray, J., & Farrington, D. P. (2005). Parental imprisonment: Effects on boys' antisocial behaviour and delinquency through the life-course. *Journal of Child Psychology & Psychiatry, 46*, 1269–1278.

Negriff, S., Susman, E., & Trickett, P. (2011). The developmental pathway from pubertal timing to delinquency and sexual activity from early to late adolescence. *Journal of Youth & Adolescence, 40*, 1343–1356.

Pepler, D. J., Jiang, D., Craig, W. M., & Connolly, J. (2010). Developmental trajectories of girls' and boys' delinquency and associated problems. *Journal of Abnormal Child Psychology, 38*, 1033–1044.

Piquero, A. R., & Brezina, T. (2001). Testing Moffitt's account of adolescence-limited delinquency. *Criminology, 93*, 353–370.

Piquero, A. R., Brame, R., Mazerolle, R., & Haapanen, R. (2002). Crime in emerging adulthood. *Criminology, 40*, 137–169.

Piquero, A. R., Farrington, D. P., Welsh, B. C., Tremblay, R., & Jennings, W. G. (2009). Effects of early family/parent training programs on antisocial behavior and delinquency. *Journal of Experimental Criminology, 5*(2), 83–120.

Polier, G. G., Vloet, T. D., & Herpertz-Dahlmann, B. B. (2012). ADHD and delinquency—a developmental perspective. *Behavioral Sciences & the Law, 30*(2), 121–139.

Sampson, R. J., & Laub, J. H. (2003). Life-course desisters? Trajectories of crime among delinquent boys followed to age 70. *Criminology, 41*, 555–592.

Sampson, R. J., Laub, J. H., & Wimer, C. (2006). Does marriage reduce crime? A counterfactual approach to within-individual causal effects. *Criminology, 44*, 465–508.

Spano, R., Rivera, C., & Bolland, J. M. (2010). Are chronic exposure to violence and chronic behavior closely related developmental processes during adolescence? *Criminal Justice and Behavior, 37*, 1160–1179.

Staff, J., & Uggen, C. (2003). The fruits of good work: Early work experiences and adolescent deviance. *Journal of Research in Crime & Delinquency, 40*, 263–290.

Uggen, C. (2000). Work as a turning point in the life course of criminals: A duration model of age, employment, and recidivism. *American Sociological Review, 67*, 529–546.

Ulmer, J. T., Desmond, S. A., Jang, S., & Johnson, B. R. (2010). Teenage religiosity and changes in marijuana use during the transition to adulthood. *Interdisciplinary Journal of Research on Religion*, 61–19.

Ulmer, J. T., Desmond, S. A., Jang, S., & Johnson, B. R. (2012). Religious involvement and dynamics of marijuana use: Initiation, persistence, and desistence. *Deviant Behavior, 33*, 448–468.

Wright, B. R., Caspi, A., Moffitt, T. E., & Silva, P. A. (2001). The effects of social ties on crime vary by criminal propensity: A life-course model of interdependence. *Criminology, 39*, 321–352.

Wright, J. P., Cullen, F. T., & Williams, N. (2002). The embeddedness of adolescent employment and participation in delinquency: A life course perspective. *Western Criminology Review, 4*(1), 1–19.

Zhang, L., Wieczorek, W. F., & Welte, J. W. (2011). Early onset of delinquency and the trajectory of alcohol-impaired driving among young males. *Addictive Behaviors, 36*, 1154–1159.

Interactional Theory (from 2000)

Brame, R., Bushway, S., Paternoster, R., & Thornberry, T. (2005). Temporal linkages in violent and nonviolent criminal activity. *Journal of Quantitative Criminology, 21,* 149–174.

Gault-Sherman, M. (2012). It's a two-way street: The bidirectional relationship between parenting and delinquency. *Journal of Youth & Adolescence, 41,* 121–145.

Henry, K., Knight, K., & Thornberry, T. (2012). School disengagement as a predictor of dropout, delinquency, and problem substance use during adolescence and early adulthood. *Journal of Youth & Adolescence, 41,* 156–166.

Henry, K., Thornberry, T., & Huizinga, D. (2009). A discrete-time survival analysis of the relationship between truancy and the onset of marijuana use. *Journal of Studies on Alcohol and Drugs, 70,* 5–15.

Howell, J. C., & Egley Jr., A. (2005). Moving risk factors into developmental theories of gang membership. *Youth Violence & Juvenile Justice, 3,* 334–354.

Ireland, T. O., Smith, C. A., & Thornberry, T. P. (2002). Developmental issues in the impact of child maltreatment on later delinquency and drug use. *Criminology, 40,* 359–400.

Jang, S. J. (1999). Age-varying effects of family, school, and peers among delinquents: A multi-level modeling test of interactional theory. *Criminology, 37,* 643–685.

Krohn, M. D., Ward, J. T., Thornberry, T. P., Lizotte, A. J., & Chu, R. (2011). The cascading effects of adolescent gang involvement across the life course. *Criminology, 49,* 991–1028.

Pogarsky, G., Lizotte, A. J., & Thornberry, T. P. (2003). The delinquency of children born to young mothers: Results from the Rochester Youth Development Study. *Criminology, 41,* 1249–1286.

Scaramella, L. V., Conger, R. D., Spoth, R., & Simons, R. L. (2002). Evaluation of a social contextual model of delinquency: A cross-study replication. *Child Development, 73,* 175–195.

Stewart, E. A., Simons, R. L., Conger, R. D., & Scaramella, L. V. (2002). Beyond the interactional relationship between delinquency and parenting practices: The contribution of legal sanctions. *Journal of Research in Crime & Delinquency, 39,* 36–59.

Thornberry, T. P. (2005). Explaining multiple patterns of offending across the life course and across generations. *Annals of the American Academy of Political & Social Science, 602,* 156–195.

Thornberry, T. P., & Henry, K. L. (2009). The interplay of school disengagement and drug use: An interactional perspective. *Monatsschrift fuer Kriminologie und Strafrechtsreform, 92(2/3),* 240–252.

Thornberry, T. P., Freeman-Gallant, A., Lizotte, A. J., Krohn, M. D., & Smith, C. A. (2003). Linked lives: The intergenerational transmission of antisocial behavior. *Journal of Abnormal Child Psychology, 31,* 171.

Thornberry, T., Freeman-Gallant, A., & Lovegrove, P. (2009). The impact of parental stressors on the intergenerational transmission of antisocial behavior. *Journal of Youth & Adolescence, 38,* 312–322.

Contemporary Integrative and Critical Theories

LEARNING OBJECTIVES

Objective 15.1: Describe what is meant by an integrative theory and why are they popular today.

Objective 15.2: Summarize the basic principles of postmodern theory.

Objective 15.3: Discuss how liberal and conservative ideologies impact social attitudes toward crime.

Objective 15.4: Define cultural criminology and its beliefs about the media.

Objective 15.5: Explain the concept of metatheory and its role in criminology.

INTRODUCTION

One of the hazards of presenting theories one after the other is that the differences among them become magnified. Too often students (and criminologists) see the various theories as separate from each other. By providing a brief look at the heritage of each theory, we have tried to show that this is really not the case. Even this, though, cannot adequately suggest the ways in which theories are related. As long as people see each theory as separate and distinct, there will be little real progress in criminology. Fortunately, several criminologists are beginning to work on the integration of theories. This final chapter discusses some of the approaches theorists have taken to criminological theory over the past 20 years.

Criminologists began exploring new theoretical constructs during the mid-to-latter 1980s. Slowly at first, and then with great rapidity, theoretical efforts began to emerge. Some of the first efforts included a "crime-as-self-help" theory proposed by Donald Black (1983) and Hal Pepinsky and Paul Jesilow's (1985) argument for a recognition of diversity in lifestyles. The main burst of theoretical energy seemed to begin about 1987 with the publication of a special theory issue of the journal *Criminology*. Since that time, new theories, new ideas, and adaptations of older theories rapidly emerged through the mid-2000s. It is only fair to add that the list of new theories does not end here. Interested readers would do well to consult the major criminological journals for other perspectives.

The theories we discuss here could be loosely grouped under the headings of integrative theories and postmodern theories. Almost all of the theories are integrative in some sense or another, and they also share an appreciation of the complexity of modern life. Many of the theories also delve into disciplines other than sociology, which previously has been the base for most criminological theorizing. Our headings, then, serve merely to group the theories rather than to purposefully separate them and should not be taken to mean that those in one category are essentially different from those in another category.

THE HERITAGE OF CONTEMPORARY THEORY

The events and influences that will affect current theoretical direction are difficult to see because of their close proximity in time to us. A few influences, however, should have a bearing on the ways theorists think. The social influences are political and economic conservatism, the development of Homeland Security, and a recognition of the necessity of rehabilitation. The intellectual influences include a new discipline specializing in criminal justice and an emphasis on quantification in mainstream criminology.

Social Influences

Since the early 1970s, society has been moving in a decidedly conservative direction. With the Iranian hostage crisis, it seemed that public attitudes came together and a conservative major- ity opinion developed. Political and religious factions claim to speak for the "silent majority," an ostensibly large group of strongly religious, conservative citizens. Whether or not this silent majority exists, there has indeed been a movement toward religious fundamentalism, even to the extent of political involvement.

A further impetus for this conservative direction can be found in the economic recessions of the 1980s and 2007–2011, the 9–11 terrorist attack, and the "wars" in Iraq and Afghanistan. Responding to fiscal necessity, many governmental programs were cut and a pragmatic approach to expenditures in the criminal justice system has been taken. In fact, criminal justice in general has taken a backseat to the Department of Homeland Security in the minds of many. National security became such an important concept to the federal government, and therefore to most U.S. citizens, that public concern over crime has fallen to its lowest levels in perhaps 40 years. If this trend continues, it will clearly sidetrack energy that might have gone into theoretical development because, at present, any academic security discipline is a decidedly nontheoretical endeavor.

In a different turn of events, some people recognized that a pure punishment-oriented approach to criminal justice was not working, and intervention strategies more closely allied with treatment are now being tried. The drug war, while still focused on law enforcement approaches, also encouraged education and treatment efforts. However, the Bush Administration remained squarely in the law-and-order camp and fostered conservative ideologies as a controlling influence. Moreover, the economic recession of 2007–2011 has, as with virtually all periods of economic difficulty before it, occasioned an attack on minorities (this time primarily Mexican Americans) under the assumption they are disproportionately responsible for crime and some part of the economic problems. Thus, it is not uncommon for the public to identify crime with "illegal immigrants."

The most important implication for criminology of this continuing conservative movement has been in the way criminals are viewed. The appreciative and sympathetic portrayal of criminals in the 1960s disappeared in favor of a view of the criminal as a rational being. A rational criminal, of course, chooses to commit crimes and is not particularly amenable to expensive rehabilitation programs. Thus, rehabilitation and other approaches are not necessary; punishing criminals by locking them up should be enough to make them think correctly. The expansion of research and literature on deterrence, just deserts, rational theories, and environmental design exemplifies the direction many criminologists chose prior to 1990. After 1990, rational thought remained in criminology but subsumed under self-concept, control-balance, and social learning theories.

A new thread, begun in corrections, seems to be making some headway. Initial concerns about the cost of building more and more prisons (and jails) led some states into looking for cheaper ways to handle the "rational" inmates. Thus, legislators hit on intervention programs designed either to help inmates think more rationally (i.e., like a conforming middle-class person) or to develop skills that would serve them once out of incarceration. The latest aspect of this movement is that the term "intervention" no longer has to be used as a proxy for rehabilitation. This means, among other things, that cognitive theories are becoming popular in treatment circles and that factors in adult life (rather than adolescence) are reentering theory.

Structural theories have made a return, albeit with only moderate levels of popularity. Those theories under the social disorganization and ecology framework (see Bursik, 1988; Bursik & Grasmick, 1993; Sampson, 2002; Sampson, Raudenbush, & Earls, 1997) are being pursued as neighborhood effects on crime and deviance are being considered. This is encouraged by (1) the popular framework of community-oriented policing, (2) a governmental embrace of the "broken windows" concept and (3) an understanding of the utility of environmental criminology to crime analysis.

Further, both gender-informed theories and new variations on conflict theories, particularly postmodern perspectives, demonstrate a greater degree of vitality than was the case in the 1980s. Nonetheless, given the current atmosphere, that rational choice and process-oriented theories are dominant. This means that criminological theory is now largely focusing on the various processes of how one becomes criminal. These processes, given a conservative framework, tend to emphasize traditional values and institutions: schools, family, friends, and work. Indeed, the most popular direction in new theories (self-control, for the past 20 years) focuses restraining natural impulsivity through the family and child-rearing practices. On the whole, social control theories and integrative theories incorporating social control ideas remain popular.

INTEGRATIVE THEORIES

Directions for Integrative Theories

At the same time an interest in new theorizing began expanding, other criminologists concerned with the state of existing mainstream theories began to search for ways to return to criminological truisms. The easiest way to accomplish this, some argued, was to begin the process of integrating theories. The two most popular theories of the 1970s and 1980s, social control and social learning, were among the first candidates for integration (see the epilogue to Chapter 11). Thus, Elliott, Ageton, & Canter (1979), Elliott, Huizinga, & Ageton (1985) and Edwards (1992) contributed a theory derived from social control, strain, and social learning perspectives (Edwards also added labeling to the mix). Others attempted integration of social learning with biological traits (Wilson & Herrnstein, 1985), biology with social control (Beaver, DeLisi, Vaughn, & Wright, 2010; Guo, Roettger, & Cai, 2008), conflict with subculture (Ferrell, 1999; Schwendinger & Schwendinger, 1985), strain, social control, and social learning (Bao, Haas, Chen, & Pi, 2012), and, perhaps the most popular integration, social control with deterrence (Paternoster, 1989; Stafford & Warr, 1993).

In addition, some theorists noted that theories do not necessarily compete with each other and advanced an argument that theories speak to varied levels of explanation (Short, 1985, 1989, 1998; Williams, 1984). Robert Merton (Cullen & Messner, 2007, pp 16–17) even thought that theoretical assumptions were rarely stringent enough to preclude integration. Thus, as long as assumptions are reasonably compatible, there is no need to cast out one theory to accept another. In fact, if most theories speak to different levels, then one task of criminology is to determine how theories might be organized into a coherent whole.

Not everyone is in favor of integration, and some theorists have claimed that the process of integration is doomed to failure. Travis Hirschi (1979), for example, argues that the assumptions of most major theories are fundamentally incompatible. Accordingly, he discourages integration and suggests instead that effort be put into the creation of new theory.

The way in which theories are integrated is also of interest. It is possible to put theories together in a sequential, straight-line fashion, referred to as an end-to-end model (Hirschi, 1979). In this model, a structural, macrolevel theory would precede a middle-level theory (bridging theory), and a microtheory might conclude the process. Thus, social structure might produce social disorganization (anomie theory), disorganization might affect the quality of general relationships of groups in urban areas (differential opportunity), and those relationships might result in inadequate child-rearing practices leading to greater levels of delinquency (low self-concept theory). Another approach is to borrow concepts from several theories without regard to either the assumptions or the general thrust of the theories. These concepts are then put together in a new fashion. This approach is called a fully integrated model. For example, one such model might put together gender roles, social disorganization, attachment to the family, and differential association. This tentative model might suggest that males and females react to social disorganization differently by relying more or less on the family for primary relationships. Social disorganization might push males to spend more time outside of the family, while females might react with greater family attachment. The associations thus built provide differential definitions for delinquent behavior, with males having proportionately higher numbers of delinquent definitions. We do not suggest that either of these two integrative examples is necessarily useful as a theory of delinquency, but they illustrate the difference between the two approaches.

Some of the theories discussed here are really integrations of two or more previous theories. Albert Cohen, and Richard Cloward and Lloyd Ohlin, for example, integrated Chicago School approaches with the anomie tradition. The subculture of violence theory proposed by Marvin Wolfgang and Franco Ferracuti attempted to synthesize most of the theoretical work of its day. More recent work has focused on combining the theories of social control and social learning or both of these with anomie theory. Even conflict and consensus versions of theory may prove to be more compatible than the field has thought. One of the obvious problems of integrating theories is the level of complexity generated and that is best exemplified by evolutionary ecology theory (Cohen & Machalek, 1988; Vila, 1994; Vila & Cohen, 1993), which is so complex that it is virtually impossible to test.

As has been the case in sociology, criminology has recently become concerned with metatheory. Metatheories tell us how to put unit theories together, or they specify the things that should be included in unit theories about a particular subject. As noted in Chapter 1, unit theories are explanations of specific phenomena; therefore, all of the theories we have discussed to this point are unit theories.

In general, metatheory is concerned with the organization of principles that can be used to make sense of theories. Metatheory is not directly testable and for that reason is rejected by some critics (e.g., Gibbs, 1989). It does, however, have its uses, particularly in the identification of levels of explanation of various theories (Short, 1989). Unless theoretical assumptions and points of focus are clearly identified, there is little to prevent improper tests and integration of those theories. Some theories, for instance, focus on either crime or criminal behavior, two rather different phenomena that are often treated as if they were identical.

Joan McCord (1989) is concerned that we may integrate theories without having appropriate criteria to measure their adequacy. Because integrative theorizing appears to be in vogue, McCord's concern may be valid. In one documentation of this trend, Steven Messner, Marvin Krohn, and Allan Liska (1989) published a collection of papers presented at a 1987 conference on theoretical integration. The authors of the various papers represent most of the major criminological theoreticians and they discuss microlevel, macrolevel, and cross-level integration. On the whole, there seems to be a consensus that there are too many problems for successful integration to take place (see, especially, the papers by Hirschi, Thornberry, Swigert, Gibbs, Meier, Short, and Giordano).

However, not all of the integrative theoretical enterprise originates when someone develops a conceptual perspective and brings several theories together. In fact, integrative theory frequently occurs in the process of research testing theories. A good example of the way in which such integration occurs is found in a recent research article by Holtfreter, Reisig, and Pratt (2008). Many theorists see a natural combination of lifestyle theory and low self-control (Schreck, Stewart, & Fisher, 2006) or routine activities theory and low self-control. By participating in routine activities, people are exposed to situations where someone with low self-control may be a more suitable target for victimization. Testing this idea, Holtfreter and colleagues found that those with low self-control, although no more likely to be targeted for consumer fraud than others, were more likely to ultimately end up victimized by it. In this study of 1,000 Florida residents surveyed by phone, the routine activities that were focused on were remote purchasing concepts like ordering products on the Internet, from a TV commercial, or from an unsolicited mailing, all common occurrences in our everyday life. Low self-control was measured by preferences for both high-risk behavior and immediate gratification. The researchers determined that the two theories combine well to explain consumer fraud risk, something further research might clarify in a broader range of consumer behaviors. Thus, an integrative theory was developed.

Based on the sheer numbers of research articles producing "integrative theory," such theories are clearly the dominant model in criminology. Unfortunately, while such theory is usually thoughtful, a careful and systematic construction of its theoretical elements tends to be missing. As a result, rather than refer to every research article that tweaks a theory or theories by adding a variable or two as integrative theory, we prefer to speak of integrative theories as those purposefully constructed. We briefly explore three illustrative examples of integrative theories here.

Crime and Social Context

One approach to integrative theory comes from Terance Miethe and Robert Meier (1994). Rather than line up a list of theories for integration, they look instead at the overall picture of crime. They argue that three base components exist in crime: the offender, the victim, and facilitating contexts (situations). Miethe and Meier bring these components together by using concepts from theories of rationally motivated offenders, routine activities perspectives related to victimization, and ecological concepts in order to structure social contexts. They achieve an integrative theory resembling a social disorganization perspective. A social context with low socioeconomic status, population mobility, ethnic heterogeneity, and family disruption facilitates both offender motivation and criminal opportunity. These factors influence youths' ties to conventional institutions of social control, the level of community supervision, and the ability to articulate and achieve communal goals. Thus, crime rates are primarily a function of a socially disorganized area's effect on social control and criminal opportunities. Such an area produces and brings together offenders and victims in the same time and space.

Control Balance Theory

Charles Tittle (1995, 2004) has developed a general theory of crime to compete with Gottfredson and Hirschi's version. Called control balance theory, it combines ideas from control and deterrence theories, some "propensity" theories, and subjective theories. Its major concept is that of "balancing" control—the amount of control people exercise as opposed to the amount of control to which they are subjected. Tittle refers to the amount of control from these two sources as the "control ratio." When there is a control imbalance, either a deficit or surplus, deviance is more likely to occur. Control deficits are more likely to lead to street crime; control surpluses are more likely to lead to white-collar crime.

Rather than pointing to the "causes" of crime, Tittle refers to the *probability* of deviance (or a specific form of it) occurring. The theory does not merely balance the two forms of control, however. Tittle recognizes the complexity of deviance and incorporates several other concepts: basic human impulses or preferences, desire for autonomy; predisposition toward deviant motivation; and feelings of debasement, situational risk, seriousness, and opportunity. A control balance usually indicates that a person will remain conforming. However, because control balance theory assumes that everyone wants more control in life, assessments will be made about the feasibility and potential effectiveness of the various ways of remediating one's perceived control imbalance. Thus, deviant behavior is designed to alter the individual's control ratio. A mere control imbalance, however, is not sufficient to produce deviance—a motivation-producing provocation is necessary.

Tittle categorizes deviance into two types, "autonomous," which involves no direct confrontation with others and is often committed through a third party, organization, or structural arrangement, and "repressive," which can be predatory, defiant, or submissive. Both of these crime types can be viewed along a continuum of seriousness that takes into consideration the amount of harm caused. In this perspective, examining only the form of deviance may not directly explain the deviant's motivation because the control-ratio motivation serves a specific purpose for the individual that may not otherwise be apparent. When the control ratio is unbalanced, counter-control (the control one is subjected to) is important in preventing deviance.

Tittle has recently revised the theory (2004) and included the concept of control balance desirability, which ranges over a continuum of more to less serious based on four components: the individual's control ratio and self-control, opportunity, and the potential for attracting outside countercontrol measures. Control balance desirability itself is composed of two elements: an act's probability of changing the individual's control imbalance and the necessity for direct, personal contact with a victim or object. Overall, the theory's components converge to produce deviant behaviors, but within predictable ranges of deviance.

Institutional Anomie Theory

A second contemporary adaptation of anomie or strain theory comes from Steven Messner and Richard Rosenfeld (2007; Messner, Thome, & Rosenfeld, 2008). Given the traditional Mertonian scheme—that stratification systems create strain and thereby yield anomic conditions—they argue that an entire level of noneconomic institutions has been omitted. A more rounded picture of structural constraints on deviance includes the contributions of such institutions as the family, schools, religion, and law. For anomie to work, not only is a disjunction of goals and means necessary, but social institutions must also be weakened. Messner and Rosenfeld posit that a disjunction affects these institutions in such a way as to contribute to a loss of control; that is, an anomic environment weakens the family's control over its members and thus its power to curtail deviant behavior. The theory obviously incorporates concepts from control theory and provides a bridge from cultural controls (old anomie/strain versions) to more personal levels of control.

Messner and Rosenfeld clarify and elaborate on the theory (Messner, 2012; Messner, Thome, & Rosenfeld, 2008) by further explaining what is meant by social institutions and incorporating both subjective and objective dimensions to those institutions. Social institutions are the product of norms, regulations, and rules derived from a common societal value system. Thus, economic systems, religion, families, and schools (to name a few institutions) are institutions because they espouse, and even enforce, those norms. Because social institutions help define means–goals relationships, they guide action by individuals, who in turn determine suitable means of reaching goals. Institutions do this largely through incorporating moral authority and incentives. When economic institutions are dominant in a society, the moral authority of other institutions is weakened and their ability to regulate behavior (social control) decreases and the potential for crime (particularly violence) increases. Individuals in such a society will react more strongly to economic control if their own internal controls are weak with regard to morality and will pursue actions, including violence, that are most expedient in the pursuit of their goals.

Thinking about Integrative Theory

Perhaps as much as anything, criminology needs to take stock of the theories it has already developed. The same variables have been used time and again to explain crime and delinquency, yet each time the claim was that a new theory was being developed, although not necessarily by the authors themselves. It may even be that we have enough theories and just need to determine exactly what they explain and the contexts in which they work best. At this point, it makes sense to begin to determine exactly how and where existing theories fit together, something we have tried to do in this book by classifying the theories as we have discussed them. Macrotheories obviously do not compete with microtheories. Structural theories may be compatible with and explain the society in which processual theories operate. Thus, a good starting point might be to integrate some of these theories.

There is also the strong possibility that mere integration of theoretical components may not be enough. The integration of critical aspects of the crime/criminal/victim/environment relationship may be required. This concept has been termed a "criminal event" (Sacco, Kennedy, & Plass, 1995; Williams, 1999) in order to get past the usual visualization of what a criminological theory might contain. Rather than focusing on explaining criminal/delinquent behavior, theories may need to incorporate a combination of what motivates the criminal (the usual criminological focus), what the environment contains, who the victim is and how he or she behaves, who reacts to the event, and perhaps even how law creation affects these other components. It doesn't seem to make sense to explain only one component of a criminal event in isolation. But, as we have already observed, such a conceptualization of what should be explained increases the complexity of the theoretical task and makes empirical testing even more difficult. When that happens, a theory seems to be acknowledged and then ignored.

POSTMODERN THEORIES

New alternatives to conventional theories are emerging under the general rubric of *postmodern theory*. Although the perspective is confusing, all postmodernism is primarily a reaction and alternative to "modernism," a term for the positivistic theories of the past century. Thus, "post"-modernism means that which comes after and succeeds positivistic approaches. In order to be an alternative to positivism, the perspective needs to reject the notion of objectivism (facts are independent of perspective), reject empiricism (facts are observable and measurable), and locate problems and issues in subjective and nonlinear causes. There appear to be three major postmodern directions: the use of linguistic theory (or semiotics), chaos-based theory, and cultural criminology.

Semiotic Theories

A semiotic theory (see Arrigo, 1996; Milovanovic, 1997a) trades primarily on the writings of Jacques Lacan (1981), a French psychoanalyst. This approach defines reality as the subjective way in which people understand the world about them. The "understanding" is primarily formed by the concepts and metaphors in language. For instance, one's role and place in society is structured by the language concepts of that society. Similarly, the reality of the criminal justice system is created by the metaphors and linguistic concepts essential to the workings of the criminal justice system. These theorists note that the created reality is such that those accused of crime are inherently disadvantaged in the legal process. This happens, for example, through the association of evil with crime, irrationality with criminality, and good with the prosecution. An appreciation of the subjective reality of legal structures and concepts adds to an understanding of crime, particularly the structuring of responses to crime. As has been the case with most critical theory, however, there seems to be little likelihood that mainstream criminology will see fit to incorporate these postmodern concepts.

Chaos Theories

The chaos-based form of postmodern theory (see Milovanovic, 1997b; Walker, 2007; Walters, 1999; Williams, 1999) is now almost 20 years old with some of the first commentary on the subject by T. R. Young (1991, 1992). On the whole, chaos theories offer a radically different view of the world, yet they do not have the intellectual and conceptual baggage of most radical/critical theory. As far as the traditional conflict/consensus debate goes, chaos theories are not inherently on one side or the other. Their foundation in the natural sciences lies in highly complex mathematical reasoning, although that has not necessarily been the approach taken by those in the social sciences who use chaos as a mode of understanding reality. As a result, there is the possibility of postmodern ideas being reflected within the existing positivist (modern) framework. Another name for the perspective, at least from physics and related fields, is complexity theory. The approach is currently being used in several social science fields and there are even journals devoted to its application within those fields (see Van Dijkum & Klandsheer [2000] for an example of a dynamic modeling analysis with delinquents).

The general idea is that highly complex systems are difficult to model in rather simplistic, but common, linear analyses and the interaction of hundreds (perhaps thousands) of variables makes static analysis (analyses that do not incorporate time and change) virtually worthless. Thus, chaotic systems are nonlinear, dynamic representations of reality (which is why the general approach is called complexity theory). In addition, there are no ideological positions that require variables from only one discipline (actually, multidisciplinary models are common). The main problem with such theories is that traditional analytical techniques are virtually worthless, making the approach a challenge to the dominant analytical paradigm. That problem, however, is being resolved with new approaches and techniques, particularly in the development of new forms of statistical analysis. Postmodern criminological varieties of chaos theory have largely ignored the mathematical base of the physical science version and, instead, reflect on the cultures, values, and social institutions that chaos-based social systems might yield.

Cultural Criminology

Theories under this general heading differ from most of the theories we discuss in this book in their emphasis on understanding the motives and intents of the people involved in committing crime and controlling crime. This perspective is often referred to as a phenomenological one, or a subjective approach to studying social phenomena. Rather than predict criminality or focus on differences in crime rates, subjective theories shun statistics and focus on describing the *essence* of behavior or why people do certain things. Cultural criminology has, thus far, been presented as a critical alternative to what these theorists refer to as administrative criminology and even to radical criminology itself (but see Spencer, 2011, for an argument that labeling theory is very similar).

Jeff Ferrell is (at least on the American side of the Atlantic) the person most closely associated with this new form of both theory and method in criminology. He helped develop a new cultural criminology (Ferrell, 1999; Ferrell, Hayward, Morrison, & Presdee, 2006; Ferrell, Hayward, & Young, 2008; Ferrell & Sanders, 1995) in which the focus is on the interaction of cultural and subcultural dynamics with crime and crime control. The meaning of crime as a constructed event is set in a contest between subcultural, social, and crime control interests and behaviors. Cultural criminologists see crime as situated in everyday events of subcultural expression and attempts by the crime control industry to contain those expressions. Crime itself is viewed as a swirl of emotion and meaning, as experienced by those enveloped by the event. The control of larger meanings (social perspectives) and the primary presentation of those meanings in a media-saturated society are primarily via the media. The responses of those presented as criminals are interpreted by the media, as are the responses of the crime-control industry.

The media use crime and crime control as a commodity to sell to consumers; thus, they have a strong interest in how the "story" of crime/control is presented. Ultimately, the result is the creation of images that are interpreted versions of previous images, which are themselves interpreted versions of images, and so on. Crime is, then, more of a constructed phenomenon than a real one. In short, cultural criminologists argue that there is no simple linear pattern of deterministic action and reaction as most positivist theories would have it. Thus, the real issue to be studied is the contested versions of the crime images: Who uses images to their advantage, who contests the images, and who manipulates the images? Crime, for cultural criminologists, is more of a defined issue than a real behavior or concept.

Seduction of Crime

A good example of a phenomenological exploration of meanings is found in *Seductions of Crime: Moral and Sensual Attractions in Doing Evil*, by Jack Katz (1988). Katz offers a critique of positivist criminology, largely by noting that many of the people predicted to commit crime do not actually do so. On the other hand, many of those who are not predicted to commit crime end up becoming criminals. In addition, he points out that the people predicted to become criminals often do not commit crimes for long periods of time, even though the background factors (social class, race, employment) remain the same. Katz's final critique, and the one most central to his theory, is that the standard background factors (the variables of anomie, differential association, etc.) cannot predict which individuals will engage in crime.

Katz's theory of violent crime revolves around the notion that the experiential foreground (what is happening at the moment) is crucial to the choice to engage in criminal action. Perhaps the term "choice" is not exactly correct here, because Katz really means that certain events and situations are "given" the power to seduce an individual into action. Different crimes have different forms of seduction, but they are all passionate, exciting, and relevant to the current personal identity of the offender. In a sense, crime is as Chicago School researcher Frederic Thrasher (1927) once described gang delinquency—it can be fun.

But the essence of violent forms of crime is more than just fun, in that the offender transcends normal life by becoming a "badass," or becoming tough, mean, and chaotic. By being unpredictable and chaotic, the robber establishes himself or herself as beyond the normal experience of victims and uses the threat of chaos to usurp the orderly lifestyle of victims. By being "alien," the badass generates a posture that transcends abnormal morality and demonstrates that he or she comes from a "morally alien place" (Katz, 1988, p. 88). In addition, the offender becomes "hard," thereby denying others' attempts at reestablishing control over the situation. Thus, the individual creates "an angle of moral superiority over the intended victim" (Katz, 1988, p. 169) and the system at large. Regarding murder, the killer is moved from the "eternally humiliating situation" to passionate rage and, finally, to a "righteous slaughter." Katz describes the humiliating situation as not simply a humiliation of the individual (the potential killer), but as an affront to his or her "eternal human value." Rage, then, is less unbridled than it is a focused effort to redeem oneself, generate power, and defend the eternal value. Thus, the term "righteous slaughter" is used to mean that the murder has been undertaken as a last stand to correct a wrong. Katz makes similar observations about shoplifting and youth gangs.

Katz's phenomenological perspective requires that one understand the situation from the view of the offender. Without this focus, the offense appears irrational. The problem is that Katz not only has to understand and appreciate these offenses from the perspective of the offender, but that he also has to assume the motives and intents of the offenders he has studied are essentially the same for other offenders. This is the problem of generalizability, and we do not know whether all, most, or only a few offenders share these meanings. The advantage of Katz's position is that it sensitizes criminologists to alternative meanings of deviance. Rationality from the point of view of the offender can be vastly different from the things that the observer (or victim) believes about the offender. Moreover, this perspective adds a spiritual flavor to the gains of crime: offenders attempt to construct their own worlds, at least temporarily. Because most criminologists prefer objective and deterministic perspectives, Katz's theory and the newer cultural criminology which it reflects has been severely critiqued. However, it reflects much of the postmodern mood of society and, in particular, a grounding of knowledge and truth in experiential settings and a rejection of scientific (modern) attempts to understand the world as falsely applied to humans.

CONCLUSIONS

This brief sampling of modern theories should give the reader a feeling for what is now being done in criminology. As may be seen, it took a merger of perspectives, disciplines, and even methodologies to generate this level of creativity. On the whole, these theories are more complex and true to life than previous theorizing. One of the by-products of such complexity is, unfortunately, that they are generally difficult to test. Some even require the development of new methodologies and statistical analyses in order to determine whether they are correct.

The theoretical periods that seemed to be demarcated by the 1970s may have simply been the end of a paradigm (Kuhn, 1970) and the beginning of a new one based on new methodologies and modes of analysis. Buoyed by new evidence produced by environmental design and victimization research of the 1980s, some criminologists began to conceive of criminals as rational individuals who made their own behavioral choices from a patchwork of opportunity. Others, informed by advances in feminist thought, used age-old evidence on male/female crime to create gender-based explanations of socialization, power, and lifestyle differentials as they affect criminality. Even the concept of crime itself has been questioned, and terrorism became a topic worthy of discussion (Akers & Silverman, 2004; Ruggiero, 2005; Savelsberg, 2006; Turk, 1989, 2004).[1] Finally, some attempted to find new ways to reconstruct the old versions of criminological theories and work on deterrence became more sophisticated (Matsueda, Kreager, & Huizinga, 2006; Matthews & Agnew, 2008; Ogilvie & Stewart, 2010; Piquero & Pogarsky, 2002; Stafford & Warr, 1993).

One new perspective seems to have grabbed some scholars relatively new to the criminological field. Tired of the orderly way in which mainstream theories relegated deviance to objective existence, Katz (1988) and Ferrell (1999) insist that crime is best understood as a subjective experience, a "seduction into evil" or a way of contesting the reality others would place on relatively powerless people. This is what we have previously referred to as postmodern theory or, in the case of Ferrell's approach, cultural criminology (see Ferrell, Hayward, & Young, 2008; Ferrell & Sanders, 1995). Perhaps because of a degree of antiscientific sentiment emerging among members of the public, it is possible that newer scholars will be more willing to shed the mantle of pure science that older scholars ascribe to. If this happens, or if at least some critical number of scholars argue against the reality of objective (and largely data-driven) evidence, then we may begin to see more subjective research with substantially different understandings (evidence) of deviance than the past 50 years of criminological theory has attempted to explain. Postmodern theory, if others can get past problems of interpreting its language, may emerge as a challenge to the conventional theoretical field.

If one counts the myriad of research-produced integrative theories, we now have a relatively large number of theories being proposed. While the forms and types of theory are diverse, it is also true that there are alternative dependent variables (Scheider & Florence, 2000). Theorists are busy explaining crime in general, victim events, and fear of crime. Variety is also evident from the number of "minitheories" proposing to explain singular forms of crime (from fraud to violence to serial murder to cybercrime to property crime). While all this has been going on, some criminologists (Akers, 1998; Gottfredson & Hirschi, 1990; Sampson & Laub, 1993; Tittle, 2004) are once again saying that general theory is possible and are busy explaining crime as an overall phenomenon.

---

[1] Terrorism is a difficult topic for criminological theory. Perhaps the largest problem is the fact that crime (and thereby terrorism) is politically defined; thus, terrorism, which is usually antigovernment activity, can be defined as whatever government doesn't like. Terrorists, then, are essentially those whose activity a government objects to. In short, no motivation is required for a designation of "terrorist" and so any theory which discusses motivation is at a loss. On the other hand, conflict-oriented theories do well in explaining terrorism because they posit essential differences in the interests of individuals, groups and governments and rely on power differentials to explain criminalization (in this case, terroristic activities). The other possibility we see is an attempt to explain terrorism solely in terms of willingness to use violent behavior to achieve ends, and this is possible through the use of social learning theory. For this reason, we do not include terrorism in our discussion of contemporary theories but instead refer readers to conflict theory or social learning theory. Other disciplines, including political science, are sources of theorizing on this topic and interested readers should examine their literature.

Theorists now appear to be entertaining new evidence on criminality while at the same time reconceptualizing and reassessing old evidence. However, the direction of theory appears to be set, at least for the next few years. Judging from the number of research studies and commentaries in the criminological literature, self-control, social learning, and developmental theories, appear to have "won" the battle for theoretical supremacy. We may yet have more complex and interdisciplinary theories on the horizon but it may require a suspension of the sociological domination of criminology coupled with the development of new methodologies to test complex theories.

What Does This Mean for Students of Criminology?

All these different theories, and the current attempts to integrate them, often leave students of criminology puzzled: How can there be so many different explanations of the same thing? One answer lies in the fact that crime is a very complex phenomenon. Even the determination of whether behavior is criminal is difficult. Further, if a criminal act occurs but we do not know it (no information on either the crime or the criminal—think about many forms of cybercrime), how can we begin to account for it in our theories? If a legislature passes a law that makes an act a crime, was the same act a criminal one before the passing of the law? This complexity means that scholars look at the reality of crime and see different things. In part what they see is a product of what they are prepared to see, and what they propose as an answer or cause is a product of what they are prepared to propose. In other instances, evidence is gathered based on what is possible to measure using certain types of research methodology and how it can be analyzed; thus, what we know and try to explain is at least partially governed by our research techniques.

A second answer is that theories attempt to explain different pieces of the crime puzzle. This is the level-of-explanation problem we discussed in Chapter 1. Some theories attempt to explain how rates of crime differ from one group to another, others deal with the making of laws, and still others try to account for individual propensities toward crime. One of the reasons for the classification schemes at the end of each chapter is to make readers aware of the varying foci of the theories.

Yet another reason for the number of theories is embedded in the assumptions we make about human nature and the way the world functions. If you believe that people are basically self-interested (as Travis Hirschi does), then deviance requires no real explanation and conformity needs explaining. On the other hand, if you believe that people are basically social creatures and conformity is natural (as Albert Cohen does), then conformity needs no explanation and deviance needs explaining. Other assumptions about the nature of society, whether crime largely belongs to the lower class, and whether gender is an important factor, lead to certain constructions of theory and not others.

The fact is that we will never all see the world the same way. Nevertheless, these theories of crime and delinquency are worth understanding. They help us see various facts about the crime problem and give us ammunition to create policy-related proposals to reduce crime. Without these theories, logical policies are much more difficult to produce, and there is the danger that atheoretical policies might cause unanticipated negative consequences. Most of our crime policies, of course, are a product of political expediency, and the danger of negative consequences is very real. Clearly, there are enough policy implications in the criminological theories we have discussed here to create a wide range of programs to suit almost any need. Through your acquaintance with these theories, perhaps you will be able to influence the direction of crime policy in your community.

Questions and Weblinks

Critical Thinking Questions

1. Katz argues that many forms of crime are seductively exciting. Can you think of current examples from the media that might support his argument?
2. Why is theory integration important for criminology today?

3. Do some people seem to have a propensity to commit crime? Why do some people seem to lack a "control balance"?

Practice Essay Questions

1. Describe what is meant by postmodern theory. Provide two examples discussed in this section.
2. What does Katz mean by the "seduction of crime"? How valid do you think his interpretations of behavior are?

3. Which theories seem to lend themselves to integration and what are the two ways used to model the integration process?

Related Websites

http://www.allaboutphilosophy.org/postmodernism.htm
http://blogs.kent.ac.uk/culturalcriminology/

http://empireofscrounge.blogspot.com/

Bibliography

Akers, R. L. (1998). *Social learning and social structure: A general theory of crime and deviance.* Boston: Northeastern University Press.

Akers, R. L., & Silverman, A. (2004). Toward a social learning model of violence and terrorism. In M. A. Zahn, H. H. Brownstein, & S. L. Jackson (Eds.), *Violence: From theory to research* (pp. 19–35). Cincinnati, OH: LexisNexis-Anderson.

Arrigo, B. (1996). The behavior of law and psychiatry: Rethinking knowledge construction and the guilty-but-mentally-ill verdict. *Criminal Justice and Behavior, 23,* 572–592.

Bao, W-N., Haas, A., Chen, X., & Pi, Y. (2012). Repeated strains, social control, social learning, and delinquency: Testing an integrated model of general strain theory in China. *Youth & Society, xx*(x), 1–23.

Beaver, K. M., DeLisi, M., Vaughn, M. G., & Wright, J. (2010). The intersection of genes and neuropsychological deficits in the prediction of adolescent delinquency and low self-control. *International Journal of Offender Therapy & Comparative Criminology, 54,* 22–42.

Black, D. (1983). Crime as social control. *American Sociological Review, 48,* 34–45.

Bursik, R. J., Jr. (1988). Social disorganization and theories of crime and delinquency: Problems and prospects. *Criminology, 26,* 519–551.

Bursik, R. J., Jr., & Grasmick, H. G. (1993). *Neighborhoods and crime: The dimensions of effective community control.* New York: Lexington.

Cohen, L. E., & Machalek, R. (1988). A general theory of expropriative crime: An evolutionary ecological approach. *American Journal of Sociology, 94,* 465–501.

Cullen, F. T., & Messner, S. F. (2007). The making of criminology revisited: An oral history of Merton's anomie paradigm. *Theoretical Criminology, 11,* 5–37.

Edwards, W. J. (1992). Predicting juvenile delinquency: A review of correlates and a confirmation by recent research based on an integrated theoretical model. *Justice Quarterly, 9,* 553–583.

Elliott, D. S., Ageton, S. S., & Canter, R. J. (1979). An integrated theoretical perspective on delinquent behavior. *Journal of Research in Crime & Delinquency, 16,* 3–27.

Elliott, D. S., Huizinga, D., & Ageton, S. S. (1985). *Explaining delinquency and drug use.* Beverly Hills, CA: Sage.

Ferrell, J. (1999). Cultural criminology. *Annual Review of Sociology, 25,* 395–418.

Ferrell, J., Hayward, K., & Young, J. (2008). *Cultural criminology: An invitation.* Thousand Oaks, CA: Sage.

Ferrell, J., Hayward, K., Morrison, W., & Presdee, M. (Eds.) (2006). *Cultural criminology unleashed.* London: Cavendish/Glasshouse.

Ferrell, J., & Sanders, C. R. (Eds.) (1995). *Cultural criminology.* Boston: Northeastern University Press.

Gibbs, J. P. (1989). Three perennial issues in the sociology of deviance. In S. F. Messner, M. D. Krohn, & A. E. Liska (Eds.), *Theoretical integration in the study of deviance and crime: Problems and prospects* (pp. 179–198). Albany, NY: State University of New York Press.

Gottfredson, M., & Hirschi, T. (1990). *A general theory of crime.* Stanford, CA: Stanford University Press.

Guo, G., Roettger, M. E., & Cai, T. (2008). The integration of genetic propensities into social-control models of delinquency and violence among male youths. *American Sociological Review, 73,* 543–568.

Hirschi, T. (1979). Separate and unequal is better. *Journal of Research in Crime & Delinquency, 16,* 34–38.

Holtfreter, K., Reisig, M., & Pratt, T. (2008). Low self-control, routine activities, and fraud victimization. *Criminology, 46*(1), 189–220.

Katz, J. (1988). *Seductions of crime: Moral and sensual attractions in doing evil.* New York: Basic Books.

Kuhn, T. (1970). *The structure of scientific revolutions* (2nd ed.). Chicago: University of Chicago Press.

Lacan, J. (1981). *The four fundamental concepts of psychoanalysis.* New York: Norton.

Matsueda, R. L., Kreager, D. A., & Huizinga, D. (2006). Deterring delinquents: A rational choice model of theft and violence. *American Sociological Review, 71,* 95–122.

Matthews, S. K., & Agnew, R. (2008). Extending deterrence theory: Do delinquent peers condition the relationship between perceptions of getting caught and offending? *Journal of Research in Crime & Delinquency, 45,* 91–118.

McCord, J. (1989). Theory, pseudotheory, and metatheory. *Advances in Criminological Theory, 1,* 127–145.

Messner, S. F. (2012). Morality, markets, and the ASC Presidential address to the American Society of Criminology. *Criminology, 50,* 5–25.

Messner, S. F., & Rosenfeld, R. (2007). *Crime and the American dream* (4th ed.). Belmont, CA: Wadsworth.

Messner, S. F., Krohn, M. D., & Liska, A. E. (Eds.). (1989). *Theoretical integration in the study of deviance and crime: Problems and prospects.* Albany, NY: State University of New York Press.

Messner, S. F., Thome, H., & Rosenfeld, R. (2008). Institutions, anomie, and violent crime: Clarifying and elaborating institutional-anomie theory. *International Journal of Conflict & Violence, 2,* 163–181.

Miethe, T., & Meier, R. F. (1994). *Crime and its social context: Toward an integrated theory of offenders, victims, and situations.* Albany, NY: State University of New York Press.

Milovanovic, D. (1997a). *Postmodern criminology.* New York: Garland.

Milovanovic, D. (Ed.) (1997b). *Chaos, criminology and social justice: The new orderly (dis)order.* Westport, CT: Praeger.

Ogilvie, J., & Stewart, A. (2010). The integration of rational choice and self-efficacy theories: A situational analysis of student misconduct. *Australian & New Zealand Journal of Criminology, 43,* 130–155.

Paternoster, R. (1989). Absolute and restrictive deterrence in a panel of youth: Explaining the onset, persistence/desistance, and frequency of delinquent offending. *Social Problems, 36,* 289–309.

Pepinsky, H. E., & Jesilow, P. (1985). *Myths that cause crime* (2nd ed.). Cabin John, MD: Seven Locks Press.

Piquero, A., & Pogarsky, G. (2002). Beyond Stafford and Warr's reconceptualization of deterrence: Personal & vicarious experiences, impulsivity, & offending behavior. *Journal of Research in Crime & Delinquency, 39,* 153–186.

Ruggiero, V. (2005). Political violence: A criminological analysis. In M. Natarajan (Ed.) *Introduction to international criminal justice* (pp. 35–41). NY: McGraw Hill.

Sacco, V. F., Kennedy, L., & Plass, P. (1995). *Criminal event: An introduction to criminology.* Belmont, CA: Wadsworth.

Sampson, R. J. (2002). Transcending tradition: New directions in community research, Chicago style. *Criminology, 40,* 213–230.

Sampson, R. J., & Laub, J. H. (1993). *Crime in the making: Pathways and turning points through life.* Cambridge, MA: Harvard University Press.

Sampson, R. J., Raudenbush, S. W., & Earls, F. (1997). Neighborhoods and violent crime: A multilevel study of collective efficacy. *Science, 277,* 918–924.

Savelsberg, J. (2006). Underused potentials for criminology: Applying the sociology of knowledge to terrorism. *Crime, Law & Social Change, 46*(1/2), 35–50.

Scheider, M. C., & Florence, J. M. (2000). Are we explaining different things? The failure to specify the dependent variable in criminology. *Deviant Behavior, 21,* 245–269.

Schreck, C., Stewart, E., & Fisher, B. (2006). Self-control, victimization, and their influence on risky lifestyles: A longitudinal analysis using panel data. *Journal of Quantitative Criminology, 22,* 319–340.

Schwendinger, H., & Schwendinger, J. S. (1985). *Adolescent subcultures and delinquency.* New York: Praeger.

Short, J. F., Jr. (1985). The level of explanation problem in criminology. In R. F. Meier (Ed.), *Theoretical methods in criminology* (pp. 51–72). Beverly Hills, CA: Sage.

Short, J. F., Jr. (1989). Exploring integration of theoretical levels of explanation: Notes on gang delinquency. In S. F. Messner, M. D. Krohn, & A. E. Liska (Eds.), *Theoretical integration in the study of deviance and crime: Problems and prospects* (pp. 243–259). Albany, NY: State University of New York Press.

Short, J. F., Jr. (1998). The level of explanation problem revisited: The American Society of Criminology 1997 Presidential Address. *Criminology, 36,* 3–36.

Spencer, D. (2011). Cultural criminology: An invitation… to what?. *Critical Criminology, 19*(3), 197–212.

Stafford M. C., & Warr, M. (1993). A reconceptualization of general and specific deterrence. *Journal of Research in Crime & Delinquency, 30,* 123–135.

Thrasher, F. M. (1927). *The gang.* Chicago, IL: University of Chicago Press.

Tittle, C. R. (1995). *Control balance: Toward a general theory of deviance.* Boulder, CO: Westview.

Tittle, C. R. (2004). Refining control balance theory. *Theoretical Criminology, 8,* 395–428.

Turk, A. T. (1989). Notes on criminology and terrorism. In W. S. Laufer, & F. Adler (Eds.), *Advances in criminological theory* (Vol. 1, pp. 17–29). New Brunswick, NJ: Transaction.

Turk, A. T. (2004). Sociology of terrorism. *Annual Review of Sociology, 30,* 271–286.

Van Dijkum, C., & Klandsheer, H. (2000). Experimenting with a nonlinear dynamic model of juvenile criminal behavior. *Simulation and Gaming,* 479–491.

Vila, B. J. (1994). A general paradigm for understanding criminal behavior: Extending evolutionary ecological theory. *Criminology, 32,* 311–359.

Vila, B. J., & Cohen, L. E. (1993). Crime as strategy: Testing an evolutionary ecological theory of expropriative crime. *American Journal of Sociology, 98,* 873–912.

Walker, J. T. (2007). Advancing science and research in criminal justice/criminology: Complex systems theory and non-linear analyses. *Justice Quarterly, 24,* 555–581.

Walters, G. D. (1999). Crime and chaos: Applying non-linear dynamic principles to problems in criminology. *International Journal of Offender Therapy and Comparative Criminology, 43,* 134–153.

Williams, F. P., III. (1984). The demise of the criminological imagination: A critique of recent criminology. *Justice Quarterly, 1,* 91–104.

Williams, F. P., III. (1999). *Imagining criminology: An alternative paradigm.* New York: Garland.

Wilson, J. Q., & Herrnstein, R. (1985). *Crime and human nature.* New York: Simon and Schuster.

Young, T. R. (1991). Chaos and crime: Nonlinear and fractal forms of crime. *Critical Criminologist, 3,* 3–4, 10–11, 13–14.

Young, T. R. (1992). Chaos theory and human agency. *Humanity and Society, 16,* 441–460.

Research Bibliography

Institutional Anomie Theory (from 2000)

Batton, C., & Jensen, G. (2002). Decommodification and homicide rates in the 20th-Century United States. *Homicide Studies, 6,* 6–38.

Baumer, E. P., & Gustafson, R. (2007). Social organization and instrumental crime: Assessing the empirical validity of classic and contemporary anomie theories. *Criminology, 45,* 617–663.

Bernburg, J. (2002). Anomie, social change and crime. A theoretical examination of institutional-anomie theory. *The British Journal of Criminology, 42,* 729–742.

Bjerregaard, B., & Cochran, J. K. (2008a). A cross-national test of institutional anomie theory: Does the strength of other social institutions mediate or moderate the effects of the economy on the rate of crime? *Western Criminology Review, 9*(1), 31–48.

Bjerregaard, B., & Cochran, J. K. (2008b). Want amid plenty: Developing and testing a cross-national measure of anomie. *International Journal of Conflict and Violence, 2,* 182–193.

Burkatzki, E. (2008). Is the market eroding moral norms? A micro-analytical validation of some ideas from anomie theory. *International Journal of Conflict and Violence, 2*(2), 268–287.

Cancino, J., Varano, S., Schafer, J. A., & Enriquez, R. (2007). An ecological assessment of property and violent crime rates across a Latino urban landscape: The role of social disorganization and institutional anomie theory. *Western Criminology Review, 8,* 69–87.

Cernkovich, S. A., Giordano, P. C., & Rudolph, J. L. (2000). Race, crime, and the American dream. *Journal of Research in Crime & Delinquency, 37,* 131–169.

Chamlin, M. B., & Cochran, J. K. (2007). An evaluation of the assumptions that underlie institutional anomie theory. *Theoretical Criminology, 11*(1), 39–61.

Frerichs, S, Münch, R., & Sander, M. (2008). Anomic crime in post-welfarist societies: Cult of the individual, integration patterns, and rates of violent crime. *International Journal of Conflict and Violence, 2,* 194–214.

Jensen, G. (2002). Institutional anomie and societal variations in crime: A critical appraisal. *International Journal of Sociology & Social Policy, 22*(7–8), 45–74.

Karstedt, S., & Farrall, S. (2006). The moral economy of everyday crime. *The British Journal of Criminology, 46,* 1011–1036.

Kim, S., & Pridemore, W. (2005a). Poverty, socioeconomic change, institutional anomie, and homicide. *Social Science Quarterly, 86,* 1377–1398.

Kim, S., & Pridemore, W. (2005b). Social change, institutional anomie and serious property crime in transitional Russia. *The British Journal of Criminology, 45,* 81–97.

Legge, S., Davidov, E., & Schmidt, P. (2008). Anomia: Empirical analyses of the level and development of the individual experience of anomie in the German population. *International Journal of Conflict and Violence, 2,* 248–267.

Maume, M. O., & Lee, M. R. (2003). Social institutions and violence: A sub-national test of institutional anomie theory. *Criminology, 41,* 1137–1172.

Muftic, L. (2006). Advancing institutional anomie theory: A microlevel examination connecting culture, institutions, and deviance. *International Journal of Offender Therapy and Comparative Criminology, 50,* 630–653.

Messner, S. F., Thome, H., & Rosenfeld, R. (2008). Institutions, anomie, and violent crime: Clarifying and elaborating institutional-anomie theory. *International Journal of Conflict & Violence, 2,* 163–181.

Sang-Weon, K., & Pridemore, W. (2005). Social change, institutional anomie, and serious property crime in transitional Russia. *British Journal of Criminology, 45,* 81–97.

Savolainen, J. (2000). Inequality, welfare state, and homicide: Further support for the institutional anomie theory. *Criminology, 38,* 1021–1042.

Schoepfer, A., & Piquero, N. (2006). Exploring white-collar crime and the American dream: A partial test of institutional anomie theory. *Journal of Criminal Justice, 34,* 227–235.

Stack, S., & Wasserman, I. (2007). Economic strain and suicide risk: A qualitative analysis. *Suicide & Life-Threatening Behavior, 37,* 103–112.

Stucky, T. D. (2003). Local politics and violent crime in U.S. cities. *Criminology, 41,* 1101–1136.

Stults, B. J., & Baumer, E. P. (2008). Assessing the relevance of anomie theory for explaining spatial variation in lethal criminal violence: An aggregate-level analysis of homicide within the United States. *International Journal of Conflict and Violence, 2,* 215–247.

Zhao, L. (2008). Anomie theory and crime in a transitional China (1978—). *International Criminal Justice Review, 18,* 137–157.

Control Balance Theory (from 2000)

Baron, S. W. (2010). Street youths' control imbalance and soft and hard drug use. *Journal of Criminal Justice, 38,* 903–912.

Delisi, M., & Hochstetler, A. (2002). An exploratory assessment of Tittle's control balance theory: Results from the National Youth Survey. *Criminal Justice Studies, 15,* 261–272.

Hickman, M. J., Piquero, A. R., Lawton, B. A., & Greene, J. R. (2001). Applying Tittle's control balance theory to police deviance. *Policing: An International Journal of Police Strategies & Management, 24,* 497–520.

Hickman, M., & Piquero, A. R. (2001). Exploring the relationship between gender, control ratios, and deviance. *Deviant Behavior, 22,* 323–351.

Piquero, A. R., & Hickman, M. (2003). Extending control balance theory to account for victimization. *Criminal Justice and Behavior, 30,* 282–301.

Piquero, A. R., MacIntosh, R., & Hickman, M. (2001). Applying Rasch modeling to the validity of a control balance scale. *Journal of Criminal Justice, 29,* 493–505.

Williams, K. S. (2008). Using Tittle's control balance theory to understand computer crime and deviance. *International Review of Law, Computers & Technology, 22*(1/2), 145–155.

INDEX

A

Aaltonen, M., 217
Abrahamsen, D., 33
Abril, J. C., 142
Ackerman, J., 159
Adams, M. S., 125
Adler, F., 7, 13, 148–149, 153, 156, 157, 235
Adolescent subcultures. *See* Subculture Theory
af Klinteberg, B., 44
Agerbo, E. E., 44
Ageton, S. S., 8, 13, 223, 233
Agha, S., 159
Agnew, R., 9, 12, 13, 86, 87, 89, 204, 205, 212, 213, 215, 231, 234
Aichhorn, A., 33, 40
Aigner, M., 43
Akers, R. L., 3, 4, 13, 72, 74, 171, 172, 177, 178, 182, 184, 186, 187, 188, 189, 207–208, 213, 231, 233
Akins, S., 188
Alarid, L. F., 75, 174, 188
Albanese, J. S., 202
Albonetti, C. A., 125, 148, 156
Aldarondo, E., 24
Alden, H., 189
Aleva, L., 44
Alexander, F., 33, 40
Allen, F. A., 31, 40
Alshalan, A., 202
Al-Talib, N. I., 125
Alvarez-Rivera, L. L., 189
Alvi, S., 202
Amato, P. R., 215
Ambah, F. S., 210, 213
Amster, R., 139, 140, 141
Anderson, J. F., 144
Anderson, A. L., 190, 233
Anderson, T., 156, 158
Andresen, M. A., 200
Anger, general strain theory, 204–205
Anomie theory
    aspirations, 86
    general strain theory, 86, 87
    goals, 87
    institutional strain theory, 87
    means, 86, 87
    modes of adaptation, 86
        conformity, 82, 83
        innovation, 82
        rebellion, 82, 83
        retreatism, 82, 83
        ritualism, 82
Anthropology, 29, 30, 48
Antonaccio, O., 26, 142, 202
Antonopoulos, G. A., 166, 172, 175
Anwar, S., 24

Applegate, B. K., 24
Aragones, A. A., 125
Aristocracy, 15–16
Armstrong, T., 215
Arneklev, B. J., 25, 120, 124
Arneklev, B.K., 208, 214
Arrigo, B., 158, 228, 233
Arsovska, J., 143
Asbridge, M., 202
Asencio, E. K., 125
Ashley-Montagu, M. F., 79, 80, 89
Åslund, C. C., 43
Atavism, 31
Attachment, 168
Austin, J., 122, 124
Austin, T., 80, 89, 128, 130, 139
Averdijk, M., 200, 202
Aversive stimuli, 179

B

Baay, P., 174
Bachman, R., 61
Bada, H., 44
Bailey, W. C., 24, 25
Baker, J. O., 215
Balkwell, J., 143
Ball, R. A., 86, 89, 92, 107, 111, 122, 124, 166, 172
Bandura, A., 39, 40, 180, 188
Bankston, C. L., III, 125
Bao, W-N., 188, 223, 233
Barak, G., 63
Barkataki, I., 44
Barker, E. D., 158
Barlow, D. E., 143
Barlow, M. H., 143
Barnes, H. E., 16, 23
Barnes, J. C., 107, 218
Baron, S. W., 75, 90, 215, 236
Bartollas, C., 167, 172
Bartusch, D. J., 62, 125
Baskin, D., 126
Batton, C., 235
Baumeister, R. F., 173, 214, 215
Baumer, E. P., 90, 215, 235, 236
Beauchaine, T. P., 44
Beauregard, E., 186, 188, 189, 200
Beaver, K. M., 37, 41, 43, 107, 188, 208, 213, 215, 216, 218, 223, 233
Beccaria, C., 14, 15, 17, 18–19, 23, 24
Beccaria, Cesare, 14, 15, 17, 18, 19
Beck, E. M., 144
Becker, G. S., 193, 198
Becker, H. S., 111, 112, 113, 114, 117, 124
Becker, R., 202
Becker, S., 158
Beckett, K., 143

Beichner, D., 159
Beirne, P., 7, 13, 18, 23
Belknap, J., 155, 157
Bellair, P. E., 62, 188
Belliston, L. M., 201, 218
Bell, J., 190
Bell, N. J., 219
Benda, B. B., 188, 216
Bendalak, Y., 201
Bender, K., 218
Benson, B., 24
Benson, M. L., 208, 213
Bentham, J., 14, 16, 17, 18, 19, 20, 23
Berdahi, T. A., 174
Berg, J., 201
Berk, R. A., 24, 26
Bernard, T. J., 29, 130, 142, 171, 173
Bernasco, W., 202
Bernburg, J. G., 62, 90, 107, 125, 126, 235
Beth, A. S., 144
Betts, S. C., 174
Beyers, J. M., 218
Bhai, A. S., 202
Bihrle, S., 44
Bijleveld, C. H., 44, 216
Binder, A., 122, 124
Biological theory
    anomaly, 31
    atavism, 31
    body types, 32
    born criminal, 30, 31
    brain, 30, 36, 37
    concordance, 33
    criminal personality, 37
    degeneracy, 30
    diet, 36
    epilepsy, 30
    evolution, 29
    evolutionary theories, 37
    feeblemindedness, 32, 36
    genetic studies, 32
    heredity, 32
    intelligence, 32, 36
    myelin, 37
    occasional criminal, 30
    phrenology, 30
    physiognomy, 30
    somatotypes, 32
    twin studies, 32, 33
Biosocial theory, 35, 36
Bird, H., 159
Birks, D., 24
Biswas, A., 45
Bjerregaard, B., 90, 235
Blackburn, A. G., 186, 188, 190
Black, D., 221, 233
Blackwell, B., 158

Blalock, H. M., Jr, 4, 13, 132, 141
Blankenship, M., 73, 74, 76, 175
Block, C. R., 158
Block, R., 202
Blokland, A. A. J., 158
Blomberg, T. G., 122, 124
Blumer, H., 51, 59
Blumstein, A., 24
Boardman, J. D., 43
Boba, R. L., 194, 199
Bobbess, L. N., 139, 141, 143
Bodapati, M., 144
Body types, 32
Boehnke, K., 107
Bohlander, E. W., 134, 142
Bohm, R. M., 134, 135, 141
Boies, J. L., 143
Boisvert, D., 216, 217
Bolland, J. M., 219
Bolton, A., 201
Boman, J. H., 189, 216
Bond, to the moral order. *See* Social
    control theory
Bonger, W. A., 128, 141
Boone, A. L., 215
Booth, J. A., 174, 216
Bordua, D. J., 94, 106
Borg, M., 189
Born criminal, 30, 31
Bossler, A. M., 189, 200
Botchkovar, E., 26
Bottcher, J., 151, 154, 156, 158, 189
Bottoms, A. E., 57, 59
Botvin, G. J., 219
Boudreaux, M. C., 200
Bouffard, J. A., 174, 202, 208, 214, 217
Bourgeoisie, 133, 134
Boutwell, B. B., 43
Bowen, N. K., 61
Bowers, K., 202
Braithwaite, J., 90, 103, 106, 120–121, 124,
    192, 199
Brame, R., 126, 216, 217, 219
Branje, S. S., 219
Brannigan, A., 216
Brantingham, P. J., 198, 199
Brantingham, P. L., 198, 199
Breault, K. D., 62
Brent, J., 25
Brezina, T., 125, 189, 215, 219
Briar, S., 166, 173
Bridging theories, 7, 95, 99, 224
Bright, C. L., 158
Brinson, T. E., 144
Britt, C. L., 213
Broidy, L. M., 205, 213, 214, 215, 218
Broken windows, 223
Bromley, R. D. F., 62
Bronner, A., 33, 42
Brook, D. W., 218
Brook, J. S., 218
Brownfield, D., 104, 125, 174, 189

Brown, G. L., 61
Brown, M. C., 143
Brownmiller, S., 153, 156
Brownsberger, W., 143
Brown, S. E., 80, 89, 104, 105, 106, 192, 199
Brownstein, H. H., 233
Brown, W. K., 125
Brubaker, S. J., 159
Brugman, G., 44
Brunet, J. R., 200
Bry, J., 202
Bry, R., 202
Bui, H. N., 61
Buist, K. L., 44
Bulmer, M., 48, 59
Bulten, E., 39, 41
Burchfield, K. B., 126
Burgess, E. W., 48, 49, 52, 59, 60, 97
Burgess, R. L., 72, 74, 178, 182, 188
Burkatzki, E., 235
Burke, P. J., 125
Burke, A. S., 158
Burkett, S. R., 24
Burks, B. E., 166, 173, 175
Burnett, K. F., 44
Burruss, G. W., 186, 188, 189
Bursik, R. J., Jr, 25, 57, 58, 59, 61, 120, 124,
    208, 214, 223, 233
Burt, C., 32, 41
Burton, V. S., Jr, 75, 174, 178, 205, 213, 215
Bushway, S. D., 218, 219
Butcher, K., 143
Button, T. M., 43
Buzawa, C. G., 24
Buzawa, E. S., 24
Buzzell, T., 166, 173, 175, 213, 216
Byrne, J., 60

C

Cai, T., 44, 223, 234
Caldas, S. J., 125
Campbell, A., 24
Cancino, J., 62, 235
Canela-Cacho, J. A., 24
Canino, G., 159
Canter, R. J., 148, 156, 223, 233
Cantillon, D., 61, 126
Cantor, D., 62
Cao, L., 90
Capable guardian, 194, 198
Capaldi, D. M., 190
Capece, M., 189
Capital punishment, 19, 22, 53, 139, 210
Caplan, J., 24
Capowich, G. E., 215
Carbonneau, R., 158
Cardone, C., 202
Carr, P., 12, 13
Caspi, A., 202, 218, 219
Cass, A. I., 200
Catalano, R. F., 218
Catell, P., 32, 41

Cauffman, E., 44, 218
Caulfiend, L., 45
Cechaviciute, I., 166, 173
Cecil, D. K., 158
Cernkovich, S., 149, 156, 174, 218, 235
Chambers, J. M., 62
Chambliss, W. B., 133, 141
Chambliss, W. J., 192, 199
Chamlin, M. B., 25, 143, 236
Chang, E., 217
Chan, H. C., 159, 174, 186, 188, 189, 200
Chapman, J. R., 152, 156
Chappell, A. T., 189
Chapple, C. L., 174, 216
Chauvin, C. D., 108
Chayet, E., 26
Chen, H-T., 125
Chen, J., 73, 75
Chen, X., 188, 223, 233
Chesney-Lind, M., 145, 147, 148, 150, 152,
    153, 156, 157
Cheung, N., 125, 208, 216
Cheung, Y., 125, 208, 215, 216, 218
Chicago School
    concentric zones, 49
    conduct norms, 53, 54, 55
    cultural transmission, 50, 51, 57
    culture conflict, 52–55
    definition of the situation, 52
    ecological theory, 57
    immigration, 47
    life history, 46, 48, 50
    symbolic interactionism, 51–52, 55, 57
Child-rearing practices, 206, 207, 223, 224
Childs, K. K., 189
Chin-Chih, C., 44
Chiricos, T. G., 143, 144, 202
Chivalry, 147–148, 152
Christensen, T., 175
Christiansen, K. O., 33, 35, 41, 42
Chui, W., 174
Chu, R., 220
Church, 15, 16, 17, 169
Church, I. T., 75
Church, W. T., 75
Cicourel, A. V., 113, 124
Clarke, R. V., 193, 195, 199
Clason, D. L., 217
Classical School
    capital punishment, 19, 22
    civil rights, 14, 18, 21
    determinate sentencing, 14
    deterrence. *See also* Deterrence
    due process, 14, 18, 19, 20, 21
    felicific calculus, 18
    free will, 14, 17, 20, 21
    hedonism, 16, 17
    human dignity, 17
    just deserts, 22
    law, 14, 15, 16, 17, 18, 20, 21
    punishment, 15, 17, 18, 19, 20, 21
    rationality, 14, 17, 18, 20

social contract, 16, 17, 18, 19, 21
  utilitarianism, 14, 16
Clear, T., 62, 124
Cleary, S., 208, 213
Cloward, R. A., 72, 86, 89, 91, 92, 96–99,
  100, 103, 105, 106, 181, 224
Cobbina, J. E., 107
Cochran, J. K., 90, 190, 215, 235, 236
Cohen, J. W., 107
Cohen, A. K., 72, 85, 86, 89, 91, 92, 93–95,
  100, 103, 104, 106, 107, 181, 224, 232
Cohen, L. E., 57, 61, 63, 193, 194, 199
Cohn, E. G., 26, 108, 202
Cohn, E. S., 217
Cohort, 203, 210
Collective solution, 94
Collins, D., 26
Collins, W., 44
Colvin, M., 135, 141, 201
Comasco, E. E., 43
Commitment, 101, 103, 139, 164, 166, 168,
  170, 171, 182, 210, 211
Community crime careers, 57
Concentric zone theory, 49
Conditioning, 39, 102, 181, 183
Conduct norms, 53, 54, 55
Conflict subculture, 98
Conflict theory
  anarchism, 133, 136, 137
  authority-subject relationship, 131
  bourgeoisie, 133, 134
  capitalism, 134
  class struggle, 133, 134, 138
  discrimination, 132, 138, 139
  false consciousness, 133
  family disorganization, 134, 135
  left realism, 133, 135–136
  legal images, 131
  living time, 131
  Marxist criminology, 133–134
  mode of production, 133–134
  pluralist, 127, 128, 129–132, 133, 137
  political economy, 134, 138, 139
  power, 127, 128, 129, 130, 131, 132, 133,
    134, 137, 138, 139
  power-control theory, 151
  proletariat, 133, 134
  resources, 129, 130, 133, 134, 135, 137,
    138, 139, 140
  social dynamite, 134, 135
  social junk, 134
  social reality, 131, 132
  surplus labor, 134, 135
  surplus value, 134, 135
  underclass, 154
  vested interests, 129, 139
Conformity, mode of adaptation, 82, 83
Conger, R. D., 126, 220
Connolly, J., 219
Consensus model, 100
Conservatism, 10, 161, 203, 204, 222
Constitutive criminology, 139

Containment, 163–164
Control balance theory, 226
Control theory. *See* Social control theory
Cook, S., 157
Copes, H., 75, 104, 107, 175
Corley, R. P., 43
Cornish, D. B., 193, 195, 196, 199
Corporate crime, 73, 152
Corsaro, N., 201
Cortes, J., 32, 33, 41
Corwyn, R. F., 188
Coser, L., 128, 141
Costa, C., 26, 162
Costello, B. J., 175
Cote, S., 12, 13
Covington, J., 63
CPTED. *See* Environmental Design
Craig, W. M., 219
Crank, J., 24
Crawford, C., 144
Crawford, L. A., 201
Cressey, D. R., 64, 67, 68, 70, 71, 72,
  73, 74, 75
Cressey, P. F., 47, 59
Cretacci, M. A., 174, 208, 213, 216
Crime analysis, 223
Criminal careers, 57, 68, 210
Criminal subculture, 98
Critical criminology, 139
Critical incident metatheory, 8
Cromwell, P., 175
Crosnoe, R., 75, 174, 218
Crosswhite, J. M., 175
Crowe, R. R., 33, 41
Cues, learning, 179, 181, 182, 183, 185
Cullen, F. T., 12, 13, 62, 75, 79, 80, 85, 86,
  89, 91, 92, 99, 106, 107, 111, 122,
  124, 174, 188, 200, 205, 208, 210,
  213, 214, 215, 217, 219, 224, 233
Cultural criminology, 139, 228, 229,
  230, 231
Cultural transmission, 50, 51, 57, 67
Culture conflict, 52–55, 66, 67, 68, 70,
  102, 109, 164
Curran, D., 12, 13, 148, 156
Curry, J. P., 148, 157
Curry, T. R., 159
Cuvelier, S. J., 201
Cynical deviant, 121

D

Dahrendorf, R., 128, 141
Daigle, L. E., 188, 200
Dalal, A. S., 73, 74
D'Alessio, S. J., 144
Dalgaard, O. S., 33, 41
Daly, K., 145, 148, 150, 152, 153, 156–157
Damphousse, K. R., 125
Danner, M., 152, 154, 157
D'Antonio-Del Rio, J. M., 108
Das, M., 44
Datesman, S., 152, 157

Daudistel, H. C., 143
Davenport, E., 25
Davey, J. D., 26
Davidov, E., 236
Davidson, W. S., II, 61
Davis, S. M., 159
Deane, G., 26, 144
Dean, K. K., 44
DeBaryshe, B. D., 209, 214
Debets, S. C., 107
Debro, J., 112, 113, 124
De Bruyn, E. J., 45
Decker, S. H., 24
Decriminalization, 16, 122, 123, 128
Defensible space
  territoriality, 57
Definition of the situation, 52
Deflem, M., 85, 89
DeFleur, M. L., 5, 13, 178, 188
DeFronzo, J., 61
de Goede, M., 44
Degree of integration, 97, 99
Deinstitutionalization, 122, 123
DeJong, C., 159
de Keijser, J. W., 107
de Kemp, R. T., 216
Dekeseredy, W. S., 135, 136, 141, 202
De Li, S., 174, 216
DeLisi, M., 43, 75, 188, 208, 213, 215, 216,
  218, 223, 233, 236
Delone, M., 143
Dembo, R., 215
Dennis, J. P., 158
Denq, F., 143
Deprivation, 86, 105, 136, 166, 180
Deregulation, 77, 79, 80
Desmond, S. A., 219
Deterrence. *See also* Classical School
  celerity, 17, 18
  certainty, 16, 17, 18
  death penalty, 1, 19, 21
  evidence of, 14, 18
  general, 17
  severity, 17, 18
  specific, 17
Dewees, M. A., 150, 157
Dietrick, D. C., 94, 107
Differential anticipation, 185
Differential association theory
  association, 64–73
  culture conflict, 52–55, 66, 67, 68, 70
  definitions for behavior, 53, 73
  differential social organization, 68,
    69, 70, 73
  excess of definitions, 69
  patterns of association, 70
  systematic criminal behavior, 68
Differential identification, 72, 102
Differential opportunity theory. *See*
  Subculture theory
Differential reinforcement, 180, 181,
  183, 185

Ding, F., 174, 208, 213, 216
Dingemans, P., 45
Dinitz, S., 163, 164, 173, 174
Discriminative stimuli, 179, 182, 184, 186, 187
Disjunction, 83, 86, 227
Dmitrieva, J., 44
Dobash, R. E., 153, 157
Dobash, R. P., 153, 157
Dodder, R. A., 174
Dodge, K. A., 219
Doherty, E. E., 174, 189, 216, 218
Dollard, J., 80, 89
Dölling, D., 24
Donovan, G. H., 200
Dornbusch, S. M., 75, 174
Dotter, D., 66, 74
Doucet, J. M., 108
Downs, W. R., 125
Drift, 161, 165, 193
Dubin, R., 86, 89
Due process, 14, 18, 19, 20, 21, 34, 122, 139
Duffield, D. W., 62
Dugdale, R. L., 32, 36, 41
Dunaway, R. G., 205, 213, 217
Dundes, L., 24
Dunford, F. W., 24, 122, 124
D'Unger, A. V., 154, 157
Dunlop, L. C., 218
Duration, of associations, 69
Durkheim, E., 48, 77, 78, 79, 89, 162, 163, 167, 173
Dwyer, S., 43

E

Eamon, M., 216
Earls, F., 62, 63, 223, 234
Eck, E. B., 202
Eck, J. E., 195, 199, 200, 201, 202
Ectomorph, 32
Edelman, B., 139, 141
Edgerton, R., 48, 59
Edmonds, W. A., 44
Edwards, W. J., 223, 233
Egley Jr., A., 220
Eher, R., 43
Ehrlich, I., 193, 199
Einat, T., 61
Eisner, M., 216
Eitle, D., 144, 215
Ekland-Olson, S., 25
Eklund, J. M., 44
Elffers, H., 202
Eliason, S. L., 200
Elifson, K. W., 217
Elis, L. A., 24
Elliott, A., 61
Elliott, D. S., 8, 13, 24, 61, 87, 89, 223, 233
Ellis, L., 33, 41
Ellwanger, S., 215
Elonheimo, H., 44
El-Sheikh, M., 43

Embry, R., 158
Empey, L. T., 105, 106, 122, 124, 160, 173
End-to-end integrative theory model, 224
Endomorph, 32
Engel, R. S., 108
Engels, R. E., 216
Eng, A. L., 201
Enlightenment, 17, 29
Ennis, L., 166, 173
Enriquez, R., 235
Ensminger, M. E., 189
Enter-Wright, B. R., 218
Entorf, H., 24
Environmental Design, 57, 58, 160, 180, 181, 186, 197, 198, 209, 223, 231
Erath, S., 43, 218
Erickson, K. G., 75, 174
Erickson, M. L., 105, 106
Esbensen, F.-A., 57, 59, 88, 89, 105, 106, 192, 199, 217
Estabrook, A., 32, 41
Estrada, F., 158
Eugenics, 29, 32
Evans, T. D., 205, 213, 215
Event, criminal, 1, 194, 197, 209, 227
Evolutionary ecology theory, 57, 224
Explanation, level of, 8, 87, 232
Exum, M., 202
Eyo, I. E., 174
Eysenck, H. J., 38, 41
Ezinga, M. J., 44, 216

F

Fagan, J., 68, 74
Farb, A., 219
Farrall, S., 236
Farrell, A., 174, 216
Farrell, G., 202
Farrell, R. A., 129, 141
Farrington, D. P., 210, 213, 219
Farris, R. E. L., 49, 59
Fazel, S., 43
Featherstone, R. A., 85, 89, 175
Feinman, C., 150, 152, 157
Feldman, R., 126
Fell, B. D., 189
Felson, M., 57, 193, 194, 195, 199, 208, 213
Female offenders. *See also* Gender theory
Feminist perspectives, 145, 152, 154, 155
Ferracuti, F., 102, 103, 107, 192, 224
Ferrell, J., 133, 136, 140, 141, 223, 229, 231, 233, 234
Ferri, E., 30, 31, 41
Finkenauer, C., 216
Finkenauer, J. O., 107
Fischer, C. S., 104, 106
Fishbein, D. H., 36, 41
Fisher, B. S., 200, 201, 202, 225, 234
Fiske, S. T., 144
Fleming, C. B., 218
Fletcher, R., 29, 41
Flora, S., 44

Florence, J. M., 231, 234
Focal concerns, 91, 100–102
Folkways, 48, 150
Fontaine, N., 158
Forde, D. R., 62
Ford, J. A., 218
Forrest, W., 189, 216
Foss, D., 208, 213, 216
Foster, H., 159, 175, 218
Fowler, S. K., 215
Fox, K. C., 159
Fraser, M. W., 61
Frazier, E. F., 51, 59
Freeman-Gallant, A., 220
Freeman, J. E., 26
Free will, 14, 17, 20, 21, 27, 30, 34, 193, 196, 197
Freilich, J. D., 143, 195, 197, 199, 201
French, M. T., 202
Freng, A., 144
Frequency, of associations, 69
Frerichs, S., 236
Frieburger, T. L., 158
Friedlander, K., 33, 41
Friedrichs, D. O., 208, 213
Fritsche, I., 175
Frottier, P., 43
Fruehwald, S. S., 43
Fuhua, Z., 175
Fully integrative theory model, 227

G

Gaarder, E., 155, 157
Gabbidon, S., 51, 60, 143
Gainey, R. R., 63, 201
Galliher, J., 66, 67, 74
Gangs, 31, 47, 91, 92, 93, 94, 96, 97, 98, 100, 101, 102, 104, 185, 230
Gannon-Rowley, T., 62
Garase, M., 205, 213
Gardiner, L., 43
Garfinkel, H., 114, 124
Garofalo, J., 193, 199, 206, 214
Garofalo, R., 30, 31, 40, 41
Gartin, P. R., 25, 26
Gastil, R. D., 104, 106
Gatti, F. M., 32, 33, 41
Gau, J. M., 188
Gault-Sherman, M., 220
Gauthier, D. K., 175
Gaylord, M. S., 66, 67, 74
Geis, G., 88, 89, 105, 106, 122, 124, 192, 199, 208, 213
Gelsthorpe, L., 158
Gender theory
    chivalry, 147–148
    economic marginalization, 150
    liberal feminism, 152–153
    liberation, 148–150
    Marxist feminism, 153–154
    paternalism, 147

radical feminism, 153
sexism, 148
socialist feminism, 154
General deterrence, 17
General strain theory, 86, 87, 204–205
General theory, of crime. *See* Low self-
control theory; Social control theory
Genes, 37, 211
Geographical criminology, 57
George, C., 207, 213
Gerber, J., 175, 217
Gertz, M. G., 25, 143, 144
Giacopassi, D., 202
Gibbons, D. C., 66, 74, 129, 141
Gibbs, J. P., 4, 9, 13, 224, 225, 234
Gibson, C. L., 43, 189, 216
Gilbert, E., 150, 157
Gilbertson, T. A., 195, 199
Gilliland, K., 195, 199, 200
Giordano, P. C., 72, 74, 149, 156, 174, 189,
210, 213, 218, 225, 235
Glaser, D., 72, 74, 185, 188
Glueck, E. T., 32, 41, 204, 209, 213
Glueck, S., 32, 41, 204, 209, 213
Gnagy, E. M., 45
Goals, 77, 78, 79, 80, 81, 82, 83, 84, 85, 86,
87, 94, 95, 96, 99, 101, 102, 103, 105,
145, 187, 204, 205, 210, 226, 227
Goddard, H. H., 32, 36, 41
Goffman, E., 115, 124
Gold, M., 3, 13
Goldweber, A., 44
Gomez-Fraguela, J. A., 217
Gongaware, T. B., 66, 74
Goode, E., 208, 213
Goodstein, L., 159
Gordon, D. M., 133, 141, 192, 199
Gordon, R. A., 36, 41
Goring, C. B., 32, 41
Gorton, J., 143
Goswami, S., 44
Goto, S. G., 189
Gottfredson, D. C., 61
Gottfredson, G. D., 61
Gottfredson, M. R., 163, 170, 171, 173,
193, 199, 205, 206, 207, 208, 209,
210, 212, 213, 214, 215, 217, 218,
226, 231
Gottfredson, S. D., 57, 61
Gould, L. C., 25
Gouldner, A. W., 9, 13
Gove, W. R., 113, 124
Graber, J. A., 219
Graeve, C. M., 216
Grann, M., 43
Grasmick, H. G., 25, 61, 120, 124, 208, 214,
217, 223, 233
Grauerholz, L., 61
Graves, J. B., 143
Gray-Ray, P., 125, 208, 214
Gray, T., 25
Great Depression, 47, 65, 79, 132

Great Society, 40, 105, 110, 161, 178
Greenberg, D. F., 128, 134, 141, 170, 173
Greene, H. T., 51, 60
Greene, J. R., 51, 236
Green, K. M., 189
Green, L., 26
Greenleaf, R. G., 143
Gremmel, W., 216
Griesinger, H., 26
Griffin, C., 125
Griffin, S., 153, 157
Griskevicius, V., 44
Groff, E. R., 200
Groholt, B., 45
Groves, B. W., 50, 60
Groves, W. B., 143
Gruhl, J., 148, 158
Grunden, L., 219
Guang, G., 44
Gudjonsson, G. H., 38, 41
Guerette, R. T., 25, 200, 202
Guerry, A. M., 30, 33, 41
Gulledge, L. M., 189
Gumbhir, V. K., 139, 141
Gunes, I., 174
Gunnison, E., 217, 218
Gunter, W. D., 75
Guo, G., 44, 223, 234
Gusfield, J., 121, 124
Gustafson, R., 215, 235
Gutierrez-Lobos, K. K., 43

H

Haapanen, R., 219
Haas, A., 188, 223, 233
Hackney, S., 104, 107
Hagan, J., 107, 125, 151, 157,
159, 218
Halfpenny, P., 29, 41
Hall, G. P., 43
Hamdani, A., 25
Hamilton, E. E., 25
Hamm, M. S., 103, 107
Hammond, J., 44
Hannon, L., 108
Hanson, R. K., 218
Harachi, T. W., 218
Harary, F., 86, 89
Harden, K., 44
Harred, J. L., 166, 173, 175
Harries, K. D., 61
Hathaway, S. R., 33, 41
Hawkins, D. F., 132, 141
Hawkins, J. D., 214
Hawley, A., 193, 199
Hay, C., 174, 189, 216
Hayes, H., 200
Hayes, R., 202
Haynes, S. H., 190
Haynie, D. L., 72, 74, 75, 150, 158, 189
Hayward, K., 229, 231, 234
Head Start Program, 40, 105, 139

Healy, W., 33, 40, 42
Heckert, A., 125
Heckert, D., 125
Hedonism, 16, 17, 38, 94
Hedonistic calculus, 20, 38, 187, 193
Heide, K. M., 159, 186, 188, 189, 200
Heidensohn, F., 75
Heimer, K., 62
Heintze, I., 202
Helenius, H., 44
Hennigan, K., 25
Henry, K. L., 220
Henry, S., 23, 32, 42
Hensley, C., 190, 208, 214
Henson, B., 200, 201
Hermann, D., 24
Herpertz-Dahlmann, B. B., 219
Herrnstein, R. J., 35, 36, 43, 223, 235
Herzog, S., 61
Hesseling, R. B. P., 62
Hessing, D., 201, 218
Hewitt, J. K., 43
Hewitt, P., 118, 124
Hickman, M., 236
Higgins, G. E., 75, 175, 186, 188, 189,
201, 216
Hindelang, M. J., 36, 42, 193, 195, 199,
206, 214
Hinduja, S., 166, 173, 175, 185, 188
Hinnant, J., 43, 218
Hipp, J. R., 139, 141, 143
Hirschfield, A., 202
Hirschi, T., 8, 13, 36, 42, 72, 84, 85, 89,
160, 161, 162, 163, 167–168, 170,
171, 173, 195, 199, 205, 206, 207,
208, 209, 212, 213, 214, 224, 225,
231, 232, 234
Hobbesian view, 169
Hochstetler, A., 75, 216, 236
Hodges, S. H., 176
Hoeve, M., 175
Hoffmann, J. P., 218
Hoge, D. R., 174
Holmes, M. D., 143, 144
Holtfreter, K., 200, 201, 225, 234
Holt, T. J., 74, 186, 188, 189, 200
Hong-Ning, F., 45
Hooten, E. A., 32, 42
Hope, T. L., 174
Hosch, H. M., 143
Hot spots, 57, 58, 194
Hough, J. M., 193, 199
Howard, G. J., 143
Howard, J., 16, 19, 24
Howell, J. C., 220
Hsieh, E., 217
Huebner, A. J., 174
Hughes, E. C., 112, 117, 124
Hughes, M., 62
Huizinga, D., 8, 13, 24, 57, 59, 61, 220,
223, 231, 233, 234
Hunter, A., 57, 60

Hussey, D., 201
Hussmann, J., 44
Hutchings, A., 200
Hutchings, B., 33, 35, 42
Hwang, H., 76
Hwang, S., 189

I

I-Chun Kuo, S., 44
Ilhong, Y., 44
Illegitimate opportunity structure, 84, 96, 99
Imitation, 39, 180, 183
Imitation theory, 39, 180, 183
Impulsiveness, 31
Incivility, 57
Ingram, J. R., 166, 173, 175
Ingram, A. L., 62
Innovation, 82, 111, 135
Institutional strain theory, 87
Integrative theory, 225, 227
Intensity, of associations, 72
Interactional theory, 211
Interest groups, 18, 129
Intravia, J., 216
Involvement, 84, 115, 168, 170, 171, 196, 205, 211, 222
Ireland, C. A., 39, 42
Ireland, J. L., 39, 42
Ireland, T. O., 220
Italian School. *See* Positive School

J

Jackson, A., 195, 199, 200
Jackson, D. B., 44
Jackson, S. L., 233
Jacobs, B. A., 25
Jacobs, D., 144
Jaggers, J. W., 75
Jamieson, K. M., 143
Jang, S. J., 219, 220
Janssens, J. M., 45
Jarjoura, G. R., 126
Jasinski, J. L., 201
Javis, J. P., 200
Jeffery, C. R., 14, 24, 35, 36, 42, 57, 60, 64, 72, 74, 177, 178, 180, 181, 184, 186, 188
Jeglum-Bartusch, D., 62
Jenkins, P., 19, 24
Jennings, W. G., 159, 189, 214, 219
Jeong, S., 216
Jesilow, P., 133, 142, 234
Jiang, D., 219
Jianhong, L., 107, 201
Jing, L., 44
Jinseong, C., 44
Job Corps, 40, 105
Johansson, P., 159
Johnson, B. R., 201, 218, 219
Johnson, M. C., 218
Johnson, R. J., 125

Johnson, S., 202
Jones, S., 190, 216, 217
Jones, T., 45, 136, 141
Joo, H., 201
Joo-Hee, J., 25
Jukes, 32
Junger, M., 201, 218

K

Kahan, D., 62
Kallikak family, 32
Kant, I., 16, 24
Kaplan, A., 29, 42
Kaplan, H. B., 125, 126
Karacki, L., 171, 173
Karlis, D., 26
Karstedt, S., 159, 236
Katz, G., 85, 89
Katz, J., 41, 229, 230, 231
Katz, R. S., 219
Kaufman, J. M., 76
Kaukinen, C., 147, 157
Keane, C., 217
Kelling, G. L., 57, 61
Kelly, S., 62
Kelly, W. R., 25
Kempf-Leonard, K., 159
Kennedy, L.W., 24, 62, 199, 200, 227, 234
Kennedy, T. D., 44
Kenney, J., 125
Kenny, D. T., 166, 173
Kent, S. L., 144
Kerbo, H. R., 76
Kerpelman, J. L., 159, 174, 175
Khoo, A. C. E., 166, 173
Kierkus, C. A., 201
Kieso, D., 139, 141
Kim, I., 24
Kim, S., 236
Kim, T. E., 189
Kinsey, K. A., 120, 124
Kirchgässner, G., 25
Kirkegaard-Sorensen, L., 35, 42
Kissner, J., 76, 207, 214, 217
Kitsuse, J. I., 94, 107, 113, 124
Kjelsberg, E., 45
Klandsheer, H., 228, 235
Klap, R., 24
Kleck, G., 144, 202
Klein, D., 146, 153, 157
Klein, M. W., 124
Klement, A., 25
Klette, H., 25
Knight, K., 220
Knutsson, J., 199, 200
Kobayashi, E., 76
Kobrin, S., 47, 57, 60, 93, 97, 98, 107
Kohfeld, C. W., 24
Konty, M., 90
Koons-Witt, B. A., 147, 150, 157, 158, 159
Koper, C. S., 25
Kornhauser, R. R., 13, 60, 89

Koski, C., 24
Kowlaski, G. S., 62
Kposowa, A. J., 62
Kramer, J., 147, 157
Krause, W., 155, 157
Kreager, D. A., 108, 175, 231, 234
Kress, J., 153, 157
Kretschmer, E., 32, 42
Kringlen, E., 33, 41
Krisberg, B., 122, 124
Kristiansson, M., 37, 43
Krohn, M. D., 43, 62, 125, 126, 143, 148, 157, 173, 187, 211, 215, 220, 225, 234, 235
Kroneberg, C., 202
Krull, C., 217
Kuhn, T., 5, 13, 231, 234
Kumari, V., 44
Kumar, R., 44
Kuntsche, E., 175
Kuo, S., 44, 201

L

Laak, J., 44
Labeling theory. *See also* Symbolic interactionism
   career deviant, 114
   criminogenesis, 115
   deviance amplification, 114
   grounded labeling, 121
   master status, 117–118
   retrospective interpretation, 117–118
   secondary deviance, 116–117, 118, 119
   self-concept, 114, 116, 117, 119
   stigma, 110, 115, 116, 117, 120
Lacan, J., 228, 234
LaCasse, L., 44
LaFree, G. D., 120, 124, 143
LaGasse, L. L., 44
LaGrange, T. C., 175, 217
Laird, J. L., 174
Lance, L. M., 189
Landau, S. F., 201
Landes, W., 198
Lane, J., 107
Lange, J., 32, 42
Lanier, M., 23, 42
Lanza-Kaduce, L., 143, 189
Laub, J. H., 47, 53, 57, 60, 93, 95, 97, 107, 173, 208, 209, 210, 212, 214, 219, 231, 234
Laufer, W., 7, 13, 235
Lauritsen, J., 144
Lavikainen, H., 217
Lawrence, R. G., 143
Lawton, B. A., 201, 236
Learning theory. *See* Social learning theory
Lee, D. R., 107
Lee, G., 159, 189
Lee, J., 219
Lee, L. J., 126, 143
Lee, M. R., 143, 202, 236

Lee, N., 62
Left realism, 133, 135–136
Legge, S., 236
Legitimate opportunity structure, 84, 96, 99
Leiber, M. J., 143, 159, 175
Lemert, E. M., 111, 116, 122, 124
Lencz, T., 44
Lening, Z., 201
Leonard, E., 29, 146, 157, 159
Leppert, J. J., 43
Lester, B. M., 44
Liberal feminism, 152–153
Liem, M., 174
Life-course theory
  persistent offenders, 210, 211
  social capital, 210
  trajectories, 209
  transitions, 209
  turning points, 210
Life history, 46, 48, 50, 66
Lifestyle, theory, 171, 193, 195, 225
Like-Haislip, T. Z., 107
Liljeberg, J., 44
Lilly, J. R., 86, 89, 107, 122, 124
Lindenberg, S., 175
Lintonen, T., 217
Liska, A., 62, 157, 173, 187, 225, 234, 235
Liu, B., 144
Liu, J., 62
Liu, R. X., 189
Liu, X., 126
Lizotte, A. J., 25, 43, 62, 126, 143, 211,
  215, 220
Lloyd, M., 54, 60
Lo, C. C., 189
Locke, J., 16, 24
Loeber, R., 218
Logie, R., 24
Lombroso, C., 27, 30, 42
Lombroso-Ferrero, G., 42
Lonardo, R. A., 174, 189
Long, J. R., 174
Longmore, M. A., 72, 74, 174, 189, 210, 213
Longshore, D., 217
Lopes, G., 62, 126
Lord, W. D., 200
Lott, J. R., Jr, 25
Lotz, R., 126
Loughran, T. A., 24
Lovegrove, P., 200
Lowenkamp, C. T., 62
Low self-control, 155, 163, 206, 207, 208,
  209, 225
Low self-control theory, 155, 207, 209
Lubeck, S. G., 105, 106
Luckenbill, D. F., 64, 75
Luengo, M. A., 217
Lutya, T., 201
Lynam, D., 217
Lynch, J. P., 62
Lynch, A. M., 143
Lynch, M. J., 143

Lynd, H. M., 80, 89
Lynd, R. S., 80, 89
Lynne-Landsman, S. D., 219
Lynskey, D. P., 217
Lyons, P. M., Jr, 158

M

Maahs, J., 7, 13, 37, 42, 215
MacDonald, J. M., 148, 157
Machalek, R., 224, 233
MacIntosh, R., 236
Mackenzie, S., 107
Mack, K. Y., 175
MacLean, B. D., 136, 141, 143
MacPhail, D. D., 39, 42
Madensen, T. D., 188
Maestro, M. T., 16, 17, 24
Maguire, B., 143
Mahoney, M., 186, 188, 189
Mailley, J., 202
Maimon, D., 202
Malakondaiah, M. M., 107
Maldonado-Molina, M. M., 159
Malesky, L. A., Jr, 166, 173
Mallicoat, S. L., 148, 157
Malone, P. S., 219
Malsch, M., 107
Maltz, M. D., 25
Manasse, M. E., 217
Mangold, G., 148, 157
Manning, W. D., 72, 74, 174, 189
Marcum, C. D., 175, 201
Margaryan, S., 217
Margolin, L., 126
Markert, J., 139, 141, 144
Markowitz, F. E., 62
Marongiu, P., 19, 24
Marsh, F. H., 41
Martinez, R., 143
Martin, R., 89, 90
Martin, S., 25
Maruna, S., 104, 107
Marvel, T. B., 25
Marxist criminology.*See* Conflict theory,
  Marxist criminology
Marxist feminism, 153–154
Mason, W. A., 217
Master status, 117–118
Matjasko, J., 219
Matsuda, K. N., 25
Matsueda, R. L., 62, 125, 126, 231, 234
Matthews, R. A., 76
Matthews, S. K., 231, 234
Matza, D., 46, 60, 104, 107, 119, 124, 161,
  164, 165, 167, 173, 193, 199
Maughan, D., 45
Maume, M. O., 202, 236
Maxson, C. L., 25
Mayhew, P. M., 193, 199
May, J. D., 215
Mazerolle, P., 205, 214, 215, 218, 219
McAra, L., 126

McBarnet, D., 126
McCartan, L. M., 217, 218
McCarthy, B., 69, 74, 159, 218
McCarthy, J. D., 174
McCluskey, J. D., 76
McCord, J., 225, 234
McCorkel, J. A., 158
McDowall, D., 25, 62
McEntire, R., 144
McGarrell, E. F., 159
McGloin, J. M., 37, 42, 108, 189, 200,
  202, 217
McKay, H. D., 48, 50, 51, 55, 57, 58, 60, 61,
  66, 67, 75, 79, 94, 142
McKenzie, R. D., 59
McNeil, R. J., III, 61
McQuillan, J. A., 174
McShane, M. D., 12, 13, 155, 157
McVie, S., 126
Mead, G. H., 52, 60, 66
Mead, H. K., 44, 111
Means.*See* Anomie theory
Meares, T., 62
Mears, D. P., 202
Mechanical solidarity, 77
Mednick, S. A., 33, 35, 41, 42
Meeker, J. W., 107
Meeks, J. W., 62
Meeus, W. W., 219
Mehlkop, G., 202
Meier, R. F., 13, 192, 199, 200, 225, 234, 235
Meldrum, R. C., 217, 218
Mellin, E. A., 45
Melossi, D., 121, 124, 135
Menard, S., 37, 42, 175, 217, 218
Mendes, S., 26
Mendez, V., 219
Mendle, J., 44
Meneses, R., 186, 188, 189
Merkens, H., 107
Merritt, R., 43
Mesomorph, 32
Messerschmidt, J., 7, 13, 151, 152, 154, 157
Messing, N., 217
Messner, S. F., 63, 79, 80, 85, 87, 89, 126,
  143, 150, 157, 158, 159, 173, 187,
  201, 215, 224, 225, 226, 227, 233,
  234, 235, 236
Metatheory, 6, 8, 9, 10, 224
Metzner, R., 32, 41
Michalowski, R. J., 134, 139, 142
Middle-class measuring rod, 94
Middleton, Z., 208, 213, 216
Miethe, T. D., 62, 225, 234
Miles-Doan, R., 62
Miller, H. V., 189
Miller, J. G., 123, 124
Miller, J M., 189, 216
Miller, K. S., 142
Miller, S., 219
Miller, W. B., 102, 107
Miller, W. J., 76

Milovanovic, D., 228, 234
Mingus, W., 126
Minke, L., 76
Mitchell, B. C., 144
MMPI (Minnesota Multiphasic Personality Inventory), 33
Mobilization for Youth, 96, 97, 105
Modeling, 39, 180, 183, 186, 211, 228
Modes, of adaptation, 82–83, 85, 86
Moe, A. M., 152, 157
Moffitt, T. E., 35, 42, 202, 210, 211, 214, 218, 219
Molina, B. G., 45
Monachesi, E. D., 33, 41
Monserud, M. A., 175
Montalbano, W., 149, 157
Montesquieu, C. L. De Secondat, 17, 24
Moody, C. E., 25
Moon, B., 76
Moore, E., 208, 213
Moore, L. D., 159
Moore, S. C., 45
Moran, R., 197, 199
Mordre, M., 45
Morenoff, J. D., 62
Moriarty, L. J., 62
Morris, A., 158
Morris, G. D., 217
Morrison, W., 229, 234
Morris, R. G., 175, 186, 188, 190
Morse, B. J., 37, 42
Mortensen, P. B., 44
Moses, E. R., 51, 60
Mosher, C., 188
Motivated offender, 194, 225
Motivation, 86, 101, 102, 121, 151, 154, 167, 195, 196, 206, 225, 226, 231
Moynihan, D. P., 105, 107
Mueller, G., 7, 13, 173
Muftic, L., 236
Mullins, C. W., 150, 157
Mulvey, E. P., 216
Münch, R., 236
Munoz, E., 144
Murphy, B., 118, 124
Murphy, D., 86, 89
Murphy, S., 26
Murray, C., 92, 107
Murray, J., 219
Murray, R. M., 44
Murty, K., 107
Mustaine, E. E., 197, 199, 201
Mustard, D. B., 25, 159
Mutchnick, R., 80, 89
Myer, A., 143
Myers, M., 144
Myhre, A., 45

N

Naffine, N., 150, 157
Nagin, D. S., 25
Nakhaie, M. R., 175, 217

Narayan, V. M., 44
Narr, K. L., 44
National Commission on the Causes and Prevention of Violence, 128
Natural rights, 21
Navarro, J. N., 201
Near group, 104
Nederlof, E., 45
Needham, B., 219
Neff, J., 190
Negative punishment, 179
Negative reinforcement, 179, 182
Negi, N. J., 158
Negriff, S., 219
Nelson-Kilger, S., 148, 157
Nelson, A. L., 62
Nelson, M. S., 217
Neoclassical, 192
Nettelbeck, T., 190
Nettler, G., 41, 55, 60
Neutralizations, 104, 161, 164, 165, 166, 168, 172, 183
Newman, G., 19, 24, 143
Newman, O., 57, 60
Nichols, T. R., 219
Niemelä, S., 44
Nieuwbeerta, P., 26, 158, 174, 201
Nijman, H., 39, 41
Nilsson, A., 158
Nilsson, K. K., 43
Nisbet, R. A., 11, 13
Noble, G., 126
Noble, R. L., 139, 142
Nofziger, S., 159
Nordquist, N. N., 43
Novak, K. B., 201
Nrop, K., 143
Nye, F. I., 3, 13, 111, 125, 161, 162, 173

O

Oakes, P. J., 166, 173
Oberwittler, D., 201
O'Connell, D., 25, 212, 214
Odgers, C. L., 159
O'Donnell, P., 190
Oei, K., 45
Official statistics, 5, 6, 65, 111, 113
Ogilvie, J., 231, 234
O'Grady, W., 202
Ohlin, L. E., 72, 86, 89, 91, 92, 96, 97, 98, 99, 100, 103, 105, 106, 107, 181, 224
Olsen, M., 77, 89
O'Maolchatha, A., 139, 142
O'Neill, L., 202
Operant learning
  conditioning, 39
  theory, 39, 179, 180
Opportunity, 1, 7, 47, 57, 65, 69, 84, 92, 96, 97, 98, 99, 100, 101, 105, 120, 129, 146, 150, 161, 167, 193, 194, 196, 206, 207, 224, 225, 226, 231

Opportunity structure, 84, 96, 98, 99, 100, 150
Orcutt, J. D., 113, 124, 186, 188, 190
Oreland, L. L., 43
Organic society, 78
Organized crime, 47, 68, 93, 98, 99, 149, 164
Ormel, J., 175
Osgood, D. W., 62, 189, 190
Ostrowsky, M., 215
Ousey, G. C., 108
Overbeek, G. J., 216, 219
Oxford, M. L., 218
Ozbay, O., 175
Ozcan, Y. Z., 175
Ozer, M., 108

P

Padavic, I., 159
Pager, D., 144
Palk, G. R., 26
Palloni, A., 125
Paradigm, 11, 93, 162, 193, 229, 231
Parker, K. F., 150, 157, 158
Parker, L., 25
Park, R. E., 48, 49, 52, 59, 60, 66
Park, S., 44
Parmelee, M., 30, 42
Parry, L., 190
Parsons, T., 80, 89, 93
Patchin, J., 215
Pate, A. M., 25
Paternalism, 147, 148, 152
Paternoster, R., 21, 24, 25, 126, 202, 205, 214, 217, 220, 223, 234
Patterned delinquent behavior, 38, 55, 84, 195
Patterson, G. R., 190, 209, 214
Paul, J., 176
Pauly, J., 135, 141
Pauwels, L., 217
Payne, A., 190
Payne, B. K., 201
Payne, G. L., 215
Peacemaking criminology, 139
Pearce, S., 190
Pearson, F. S., 8, 13
Pedi, S. J., 126
Peguero, A. A., 175, 201
Pelham, W. E., 45
Pepinsky, H. E., 133, 142, 221, 234
Pepler, D. J., 219
Peralta, R. L., 159
Peretti-Watel, P., 166, 173, 175
Perez, D. A., 143
Perkins, D. D., 62
Perone, D., 217
Petee, T. A., 62
Peterson, D., 217
Peterson, A. G., 108
Peterson, R. D., 25
Peterson, S., 24
Petrocelli, M., 144

Petrossian, G., 24
Petrovic, M., 159
Pevalin, D. J., 216
Pfau-Vicent, B. A., 174
Pfingst, L., 143
Pfohl, S. J., 105, 107
Philipson, J., 43
Phillipson, C., 209, 214
Phrenology, 30
Phythian, K., 217
Pickering, L., 201, 218
Piehl, A., 143
Piliavin, I., 166, 173
Pink collar crime, 150
Piquero, N., 73, 74, 76, 175, 202, 205, 214, 236
Piquero, A. R., 25, 144, 158, 159, 189, 208, 210, 214, 215, 216, 217, 218, 219, 231, 234, 236
Pi, Y., 188, 223, 233
Pizarro, J. M., 159, 201
Plass, P., 227, 234
Platt, T., 133, 134, 135, 142
Pluralism, conflict, 119
Pogarsky, G., 25, 220, 231, 234
Pogrebin, M. R., 62
Polier, G. G., 219
Polk, K., 207, 214
Pollock, J. M., 159
Pollock, W., 201
Poole, E. D., 62
Popp, A. M., 175, 201
Positive punishment, 179
Positive reinforcement, 179, 182
Positive School. *See also* Biological theory; Psychological theory
  determinism, 55
  natural crime, 31
Postmodern theory, 228, 231
Poverty, 36, 48, 86, 92, 96, 97, 105, 136, 150, 181, 209
Power-control theory, 151, 155
Power-threat, 132
Poynting, S., 126
Pratt, T. C., 37, 42, 62, 185, 188, 200, 201, 208, 214, 217, 218, 225, 234
Presdee, M., 229, 234
President's Commission on Law Enforcement and the Administration of Justice, 97
Prestemon, J. P., 200
Pridemore, W., 236
Primary conflict, 54
Primary deviance, 116
Priority, of associations, 69
Process theory, 8, 233
Proletariat, 133, 134
Propensity-event, 205
Psychoanalysis, 28
Psychological theory. *See also* Positive School
  emotional trauma, 33

extroversion, 38
feeblemindedness, 32, 36
insanity, 31
neuroticism, 38
pathology, 39
personality, 38–39
psychopathology, 37
psychoticism, 38
unconscious conflict, 33
Pullmann, M. M., 45
Punishment, 15, 17, 18, 19, 20, 21, 22, 34, 36, 39, 53, 73, 120, 123, 131, 139, 162, 166, 177, 178, 179, 182, 183, 185, 186, 187, 192, 197, 210, 222
Pure deviant, 113–114
Pyrooz, D. C., 76, 217

Q
Quetelet, A., 30, 33, 42
Quillian, L., 144
Quinney, R., 5, 13, 128, 131, 132, 133, 134, 135, 138, 142, 178, 182, 188, 192, 199

R
Rader, N. E., 190
Radical criminology, 135, 136, 139, 153, 229
Radical feminism, 153
Radical theory, 136
Radosh, P., 149, 152, 153, 154, 158
Rafter, N., 12, 13, 32, 34, 42
Raine, A., 37, 39, 42, 44
Rainey, R., 63
Ramirez, E., 24
Ramsey, E., 209, 214
Rankin, B., 61
Rasmussen, D. W., 24
Rational theory. *See also* Classical School
  cognitive theory, 191
  lifestyle, 195
  rationality, 195
  routine activities, 193–195
    guardians, 194
    motivated offenders, 194
    surveillance, 198
    targets, 194
Raudenbush, S. W., 62, 63, 223, 234
Ray, M. C., 125, 214
Reaction-formation, 94, 95, 96
Realist criminology, 135, 139
Rebellion, mode of adaptation, 82, 83
Rebellon, C. J., 76, 190, 217
Recidivism, 212
Reckdenwald, A., 150, 158
Reckless, W. C., 161, 163, 164, 173
Recreation, 58, 85, 168, 171
Reed, G. E., 208, 214
Reid, S. T., 7, 13
Reinarman, C., 68, 74
Reinforcement, 164, 177, 179, 180, 181, 182, 183, 184, 185
Reingle, J., 214
Reintegrative shaming, 120–121, 122

Reisig, M. D., 62, 200, 201, 225, 234
Reiss, A. J., Jr, 3, 13, 50, 53, 57, 58, 59, 60, 161, 163, 173
Relative deprivation, 86
Relin, D. O., 171, 173
Rengifo, A. F., 201
Ren, L., 90
Renzetti, C., 12, 13, 159
Restivo, E., 174
Restorative justice, 123, 139
Retreatism, mode of adaptation, 82, 83
Retreatist gangs, 82, 85, 97, 98, 99
Reynald, D. M., 202
Reynolds, A. J., 44
Reyns, B. W., 200, 201
Rhee, S., 43
Rhodes, A. L., 3, 13
Rice, S. K., 144, 174
Richards, M., 190
Rich, R. C., 62
Ricketts, M. L., 175, 186, 188, 189, 201, 216
Rickles, M., 159
Ritualism, mode of adaptation, 82
Ritzer, G., 157, 213, 214
Rivera, C. J., 125, 174, 208, 213, 216, 219
Roberts, J., 174
Robertson, C. T., 125
Robertson, J., 125
Robinson, M., 86, 89
Rocque, M., 37, 39, 42
Rodriguez, O., 150, 158
Rodriguez, S. F., 159
Roettger, M. E., 44, 223, 234
Rogan, D. P., 26
Romero, E., 190, 217
Rommes, E. M., 216
Roscigno, V. J., 188
Rose, D., 62, 120, 124
Rosemary, D. F., 62
Rosenfeld, R., 87, 89, 143, 226, 227, 234, 236
Rosenhan, D. L., 117, 124
Rossby, P., 44
Ross, C. E., 189
Ross, H. L., 25
Rothman, D., 28, 42
Rotton, J., 108, 202
Rouhana, N. N., 144
Routine activities, 193–195
Routine activity theory. *See* Rational theory
Rubenstone, E., 218
Rudolph, J. L., 174, 235
Ruggiero, V., 231, 234
Rupp, T., 24
Ryan, J. P., 175

S
Saar, N. S., 218
Sacco, V. F., 157, 199, 200, 227, 234
Salmi, V., 217
Salotti, S., 190
Samenow, S. E., 37, 38, 43, 192, 200
Sample, L., 159

Sampson, R. J., 50, 56, 57, 58, 60, 62, 63, 144, 173, 208, 209, 210, 212, 214, 219, 223, 231, 234
Sanchez, L., 159
Sander, M., 236
Sanders, C. R., 229, 231, 234
Sandstad, B., 45
Sang-Weon, K., 236
Santana, S. A., 25, 200, 202
Saridakis, G., 26
Satiation, 180
Saulters-Tubbs, C., 148, 158
Savelsberg, J., 231, 234
Savitz, L. D., 29, 42
Savolainen, J., 236
Scaramella, L. V., 126, 220
Scarpitti, F. R., 152, 157
Schafer, J. A., 235
Schafer, S., 30, 43
Scheff, T. J., 120, 124
Scheider, M. C., 231, 234
Schlapp, M. G., 32, 43
Schmidt, J., 26
Schmidt, N. M., 62, 126
Schmidt, P., 236
Schoepfer, A., 236
Scholte, R. J., 216
Schram, P. J., 150, 158
Schreck, C. J., 108, 201, 216, 225, 234
Schroeder, R. D., 210, 213
Schuerman, L., 57, 60
Schuessler, K., 66, 70, 75
Schulsinger, F., 33, 43
Schur, E. M., 117, 120, 123, 125
Schwabe, A. M., 186, 188, 190
Schwartz, J., 159
Schwartz, M. D., 141, 202, 208, 213
Schwartz, R. D., 115, 125
Schweitzer, J. H., 61
Schwendinger, H., 134, 142, 223, 234
Schwendinger, J., 134, 142, 223, 234
Scott, M. L., 202
Scull, A. T., 123, 125
Sealock, M. D., 205, 214, 215
Secret deviant, 114
Seductions of crime, 229
Seffrin, P. M., 210, 213
Seidman, R. B., 133, 141
Self-concept, 32, 33, 52, 114, 116, 117, 119, 164, 223, 224, 232
Self-control, 37, 163, 164, 171, 204, 205, 206, 207, 208, 209, 223, 225, 226
Self-control theory, 155, 171, 204, 205, 206, 207, 208, 209, 212
Self-interest, 19, 21, 38, 135, 167, 169, 170, 205, 207, 232
Self-report studies, 3, 5, 103, 104, 111, 148, 162, 169, 170, 192
Sellers, B. G., 159
Sellers, C., 4, 13, 186, 188, 190, 215
Sellin, T., 53, 60, 66, 75
Seward, R., 174

Sexism, 140, 147, 148, 153
Shaming. *See also* Labeling theory; Integrative theory
Shankaran, S., 44
Shannon, K. E., 44
Sharma, R., 73, 74
Shaw, C. R., 48, 49, 50, 51, 55, 57, 58, 60, 61, 63, 66, 75, 79, 93
Shelden, A., 24
Shelden, R. G., 148, 156
Sheldon, W. H., 32, 43
Sherman, L. W., 26, 125, 126
Shermer, L., 217
Sheu, C., 201
Shihadeh, E. S., 63
Shih, J. C., 44
Shockley, W., 36, 43
Short, J. F., Jr, 13, 48, 60, 61, 104, 106, 111, 125, 166, 173, 224, 225, 235
Sibley, M. H., 45
Siennick, S. E., 126
Silva, P. A., 218, 219
Silver, E., 63
Silverman, R. A., 62, 175, 217
Simon, R. J., 149, 158
Simons, R. L., 126, 220
Simpson, J. A., 44
Simpson, S. S., 24, 25, 152, 158, 202
Sims, R., 175
Singer, S. D., 190
Sitren, A. H., 26
Situational crime prevention, 52
Skolnick, J. H., 115, 125
Smart, C., 153, 158
Smith-Adcock, S., 159, 174
Smith, B. L., 144
Smith, B. W., 144
Smith, C. A., 63, 215, 220
Smith, C. L., 188
Smith, E. H., 32, 43
Smith, M., 144
Smith, P. T., 26
Smith, S., 202
Snipes, J. B., 129, 142
Snodgrass, J., 66, 75
Sobolewski, J. M., 215
Sobral, J., 217
Socia, K. M., 26
Social contract, 16, 17, 18, 19, 21
Social control theory. *See also* Self-control theory
  bonds, elements of the, 168–169
    attachment, 168
    belief, 168
    commitment, 168
    involvement, 168
  boundary maintenance, 162
  child-rearing practices, 206
  containment, 163
  drift, 161, 165
  moral order, 165, 169
  propensity-event, 205

self-concept, 164
self-control, 163, 164, 204, 205
stakes in conformity, 171
Social disorganization. *See also* Chicago School
Social dynamite, 134
Social ecology, 233
Socialist feminism, 152, 154
Socialization, 36, 37, 102, 134, 161, 163, 170, 181, 187, 206, 231
Social junk, 134
Social learning theory
  behavior modification, 178, 186, 187
  cues, 179, 181, 182, 183, 185
  deprivation, 180
  differential reinforcement, 180–181, 183, 185
  discriminative stimuli, 179, 182, 184, 186, 187
  imitation, 180, 183
  modeling, 180, 183, 186
  neutralizing definitions, 182
  reinforcement, 179, 180, 181, 182, 183, 184, 185
  satiation, 180
  schedule of consequences, 179
Social reality of crime. *See also* Conflict theory
Social statistics. *See also* Chicago School
Social structure, 2, 5, 7, 8, 9, 33, 58, 79, 80, 81, 83, 84, 86, 87, 93, 94, 95, 119, 134, 137, 138, 152, 169, 182, 185, 186, 195, 196, 197, 224
Societal reaction theory.*See* Labeling theory
Societal reaction. *See also* Labeling theory; Symbolic interactionism
Society of saints, 162
Sociobiology, 160, 180, 181
Soft free will, 193, 196
Solomon, E. P., 159
Somatotypes, 32
Sommers, I., 126
Sorokin, P. A., 80, 89
Sourander, A., 44
Southernness hypothesis, 104
Spano, R., 195, 197, 199, 201, 219
Spears, J. W., 159
Specific deterrence, 17
Spencer, D., 229, 235
Spengler, H., 26
Spitzer, S., 33, 34, 142, 192, 199
Spohn, C., 148, 158, 159
Spoth, R., 220
Stack, S., 26, 35, 42, 63, 236
Staff, J., 108, 219
Stafford, M. C., 25, 26, 223, 231, 234, 235
Stallings, M. C., 43
Stark, R., 57, 61
State-organized crime, 47, 68, 93, 98, 149, 164

Status-frustration, 94, 95
Steele, J. L., 159
Steffensmeier, D. J., 63, 150, 158, 159
Steffensmeier, R. H., 149, 158
Steinberg, L., 44
Stein, R. E., 201
Stengel, K. M., 201
Stenius, V., 200
Sterk, C., 217
Stern, S. B., 63
Stevens, H. H., 44
Stewart, A., 24, 231, 234
Stewart, E. A., 108, 126, 217, 220, 225, 234
Stigma, 110, 122
Stiles, B. L., 126
Stitt, G., 202
Stolzenberg, L., 61, 144
Strain, 8, 9, 84, 87, 95, 99, 204
Strain theory.*See* Anomie theory
Strodtbeck, F. L., 166, 173
Structural-functionalism.*See* Anomie theory
Structural theory, 9, 84, 95, 204
Stucky, T. D., 236
Stults, B. J., 90, 144, 174, 236
Sturman, A., 193, 199
Subculture theory
    collective solution, 94
    delinquent subculture, 9, 92, 93, 94, 95,
        96, 97, 98, 99, 102, 103, 104
    differential opportunity, 7, 57, 84, 92, 96,
        99, 105, 129, 224
        conflict subculture, 98
        criminal subculture, 98
        integrated community, 93, 98
        retreatist subculture, 98
    focal concerns, 100–102
    middle-class measuring rod, 94
    neutralizations, 104
    parent subculture, 104
    reaction-formation, 94, 95, 96
    status-frustration, 94, 95
    subterranean values, 104, 165
Subculture of violence, 91, 102, 103, 104, 224
Suitable target, 194, 225
Sullivan, C. J., 189, 190, 217
Sung Joon, J., 190
Sung, S., 44
Sung-suk Violet, Y., 201
Sun, I. Y., 63
Surplus population, 135
Susman, E., 219
Su, S. S., 205, 214
Sutherland, E. H., 51, 53, 61, 64, 65, 66–67,
        68, 69–70, 71, 72, 74, 75, 79, 92, 93,
        94, 97, 116, 164, 165, 180, 182
Svensson, R., 201, 217
Swigert, V. L., 129, 141, 225
Sykes, G. M., 104, 107, 129, 142, 161, 164,
        165, 166, 167, 173
Symbolic interactionism.*See* Chicago
        School; Labeling theory
Symons, F. J., 44

T
Tabar, P., 126
Tangne, J. P., 215
Tannenbaum, F., 111, 112, 125
Tapia, M., 126
Tarde, G., 33, 43
Tarr, D. B., 108
Tauchen, H., 26
Tavares, A., 26
Taylor, J. K., 75
Taylor, M., 144
Taylor, P., 44
Taylor, R. B., 57, 61, 62, 63, 75
Techniques of neutralization.*See* Social
        control theory
Teevan, J., 157
Teilman, K. S., 124
Terrill, W., 144
Teske, R., 159
Testa, M. F., 175
Tewksbury, R., 75, 197, 199, 201, 216
Theory
    bridging theory, 7, 95, 99, 224
    conceptual absorption, 186
    conflict-oriented, 128, 151, 155, 231
    consensus-oriented, 99, 119, 137,
        184, 196
    integrated, 122, 150, 171, 211
    intellectual context, 10, 11, 12
    interdisciplinary, 36, 232
    levels of explanation, 8
    logical soundness, 4, 5, 6
    macrotheory, 7, 55, 84, 95, 136, 137
    metatheory, 6, 8, 9, 10, 224
    microtheory, 7, 70, 95, 119, 136, 184, 224
    popularity, 204
    sensitizing ability, 5
    social context, 9–10, 225
    unit theory, 6
Thomas, C. J., 62
Thomas, J., 142
Thomas, O., 126
Thomas, W. I., 48, 61
Thome, H., 226, 227, 234, 236
Thompson, K., 41, 125, 174, 189
Thompson, M., 159
Thompson, P. M., 44
Thompson, W. E., 173, 174, 175
Thomson, E., 26
Thorlindsson, T. T., 107, 200
Thornberry, T. P., 211, 214, 215, 219,
        220, 225
Thrasher, F. M., 230, 235
Thurman, Q., 175
Tibbetts, S., 73, 74, 76, 175, 216
Tienda, M., 63
Tifft, L. L., 133, 136, 142, 192, 199
Tilley, N., 202
Tillyer, M., 195, 199, 201, 202
Tinga, F., 175
Tita, G. E., 139, 141, 143

Tittle, C., 26, 37, 43, 58, 61, 103, 107, 142,
        207, 208, 214, 215, 226, 231, 235
Tobin, K., 211, 215
Toby, J., 166, 171, 173
Toga, A. W., 44
Tolnay, S. E., 26, 144
Tonry, M., 59, 60, 61
Topalli, V., 166, 173, 176
Townsley, M., 24
Toy, C., 63
Traub, S. H., 26
Tremblay, R. E., 158, 219
Trickett, P., 219
Triplett, R. A., 63, 126
Trivizas, E., 26
Tseloni, A., 26, 143, 202
T'Sjoen, G., 76
Tung, Y-K., 208, 214
Tunnell, K. D., 26, 196, 199
Turk, A. T., 128, 130, 131, 139, 142, 143,
        231, 235
Turner, M. G., 217, 218
Turner, R. J., 215

U
Uggen, C., 219
Ulmer, J. T., 76, 147, 157, 219
Ulsperger, J. S., 176
Uludag, S., 201
Urbanization, 47, 56, 92
Utilitarian, 135

V
Valier, C., 47, 61
Van Dam, C., 45
van der Ham. A., 45
van der Staak, C., 39, 41
van der Werff, C., 158
Vanderwood, P. J., 126
Van Dijkum, C., 228, 235
Vandiver, D. M., 159
Vandiver, M., 202
Van Gundy, K. T., 217
van Leuven, M., 44
van Os, R., 158
van San, M., 176
Varano, S. P., 174, 216, 235
Vaske, J., 216
Vasquez, B. E., 62, 126
Vaughn, M. G., 43, 208, 213, 215, 218,
        223, 233
Vaughn, M. S., 143
Vazonyi, A., 218
Veenstra, R., 175
Velez, M. B., 63, 188
Veneziano, C., 26
Veneziano, L., 26, 195, 199, 200
Verduyn, P., 143
Vermeersch, H., 76
Vermulst, A. A., 216
Verrill, S., 186, 188, 190
Veysey, B. M., 63

Victimization statistics, 192, 193
Victims, 32, 39, 83, 113, 118, 136, 145, 155, 192, 194, 195, 197, 198, 208, 226, 230
Vila, B. J., 61, 63, 224, 235
Villemez, W. J., 103, 107
Vincke, J. J., 76
Virginia Bill of Rights, 20
Visher, C. A., 25, 148, 158
Vitaro, F., 158
Vito, G., 7, 13
Vloet, T. D., 219
Vocabulary of motives, 72
Vohs, K. D., 173, 214
Vold, G. B., 66, 75, 127, 129, 130, 142
Voss, H., 87, 89
Vowell, P., 73, 75

W

Wade, T. J., 216
Wadsworth, T., 175
Waggoner, M., 32, 43
Wagner, D. G., 6, 13
Wahlund, K., 37, 43
Waite, D., 190
Wai Ting Cheung, N., 208, 215, 218
Waldner, L. K., 201
Waldorf, D., 26
Walker, J. T., 63, 228, 235
Wallace, L. H., 215
Walsh, A., 37, 43, 44, 126
Walsh, E. E., 44
Walters, G. D., 38, 43, 190, 191, 199, 228, 235
Wandersman, A., 62
Wang, S., 190
Ward, D. A., 24, 37, 43, 217
Ward, J. T., 220
Ward, S. K., 158
Wareham, J., 215
Waring, E., 26
Warner, B. D., 63, 143, 215
Warr, M., 223, 231, 235
Waschbusch, D. A., 45
Wasserman, I., 236
Watling, C. N., 26
Watson, W., 219
Weerman, F. M., 44, 175, 216, 217, 218
Weidner, R., 144

Weiner, N. A., 8, 13
Weisburd, D., 26
Weisheit, R. A., 63
Weitzer, R., 144
Welch, K., 143
Welch, S., 148, 158
Wellford, C. F., 110, 125
Wells, E. L., 63
Welsh, B. C., 37, 39, 42, 219
Welte, J. W., 219
Westenberg, P. M., 44, 216
Western, B., 24
Whaley, R. B., 150, 158
Wharton, T., 75
White-collar crime, 65, 73, 140, 149, 150, 170, 205, 226
Whiteford, S. W., 174
Whitehead, J. T., 192, 200
White, H. R., 205, 213
White, N. A., 214
White, T. W., 38, 49, 191, 199
Whyte, W. F., 47, 61
Widom, C., 44
Wiebe, R. P., 218
Wieczorek, W. F., 219
Wiersema, B., 25
Wiersma, E., 26
Wiesner, M., 190
Wikström, P. H., 26
Wilcox, P., 200, 202, 214, 217
Wildeman, J., 138, 142
Wiles, P., 57, 59
Wilkins, L. T., 114, 125
Wilkinson, D., 45
Williams, J. J., 144
Williams, J. M., 218
Williams, K. S., 236
Williams, N., 210, 215, 219
Williams, F. P., III, 7, 10, 13, 132, 142, 162, 173, 192, 200, 224, 227, 235
Wilson, C., 190
Wilson, J. Q., 35, 36, 43, 57, 61, 192, 200, 223, 235
Wilson, A. L., 189
Wilson, W. J., 61
Wimer, C., 219
Windle, M., 217
Windlin, B., 175

Winfree, L. T., Jr, 217
Winterdyk, J. A., 166, 172, 175
Wirth, L., 52, 53, 60, 61, 66, 75
Wittebrood, K., 26, 201
Witte, A. D., 26
Wodarski, J., 126
Wolf, A., 126
Wolfe, S. E., 175
Wolfgang, M. E., 74, 91, 92, 102, 103, 107, 224
Women's liberation, 146, 149, 152, 153
Wonders, N., 154, 158
Wong, C. A., 174
Wood, P. B., 217
Woods, R. P., 44
Work, M., 61
Wright, B. E., 202
Wright, B. R., 218, 219
Wright, J. P., 43, 188, 208, 213, 215, 216, 219
Wright, R. A., 157

X

Xiao-Ming, O., 44
Xu, X., 208, 214

Y

Yablonsky, L., 104, 107
Yalda, C. A., 201
Yarbrough, A., 190
Yeager, P. C., 208, 214
Yochelson, S., 37, 38, 43, 192, 200
Young, J. N., 217, 218
Young, T. R., 90, 235
Young, V., 60

Z

Zahn, M. A., 233
Zdun, S., 108
Zhang, C., 218
Zhang, L., 126, 219
Zhao, J., 90, 201
Zhao, L., 90, 236
Zhao, R., 90
Zhong, H., 159
Zimmerman, G. M., 159
Ziya-Ozcan, Y., 175
Znaneicki, F., 48, 61